# WordPerfect® 7 For Windows® 95 For Dummies

P9-APK-410

Cheat Sheet

## General Information

To start WordPerfect, click on Start in the Windows 95 taskbar and choose Corel WordPerfect Suite 7⇨Corel WordPerfect.

To leave WordPerfect, choose File from the menu bar and then choose Exit. (Or press Alt+F and then X.)

When we say "press Alt+*some key*" or "press Ctrl+*some key,*" it means to hold down the Alt or Ctrl key (like a Shift key) while you type another key and then release it.

| While you are typing | Press this key |
| --- | --- |
| For help | F1 |
| To erase the character you just typed | Backspace |
| To erase the character to the right of your cursor (insertion point) | Delete |
| To start a new paragraph | Enter |
| To start a new page | Ctrl+Enter |
| To indent the first line of a paragraph | Tab |
| To indent all the lines in a paragraph | Move your cursor to the beginning of the paragraph and press F7 |
| To center a title | Move your cursor to the beginning of the title and then press Shift+F7 |

## Mouse Droppings

| To do this | Do this with your mouse |
| --- | --- |
| Select (highlight) text | Click in the text, hold down the button, and drag |
| Select a word | Double-click on the word |
| Select a sentence | Click once in the left margin |
| Select a paragraph | Double-click in the left margin |
| Move text or graphics | Select it and then click on it and drag |
| See a QuickMenu | Click the right button in the text or left margin |
| Change font | Click on font name in the Power Bar |
| Go somewhere | Double-click on position area of status bar |
| Close a file | Click on the right end of the menu bar |
| Exit from WordPerfect | Click on the right end of the title bar |

## . . . For Dummies: #1 Computer Book Series for Beginners

*Cheat Sheet*

## Getting Around Your Document

**The following keys move the cursor around your screen:**

| | |
|---|---|
| Up | Up one line |
| Down | Down one line |
| Left | Left one character |
| Right | Right one character |
| Ctrl+Left | Left one word |
| Ctrl+Right | Right one word |
| Home | Beginning of the line |
| End | End of the line |
| PgUp | Top of the screen or up one screenful |
| PgDn | Bottom of the screen or down one screenful |
| Ctrl+Home | Beginning of the document |
| Ctrl+End | End of the document |

## Kommon Kwick Key Kombinations

**These quick key combinations help you manage your files and text:**

| | |
|---|---|
| Ctrl+C | Copy to Clipboard |
| Ctrl+X | Cut to Clipboard |
| Ctrl+V | Paste from Clipboard |
| Ctrl+S or Shift+F3 | Save document |
| F3 | Save with new name |
| Ctrl+Shift+S | Save all open documents |
| Ctrl+P or F5 | Print document |
| F4 or Ctrl+O | Open document |
| Shift+F4 or Ctrl+N | New document |
| Ctrl+F4 | Close document |
| Alt+F4 | Exit from WordPerfect |
| Ctrl+B | Boldface |
| Ctrl+I | Italics |
| Ctrl+U | Underline |
| Ctrl+F1 | Spell-check |
| Alt+F3 | Reveal Codes |
| Ctrl+F or F9 | Font dialog box |
| Ctrl+G | Go To |
| Ctrl+K | Change capitalization |
| Ctrl+W | Weird characters |

## Helpful Tips

- Tell WordPerfect what you have in mind. Never type page numbers yourself, use lots of tabs to create a table, or type multiple columns of text yourself. Instead, use WordPerfect's multitude of features, such as page numbering, tables, or columns.

- Save your documents often by pressing Ctrl+S. To save all your open documents, press Ctrl+Shift+S.

## Recovering from Errors

| | |
|---|---|
| If you don't like what's going on | Press Esc a few times |
| If you have just deleted something and you want it back | Press Ctrl+Shift+Z or Alt+Backspace |
| If you have just given a command and you want to undo it | Press Ctrl+Z |

## *. . . For Dummies: #1 Computer Book Series for Beginners*

 ®

# References for the Rest of Us! ®

## COMPUTER BOOK SERIES FROM IDG

Are you intimidated and confused by computers? Do you find that traditional manuals are overloaded with technical details you'll never use? Do your friends and family always call you to fix simple problems on their PCs? Then the *...For Dummies®* computer book series from IDG Books Worldwide is for you.

*...For Dummies* books are written for those frustrated computer users who know they aren't really dumb but find that PC hardware, software, and indeed the unique vocabulary of computing make them feel helpless. *...For Dummies* books use a lighthearted approach, a down-to-earth style, and even cartoons and humorous icons to diffuse computer novices' fears and build their confidence. Lighthearted but not lightweight, these books are a perfect survival guide for anyone forced to use a computer.

> **"I like my copy so much I told friends; now they bought copies."**
>
> **Irene C., Orwell, Ohio**

> **"Quick, concise, nontechnical, and humorous."**
>
> **Jay A., Elburn, Illinois**

> **"Thanks, I needed this book. Now I can sleep at night."**
>
> **Robin F., British Columbia, Canada**

Already, hundreds of thousands of satisfied readers agree. They have made *...For Dummies* books the #1 introductory level computer book series and have written asking for more. So, if you're looking for the most fun and easy way to learn about computers, look to *...For Dummies* books to give you a helping hand.

7/96

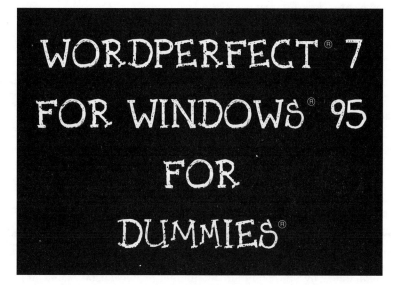

# WORDPERFECT® 7 FOR WINDOWS® 95 FOR DUMMIES®

## by Margaret Levine Young
## and
## David C. Kay

IDG Books Worldwide, Inc.
An International Data Group Company

Foster City, CA ♦ Chicago, IL ♦ Indianapolis, IN ♦ Southlake, TX

**WordPerfect® 7 For Windows® 95 For Dummies®**

Published by
**IDG Books Worldwide, Inc.**
An International Data Group Company
919 E. Hillsdale Blvd.
Suite 400
Foster City, CA 94404
http://www.dummies.com (Dummies Press Web Site)

Library of Congress Catalog Card No.: 96-75124

ISBN: 1-56884-949-4

Printed in the United States of America

10 9 8 7 6 5 4 3 2 1

1B/QR/QY/ZW/IN

Distributed in the United States by IDG Books Worldwide, Inc.

Distributed by Macmillan Canada for Canada; by Contemporanea de Ediciones for Venezuela; by Distribuidora Cuspide for Argentina; by CITEC for Brazil; by Ediciones ZETA S.C.R. Ltda. for Peru; by Editorial Limusa SA for Mexico; by Transworld Publishers Limited in the United Kingdom and Europe; by Academic Bookshop for Egypt; by Levant Distributors S.A.R.L. for Lebanon; by Al Jassim for Saudi Arabia; by Simron Pty. Ltd. for South Africa; by Pustak Mahal for India; by The Computer Bookshop for India; by Toppan Company Ltd. for Japan; by Addison Wesley Publishing Company for Korea; by Longman Singapore Publishers Ltd. for Singapore, Malaysia, Thailand, and Indonesia; by Unalis Corporation for Taiwan; by WS Computer Publishing Company, Inc. for the Philippines; by WoodsLane Pty. Ltd. for Australia; by WoodsLane Enterprises Ltd. for New Zealand. Authorized Sales Agent: Anthony Rudkin Associates for the Middle East and North Africa.

For general information on IDG Books Worldwide's books in the U.S., please call our Consumer Customer Service department at 800-762-2974. For reseller information, including discounts and premium sales, please call our Reseller Customer Service department at 800-434-3422.

For information on where to purchase IDG Books Worldwide's books outside the U.S., contact IDG Books Worldwide's International Sales department at 415-655-3172 or fax 415-655-3295.

For information on foreign language translations, contact IDG Books Worldwide's Foreign & Subsidiary Rights department at 415-655-3021 or fax 415-655-3281.

For sales inquiries and special prices for bulk quantities, contact IDG Books Worldwide's Sales department at 415-655-3200 or write to the address above.

For information on using IDG Books Worldwide's books in the classroom or for ordering examination copies, contact IDG Books Worldwide's Educational Sales department at 800-434-2086 or fax 817-251-8174.

For authorization to photocopy items for corporate, personal, or educational use, please contact Copyright Clearance Center, 222 Rosewood Drive, Danvers, MA 01923, or fax 508-750-4470.

# About the Author

## Margaret Levine Young

Unlike most of her peers in that mid-30-something bracket, Margaret Levine Young was exposed to computers at an early age. In high school, she got into a computer club known as the Resistors. "We were a group of kids who spent all day Saturday together in a barn fooling around on three computers that ran on vacuum tubes." Their goal, she admits, was to do language processing "so that the computers could make smart-aleck remarks back to us."

Although Levine got into computers "for fun" and because "my brother did," she stayed in the field through college, graduating from Yale with a degree in computer science. She was one of the first microcomputer managers in the early 1980s and was placed in charge of the MIS division for Columbia Pictures.

Since then, Levine has written 15 other computer books, and this is her third book written with coauthor Dave Kay. "We've known each other for a long time, but Dave is funnier than I am," she says. "Each of us did a chapter and then we'd pass them back and forth on the modem. I love writing . . .*For Dummies* books because I can write the way I think. It's fun being able to say: This is important, but you can forget about it."

Oh, by the way, Levine also met her future husband in the Resistors, and her other passion is her children, Meg and Zac. She loves gardening, "anything to do with eating," and wandering the Amazon, which she periodically revisits.

## David C. Kay

Dave Kay is a writer, engineer, and aspiring artist, combining professions in the same way as his favorite business establishment, Acton Muffler, Brake, and Ice Cream (now defunct). This is Kay's tenth computer book including *VRML and 3D on the Web For Dummies,* and various editions of *Works For Windows For Dummies, WordPerfect For Windows For Dummies, MORE WordPerfect For Windows For Dummies,* and *Graphics File Formats.*

In his other life, as the Poo-bah of Bright Leaf Communications, he creates promotional copy, graphics, and Web sites for high-tech firms. In his spare time, he studies human and animal tracking, munches edible wildplants, makes strange blobs from molten glass, hikes in whatever mountains he can get to, and longs to return to New Zealand and track kiwis and hedgehogs in Wanaka. He hates writing about himself in the third person like this and will stop now.

Welcome to the world of IDG Books Worldwide.

IDG Books Worldwide, Inc., is a subsidiary of International Data Group, the world's largest publisher of computer-related information and the leading global provider of information services on information technology. IDG was founded more than 25 years ago and now employs more than 8,500 people worldwide. IDG publishes more than 270 computer publications in over 75 countries (see listing below). More than 90 million people read one or more IDG publications each month.

Launched in 1990, IDG Books Worldwide is today the #1 publisher of best-selling computer books in the United States. We are proud to have received eight awards from the Computer Press Association in recognition of editorial excellence and three from *Computer Currents'* First Annual Readers' Choice Awards, and our best-selling . . .*For Dummies*® series has more than 25 million copies in print with translations in 28 languages. IDG Books Worldwide, through a joint venture with IDG's Hi-Tech Beijing, became the first U.S. publisher to publish a computer book in the People's Republic of China. In record time, IDG Books Worldwide has become the first choice for millions of readers around the world who want to learn how to better manage their businesses.

Our mission is simple: Every one of our books is designed to bring extra value and skill-building instructions to the reader. Our books are written by experts who understand and care about our readers. The knowledge base of our editorial staff comes from years of experience in publishing, education, and journalism — experience which we use to produce books for the '90s. In short, we care about books, so we attract the best people. We devote special attention to details such as audience, interior design, use of icons, and illustrations. And because we use an efficient process of authoring, editing, and desktop publishing our books electronically, we can spend more time ensuring superior content and spend less time on the technicalities of making books.

You can count on our commitment to deliver high-quality books at competitive prices on topics you want to read about. At IDG Books Worldwide, we continue in the IDG tradition of delivering quality for more than 25 years. You'll find no better book on a subject than one from IDG Books Worldwide.

*John J. Kilcullen*

John Kilcullen
President and CEO
IDG Books Worldwide, Inc.

IDG Books Worldwide, Inc., is a subsidiary of International Data Group, the world's largest publisher of computer-related information and the leading global provider of information services on information technology. International Data Group publishes over 270 computer publications in over 75 countries. Ninety million people read one or more International Data Group publications each month. International Data Group's publications include: **ARGENTINA:** Annuario de Informatica, Computerworld Argentina, Infoworld, PC World Argentina; **AUSTRALIA:** Australian Macworld, au.World, Client/Server Journal, Computer Living, Computerworld, Computerworld 100, Digital News, Network World, PC World, Publishing Essentials, Reseller, WebMaster; **AUSTRIA:** Computerwelt Osterreich, Networks Austria, PC Tip; **BELARUS:** PC World Belarus; **BELGIUM:** Data News; **BRAZIL:** Annuário de Informática, Computerworld Brazil, Connections, Super Game Power, Macworld, PC World Brazil, Publish Brazil, SUPERGAME; **BULGARIA:** Computerworld Bulgaria, Networkworld/Bulgaria, PC & MacWorld Bulgaria; **CANADA:** CIO Canada, Client/Server World, ComputerWorld Canada, InfoCanada, Network World Canada; **CHILE:** Computerworld Chile, PC World Chile; **COLOMBIA:** Computerworld Colombia, PC World Colombia; **COSTA RICA:** PC World Costa Rica/Nicaragua; **THE CZECH AND SLOVAK REPUBLICS:** Computerworld Czechoslovakia, Elektronika Czechoslovakia, PC World Czechoslovakia; **DENMARK:** Communications World, Computerworld Danmark, Macworld Danmark, PC Privat Danmark, PC World Danmark, PC World Danmark Supplements, TECH World; **DOMINICAN REPUBLIC:** PC World Republica Dominicana; **ECUADOR:** PC World Ecuador; **EGYPT:** Computerworld Middle East, PC World Middle East; **EL SALVADOR:** PC World Centro America; **FINLAND:** MikroPC, Tietoverkko, Tietoviikko; **FRANCE:** Distributique, Golden, Hebdo-Distributique, Info PC, Le Guide du Monde Informatique, Le Monde Informatique, Reseaux & Telecoms; **GERMANY:** Computer Partner, Computerwoche, Computerwoche Extra, Computerwoche Focus, Electronic Entertainment, GamePro, I/M Information Management, Macwelt, PC Welt; **GREECE:** GamePro, Multimedia World; **GUATEMALA:** PC World Centro America; **HONDURAS:** PC World Centro America; **HONG KONG:** Computerworld Hong Kong, PCWorld Hong Kong, Publish in Asia; **HUNGARY:** ABCD CD-ROM, Computerworld Szamitastechnika, PC & Mac World Hungary, PC-X Magazine; **ICELAND:** Tolvuheimur/PC World Island; **INDIA:** Computerworld India, PC World India, Publish in Asia; **INDONESIA:** InfoKomputer PC World, Komputek Computerworld, Publish in Asia; **IRELAND:** ComputerScope, PC Live!; **ISRAEL:** People & Computers; **ITALY:** Computerworld Italia, Computerworld Italia Special Editions, Macworld Italia, Networking Italia, PC Shopping, PC World Italia, PC World/Walt Disney; **JAPAN:** Macworld Japan, Nikkei Personal Computing, SunWorld Japan, Windows World Japan; **KENYA:** East African Computer News; **KOREA:** Hi-Tech Information/Computerworld, Macworld Korea, PC World Korea; **MACEDONIA:** PC World Macedonia; **MALAYSIA:** Computerworld Malaysia, PC World Malaysia, Publish in Asia; **MEXICO:** Computerworld Mexico, Macworld, PC World Mexico; **MYANMAR:** PC World Myanmar; **NETHERLANDS:** Computable, Computer! Totaal, LAN Magazine, LanWorld Buyers Guide, Macworld, Net Magazine, Totaal! Beurskrant; **NEW ZEALAND:** Absolute Beginner's Guide, Computer Buyer, Computer Industry Directory, Computerworld New Zealand, Electronic Entertainment, MTB, Network World, PC World New Zealand; **NICARAGUA:** PC World Costa Rica/Nicaragua; **NIGERIA:** PC World Nigeria; **NORWAY:** CAD/CAM Norge, Computerworld Norge, Computerworld Privat (Datamagasinet), CW Rapport Norge, IDG's KURSGUIDE, Macworld Norge, Multimediaworld, PC World Ekspress, PC World Nettverk, PC World Norge, PC World's Produktguide; **PAKISTAN:** Computerworld Pakistan, PC World Pakistan; **PANAMA:** PC World Panama; **P. R. OF CHINA:** China Computer Users, China Computerworld, China Infoworld, Computer & Communication, Electronic Design China, Electronics Today, Electronics Weekly, Game Camp, PC World China, Popular Computer Weekly, Software Weekly, Software World, Telecom World; **PERU:** Computerworld Peru, PC World Profesional Peru, PC World Peru; **PHILIPPINES:** Computerworld Philippines, PC World Philippines, Publish in Asia; **POLAND:** Computerworld Poland, Computerworld Special Report, Macworld, Networld, PC World Komputer; **PORTUGAL:** Cerebro/PC World, Computerworld/Correio Informático, MacIn/PCIn, Multimedia World Portugal; **PUERTO RICO:** PC World Puerto Rico; **ROMANIA:** Computerworld Romania, PC World Romania, Telecom Romania; **RUSSIA:** Computerworld Russia, Mir PK, Sety; **SINGAPORE:** Computerworld Singapore, PC World Singapore, Publish in Asia; **SLOVENIA:** MONITOR; **SOUTH AFRICA:** Computing S.A., InfoWorld S.A., Network World S.A., Software World; **SPAIN:** Computerworld España, COMUNICACIONES WORLD, Dealer World, Macworld España, PC World España; **SWEDEN:** CAP&Design, Computer Sweden, Corporate Computing, MacWorld, Maxi Data, MikroDatorn, Nätverk & Kommunikation, PC/Aktiv, PC World, Windows World; **SWITZERLAND:** Computerworld Schweiz, Macworld Schweiz, PCtip; **TAIWAN:** Computerworld Taiwan, Macworld Taiwan, PC World Taiwan, Publish Taiwan, Windows World; **THAILAND:** Thai Computerworld, PC World Thailand, Publish in Asia; **TURKEY:** Computerworld Monitör, MACWORLD Turkiye, PC Games, PC WORLD Turkiye; **UKRAINE:** Computerworld Kiev, Computers & Software, Multimedia World Ukraine, PC World Ukraine; **UNITED KINGDOM:** Acorn User, Amiga Action, Amiga Computing, Appletalk, CD-ROM Now, Computing, GamePro, Macaction, Macworld, Network News, Parents and Computers, PC Home, PSX Pro UK, The WEB; **UNITED STATES:** Cable in the Classroom, CD Review, CIO Magazine, Computerworld, Computerworld Client/Server Journal, Digital Video Magazine, DOS World, Electronic Entertainment, Federal Computer Week, GamePro, InfoWorld, I+Way, JavaWorld, Macworld, Maximize, Multimedia World, Netscape World, Network World, PC World, Publish, SunWorld Online, SWATPro Magazine, Video Event, WebMaster; **URUGUAY:** PC World Uruguay; **VENEZUELA:** Computerworld Venezuela, PC World Venezuela; and **VIETNAM:** PC World Vietnam. 7/8/96

# Dedication

We would like to dedicate this book to our parents: To Ginny and Bob Levine, who were always both knowledgeable and funny, and to Hester and Harold Kay, who always taught that "if you can read, you can do anything!" (They didn't say anything about writing.)

Who knows? Maybe someday we'll surprise our parents and get real jobs.

# Acknowledgments

We would like to thank Jordan Young, Katy Weeks, Matt Wagner, Bill Gladstone, Steve Emmerich, the folks at IDG Books, and our ever-patient friends and families.

We are indebted to Dan Gookin, author of the first book in the . . .*For Dummies* series. His irreverent style and deep knowledge of software combine to create winning books. We are honored to follow in the footsteps of this original dummy.

## Publisher's Acknowledgments

We're proud of this book; please send us your comments about it by using the Reader Response Card at the back of the book or by e-mailing us at feedback/dummies@idgbooks.com. Some of the people who helped bring this book to market include the following:

### Acquisitions, Development, & Editorial

**Project Editor:** Colleen Rainsberger

**Acquisitions Editor:** Tammy Goldfeld

**Product Development Manager:** Mary Bednarek

**Copy Editors:** Kathy Simpson, Kelly Ewing, Christine Meloy Beck, Tim Gallan, Diane L. Giangrossi, Pamela Mourouzis, Rebecca Whitney

**Technical Editor:** Allen Clark

**Editorial Managers:** Mary C. Corder and Seta K. Frantz

**Editorial Assistant:** Chris H. Collins

### Production

**Project Coordinator:** Regina Snyder

**Layout and Graphics:** Cameron Booker, Maridee V. Ennis, Todd Klemme, Jane E. Martin, Gina Scott

**Proofreaders:** Michael Bolinger, Rob Springer, Karen York

**Indexer:** Anne Leach

### General & Administrative

**IDG Books Worldwide, Inc.:** John Kilcullen, President & CEO; Steven Berkowitz, COO & Publisher

**Dummies, Inc.:** Milissa Koloski, Executive Vice President & Publisher

**Dummies Technology Press & Dummies Editorial:** Diane Graves Steele, Associate Publisher; Judith A. Taylor, Brand Manager; Myra Immell, Editorial Director

**Dummies Trade Press:** Kathleen A. Welton, Vice President & Publisher; Stacy S. Collins, Brand Manager

**IDG Books Production for Dummies Press:** Beth Jenkins, Production Director; Cindy L. Phipps, Supervisor of Project Coordination; Kathie S. Schutte, Supervisor of Page Layout; Shelley Lea, Supervisor of Graphics and Design

**Dummies Packaging & Book Design:** Erin McDermit, Packaging Coordinator; Patti Sandez, Packaging Assistant; Kavish+Kavish, Cover Design

◆

The publisher would like to give special thanks to Patrick J. McGovern, without whom this book would not have been possible.

◆

# Contents at a Glance

# Cartoons at a Glance

*By Rich Tennant • Fax: 508-546-7747 • E-mail:* the5wave@tiac.net

page 7

page 91

page 385

page 187

page 337

# Table of Contents

## Chapter 11: Documents with Style ...................................................... 171

## Part III: Things You Can Do with Documents ........................... 187

## Chapter 12: On Paper at Last: Printing Stuff ........................................ 189

## Chapter 13: Juggling Documents on Your Screen ................................ 203

## Chapter 21: Fun with Windows 95 ........................................... 357

## Chapter 22: Solving Printing Problems ................................... 365

## Chapter 23: Don't Panic! Read This Chapter! ......................... 375

# Introduction

*I*f you thought that the idea of word processing was to write, not to do amazing things on a computer. . .

If you ever secretly wondered who the heck uses all those features advertised on the box your software came in. . .

If you ever had to humiliate yourself in front of some computer wizard just to get words on paper. . .

Congratulations — you're a "dummy!" Dummies are an underground group of people smart enough to say, "Call me what you will — I just want to get some work done, please!" If you're that sort of person, this book is for you.

This book is a reference book, so the idea is to thumb through it whenever you have a question. It's also a book that can be read any old way you want. So sit back, prop your feet up on your wastebasket, and let the vibrant, yellow cover of *WordPerfect 7 For Windows 95 For Dummies* proudly proclaim your dummyhood to all who pass by.

## What Goes On in This Book

In this book, we do the following:

- ✔ Start from the beginning, in case you're a beginner. We use genuine English words, not cryptic technobabble.

- ✔ Separate the basics from the fancy stuff so that you can get real work done.

- ✔ Lead you through the maze of buttons, commands, icons, menus, mice, and windows that make up WordPerfect for Windows.

- ✔ Give you just enough of the fancy stuff to look good — or to convince your boss or spouse that WordPerfect was worth the big bucks you paid for it.

True to the . . .*For Dummies* philosophy, this book refuses to take software too seriously. Software is, as one enlightened friend says, "not the Salk vaccine." Software does, however, sometimes provide a localized pain not dissimilar to that engendered by certain inoculations.

What we do take seriously is helping you get your work done. So this book addresses the following topics:

- ✔ Using the keyboard and the mouse
- ✔ Learning what's with all those buttons on-screen
- ✔ Cutting and pasting
- ✔ Saving your work
- ✔ Using different typefaces
- ✔ Finding a file when you have forgotten its name
- ✔ Dealing with printing problems
- ✔ Printing envelopes
- ✔ Popular documents and how to make them

When there's something to watch out for, this book tells you about it. When something really isn't important, it tells you that too.

Probably just as important as what's in this book is what isn't in it. It has no long, technical explanations of underlying principles; no huge tables of the 47 things that feature X can do; and no eyecharts of commands and keystrokes organized in some useless manner, such as alphabetically.

# How to Use This Book

No one, absolutely no one, wants to sit down and read a book before beginning to use his software. So don't. If you know how to do anything at all in WordPerfect, go to it!

Because this book is a reference book, when some feature in WordPerfect has you tying knots in your mouse cord, you can just look up what you want in the table of contents or the index.

If your brow is already furrowing while you're just looking at the pictures of WordPerfect on the box, check out the earlier chapters first. These chapters speak of mice and menus and similar basics, so they're written for beginners. If you're new to Windows or even to computers, you probably should start there. These chapters help you get used to the what, why, and how of giving commands to WordPerfect. After you understand the basics, though, you don't have to read the chapters in any sequence.

This book stands by itself. (No one else will get near it!) It does not, for example, require you to read the WordPerfect for Windows manual. It may occasionally refer you to a companion book in this series — *Windows 95 For Dummies,* by

Andy Rathbone (published by IDG Books Worldwide, Inc.), available wherever books are sold, read, or generally left lying around.

Most of what you find in this book are full, robust sentences, not cryptic abbreviations or shortcut terminology. Unfortunately, one person's full, robust sentence is another's long-winded description. This statement is true particularly when it comes to describing how to do things in the world of Windows.

If we always used such sentences as "Move the mouse so that the mouse pointer covers the word *Edit* on the menu and then press the left mouse button; a menu appears and contains the word *Cut;* move the mouse so that the mouse pointer covers the word *Cut,*" you would be comatose by Chapter 2, and this book would take on encyclopedic dimensions. So we generally restrict this sort of thing to chapters on the basics. When we get around to less basic stuff, we say such things as "Choose the Edit➪Cut command" and hope that you forgive us.

When we want you to choose a command from the menu bar and then choose another command from the menu that appears, we separate the two commands with this cute little arrow: ➪. See Chapter 2 for details.

When we want you to type something, it appears in **bold type**. On-screen messages look like this. When we suggest pressing two keys at the same time, such as the Ctrl key and the C key, we use a plus sign like this: Ctrl+C. In Chapter 2, we tell you all about choosing commands from menus and using all those interesting keys on your keyboard.

# *Who Am Us, Anyway?*

This section explains what we assume about you, our esteemed (and thanks to the joy of software, occasionally steamed) reader:

✔ You use a PC that has Windows 95 and WordPerfect 7 for Windows 95 installed.

✔ You want to write stuff and make it look nice.

✔ You don't really give a bat's eyelash about Windows 95 except what you absolutely need for your daily work.

✔ You have a "guru" available — an expert, like one of those infuriatingly clever ten-year-olds born with a computer cable for an umbilical cord, whom you can call for the really tough stuff and whom you can probably pay off in cookies.

✔ You don't have fabulous fenestration skills (Windows expertise), but you have a mouse and probably would know a window if it were pointed out to you.

- You don't intend to make WordPerfect for Windows run like something it's not, such as an earlier version of WordPerfect, by changing the way the keyboard works.

- You or the person who installed WordPerfect installed it in the standard way. WordPerfect is accommodating almost to a fault and lets itself be twisted and restructured like a ball of Silly Putty. If buttons and things on your screen don't look like the buttons in our pictures or if your keyboard doesn't work as this book describes, be suspicious that someone got clever and changed things.

Although we assume that you have a computer guru at your disposal, we also know that gurus can be hard to coax from their rock on top of the mountain. So we teach you a few of the important guru-type tricks where it's practical and suggest appropriate guru bribes where it's not.

# What You're Not Supposed to Read

Don't read anything with a picture of that nerdy-looking "Mr. Science" guy next to it (the Technical Stuff icons) unless you really feel a need to know why something is true rather than how to do something useful. (You know the Mr. Science type — full of brain-glazing explanations of how, for example, "User Preferences set under the XYZ dialog box are actually edits to the .INI file" when what you really need to know is "Press this key now.") The only good part about reading this stuff is that it can help you sound sufficiently informed to your computer wizard to induce her to do technical things for you.

# How This Book Is Organized

Unlike computer manuals, which often seem to be organized alphabetically by height, this book is organized by what you may be trying to do. It doesn't explain, for example, all the commands on the Edit menu in one chapter. Our reasoning is that the Edit commands don't necessarily have anything to do with editing and that Edit is a foolish category because isn't almost everything you do in a word processor a sort of edit anyway?

No, what this book does is break things down into the following five useful categories.

# Part I: Introducing WordPerfect 7 for Windows 95

Part I discusses the basics: your keyboard, your mouse, and the WordPerfect screen and how they all work together to let you write stuff and make it come out of your printer. Part I is the place to go for some of the basics of using WordPerfect menus, keystrokes, and buttons. It also has information about some of the fancier basics, such as searching and replacing, working with blocks of text, and spell-checking. Part I can even help you if you have never worked in Windows or never even used a computer.

# Part II: Prettying Up Your Text

If you didn't care how your text looked, you wouldn't be using a word processor, would you? What? You say that all you want to do is put something in boldface type or italics? And perhaps also center a heading? And set the margins too? *And* put in page numbers? It's all here.

# Part III: Things You Can Do with Documents

You thought that you were just *word* processing, didn't you? Hah! You are really *creating entire documents*. And now you have to live with your creation, Dr. Frankenstein. Maybe you want to print your document, for example. Or kill it off altogether by deleting it. Or move it somewhere where it can do no harm. Maybe you even want to dress it up with borders and columns and send it out into the world as junk mail! Part III talks all about this kind of stuff.

# Part IV: Help Me, Rhonda!

WordPerfect for Windows is big-time software that consumes vast portions of your computer's disk and memory space with lots of incredibly complex, sophisticated, and really clever software. Unfortunately, sometimes it's a tad too complex, sophisticated, and clever for its own good — or yours.

Go to Part IV when things don't work quite right — or at least, when they don't work the way you think that they ought to. Part IV is the place to go when things have to be done in Windows, not just in WordPerfect.

# Part V: The Part of Tens

In honor of the decimal system, the Ten Commandments, and the perfectly silly accident of fate that humans have ten fingers, Part V is where we stick other useful stuff. We would have made this part an appendix, but appendixes have no fingers and — look — just check it out. Part V is full of stuff that everyone who uses WordPerfect for Windows should know.

# Icons Used in This Book

The 1990s will be considered The Age of Icons by future historians, who probably will analyze how humanity lost its ability to read actual words. But — because we're not inclined to buck the trend and we want you to get accustomed to all the icons you have to deal with in WordPerfect — we have put them in this book, too.

What are icons? They're pictures that are far more interesting than the actual words they represent. They also take up less space than do the words, which is why they're used on computer screens in such blinding profusion.

 This icon alerts you to the sort of stuff that appeals to people who secretly like software. It's not required reading unless you're trying to date a person like that (or are already married to one).

 This icon flags useful tips or shortcuts.

 This icon suggests that we are presenting something useful to remember so that you don't wear out your book by looking it up all the time.

 This icon cheerfully denotes things that can cause trouble. (Why doesn't life come with these icons?)

# Where to Go from Here

If WordPerfect is already installed on your computer, you probably have already tried to do something in WordPerfect. You are probably annoyed, perplexed, or intrigued by the promise of something you have seen. So look it up in the table of contents or the index and see what this book has to say about it. Or peruse the table of contents and see what appeals to you. You may learn something, and it beats the heck out of working.

If you use electronic mail, we would love to hear from you! Send comments about this book to our Internet address, which is `winwp7@dummies.com`.

# Part I

## Introducing WordPerfect 7 for Windows 95

## In this part . . .

You are ready to employ the very latest in Windows word-processing technology. You have the power to create tables, graphics, columns, fonts, borders, tables of contents, illustrations, sidebars, envelopes, junk mail — you name it! In short, *you are ready to launch yourself into the blazing, glorious future of word processing* — except for one teensy little problem. You were wondering, perhaps, just wondering: How do you start the silly thing? And, um, how do you print something? Or delete a sentence? Or save your work? Good questions, pilgrim — questions that deserve answers. And here's where to find them: Part I of *WordPerfect 7 For Windows 95 For Dummies*. Read on.

# Chapter 1

# WordPerfect Basics

## In This Chapter

▶ Starting WordPerfect

▶ Minimizing the program

▶ Looking at the WordPerfect window

▶ Typing your text

▶ Naming files

▶ Getting help

▶ Editing another file

▶ Printing your document

▶ Leaving WordPerfect

*T*his chapter gets you started using WordPerfect by showing you how to perform the Big Five word-processing operations: get the program (WordPerfect) running, type some text, save the text in a file on disk, open the file again later, and print the file. By the end of this chapter, you will know how to coax WordPerfect into performing these five operations. In later chapters, we get into some refinements, such as editing the text after you type it or making it look a little spiffier.

But first, the basics.

## Starting WordPerfect

To begin using WordPerfect, you have to see it on-screen. Follow these steps:

**1. Get psyched.**

Repeat to yourself three times, "I love using the computer! This is going to be great!" — whether you believe it or not.

**2. Turn on the computer, the monitor, the printer, and whatever else looks important.**

**3. Wait for Windows 95 to start running.**

Windows 95 runs automatically when you start your computer, unless some wizard has done something peculiar to your computer. If so, go find that person and learn the magic that's necessary to get Windows 95 going on your computer. Wait until the now-familiar cloud scene disappears and the Windows 95 desktop appears. By this, we mean that lots of little doohickeys, called *icons* (pictures), are on-screen — one for each program you may want to run.

**4. Look for WordPerfect.**

Again, unless you or someone else did something too clever, you can find it by clicking on the Start button on the Windows 95 Taskbar. (If the phrase *clicking on* is unfamiliar to you, see the tip following these steps.) At the top of the menu of programs you can run should be WordPerfect Suite (or Corel Office 7, depending on what all got installed on your computer).

It may be that somebody installed Corel's Desktop Application Director (called DAD — no, we're not making this up!) on your computer. In that case, you see a little icon with a pen nib on your Taskbar. Or you may have an icon on your desktop labeled WordPerfect 7. If you can't find the program anywhere, it's probably not installed on your computer.

**5. Start WordPerfect.**

How you do this depends on where you found the program. If you found Corel Office 7 or Corel WordPerfect Suite 7 at the top of your Start menu, place the mouse pointer (the little arrow symbol that moves when you move the mouse) on it and leave it there for a second. The words `WordPerfect 7` appear beside your mouse pointer; click on them.

If you found the little icon with the pen nib on the Taskbar, you can click on it. And if you found an icon on your desktop labeled WordPerfect 7, you can *double-click* on it. (Look at the tip that follows these steps if double-clicking isn't a familiar concept.)

WordPerfect should begin to run. After a minute or so, you see the Word-Perfect screen, which is described later in this chapter. Suffice it to say that the screen is a little more complicated than a nice blank piece of paper.

If you're new to the wonderful world of mice, two terms may need some definition. When we tell you to *click on something,* you should point to it with the pointer on-screen that moves when the mouse does; then you briskly press and release the mouse button (usually, the left one). When we tell you to *double-click on something,* we mean that you should press and release the button twice in close succession. In Windows, double-clicking means, "Hey, you! You with the teeth! *Do* something!" You may need to try this procedure a few times to get the double-click at just the right speed. For more information about mice and mouse acrobatics, see Chapter 2.

---

## Running WordPerfect automagically

If you use WordPerfect 7 every day, you may want it to run automatically every time you turn on your computer. This is less important than it used to be because you've probably got that DAD bar on your Taskbar. Just click on the fountain-pen nib on the Taskbar. Still, if you want WordPerfect 7 to run without your having to do anything (while you're getting your coffee in the morning, say), ask your local computer wizard to put WordPerfect 7 in your Startup folder. A true wizard will know what this request means. You can do the same thing yourself; see Chapter 21, which discusses Windows 95, icons, and folders.

---

This list shows some things that may go wrong:

- Someone may have told Windows 95 to run WordPerfect for you automatically. If so, the program may already be visible on-screen. Go thank this person.

- WordPerfect may run automatically but may be minimized. The following section describes what to do if you see an extra WordPerfect icon lying around on your Taskbar.

- If you cannot find WordPerfect 7 in your Start menu, it may be hiding among the items in the Programs portion of this menu. See the section "Menu Madness" in Chapter 21 for information on how to find WordPerfect 7 and how to put it somewhere that's easier to find.

- If your computer, Windows 95, or (heaven forbid!) WordPerfect "crashed" the last time you were running WordPerfect, you may see a message that a timed backup document exists. If this message appears, refer to Chapter 23.

- If you have trouble getting WordPerfect to run or if you are wrestling with the Program Manager, you may want to refer to Chapter 21. If that doesn't work, check out *Windows 95 For Dummies*, by Andy Rathbone (published by IDG Books Worldwide, Inc.) — a great book that tries to clarify this stuff.

# Honey, I Shrunk the Program!

While WordPerfect is running, it can be *minimized,* which means that it shrinks into a little button on the Taskbar. You may want to minimize a program to get it out of the way temporarily while you do something else. The program's still running, ready to do your work, but it's tiny. Minimizing is similar to freeze-drying your program — you can add water later to bring it back to life.

If you want to minimize WordPerfect (and who wouldn't?), click on the little Minimize button near the upper right corner of the WordPerfect window (described in the following section). Poof! It disappears in a puff of bytes, to be replaced by a button on the Taskbar.

You get WordPerfect 7 back the same way you started it in the first place: by choosing the Taskbar⇨Start 7⇨Corel WordPerfect Suite⇨Corel WordPerfect 7 menu commands; by double-clicking on the DAD bar WordPerfect 7 icon on the Taskbar; by double-clicking on the WordPerfect 7 icon on your desktop; or by clicking on the WordPerfect 7 button on the Taskbar. WordPerfect not only jumps back into existence on your screen, but also (if you were working on a document) is just the way you left it.

# *The WordPerfect Window*

After WordPerfect is running, you see the WordPerfect window, as shown in Figure 1-1. The wide expanse of white screen corresponds to the white paper that sticks out of your old-fashioned typewriter and is probably no more inspirational.

The following list describes lots of stuff around the edges that may not be familiar to you:

- ✔ **The title bar.** The title bar is the top edge of the window, displaying the words `Corel WordPerfect - Document1`. This line tells you the name of the document you are editing and reminds you that you are, in fact, running WordPerfect (more about documents anon).

- ✔ **The WordPerfect Minimize button.** You click on this button to turn WordPerfect into an icon.

- ✔ **The WordPerfect Close button.** If you click on this button, WordPerfect 7 closes — that is, it exits, disappears, terminates, goes poof! This button is new in Windows 95. It's very useful, but it's also kind of dangerous — you may leave WordPerfect and be asked whether you want to save changes in your document. Don't panic; just choose the Cancel option and continue normally. For more information, see the section "Leaving WordPerfect" later in this chapter.

- ✔ **The menu bar.** The row of words just below the title bar is WordPerfect's main menu bar. Each word is a *command* you can choose. Later in this chapter, we tell you how to use a command to exit WordPerfect. We talk more about commands in Chapter 3.

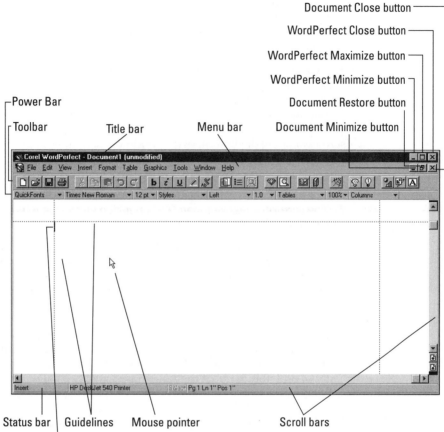

Document Close button
WordPerfect Close button
WordPerfect Maximize button
WordPerfect Minimize button
Document Restore button
Document Minimize button

Power Bar
Toolbar     Title bar     Menu bar

**Figure 1-1:**
The
WordPerfect
window.

Status bar | Guidelines   Mouse pointer          Scroll bars

Cursor (insertion point)

  ✔ **The Toolbar.** Below the menu bar is a row of gray boxes called *buttons;*
    these buttons make up the Toolbar. (Users of WordPerfect 6.0 will recog-
    nize the Toolbar as the old Power Bar, but everything has been renamed
    since version 6.0. Bummer!) The buttons usually have little pictures on
    them. Later in this chapter, you use some of these buttons to save and
    print a document. If you don't see the Toolbar on-screen, use the following
    powerful incantation to make it appear: Press Alt+V (hold down the Alt
    key while you press the V key) and then press T. We explain more about
    using commands in Chapter 2 and about determining what you want to see
    on-screen in Chapter 19.

  ✔ **The Power Bar.** Just below the Toolbar is a row of little gray boxes. If you
    click on these boxes, you can change such things as the font, type size,
    and line spacing.

✔ **The status bar.** The bottom line of the WordPerfect window shows information about what is going on right now. Each indented box on the status bar contains a different type of information, as explained in the following section.

✔ **The scroll bar.** (Why are there so many bars in WordPerfect? Maybe it's because there aren't many bars in Utah, where WordPerfect was written.) Along the right side of the window is a gray strip that helps you move around the document; you find out how to use it in Chapter 2. If your document is too wide to fit across the screen, WordPerfect displays a scroll bar along the bottom of the window too, right above the status bar.

✔ **The mouse pointer and the cursor.** The *mouse pointer* is usually a little arrow, and it shows where your mouse is pointing. The mouse pointer changes to other shapes, depending on what you are doing (see Chapter 2). The *cursor* (or *insertion point*) is a blinking vertical line that indicates where you are typing.

✔ **Dark edges.** On either side of the document, you may see dark areas that represent your desktop underneath the paper on which you are typing. The WordPerfect folks seem to have gone overboard in the realism department here, although they might have gone a step further and displayed simulated wood grain with coffee-mug rings.

Wow! There sure are lots of gizmos to look at while you are trying to type. Chapter 19 contains hints for controlling the things that clutter the WordPerfect window. Otherwise, you'll get used to all these little buttons and messages eventually — probably at about the same time a new version of WordPerfect comes along, with a whole new concept in screen clutter.

When WordPerfect is busy, the mouse pointer, which is usually a little arrow, turns into an hourglass. The sands of time fall while WordPerfect does something that it considers to be more important than listening to your commands. The hourglass means, "Wait around until I'm finished. Consider warming up your coffee in the nuke." Sooner or later (usually within a few seconds), the mouse pointer turns back into its normal pointy self, and you can get back to work.

# What's on the Status Bar?

The status bar contains squarish boxes (rectangular boxes, for those of you who remember fourth-grade geometry), each of which contains vital information about your document. You can control the kind of information that WordPerfect displays, but you're probably not interested in this rather arcane subject at the moment (see Chapter 20 if we're wrong about your insatiable curiosity). Starting from the left, here's what this gibberish means:

✓ The first box says either `Insert` or `Typeover`, depending on which
mode you use. Insert mode means that when you type, the letters are
inserted wherever the cursor is positioned. Typeover mode means that
the letters you type replace (or *type over*) the characters to the right of the
cursor. You switch between Insert and Typeover modes by pressing the
Insert (or Ins) key or by double-clicking on this box. When you are editing
something fancy, such as a table or a merge file, other information may
appear in this box. See Chapter 2 for more details.

✓ The second box shows what kind of printer you have. Double-clicking on it
displays the Select Printer dialog box so that you can use another printer,
if you have more than one. (For details on selecting a printer, see the
section "Selecting Which Printer to Use" in Chapter 22.)

✓ The third box indicates whether you have selected some text to move,
copy, delete, and so on. See Chapter 6 for information about how to select
text and what to do with it.

✓ The fourth box tells you where you are in your document, including the
page number (`Pg`), how far down the page you are (`Ln`), and where you are
across the page (`Pos`). For the most part, of course, who cares, unless you
get paid to write by the inch? Every once in a while, however, you may
want to know exactly where on the page your text will appear, and these
measurements tell you.

# Typing Something

WordPerfect is completely different from a typewriter in many ways, but in one
way, it is the same: To enter some text, you just start typing.

If you make a mistake or change your mind about the wording, move the cursor
(the slowly blinking vertical line that shows where you are typing) to the text
you want to change; then change it. You can use either the mouse or the
keyboard to get that cursor moving. (Chapter 2 explains ways to move the
cursor around.)

All the regular keys on the keyboard — the letters, numbers, and punctuation
keys — enter characters on-screen when you press them. The rest of the keys —
the function keys (F1 and its friends), Enter, Insert, Delete, and all the keys with
arrows on them — do not enter characters. Those keys do something else, and
we tell you exactly what each key does as we get to it.

Normally, you are in Insert mode, which means that whatever you type is
inserted into the text. If your cursor is between two letters and you type a new
letter, the new one is inserted between the two original letters.

To type a capital letter, first hold down one of the two Shift keys and then type
the lettter.

To type a bunch of capital letters, press (but do not hold down) the Caps Lock key. Now whatever letters you type are capitalized. To turn off Caps Lock, press the Caps Lock key again. You will notice (with a little experimentation) that Caps Lock doesn't have the slightest effect on numbers or punctuation — only on letters.

Your keyboard may have a light that indicates when Caps Lock is on. The light may even be right on the key. You can tell WordPerfect to display a little Caps Lock indicator on-screen, too, as part of the status bar (see Chapter 20).

If you want to type numbers, you can press the number keys just above the QWERTYUIOP row, or you can use the *numeric keypad,* which is the group of number keys on the right side of the keyboard. But watch out — you can also use the numeric keypad to move the cursor. (See Chapter 2 to learn how to determine when these keys do what.)

If you want to delete just a letter or two, you can move the cursor just after the letters and then press the Backspace key to wipe them out. Or you can move the cursor right *before* them and press the Delete key. Same difference — the letter disappears. See Chapter 4 to learn how to delete larger amounts of text.

Chapters 2 and 3 contain lots of information about using the keyboard and the mouse to do things in WordPerfect.

# Waxing Eloquent

After you begin typing, you can go ahead and say what you have to say. But what happens when you get to the end of the line? Unlike a typewriter, WordPerfect doesn't go "Ding!" to tell you that you are about to type off the edge of the paper and get ink on the platen. Instead, WordPerfect (like all word processors) does something called *word wrap:* It figures out that you are almost at the right margin and moves down to the next line *all by itself.* What will they think of next?

Because of the miracle of word wrap (not to be confused with plastic wrap), you don't have to keep track of where you are on the line. You can just type away, knowing that WordPerfect will move you along to the next line as needed.

*Not* pressing the Enter key at the end of each line is important. WordPerfect, like all word processors, assumes that when you press Enter, you are at the end of a paragraph, not just at the end of a line within the paragraph.

If you change the margins later or use a larger font (character style), WordPerfect even moves the words around (keeping them in order, of course) so that your paragraphs fit within the new margins. This nice side effect of word wrap is called *reformatting.*

Press Enter only when you want to begin a new paragraph; otherwise, let WordPerfect handle the line endings. Pressing Enter at the end of every line is a sure sign of a word-processing novice, and it makes computer nerds sigh and shake their heads sadly. Worse, keeping things looking right with this method eventually causes you a great deal of work and headaches.

If you want to split one paragraph into two, you can insert a paragraph mark by pressing Enter. Move your cursor just before the letter where you want the new paragraph to begin and press Enter. Voilà! WordPerfect moves the rest of the line down to a new line and reformats the rest of the paragraph to fit.

# What's in a Name?

When you type text in WordPerfect, you are making a document. A *document* is WordPerfect's fancy name for anything that's typed. A letter, a memo, a laundry list, or the next great American novel — all these things are documents to WordPerfect.

To save your document so that you can look at it, edit it, or print it later, you save it in a *file* on the disk. Each document is in one file.

Right now, the prose you have typed is in a document that WordPerfect named Document1. The text is on-screen, but it's not on disk (yet). Documents on-screen are ephemeral and disappear when you exit WordPerfect or turn off your computer — here today, gone tomorrow (or later this afternoon). Saving your documents on disk is important so that they are saved for good.

Document1 isn't a good name for a document because it doesn't give you a clue to what it's about, but it's the best that WordPerfect can do. You should give the document a more descriptive name, which you can do when you save it.

## Saving your document

There are at least three ways to save a document on disk and give it a name. We're sure that your insatiable curiosity will drive you to find out all three, but this method is our favorite. Follow these steps:

1. **Click the Save button on the Toolbar.**

   The Toolbar is the row of little buttons just below the title bar. (Refer to the section "The WordPerfect Window" and Figure 1-1, earlier in this chapter, if you can't find the Toolbar.) The Save button is the one with a tiny picture of a floppy disk. (You probably are really saving your document on a hard disk, but hard disks aren't as cute as floppy disks.) This button is probably the third from the left.

When your mouse pointer points to a button on the Toolbar, the name of the button appears in a little yellow box along with a description of the button. Thank goodness for that because many of those teeny little buttons look alike to us (and don't tell us that it's time to break down and get reading glasses!). When your mouse pointer is on the Save button, for example, you see this helpful reminder: `Save the current document - Ctrl+S`. These messages tell you the name of the button and what the button does (as though you couldn't guess from the name). Chapter 3 has more information about this subject.

As soon as you click on the Save button, a window appears on your screen, right on top of the WordPerfect window. The window is a *dialog box,* which WordPerfect displays when it wants to ask you some questions. Chapter 3 tells you more than you ever wanted to know about dialog boxes.

This particular dialog box is titled (not surprisingly) Corel Office — Save As (see Figure 1-2). You use it to tell WordPerfect where to store the document on the disk and what to call it. We talk more in Chapter 15 about where you can store documents. For now, WordPerfect suggests that you store your document in the *default document folder* — the folder to put files in unless someone says otherwise.

**2. In the box titled Name, enter a name for the document.**

One of the great reliefs of Windows 95 is the fact that filenames are no longer extremely limited in length. Feel free to name your document (almost) anything you want. There are a couple of rules, which are listed in the following section. If this is just a test document, you might name it Test.wpd.

**Figure 1-2:** WordPerfect's all-new, super-duper-tell-it-where-you-want-your-file-to-go dialog box.

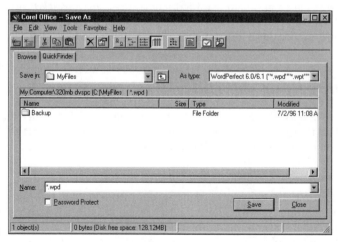

**3. Press Enter or click on the Save button.**

WordPerfect saves the document in the file you named. You can tell that this procedure worked, because the title bar displays the following line:

```
Corel WordPerfect - C:\MyFiles\test.wpd[unmodified]
```

When you save a document in a file, you can choose which folder the file should be in. See Chapter 15 to find out how to tell WordPerfect where to store it.

Save early and often. Save whenever you think of it and whenever you wonder when was the last time you saved. A save in time saves the loss of your document. You get the idea. If you kick the computer's cord out of the plug, if your 2-year-old presses the Reset button, or if you have a brain spasm that causes you to delete several paragraphs of perfectly good text, you will be happy if you know that the document is safe and sound on your disk. (See Chapter 20 to learn how to get your document back if these or other catastrophes occur.)

You can tell WordPerfect to save your document automatically every 5 or 10 minutes or at any interval you choose (see Chapter 20).

What if a file named Test.wpd *already* exists? WordPerfect, which always watches out for your interests, tells you when this happens. A dialog box appears, telling you that the file already exists and asking whether you really want to replace it (irrevocably deleting the existing file in the process). You have two — count 'em two — options here:

- ✔ **Yes:** To replace the existing file
- ✔ **No:** To enter a different name for your new file

If you are looking at the Save As dialog box and change your mind about saving the document, press the Escape (or Esc) key. This action makes the dialog box disappear.

Chapter 15 describes everything you want to know about files, including how to delete, move, copy, and rename them.

## *Filename rules*

When you enter a name for a new WordPerfect document, you must follow the rules for naming files. WordPerfect didn't make up these rules; Windows 95 did. And because people have been complaining for years about the names you could give files in Windows, those thoughtful folks at Microsoft changed the rules considerably.

The game has changed. Here are the new rules:

- Filenames can be as long as 255 characters.

- Most filenames contain a period (.). What follows the period is called an *extension,* is usually three letters, and usually describes the type of the file. WordPerfect documents use the extensions wpd (word- processing document), frm (mail-merge forms, covered in Chapter 18), and dat (mail-merge data files, also in Chapter 18).

- You can omit the extension, if you want, but you cannot omit the name.

- You can use any extension you want, but you'll find it more convenient if you use the wpd, frm, and dat extensions suggested by WordPerfect.

- You can use letters, numbers, spaces, and almost all punctuation in the name and extension. Rather than memorize which symbols are OK and which ones are no good, stick with letters, numbers, and spaces in your filenames.

- You can use either capital or small letters: Neither Windows 95 nor WordPerfect cares. In fact, they don't even distinguish between them. READ.ME, read.me, and rEaD.mE all are the same filename, as far as Windows 95 is concerned.

These three filenames, for example, are okay:

- LETTER.WPD

- Chapter 1 - First Draft.wpd

- SuperCaliFragiListicExpiAliDocious.Documents.Are.Fun.wpd

But these filenames aren't:

- "Here's Johnny" (Quotes are some of the punctuation characters you can't use in a filename.)

- \ / : * ? < > | (These are the rest of the punctuation characters you can't use in a filename.)

## *Save it again, Sam*

After you save your document and give it a name, you don't have to tell WordPerfect the name again. If you enter some more text and want to save it, you can just click on the Save button again. WordPerfect updates the file on the disk with the new version of your document, which replaces the old one.

# Getting Some Help

Clearly, you have a great deal to remember here. And you probably have better things to do than to memorize all this computer trivia. Luckily, WordPerfect can provide help when you need it — at least it can provide a description, in computerese, that may be of limited help.

Like almost all Windows programs, WordPerfect has a *Help key:* the F1 function key. Pressing F1 runs the WordPerfect Help system, which contains most of the text in the WordPerfect reference manual. Finding information in the on-line Help is usually easier than riffling through printed pages. Chapter 2 describes on-line Help.

# Editing Another File

So far, you have made a document from scratch. But frequently, you will want to edit a document that is already stored on disk. It may be a document you made earlier and saved, a document created by someone else, or a love note left on your disk by a secret admirer (secret admirers are getting more high-tech these days). Whatever the document is, you can look at it in WordPerfect. This process is called *loading* (or *opening*) the document.

These steps show you the easiest way to open a document that has been stored on the disk:

1. **Click the Open button on the Toolbar.**

   This button is the one with a tiny yellow folder on it — usually, the second button from the left.

   WordPerfect displays the Open dialog box (see Figure 1-3). Displaying this dialog box is the program's subtle way of saying that it wants to know which file you want to open.

2. **Choose a file from the list that is displayed.**

   To choose one, click on a name in the list of displayed names. WordPerfect highlights the name by displaying it in another color to show that it knows the one you want.

3. **Choose the Open button.**

   That is, click on it (or press the Enter key). WordPerfect opens the file, reads the document, and displays it on-screen.

Now you can make changes in the document, save it again, print it, or whatever!

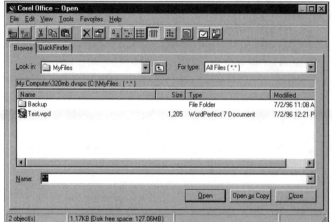

**Figure 1-3:**
Opening a
file you
made
earlier.

If the document is long, it doesn't all fit on-screen. Don't panic — it's still there. See Chapter 2 for information about how to move around in the document, including the parts that aren't currently visible.

You may want to open a file in a different folder from the one displayed in the Open dialog box. See Chapter 15 to learn how to use folders.

If the document was created by a word processor other than WordPerfect, see Chapter 14 to learn how to open it.

After you have opened a document in WordPerfect, you can see it on-screen, make changes in it, save the new version, and print it. We talk about how to print a document in the following section.

## A brief diversion for conversion

When you open a document, you may see a little box with the message that a conversion is in progress. This message usually means that the document you are opening was created in a different version of WordPerfect, such as WordPerfect for Windows 5.2 or WordPerfect for DOS. (Don'tcha love all these long names?) Each version of WordPerfect stores documents in its own way.

Not to worry — WordPerfect 7 reads these files just fine. When you save the file, WordPerfect asks which flavor of WordPerfect document you want to save it as. If you plan to give the document back to someone who uses one of these older, less technologically advanced WordPerfects, save the file in the same format it was in when you opened it (WordPerfect tells you what that version was). If you plan to keep the document, save it in WordPerfect 7 format so that you don't have to see that "Conversion in progress" message every time you open the document.

# *Printing Your Document*

After you type a document or edit it until it looks the way you want it, you probably will want to print it. After all, the goal of most word processing is to produce — on paper — a letter, memo, report, or what have you. If you work in the Paperless Office of the Future (reputed to be just down the hall from the Paperless Bathroom of the Future), you may be able to send your memo or letter electronically at the touch of a button. For the rest of us, though, paper works well (typing paper, that is).

These steps show a fast way to print your document:

1. **Save the document first, just in case something goes wrong while you are trying to print it.**

   To save, click on the Save button on the Toolbar. (Refer to the "Saving your document" section, earlier in this chapter, if you don't know what we're talking about.)

2. **Turn on your printer.**

   Good luck finding the switch!

3. **Make sure that some paper is in the printer.**

4. **Click on the Print button on the Toolbar.**

   Print is the button that shows a little printer with a piece of paper sticking out the top — usually, the fourth button from the left.

   WordPerfect displays the Print dialog box. As you can see, WordPerfect provides billions of options when it comes to printing. Stay calm.

5. **Click on the Print button.**

   WordPerfect then prints the document in all its glory.

Chapter 13 contains lots more information about printing, including the care and feeding of your printer.

If you don't like the way your polished prose looks on the page, look in Chapter 8 to learn how to choose which typeface (or typefaces) to use for the text. Chapter 9 tells you how to center and justify text, and Chapter 10 shows you how to number pages and how to print page headers and footers.

# *Leaving WordPerfect*

We know that you're having fun, but sooner or later you may need to stop running WordPerfect. Because you use Windows 95, you can run other programs at the same time you run WordPerfect. You don't have to leave WordPerfect every time you want to change the budget figures in your 1-2-3 spreadsheet, receive a fax with your fax board, or play a little game of Minesweeper. You may want to leave WordPerfect running all day so that you can switch back to it in a jiffy, but you must exit WordPerfect (and Windows 95) before you turn off your computer.

To leave WordPerfect, you use the File⇨Exit command. (Why choose File when you want to exit? This strange trait is shared by almost all Windows programs.) We talk more about how to use commands in Chapter 3, but these steps show you what you have to do:

1. **Click on the word File on the menu bar.**

   The File menu appears by dropping down from the word File. (Wonder why they call it a pull-down menu when you don't have to pull on anything?)

2. **Click on the word Exit near the bottom of the File menu.**

   If you have created or changed a document but haven't saved the document in a file, WordPerfect asks whether you want to save it now. Click on Yes to save the document, No to skip saving it, or Cancel to return to WordPerfect. Choose No only if you are sure that the document doesn't contain anything you ever want to see again.

   WordPerfect packs up and goes home, and you are probably thinking about doing the same.

 Never turn off the computer without exiting WordPerfect and Windows 95. Otherwise, you may catch these programs unawares (with their digital pants down, as it were), and they may not have saved everything on disk. When you start the computer again, you may get some complaints (see Chapter 20 for information about what to do if you see them).

If you want to exit Windows 95 and turn off the computer, you can also click on the Start button on the Taskbar. The bottom menu item is Shut Down; clicking on it tells Windows 95 that you want to do just that. But before Windows 95 departs, it politely asks all running programs to vamoose. WordPerfect takes the hint and exits, just as though you had given it the File⇨Exit command yourself. If unsaved documents are open, you get the usual messages.

# Chapter 2

# Using the Mouse and Keyboard

● ● ● ● ● ● ● ● ● ● ● ● ● ● ● ● ● ● ● ● ● ● ● ● ● ● ● ● ● ● ● ● ● ● ● ● ● ● ● ● ● ● ● ●

### In This Chapter

▶ Knowing when to mouse and when not to mouse

▶ Choosing commands from menus

▶ Using dialog boxes

▶ Using QuickMenus for even more ways to choose commands

▶ Using the button bar, the Power Bar, and the ruler bar

▶ Identifying keys on the keyboard

▶ Pressing and releasing keys

▶ Knowing when to press Enter

▶ Using Tab and the spacebar

▶ Using the Undo button

▶ Using Help

● ● ● ● ● ● ● ● ● ● ● ● ● ● ● ● ● ● ● ● ● ● ● ● ● ● ● ● ● ● ● ● ● ● ● ● ● ● ● ● ● ● ● ●

*U*sing WordPerfect for Windows is a little like dining at a fine restaurant in another country, or maybe on another planet. And as anyone who has ever ordered in a foreign restaurant knows, you can tell the waiter what you want in three ways:

✔ The difficult, old-fashioned (but highly impressive) way: Speak the language.

✔ Order by the numbers (works mainly in Chinese-American restaurants).

✔ Point at the menu and grunt.

Until recently, telling a computer what you wanted was also a matter of speaking the language: typing a command or "ordering by the numbers" by pressing a special key, such as F3. Now, however, with the advent of Windows 95, PC software is smart enough that you can just "point and grunt."

That advance came just in time, too, because the "menu" of things that today's software can do is huge — so huge that to use the old-fashioned keyboard method, you have to hold down as many as three keys at a time and develop a keyboard method that would prostrate Paderewski.

That's why you have a rodent-like object called a *mouse* next to your keyboard. (If you don't, don't panic; see the section "Mouse Anatomy and Behavior Basics," later in this chapter.) Move your mouse around, and you can point with the correspondingly moving arrow on the screen. Click a button on the mouse, and you can "grunt" electronically. (Ain't science grand?) But to avoid disgruntling the folks who have already put a great deal of effort into refining their keyboard style (such as old WordPerfect for DOS users), WordPerfect 7 for Windows 95 also allows you to order it around the old-fashioned way: by using the keyboard.

The result of all this highly obliging, verging-on-sycophantic user-friendliness is that you now have three more or less alternative ways to order WordPerfect for Windows around:

- ✔ The regular keyboard, with letters, numbers, and stuff
- ✔ The function keys, labeled F1 through F12 (some keyboards don't have F11 and F12)
- ✔ The mouse, which you can use by itself in about three ways to command WordPerfect (try not to think about this for now)

Another result of all this is that your keyboard and screen begin to resemble the cockpit of a jet fighter. As always when you face jet fighters, the important thing is not to let it intimidate you. It's a friendly jet fighter (oxymoronically speaking), and you can't crash and burn. You can't hurt any hardware on your PC, and it's pretty hard to damage the software or data either unless you're willing to answer Yes to a bunch of intimidating questions. About the worst you can do is lose whatever work you have done since the last time you used WordPerfect, and even that's pretty hard to do.

If you're already fully fenestrated (Windows-familiar) and keyboard-qualified, you can just skim the next two sections of this chapter to pick up the WordPerfect peculiarities.

## *To Mouse or Not to Mouse*

Because of the popularity of the "point and grunt" method (hereafter called point and click, to be nice), mice are taking over the world. Accept this fact, and learn to love your mouse. WordPerfect for Windows is designed for the mouse, even though you can also do almost everything by using the keyboard.

Most people eventually find a particular combination of mousifying and keyboardification that suits them. Because mice are the cat's pajamas in Windows, this book generally emphasizes the mouse method and also lists the alternatives.

We begin with your mouse.

# *Mouse Anatomy and Behavior Basics*

On PCs that have mice, the mouse generally wears two buttons; snazzy dressers may sport three. Typically, however, only one button really matters: the left one. If you have a third, middle button, consider it to be a vestige of the days when giant, Jurassic-era mice roamed the countryside and intimidated one another with their vast array of buttons. If you're left-handed, you may want to ask your system guru to change the functions of the left button to the right button. (Be sure to motivate your computer expert as needed — this task is a one-cookie task, at current guru rates.)

What about the right button? Try not to think about it — or use it — for now. If you must know, the hard-working folks at WordPerfect felt that it should carry its weight for once, so they put it to use. The right button displays something called a *QuickMenu,* whose contents change depending on where the mouse pointer is pointing. This shortcut method, designed by WordPerfect's Department of Redundancy Department, does the same things you can do in about two other ways with your mouse. We talk about this subject later.

## *Nonmouse mice*

If you cannot find your mouse, you're probably beginning to get nervous. This feeling may or may not be appropriate. You may (especially if you're using a laptop PC) have an alternative pointing device called a *trackball,* which attaches to the keyboard. This device is essentially a mouse turned upside down; you trick it into thinking that it's moving by stroking the ball that normally resides on a mouse's underside. (Stop giggling; it's true.) A trackball has a button or buttons, which are analogous to the mouse buttons we have been discussing. If you're still worried, check with the guru who bought or set up your computer.

## *Configuring your mouse*

Following are some other useful things your guru can do (if you have a can-do guru):

- ✔ Adjust how fast the pointer moves on your screen when you move the mouse. (A slow pointer makes it easier to point accurately at tiny buttons but takes more room on your desk.) The *pointer* is whatever moves when the mouse moves. It can be one of several arrow shapes, a line, a hand, or an hourglass, depending on where it is and what's going on.

- ✔ Adjust how fast you have to click the button to double-click. (We talk more about double-clicking in a minute.)

For more information about how you can save cookies by doing these things yourself, see *Windows 95 For Dummies*, by Andy Rathbone (published by IDG Books Worldwide, Inc.).

Mice have their differences, but only The Truly Technical care about those differences. You can see the most important difference by turning your mouse over to examine its intimate anatomy. If you don't find a hole with a loose ball in it, you have an optical mouse, which "sees" with its feet and needs a special pad on which to run.

## Mouse skills

The first mouse skill that you need to control WordPerfect is the ability to point and click, so we define exactly what this and related terms mean:

- ✔ **To point:** Move the pointer so that the arrow tip is on top of a word or button. (Sometimes the pointer only has to be nearby.)

- ✔ **To click on something:** Point to it and then press and release the button (usually, the left one) on the mouse.

- ✔ **To double-click:** Press and release the button twice in rapid succession. You may need some practice to learn just how fast you have to click.

- ✔ **To click and drag:** Press the mouse button and hold it down; then move the mouse while you hold down the button. This action drags something around on the screen, such as a highlight bar on a menu. Finally, when you have the thing positioned where you want it, release the button.

The following section shows you how to use the mouse to order WordPerfect around.

## Choosing Commands from Menus

Taking their cue from fine-dining establishments everywhere, Windows programs, such as WordPerfect, have more than one menu of commands. They have the computer equivalent of an appetizer menu, an aperitif menu, a bread menu, a soup menu, a wine menu, an entreé menu, a choice-of-vegetable menu, a sorbet menu, and a dessert menu.

To help you sort out these menus, the next-to-topmost line (the one that displays all the words) in your WordPerfect window lists all the available menus. This line is called the *menu bar* (see Figure 2-1).

**Figure 2-1:**
Not an
oyster bar;
not a sushi
bar — it's a
menu bar.

## *Clicking on the menu bar*

To see what's in a menu, click on a word in the menu bar. That word then gets highlighted, and a menu of commands drops down from it. Quite unreasonably (because you didn't pull anything), this menu is called a *pull-down menu*.

To try out this theory, start WordPerfect (see Chapter 1) and then click on the word File. If you pull the mouse down a little, the word New is highlighted as the WordPerfect waiter suggests the delightfully savory New command. In the little yellow bar, a cheerful description of New appears. Admire this screen, leave things as they are, and read on.

If you don't find anything you like, close the menu by clicking on the menu name again or anywhere else in the WordPerfect window. If you click on another button or menu selection, however, you get whatever you clicked on.

## Let go of that button!

Some folks, for fear that the menu they selected will disappear, continue to hold down the mouse button (particularly if they have learned to use a Macintosh computer). If their hands drift by accident while they are holding down the button, they end up selecting something when they finally release the button. If you are one of these people, read the section "Using Dialog Boxes," later in this chapter.

This alternative menu technique, called *click and drag*, is useful for former Macintosh users but confusing for the rest of us. In Windows 95, most menus are displayed until you put them away; otherwise, let go of the button before you move the mouse.

## Choosing a command

To choose a command from this menu, point and click on the command. Related commands are clumped together and separated from other command clumps by a line.

In addition to the commands, you may find other suggestive symbols — sort of like the little red dots next to the hot stuff on a Chinese menu. This list shows what a few of those symbols mean:

- ✔ **A little right-pointing triangle after the command:** If you click on one of these commands, you see a submenu. (The process is similar to choosing chicken and then being asked whether you want fried, roasted, or Szechuan.)

- ✔ **A check mark next to the command:** The check mark means that it's already on, whatever it is. You can turn it off by clicking on the command.

- ✔ **An ellipsis ( . . . ) after the command:** The ellipsis appears to tell you that the command has more to say, if you ask. It does, and if you click on it, the command gift-wraps its thoughts in attractive little dialog boxes, which are discussed in the following section.

- ✔ **An _F_ with a number, such as F3:** This is a reminder that you can perform this command without ever opening a menu. All you have to do is press the key labeled F3 (or whatever the appropriate key is) on your keyboard. The F keys are function keys, whose jobs change with every program you run. These keys are the second way of ordering WordPerfect around that we mentioned earlier. You may want to remember some of these commands to make your life easier. Pressing F3, for example, always invokes the Save As dialog box in WordPerfect for Windows.

## How we talk about menus and commands in this book

Because darn near every command in WordPerfect appears on a menu, a submenu, or a sub-submenu, it gets really tedious for us to say, "Click on Edit, and then on Select in that menu, and then on Page in the next menu," or whatever. We say it this way in the early chapters of this book until you get used to the idea. After that, though, we just say "Click on (or select, or choose) Edit➪Select➪Page." It's a little terse, but if we don't do it that way, you would be comatose with boredom by the end of a paragraph. Also, think of all the trees we're saving by making the book shorter.

## <u>W</u>hat's w<u>i</u>th <u>a</u>ll <u>t</u>hese <u>u</u>nderlined characters <u>i</u>n menu<u>s</u>?

For those of you who are already comfortable with computer keyboards, underlined characters designate the Alt+key combinations that select the command. To save a file, for example, you can press Alt+F and then press S. If the preceding information is gibberish to you, read the section "Choosing commands by using keys," later in this chapter.

# *Using Dialog Boxes*

If you click on a menu command that has an ellipsis ( . . . ) after it, you get either another menu or a *dialog box.* The dialog box shown in Figure 2-2 looks like a cross between a tax form and a VCR remote control, but it is less painful to use than either one of those things.

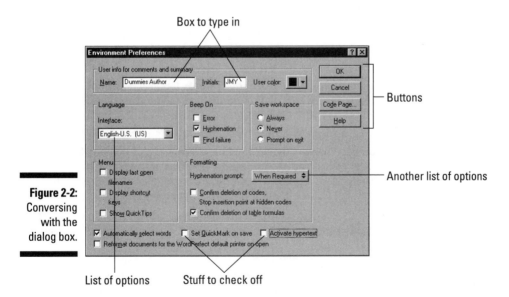

Box to type in

Buttons

Another list of options

**Figure 2-2:**
Conversing with the dialog box.

List of options       Stuff to check off

To see an example dialog box, with the <u>F</u>ile menu open, click on the Save <u>A</u>s command.

## *Those wacky dialog thingies*

This section shows some of the things (called *dialog thingies* herein) you may find in a dialog box:

> **Stuff to check off.** These items have a little box or circle to their left. This type of item can be on (selected) or off (not selected). Click on the little box or circle to select or deselect the item. The Environment Preferences dialog box, for example, has an Activate Hypertext thingy.

> **Lists of options.** You can tell which item is selected because it has a little box around it or is displayed in a different color. Click on the option you want.

> **Lists of options ( but you see only one option).** In some lists of options, WordPerfect shows only the option that is selected. To see all the options, click on the little down-pointing arrow just to the right of the selected option. In the Environment Preferences dialog box, for example, a list of languages that WordPerfect is willing to work in appears below the heading Interface.

> **Boxes in which you type.** Click on these boxes to highlight them and then type stuff. For example, you can type a name for your document's author in the Name box (refer to Figure 2-2).

> Don't press Enter when you finish typing. If you do, the dialog box closes, and WordPerfect begins executing your command immediately, even if you aren't finished.

> **Boxes with numbers you can change.** Some dialog boxes contain number settings, such as the width of a margin. To type a number, click on the number and then type the new number. To increase or decrease the number a little at a time, click on the up or down arrow next to the box.

> **Buttons you can "press" by clicking on them.** If these buttons have ellipses, guess what? You see another dialog box. If they have little triangles on them, they display a menu. The Environment Preferences dialog box, for example, has a bunch of buttons down its right side.

> **Icons that run little WordPerfect subprograms.** These icons are sort of like specialized junior waiters — one for forks and one for spoons. Double-click on these items to see them scurry.

Don't try to remember all this stuff. We talk about various instances of these dialog thingies as we go along, but you can refer to this list if you ever run into an unfamiliar one.

## Pinky finger alert!

When you use dialog boxes, you should beware of two keyboard keys: Enter and Esc, which mean the same as the OK and Cancel buttons, respectively. This caution applies even if you're typing something in a dialog thingy. Keep a watchful eye on your pinky fingers, lest they unwittingly lead you astray by pressing Enter or Esc before you are really finished with the dialog box.

## *Our favorite buttons*

Two common and important buttons are the OK and Cancel buttons. Clicking on OK means "Do it — and do it the way this box says to do it." Clicking on Cancel means "Forget it — I didn't really want to do this. Get me outta here, and ignore everything I said in this box."

"Forget it" apparently is a popular choice because Windows allows you to say the same thing in three other ways:

- ✔ Press the Esc key on the keyboard.
- ✔ Click on the X in the upper right corner of the dialog box.
- ✔ Press Alt+F4.

We're talking overkill here. We just remember to click the Cancel button or press Esc — enough is enough.

You may also see the Close button, which means basically the same thing as OK. Clicking on Close just closes the box without changing anything that hasn't already been changed.

# *Using QuickMenus for Even More Ways to Choose Commands*

If you're beginning to get a headache just thinking about the regular, plain-vanilla menu bar, give this subject a miss.

As usual, in its quest to give you more options than you would have thought possible, WordPerfect provides another way to choose commands. This method involves the use of the right mouse button. Until now, whenever we tell you to click the mouse button, we have always meant the left one.

The people who write Windows programs, however, decided that because most PC mice have two or three buttons, ignoring the additional one or two buttons would be missing an opportunity for more menus, options, and (probably) confusion.

In many Windows programs, clicking on something with the right mouse button pops up a little menu called a QuickMenu, so those wacky WordPerfect people decided to have QuickMenus too. Throughout this book, whenever clicking on something with the right mouse button displays a QuickMenu, we tell you about it. The status bar (the bar at the bottom of the screen), for example, has a QuickMenu you can hide if you get tired of looking at it.

These steps show you how to see a QuickMenu:

1. **Point to the status bar with the mouse pointer.**

2. **Click once, using the right mouse button.**

   A little box pops up, right where your mouse pointer is.

Voilà! Now that you can see a QuickMenu — specifically, the one for the status bar — what good does it do you? This QuickMenu has three options: Hide Status Bar, What's This? and Preferences. . . .

Most QuickMenus have a Preferences option that allows you to customize the way WordPerfect works. We talk about customizing WordPerfect in Chapter 20.

Each QuickMenu contains commands that have something to do with the thing you were pointing at (the status bar, in this case). This particular QuickMenu contains the command Hide Status Bar.

To choose a command, such as Hide Status Bar, from a QuickMenu, you have (as usual) a choice of methods:

   ✔ Point to the command with the mouse pointer, and click on it (either the left *or* the right mouse button will do).
   ✔ Press the underlined letter in the command (H, in this case).

Either way, WordPerfect leaps into action and performs the command. In this case, the status bar vanishes like M&Ms at a birthday party. (To get the status bar back, by the way, you can use the View⇨Toolbars/Ruler . . . Bar command and make sure that the box beside Status Bar has an X in it.)

# *Fooling with the Toolbar*

As accustomed to bars as writers traditionally are, the number of bars in WordPerfect for Windows 95 inspires even us. We are about to discuss two of these word-processing watering holes: the Toolbar and the Power Bar. As in real life (restaurants, that is), you can think of going to these bars as a way to get quick service without a menu.

The *Toolbar* is a line of buttons with pictures on them below the menu bar, as shown in Figure 2-3. The Toolbar is one of those cool icon things that make Windows programs such as WordPerfect look really impressive — like your VCR or CD player's remote control. Unlike your remote control, though, the Toolbar is very useful and simple after you get to know it.

**Figure 2-3:**
The Toolbar.
The tools
at the hard-
ware store
never looked
like this!

The first thing to know about the Toolbar is that it's not always displayed. (This knowledge should be reassuring to those who are now frantically looking for rectangular buttons with pictures on them.) The second thing to know is that the Toolbar is not the same as the Power Bar, which has even smaller buttons with words but no pictures (fortunately, for those of us whose eyes have trouble with small stuff). If you're not sure which bar you're looking at on your screen, check Figure 1-1 in Chapter 1.

If you don't see the Toolbar, you can display it by opening the View menu and clicking on Toolbars/Ruler. . . . Make sure that the box beside WordPerfect 7 Toolbar is checked, and click OK. Notice that you may not have the same buttons in your bar that we have in ours. In fact, your Power Bar might even have pictures on it. If that's the case, the person who set up your software decided to change the buttons. If he went to all that trouble, there's probably a good reason, and you should ask him to explain what he had in mind.

Toolbar buttons are quick ways to do everyday things — things you can do with menus that take longer to do that way. Some buttons are self-explanatory and pretty simple, such as Print, which prints the document. Thanks again to the Department of Redundancy Department (again), you can also print by choosing File⇨Print or by holding down the Ctrl key while you press P (Ctrl+P). Some buttons, such as Text Box, do things that are a little more complicated. If you want more explanation about a button, just move your pointer to it (don't click). A little birdie — ahem, we mean a little yellow box delivers a brief one-liner about the button and lists the function-key equivalent, if there is one.

The Very Sharp-Sighted among you will notice that if they put the pointer in the gray area around the buttons, the pointer turns into a hand. The More Adventuresome will discover that if you hold down the mouse button and move the mouse, the hand drags an outline of the Toolbar to another location. After these people release the button, the Toolbar reappears in the new location and in a chunkier form. If you find the Toolbar's original location to be annoying, you might give this technique a try.

If you decide that you don't like the adorable little pictures on the Toolbar, open the View menu, click on Toolbars/Ruler . . . and uncheck the WordPerfect 7 Toolbar.

Throughout this book, we tell you when a button on the Toolbar would be useful. In Chapter 1, for example, we used Toolbar buttons to open, save, and print documents in one fell click.

# Power Lunch at the Power Bar

The concept of something called a *Power Bar* is intriguing, although it's vaguely disconcerting to those of us who made it through the 1980s without ever having had a power lunch. Perhaps that's why we brown-bag, tuna-sandwich types find its function to be barely distinguishable from the more humble and homely-sounding Toolbar. Yet there it is.

If the Power Bar is displayed, it looks something like Figure 2-4.

## Sharpening your tools

Here's the cool thing about the Toolbar: You can tell WordPerfect which buttons you want on the bar. You can even make your own buttons. Then you can make different sets of buttons for different kinds of documents you work on — one set of buttons for writing memos, perhaps, and a different set of buttons for writing reports.

Fortunately, we don't tell you how to do all this stuff right now. But we want to warn you, in case someone else set up specialized Toolbars on your computer, in which case the buttons on your Toolbar will change mysteriously when you use different documents. If you think that this trick sounds as cool as we think it does, check out Chapter 17 for details.

**Figure 2-4:**
Powerful
buttons
on the
Power Bar.

Like the Toolbar, the Power Bar has buttons that can be changed by the Very Knowledgeable, so yours may not look like ours. If the Power Bar is not visible, open the View menu, click on Toolbars/Ruler, and make sure that the box beside Power Bar is checked. Then click on the OK button.

Also like the Toolbar, the Power Bar is a quick, convenient way to do something that would take longer to do if you used the menus. If you place the pointer on a button, the title bar provides a brief explanation of the button's function. Because some of the labels on the buttons can be a little vague ("Left"? Left what?), this explanation is quite useful.

When you click on a button on the Power Bar, a menu drops down from the button. If you click on the leftmost button, for example, you can choose the font to use for some text. This button usually starts out saying `Times New Roman`. By clicking on it, you can choose another font from a long list of fonts that come with WordPerfect, as well as fonts that come with other applications for Windows 95. (We talk more about fonts in Chapter 8.)

As with the Toolbar, if you decide that you really don't like the Power Bar, click on Toolbars/Ruler on the View menu again and *un*check the Power Bar check box.

## Using the Ruler Bar

Okay, now we're on familiar ground. Everybody knows what a ruler is, right? Ummm, maybe. The WordPerfect ruler is not your ordinary tick-marks-along-the-edge sort of thing (although it has those too). It's a behavior-controlling ruler bar (like the ones your grade-school teachers had), except that this ruler bar controls the behavior of your paragraphs. Specifically, it controls the indents and tabs of whatever paragraph you're working in (where the cursor is — not your mouse pointer). The *cursor,* or *insertion point,* is a stationary, usually blinking vertical line after which text appears when you type. The mouse pointer is an arrow shape that moves when the mouse moves. WordPerfect also has a shadow cursor that shows you where the cursor or insertion point *would* go *if* you were to click the left mouse button.

Like the various other bars, the ruler bar may or may not be displayed. Open the <u>V</u>iew menu, click on <u>T</u>oolbars/Ruler, and check or clear the box next to Ruler Bar to make the ruler bar appear or disappear (see Figure 2-5).

The light-colored bar across the top of the ruler shows your left and right margins, as well as your paragraph indents. In the bar below the actual ruler, the little triangles show tab settings. The triangles take different shapes, according to which kind of tabs they represent. When you look at your ruler, you'll find that some tabs are already set. These settings are not your fault: They are default tabs, which you can change if you want. You can add tabs, remove tabs, or move tabs around.

We discuss all this stuff in fascinating detail in Chapter 9, but the quick tour goes like this:

✔ To move a tab or paragraph margin around, you *drag* it. Point to it; press the mouse button, and hold it down. Then move the mouse. Release the button when the selected item is where you want it.

✔ To change the type of tabs you're putting in, click on the far left end of the ruler bar, where you see a small, unlabeled button. WordPerfect displays a menu of tab types. Move the mouse to drag the highlight to the type you want; then release the mouse button.

Make sure that the blinking cursor (the blinking vertical bar, not the mouse pointer) is in the correct paragraph before you set tab stops or indents with the ruler.

**Figure 2-5:**
Pay homage
to your ruler.
He's picking
up your tab.

Left margin          Right margin

Tab stop

# Using the Keyboard

What with all these bars, windows, and icons, the keyboard begins to seem rather old and dowdy. Still, it beats the heck out of trying to type with the mouse. And for those of us who are reluctant to change our ways just because some software engineer decided to give us a mouse, the keyboard still provides a fairly fast way to give commands to WordPerfect.

## Know your keys

Take a look at your keyboard. With any luck, it looks like Figure 2-6. (If your computer is a laptop, you're on your own 'cause the keys can be anywhere.)

Notice that the keyboard has different areas, each with its own role to play. The following list describes the different groups and what they do:

**Function keys.** Usually located along the top of the keyboard and labeled F1 through F10 or F12, these keys are assigned to different commands in WordPerfect. They perform many of the same commands you can call from the menu bar, Toolbar, or Power Bar. The function keys perform one set of commands when you use them by themselves and others when you use them with the *shift keys:* Alt, Ctrl, and Shift.

**Typewriter keys.** These keys have the familiar characters, numbers, and punctuation that are on your old Royal typewriter, plus a few jazzy new ones. You use these keys mostly to type stuff, but you can use them with the shift keys to issue commands.

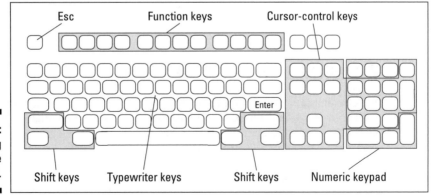

**Figure 2-6:** Interesting keys on the keyboard.

**Cursor-control keys.** These keys are the ones off to the right of the typewriter keys. Four of them have arrows on them; they move the cursor when you're typing or move the highlight that appears when you're using Windows menus or scroll bars. The others — marked Home, End, PgUp (or Page Up), and PgDn (or Page Down) — are pairs of keys that move the cursor in large gulps. The size of the gulp depends on which shift keys you're holding down, if any. See Chapter 3 for details about how to use these keys to move around in your document.

**Florida Keys.** You retire here after learning how to use WordPerfect for Windows 95. Hang out in an RV along lovely Smathers Beach in Key West, cruise Duvall Street, and watch the college kids throw up during spring break.

**Numeric-keypad keys.** The keys on this keypad basically duplicate the number keys, useful math symbols, and the Enter key. You can also use them rather than the cursor keys if you don't have any others. Just press the Num Lock button that is probably nearby, and the keypad keys become cursor keys.

**Shift keys.** The members of this shifty bunch don't do anything by themselves — only in combination with other keys, sort of like the pedals on a piano. Like the Shift key on your Smith-Corona, when the Shift, Alt, and Ctrl (pronounced Control) keys are held down, they impart new meanings to function keys and cursor-control keys, and they cause certain typewriter keys to execute commands when you press them.

**Enter key.** This key is generally marked as such or with a funny L-shaped arrow. Pressing this key ends your paragraphs when you're typing (*not* every line) or finishes a command when you're in a menu or dialog box. Some people call this key the Return key. Used with the Ctrl key, Enter inserts a page break (see Chapter 10).

**Esc key:** Called the Escape key, this little guy can help you back out of menus you didn't mean to get into.

## Pressing and releasing keys

As an example of how computer technology makes your life easier than it was with your Smith-Corona (or not, as the case usually is), you must now be careful not only about which keys you press but also about precisely how you press *and* release them. At least, that's the case with some keys.

The computer is particularly fussy about the shift keys, which work only in conjunction with other keys. All is well if you use them exactly like the Shift key on your beloved Periwinkle-Marmosette typewriter, as shown in these steps:

1. **Press the Shift key (Shift, Alt, or Ctrl, as directed) *first,* and *hold it down.***

   Don't crush it — just push it.

**2. Press the other key (F7, for example).**

**3. Finally, release both keys.**

If your fingers don't work well together, release the Shift key last.

These types of key combinations are written as Shift+F7, for example, or Ctrl+F7 or Alt+F7.

Sometimes you must press more than one shift key. This instruction is written as Ctrl+Shift+F3, but it may as well be written Shift+Ctrl+F3 because it doesn't matter in which order you press the shift keys. Just get both of 'em down before you press the last key, and release 'em all at once.

## Knowing when to press Enter

This section probably should be titled "Knowing when *not* to press Enter." In WordPerfect and any other word processor, you do *not* press the Enter key at the end of every line; you press Enter at the end of every *paragraph*. Failure to observe this rule causes you regular consternation and grief and marks you as a tyro (a novice) to all who observe your work.

Do not worry about the ends of your lines. WordPerfect takes care of most lines automatically and usually does it far better than you can (ragged right, justi-fied, whatever you need). The *only* time you should press Enter at the end of a line is when you are entering a list and the line must end before it is full.

Because pressing the Enter key marks the end of a paragraph, WordPerfect inserts a little paragraph symbol, like this: ¶. Trouble is, the symbol is invisible. To make it visible, open the <u>V</u>iew menu and click on <u>S</u>how ¶.

Whether the symbol is visible or not, it's there. If you delete it — which you can do the same way you delete any normal, visible character — your paragraph gets merged with the one below it.

## The story of Tab and the spacebar

This story sounds like an entertaining tale of Tab, the swinging Astro Kitty. Alas, although this story is about space, it's not about black holes and watering holes — it's about white space.

Like pressing Enter at the end of every line, another way to cause yourself no end of unnecessary grief is to overuse the Tab key and the spacebar to get your text where you want it. There generally are better ways to do this than the way you did it on your Stombrowski-Danglowicz steam-powered typing machine, which you fondly remember from the old days in the KGB.

The Tab and spacebar keys insert white-space characters. Like cockroaches in the Keys (Florida, that is), you may not see them, but they're there. A certain WordPerfect command is equivalent to snapping on the light switch to see these critters; it's the same command that shows the invisible paragraph mark. Choose View from the menu bar and then choose Show ¶ (you can also press Ctrl+Shift+F3).

Whoa! Suddenly, all the spaces in your document appear as little black dots, all the tabs appear as arrows, and your little paragraph markers show up at the end of each paragraph. Don't worry — your document won't look like this when it's printed. This is just a useful way to see exactly which characters you have.

There are better ways to position your text than to use a bunch of spaces and tabs, and we get into them in Chapter 9. This list tells you how to use these guys properly:

✔ Use the spacebar only between words or sentences.

✔ For the most part, you press the Tab key only to indent the *first line* of a paragraph or put white space in the middle of a sentence. (To indent an entire paragraph, click on the Indent button on the Toolbar or press the F7 key; see Chapter 9.)

If you want to create a table of words and numbers, you may have to use tabs too, or you can tell WordPerfect to help you make a table (see Chapter 16).

## *Choosing commands by using keys*

As we intimated earlier, you can use the keyboard rather than the mouse to choose commands from the menu bar. For touch typists, this method can be more efficient than mousing it because you don't have to move your fingers from that all-important home row.

To choose a command without touching the mouse, follow these steps:

1. **Look at the menu bar, and notice which character of the command is underlined.**

   The underlined character is always a letter or a number.

2. **Hold down the Alt key while you press the key; then release the Alt key.**

   Aha! WordPerfect grasps your meaning and displays the menu associated with that command. If you press Alt+V, for example, WordPerfect rolls down the View menu.

**3. Again, check the command on this menu to see which character is underlined.**

Press it, with or without the Alt key. WordPerfect has guessed that you are giving a command, so you don't have to press the Alt key to tip it off.

If you choose a command that has a little triangle after it, such as the Format⇨Line command, WordPerfect displays another little menu. Repeat step 2 to choose the command from this menu.

For commands you use frequently, you may learn the letters that invoke the command, and you can probably type them faster (even including pressing the Alt key) than you can choose the command with the mouse.

This list shows some other keys you can use while you give commands:

✔ To cancel a menu by using the keyboard, press the Esc key. Every time you press it, WordPerfect backs up one step. Keep pressing Esc until the menus go away and no command is highlighted on the menu bar.

✔ Computer-literate types may be tempted to think that the Break key cancels commands too, but in fact, WordPerfect ignores it.

✔ You can also use the keyboard to get around in dialog boxes, although this method is rather cumbersome. In every dialog box, almost every item and button has an underlined letter in its name, and pressing Alt and that letter moves the cursor there.

# *Undoing Mistakes*

Not that you're likely to make a mistake or anything, but for those of us who occasionally give the wrong command, the Toolbar has a highly useful button called Undo. Actually, it's not called anything. The button doesn't say *Undo* — it just has an icon of an arrow doing a counterclockwise U-turn.

When you click on this button (or press Ctrl+Z or choose Edit⇨Undo), WordPerfect usually can undo whatever the last command did, including deleting a bunch of characters, whether you used the Delete key, the Backspace key (see Chapter 3), or both.

WordPerfect also has a Redo button (and a matching Edit⇨Redo command). This button undoes the last Undo you did. (Confused? We are!) Redo is the clockwise U-turn button on the Toolbar.

For information about specifically undoing deletions, see Chapter 4, which discusses an even more useful ( but somewhat trickier) command called Undelete.

# *Help, Help-Help, and More Help*

Calling for help in a Windows 95 program such as WordPerfect is a little like calling for help at the Arnold Schwarzenegger–Leona Helmsley School of Lifeguard Training: Prepare to be a little overwhelmed. You don't just get information — you get an entire muscle-bound information retrieval and management system designed to meet your assistance requirements (and leave a mint on your pillow).

We're not even going to try to explain everything that this Dream Team of lifesavers can do; we just give you the simplest way to use Help. For all the fancy stuff, we recommend that you play around in Help to your heart's content. You can't break anything, and you may learn a great deal.

## *Help*

The simplest part is calling for Help. It's <u>H</u>elp on the menu bar (or press Alt+H). At this point, it's a good thing you're not literally drowning when you call for help in WordPerfect, because now you must decide precisely *how* you are going to ask for help. The <u>T</u>opic and <u>U</u>pgrade Help options are perfectly reasonable and straightforward. The Ask the <u>P</u>erfectExpert option is so cool that we talk about it in its own section (see the section "Ask the Expert," later in this chapter).

If you choose <u>H</u>elp Topics, you see a help box with four tabs at the top: Contents, Index, Find, and Show Me. Here's what happens on each of those tabs:

- ✔ **Contents.** You can click on a closed book to see the topics inside it, or you can click on one of the question marks to see the actual help for a particular topic.

- ✔ **Index.** WordPerfect Help displays a list of all topics, arranged alphabetically. As you type the first few letters of the topic you're interested in, WordPerfect displays the index entry that starts with what you typed.

- ✔ **Find.** Okay, what you were looking for wasn't in the index. You're not surprised, right? That's okay; WordPerfect Help can flip through the whole help file, looking for any word you want. But wait — this is Windows 95. The first time you try to find something, a Wizard asks you all sorts of questions about how you want to search the help file. Just click on the Next button and the Finish button, and then go get a cup of coffee while Windows 95 creates a word list. When it's done, you see a screen much like the one on the Index tab. As you type your word, WordPerfect Help shows you which words match what you typed. Click on a matching word, and WordPerfect Help shows you some help topics.

✔ **Show Me.** WordPerfect can do some tasks for you. Choose a topic from the list, and tell WordPerfect Help to play a demo of how to use a feature, guide you through it, or do it for you. Try these options; they're fun. And they sure beat the heck out of working. But if you let WordPerfect Help do the work for you, you may want to save your document first; just a word to the wise. . . . Actually, this feature is fabulous, because it works right along with you.

Whichever method you choose, you get exactly the same window full of information. Often, several items in the text appear in a list with buttons in front of them; each of these areas is itself a topic. When you click on one of these buttons, you get information on that topic. Figure 2-7 shows a sample Help window with three other Help topics on it. If you get lost in this labyrinthine Hall of Help and want to find your way back, look for a Back button at the top of the Help window and click on it.

To make the Help window go away, the easiest thing to do is click on the Close button (the little x) in the upper right corner of the screen.

**Figure 2-7:**
A sample
Help
window.

# Ask the Expert

Usually the Expert is the office WordPerfect guru. In case your office doesn't have one of these people, those thoughtful WordPerfect folks included a couple of experts, called PerfectExperts.

This is WordPerfect, so of course you can Ask the PerfectExpert in two ways: Choose Ask the PerfectExpert . . . from the Help menu or click the Ask the PerfectExpert button in Help Topics. In either case, you can type an English sentence about what you want to do, and WordPerfect Help will try to find some help topics that it thinks are relevant. This feature is simple, and quite cool. The PerfectExpert usually guesses pretty well too.

## Context-sensitive Help

If you want the Help feature to pare down the list of topics to things related to whatever you're doing right now, you can choose Context-Sensitive Help. (Imagine Arnold and Leona trying to be sensitive to your personal needs, and you get the picture.) When you're in the middle of using a menu or a dialog box, press F1. Zap! Arnold figures out exactly which topic you ought to be interested in (whether you are or not). If you press F1 with the pointer in the middle of your text, you see the same window that appears when you choose the Contents tab from the Help⇨Help Topics menu picks.

Another form of context-sensitive help is available — kind of in the Tinkerbell school of lifesaving (for you Peter Pan fans). In almost all dialog boxes, you find a button with a question mark on it near the upper right corner of the dialog box. Click on that button, and your mouse pointer turns into a little cartoon thought balloon with a question mark on it. (We cannot help but think of this as Tinkerbell. Sorry.) Click on something in the dialog box, and a Help screen tells you about it.

Tinkerbell can also help you with commands. These steps show you how to ask:

1. **Press Shift+F1.**

   Your mouse pointer turns into a little cartoon thought balloon with a question mark on it.

2. **Point to a menu command or button, and click the left mouse button.**

3. **If you're looking in a menu, continue to hold down the mouse button and drag the highlight (by moving the mouse) to whatever you want help with.**

4. **Release the mouse button.**

   Poof! Tinkerbell helps you with whatever you selected. When you exit the Help window, she goes away and doesn't come back until you press Shift+F1 again.

# Chapter 3

# Cruising the Document

· · · · · · · · · · · · · · · · · · · · · · · · · · · · · · · · · · · · · · · ·

## In This Chapter

▶ Moving around in the document

▶ Using the mouse

▶ Using the keyboard

▶ Using the Go To dialog box

· · · · · · · · · · · · · · · · · · · · · · · · · · · · · · · · · · · · · · · ·

*A*fter you type some text in your document, you undoubtedly will want to do some editing. After all, that's what word processing is all about. When you use a regular typewriter, making changes involves splashing a viscous white liquid all over your paper, yourself, and the furniture — or slicing and dicing little slips of paper, only to reassemble them with glue or tape. But those days are over, now that you have entered the Age of Word Processing — you can slice and dice your text right on the screen, with no paper cuts or white-out stains.

To be able to edit, of course, you must move your cursor (the blinking vertical bar) to the text you want to change. Your cursor is your pencil point on the page; its location determines where actions will happen. So that's what this chapter is about: moving the cursor around in your document. In later chapters, we tell you what to do when you get there, such as deleting things (Chapter 4), moving text around (Chapter 6), and making the text look different (Chapter 8).

## *Two — Count 'Em, Two — Ways*

You have, of course, two ways of navigating around your document. (Computer people like to talk about *navigation* rather than just *moving;* we must be a group of frustrated sailors.) As you use WordPerfect, you find that two is the absolute minimum number of ways to do anything, and in many cases WordPerfect provides four or five ways. (Chapter 2 tells how many ways there are to give a command.)

You can move the cursor in two general ways:

- ✔ Use the mouse to point to where you want to go.
- ✔ Use keys on the keyboard to move in the direction you indicate.

Two cursorlike things are also on the screen (as they are in most Windows 95 programs):

- ✔ **The mouse pointer.** The mouse pointer tells you where the mouse is pointing. It can change shapes and does so, depending on what WordPerfect thinks it is pointing at. Usually in WordPerfect, the pointer is a little white arrow. If WordPerfect is busy, it turns into an hourglass. And if your mouse is pointing to a place in WordPerfect where you can type, you see a gray blinking line at the place where you would be typing if you clicked the mouse. Finally, if you don't see the mouse pointer, just move the mouse a little to make it appear.

- ✔ **The insertion point.** Also called the plain old *cursor,* it tells you where your typing will appear. (We hope you don't mind that we call this thing the cursor, because it's the term we're used to.) The cursor is a slowly blinking vertical bar; you can't miss it.

The purpose of this chapter is to get the cursor into firing position so that you can take aim at some text. First, we talk about using the mouse; next, we talk about using the boring old keyboard; finally, we throw in a few other ways in which WordPerfect allows you to cruise your document.

# Mousing Around

Now that WordPerfect runs with Windows 95, it uses the snazzy Windows 95 graphical user interface — including the mouse — for just about everything except typing text. (Gee, maybe the next version will let you use the mouse to point to letters on a little picture of a keyboard. Can you imagine a slower way to type?)

## Moving nearby

If the place where you want to go to is displayed on-screen, just position the mouse pointer there and click the left mouse button. Follow these steps:

1. **Move the mouse pointer to the position where you want to work.**

   When the mouse is pointing to your text or near it, a blinking gray line appears in the text. If there's no little gray line (and it can be hard to see), you are pointing to something other than your text and you cannot move your cursor there. Move the mouse pointer to the beginning of the paragraph.

2. **Click the mouse button without moving the mouse.**

   This action tells WordPerfect to put the cursor right where the mouse pointer is.

3. **You may want to move the mouse pointer out of the way so that it doesn't obscure the text you are going to edit.**

   You don't really have to, though, because as soon as you begin typing, the mouse pointer disappears, in an effort to stay out of the way.

## *Moving to the far reaches of the document*

If you cannot see the text you want to edit, don't panic — it's still there, but it has fallen off the edge of the screen. WordPerfect displays your document as though it were written on a long scroll (imagine medieval monks or Egyptian scribes). The beginning and ending portions of the document are rolled up, and only the middle part is visible. If you want to see a different section of the text, WordPerfect unrolls the scroll for you and displays it on-screen.

You may have noticed a vertical gray bar running along the right side of the screen. Figure 3-1 shows this *scroll bar* (mentioned in Chapter 1). You use it to tell WordPerfect to roll and unroll the metaphorical scroll that contains your document.

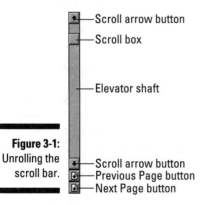

—Scroll arrow button

—Scroll box

—Elevator shaft

**Figure 3-1:**
Unrolling the
scroll bar.

—Scroll arrow button
—Previous Page button
—Next Page button

The scroll bar is similar to a little map of your document, with the full length of the scroll bar representing your entire document: The top end is the beginning of the document, and the bottom end is the end of it. The little gray box on the scroll bar (the *scroll box,* in Windows parlance) represents the part of the document you can see on-screen right now. The scroll box moves up and down the scroll bar the way an elevator moves up and down a shaft. By looking at the position of the scroll box in the scroll bar, you can tell where you are in the document — at the beginning, middle, or end.

You can also move around the document by using the scroll bar, as you may have guessed already. This list shows the things you can do to the scroll bar with your mouse:

- **Move anywhere in the document in a big hurry.** Use the mouse to drag the scroll box up and down the scroll bar. As you move the scroll box, thus scrolleth the text of the document. To drag the scroll box, point to it with your mouse pointer, press and hold down the mouse button, and move the mouse pointer up or down. The scroll box moves with the mouse pointer as long as you hold down the mouse button. When you release the button, the scroll box stays where you left it, and the document scrolls to match.

- **Move to the end of your document.** You can drag the scroll box down to the bottom of its elevator shaft.

- **Move to the beginning of the document.** Do the reverse — drag the scroll box up to the tippy-top.

- **Move forward or backward one screen of text at a time.** Click on the scroll bar (not on the scroll box). To move to the next screen of text in the document, click on the scroll bar below the scroll box. To move to the preceding screen, click above the scroll box. The scroll box moves, and the document scrolls down one screen.

- **Scroll your text one line at a time.** Click on the scroll arrow buttons — the little buttons with arrows on them at either end of the scroll bar. The button with the up-pointing arrow (at the top of the scroll bar) moves you toward the beginning of the document, and the button with the down-pointing arrow moves toward the end.

- **Move through the document page by page.** Click on the Next Page and Previous Page buttons. These buttons, which are at the bottom of the scroll bar, have little pages with up and down arrows on them. When you click on the Next Page button, WordPerfect scrolls the document so that the top of the next page is at the top of the screen. The Previous Page button scrolls so that the top of the preceding page is at the top of the screen.

Clicking on the scroll box itself doesn't do a blessed thing — not even double-clicking. If you click on the scroll bar with the *right* mouse button, however, WordPerfect pops up the scroll bar's QuickMenu. We talk about this menu at the end of this chapter.

If your document is too wide to fit across the WordPerfect window, a scroll bar runs across the bottom of the window too, right above the status bar. This scroll bar works just like the vertical scroll bar we have been talking about, except that it moves sideways and has no Next Page and Previous Page buttons.

# *Using the Keyboard, Staying Close to Home*

If you type like the wind, you probably don't want to have to move your hands from the home row of your keyboard — not even to have lunch. Your speedy fingers know where every key is, and they can hit them faster than a 2-year-old can grab an Oreo. Faster, even.

After reading about all this mouse stuff, you're probably thinking, "The mouse is cute, but it slows me down. I don't want to have to lift my hand, grope around for my mouse, and knock over my coffee cup just to see the next page of my letter." For you, dear friend, WordPerfect has navigation keys. You can forget about using the mouse; just press keys to get where you want to go.

The main keys you use are the *cursor-control keys,* which are outlined in Figure 3-2.

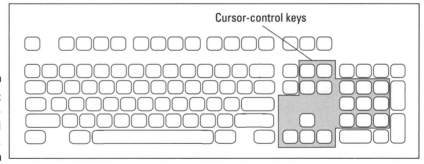

**Figure 3-2:**
The cursor-
control
keys.

These keys are

- ✔ The *arrow keys,* for moving the cursor up, down, left, and right
- ✔ The keys labeled Home, End, Page Up (or PgUp), and Page Down (or PgDn)

## *Using the arrow keys*

You can use the arrow keys — which have the little up-, down-, left-, and right-pointing arrows on them — to move up or down one line or to move left or right one character. These keys are great for positioning the cursor in an exact spot.

This list shows some of the finer points of using cursor-control keys:

- If the cursor is on the top line of the screen and you press the up-arrow key, WordPerfect does your bidding. To move up a line, WordPerfect must display that line, so it scrolls the document down a tad.

- Ditto if the cursor is on the bottom line of the screen and you press the down-arrow key.

- Don't confuse the left-arrow key with the Backspace key, which usually also has a left-pointing arrow (a longer one) on it. The Backspace key *eats* your text as it moves leftward. The left-arrow key just moves the cursor to the left and slides around below the letters like a hot knife through ice cream.

- As you move the cursor, it moves from letter to letter in your text. When you move rightward off the end of a line, the cursor moves to the left end of the next line. Unlike the mouse pointer, the cursor can go only where there is text. The cursor must have text to walk around on, as it were; you cannot move it off the text into the white void of the blank page.

---

## Lock those numbers

Your keyboard probably has two sets of arrow keys. (Sigh.) There are two of everything, as usual. One set of keys is labeled only with arrows, and the keys in this set always work as arrow keys. The keys in the other set, however, have numbers on them, too; they are part of the *numeric keypad.* These keys act like arrow keys some of the time, and you can type numbers with them the rest of the time.

To switch between these uses, you press the Num Lock key. (*Num Lock* stands for *numeric lock,* although it sounds like a wrestling grip.)

This key should be in the general vicinity of the numeric keypad (ours is right above the 7 key). When Num Lock is *on,* the numeric-keypad keys type numbers; when it is *off,* the numeric-keypad keys move the cursor. Your keyboard may have a little light that tells you whether Num Lock is on or off — the light may even be right on the Num Lock key. If not, you can tell WordPerfect to display NUM on the status bar on-screen when Num Lock is on (see Chapter 20). Just press the Num Lock key if you don't like what these keys are doing.

---

## Using Ctrl with the arrow keys

By pressing the Ctrl key while you press an arrow key, you can make the cursor move farther, as shown by the key combinations in this list:

Ctrl+up arrow | Moves the cursor to the beginning of the current paragraph; if you are already there, it moves the cursor to the beginning of the preceding paragraph.

Ctrl+down arrow | Moves the cursor down to the beginning of the next paragraph

Ctrl+left arrow | Moves the cursor left one word

Ctrl+right arrow | Moves the cursor right one word

To use the Ctrl key, press it while you press another key, as though it were the Shift key. Don't release it until you have released the other key.

## Moving farther and faster

How about those other keys we mentioned earlier — the Home, End, Page Down (or PgDn), and Page Up (or PgUp) keys? You can use them to range farther afield in your documents — an especially useful capability as they get larger (the documents, not the keys). As with the arrow keys, your keyboard probably has two sets of these keys, and you can use only the ones on the numeric keypad if the Num Lock key is turned off.

You can move to the beginning or end of the line by pressing one of these keys:

Home    Moves the cursor to the beginning of the current line

End     Moves the cursor to the end of the current line

We use the End key all the time to get back to the end of the line we are typing so that we can type some more.

You can move up or down one screen of information by pressing one of these keys:

Page Up | Moves the cursor to the top of the screen. If you are already there, it moves up one screen's worth of text and scrolls the document as it does so.

Page Down | Moves the cursor to the bottom of the screen. If you are already there, it moves down one screen of text.

To move to the beginning or end of the document, press one of these keys:

Ctrl+Home  Moves the cursor to the beginning of the document

Ctrl+End   Moves the cursor to the end of the document

If you are wondering how long a document is, press Ctrl+End to get to the end of it. Then look at the status bar to see what page you are on (the number after Pg).

# Go To Where?

WordPerfect has a Go To dialog box you can use to tell it where to go. Unfortunately, you cannot tell WordPerfect to go where you probably *want* to tell it to go, but this option is better than nothing. And it's useful for moving around in really large documents.

There are four — count 'em, four — ways to display the Go To dialog box:

✔ Choose the Edit➪Go To command from the menu.

✔ Press Ctrl+G.

✔ Use the scroll bar's QuickMenu — that is, point to the scroll bar and click the *right* mouse button to display the QuickMenu; then choose the Go To command.

✔ Double-click on the location section of the status bar (the part that gives you the page, line, and cursor position).

Actually, there are many more than four ways, because you can use the keyboard or the mouse to choose commands, but you see our point. And you see the Go To dialog box, shown in Figure 3-3.

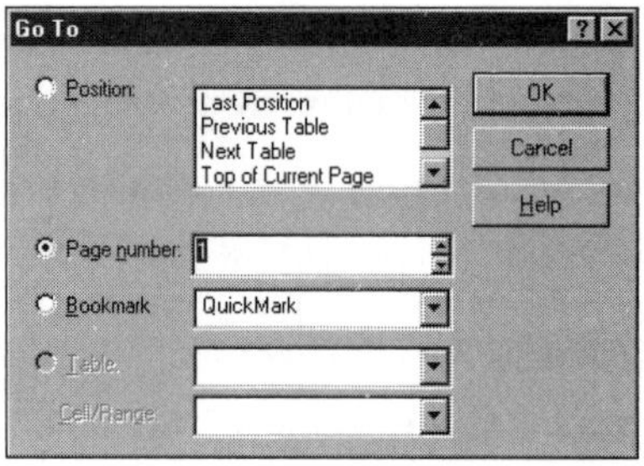

**Figure 3-3:**
Using the Go
To dialog
box to tell
WordPerfect
where to go.

| Go To | ? ☒ |
| --- | --- |
| ○ Position: | Last Position / Previous Table / Next Table / Top of Current Page | OK / Cancel / Help |
| ◉ Page number: | 1 | |
| ○ Bookmark | QuickMark | |
| ○ Table: | | |
| Cell/Range | | |

You can use four other commands to tell WordPerfect where to go: Position, Page Number, Bookmark, and Table. We talk about the last two commands later in this book, when you know what the heck bookmarks and tables are.

## *Top of the page to you!*

The following list shows you how to use the Go To dialog box to get to the top of any page in your document:

- ✔ **To move the cursor to the top of the current page:** Choose Position and then choose Top of Current Page from the list of possible positions (sounds indecent, doesn't it?). Finally, click on OK or press Enter.

- ✔ **To move the cursor to the bottom of the current page:** Do the same thing you do to move to the top, but choose Bottom of Current Page as the position.

- ✔ **To move the cursor to the top of a different page:** Choose Page Number, and enter the number of the page you want to go to. Then click on OK or press Enter.

## *Getting unlost*

If you use any of the mouse or keyboard methods described in this book to move your cursor, or if you use the search commands described in Chapter 5, you may find that you made a dreadful error and you want to go back to where you started and try again. Amazingly enough, WordPerfect has a "go back to where I started" command. (These nice little surprises keep up our faith in computers.)

To return the cursor to its most recent location, use the Go To dialog box. Choose Position and then Last Position, and click on OK or press Enter. Your cursor flies back to its earlier location like a well-trained homing pigeon.

# Chapter 4
# Trashing Your Text

. . . . . . . . . . . . . . . . . . . . . . . . . . . . . . . . . . . . . . . . . . . . .

### In This Chapter

▶ Using insert and typeover modes

▶ Dealing with one character at a time: Backspace and Delete

▶ Deleting secret codes

▶ Deleting blocks of text

▶ Undeleting

▶ Undoing versus undeleting

. . . . . . . . . . . . . . . . . . . . . . . . . . . . . . . . . . . . . . . . . . . . .

The greatest boon to writers after the discovery of caffeine has been, arguably, correction fluid. It is therefore not surprising that the word processor's capability to do correction fluid one step better by absolutely, indetectably deleting text as though it had never been there — like really, really gone — is quite popular.

## Insert and Typeover Modes

If you're replacing existing text, one of the simplest ways to delete the old stuff is to write over it. Normally, WordPerfect doesn't let you do that. When you type, the new text is inserted at the cursor position. This feature is called, not surprisingly, *insert mode*.

If you want to type over your old text, however, all you have to do is press the Insert key (it's probably above the arrow keys), and you enter *typeover mode*. Move the cursor to where you want to begin; anything you type then overwrites the old text as though it had never been there. (Old fogies can now put to rest the ghost of their typing instructors, for whom "strikeovers" were cardinal sins.)

A ghost of the former text does remain, however, in the form of character formatting, such as italics. If the original text was 20 characters in italics, the new text also is 20 characters in italics. Hmm. This situation might not be what you had in mind (see Chapter 8 to learn how to format text in italics or to get rid of this type of formatting).

To return to insert mode, just press the Insert key again.

## Typeovers and popovers

Sometimes, in the frenzy of typing, a flying finger mysteriously hits the Insert key and accidentally sends you into typeover mode, which really messes things up. Or you forget to switch back to insert mode.

If it looks like you're overtyping and you didn't want to, follow these steps:

1. **Check out the status bar at the bottom of the WordPerfect window.**

   It should tell you which mode you're in by displaying Insert or Typeover. If it doesn't and you use typeover mode frequently, get your guru to add this feature to the status bar or see Chapter 20 to learn how to do it yourself.

2. **Undo your most recent typing by choosing Edit⇨Undo from the menu (or press Ctrl+Z or click the Undo button on the Toolbar).**

   See the section "Undeleting," later in this chapter.

3. **Switch back to insert mode by pressing the Insert key.**

   Check the status bar to make sure that you're really in the right mode now.

We recommend that you stay in insert mode while you work in WordPerfect so that you don't find yourself deleting stuff by mistake. Also, some keys (such as Tab and Backspace) work a little differently in typeover mode — our descriptions refer to the way things work in insert mode.

WordPerfect has a way to replace text without changing to typeover mode. Just select the text you want to replace and then begin typing. This step deletes the original text and puts in your new text. For information about selecting text, see the section "Deleting Blocks of Text," later in this chapter, and also Chapter 6.

# Dealing with One Character at a Time: Backspace and Delete

You can delete one character at a time in these two ways:

- ✔ The Delete key deletes the character *after* the cursor.
- ✔ The Backspace key deletes the character *before* the cursor.

In either case, the text closes up behind you as you go. Surgery without scars.

Make sure that you don't have any text *selected* if you want to delete just one character at a time. Both the Backspace and Delete keys delete whatever text is selected. Selected text is indicated by highlighting (actually, it's darklighting, but who's counting?).

# Deleting Secret Codes

Feeling a tad paranoid? Can it be that everyone around you is, undetected by you, exchanging secret glances and signs? Just to add to your paranoia, be aware that WordPerfect is indeed using secret codes. And, as in your glory days in the CIA, if you lose the codes by accident, you may be in deep guacamole.

As we discuss in Chapter 11, lots of hidden, secret codes are sprinkled throughout every WordPerfect document. These codes are cryptic notes WordPerfect makes to itself to remember to, for example, "turn on boldface type here" and "turn off boldface type here."

While you are deleting text, you may also delete one or more of these secret codes. If you do, the appearance of a bunch of text then changes. Fortunately, WordPerfect prevents you from accidentally doing this in many cases (like the boldface case).

If you really, really want to, you can tell WordPerfect to show you the secret codes. Seeing them can be helpful if you're trying to recover from an unwanted deletion, but only if you like this kind of spooky stuff.

If the formatting of a block of text changes while you are deleting, you probably deleted a secret code. If you catch your mistake soon enough, you may be able to undelete it with Edit⇨Undelete or Edit⇨Undo (or with their equivalent keyboard commands, Ctrl+Shift+Z or Ctrl+Z, respectively, which we talk about later in this chapter); otherwise, just reformat it back to the way it was.

# Deleting Blocks of Text

The simplest way to delete a block of text is to *select* it (highlight it) with your mouse or keyboard and press the Delete or Backspace key. WordPerfect has other, weird ways in which you can delete, for example, a single word to the left or right, but we say, "Go with the rodent."

For the full details about selecting text, see Chapter 6. The quick summary is as follows:

1. **Position the mouse pointer.**

   Place it at the beginning or end of the text you want to delete.

2. **Click and drag the mouse pointer to the other end.**

   A block of text will be highlighted.

3. **Press the Delete or Backspace key.**

If you would rather not take your hand off the mouse to delete, just select your text, click the right button on the mouse, and then click on Delete in the QuickMenu that appears.

On the other hand, if you insist that you would rather not take your hands off the keyboard, you can also select blocks as shown in this list and then press Delete:

| | |
|---|---|
| Shift+left or right arrow | Selects from the current insertion point to the left or right, one character at a time |
| Shift+up or down arrow | Selects from the current insertion point to the same location in the line above or below it |
| Shift+Home | Selects from the current insertion point to the beginning of the line |
| Shift+End | Selects from the current insertion point to the end of the line |
| Shift+PgUp or PgDn | Selects from the current insertion point to the top or bottom of the screen |
| Ctrl+Shift+left or right arrow | Selects one word at a time to the left or right of the current insertion point (using the mouse, you can do the same thing by double-clicking on a word) |

Other nifty key combinations are available for related purposes, but they tend to be hard to remember. (Not that we think that memorizing the little goodies in the preceding list is a snap!)

If you think that you might be able to reuse the text you're deleting, you can cut it out rather than delete it and then paste it later (see Chapter 6).

# *Undeleting*

Undeleting tends to be a popular topic among beginners and old-timers alike. Maybe that's because it sounds like "undulating," which is an even more popular topic. More likely, it's because we all, at some time or another, have deleted that which we ought not to delete (and probably have not deleted that which we ought to have deleted, but that's an editorial problem).

Fortunately, WordPerfect always remembers the last three chunks of stuff you have deleted. Anything beyond that has gone to the big bit-bucket in the sky. The "chunks of stuff" WordPerfect can return from the dead are defined as the following:

- ✔ A single character, if that's all you deleted
- ✔ Contiguous characters, deleted by repeatedly pressing the Delete or Backspace key and not doing anything else in between
- ✔ A block of text deleted all at once

Any of these "last three things deleted" *can be returned to any point in the document,* not just to the place they came from. To get at them, you follow these steps:

1. **Position the cursor at the place where you want the resurrection to occur.**

   Point and click in the document to move the cursor to the right place.

2. **Click on Edit⇨Undelete from the menu bar (or press Ctrl+Shift+Z).**

   You then see the little Undelete dialog box. Also, WordPerfect shows you the most recent deletion and inserts it where your cursor is positioned. WordPerfect highlights it so that it's easy to find.

3. **If you want to keep this text in your document, click on Restore.**

   The text comes back for good, and the dialog box goes away.

4. **If it's not the deletion you want, click on Previous to move back in time.**

   The Next button moves you the other way. Notice that deletions are held like slides in a very small carousel slide projector, so if you change three times, you are back where you began.

5. **When you have the deletion you want, click on Restore. If you don't want any of them, click on Cancel.**

# *Undoing versus Undeleting*

You can also undelete by undoing, which is as simple as selecting Edit⇨Undo from the menu bar. Or you can press Ctrl+Z on the keyboard, or you can click on the button that seems to suggest a U-turn on the Toolbar, which explains all the skid marks on it.

Undoing goes back only one deletion and uses pretty much the same definition of a deletion as Undelete does:

- ✔ The character just deleted
- ✔ The block of text just deleted
- ✔ All the consecutive characters just deleted when you repeatedly pressed the Delete or Backspace key

Unlike Undelete, Undo recovers text in only the exact position where it was before. Edit⇨Undo does not recover anything unless the very last thing you did was to delete something. If you do anything to your text after deleting, the deleted stuff is gone, as far as Undo is concerned. It's history. Yesterday's news. Forgetitsville, Daddy-o. You may be able to do stuff that doesn't change your text, though, such as change the view, and Undo will still recover your deletion. If, in a fit of frustration, you press Edit⇨Undo repeatedly, all that happens is that you undo your Undo. This procedure probably will be your undoing, and leave you undo-lating, which, as we said, is more fun anyway.

Actually, there is a way to undo previous actions. Choose Edit⇨Undo/Redo History from the menu bar. You see the Undo/Redo History dialog box, listing your previous 300 actions (unbelievable!) in rather cryptic terms. Each time you click on the Undo button in this dialog box, WordPerfect undoes one more action. If you undo too far, click on the Redo button to reperform the last undone action. When you're done, click on Close to get rid of the dialog box. Whew!

# Chapter 5

# Searching for Sanity

● ● ● ● ● ● ● ● ● ● ● ● ● ● ● ● ● ● ● ● ● ● ● ● ● ● ● ● ● ● ● ● ● ● ● ● ● ● ● ● ● ● ● ● ● ● ● ● ● ● ●

### In This Chapter

▶ Finding what's lost

▶ Finding and replacing text

▶ Typing misspelled words

▶ Fixing misspelled words

▶ Checking your spelling throughout

● ● ● ● ● ● ● ● ● ● ● ● ● ● ● ● ● ● ● ● ● ● ● ● ● ● ● ● ● ● ● ● ● ● ● ● ● ● ● ● ● ● ● ● ● ● ● ● ● ● ●

*1*f you have lost your marbles, your cool, or your sense of values, you have come to the right place. WordPerfect's Find and Replace command can help you not only find them again but also replace them with something better — for example, *cottage cheese* for *marbles.* This command can even replace your besieged sense of values with a sense of direction.

For finding and replacing words, phrases, and even secret WordPerfect codes, the Edit⇨Find and Replace command is your buddy.

Those of you who are used to versions of WordPerfect before 6.1, or to many other word processors, will be surprised to find that WordPerfect uses the same command and dialog box to find something or to replace it.

## Finding What's Lost

To start your search for the word *sanity,* for example, click on the Edit⇨Find and Replace command on the menu bar or press F2. The Find and Replace Text dialog box, shown in Figure 5-1, springs to your aid.

**Figure 5-1:**
The Find and
Replace
Text dialog
box.

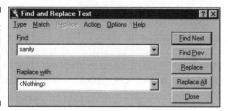

## The usual search for sanity

In the normal scheme of things, the search for the word *sanity* requires a journey of only two, or perhaps three, steps in the dialog box:

1. **Type the text you're looking for.**

   It appears in the Find window, where you can edit it (if you want to) by moving the cursor around, using the Backspace and Delete keys, and so on.

2. **Click on Find Next (or press Enter) to search toward the end of the document.**

3. **To search toward the beginning of the document, click on Find Prev.**

If the text you're looking for exists, it appears highlighted in the document window. If the text that WordPerfect found is not the precise instance of the text you want, just click on Find Next or Find Prev again until you get it.

If your quest is futile, WordPerfect displays a window saying that it cannot find the text. Reassure it that you're not mad by clicking on the OK button.

This process of choosing the direction in which to look may seem to be a bit nit-picky for your urgent quest, but it makes things faster with long documents (assuming that you have any idea at all where *sanity* lies). Direction, by the bye, is relative to the current cursor position in your document.

If you want to search for something you looked for recently, click on the down-pointing arrow to the right of the Find box. WordPerfect displays a list of recent searches you've done.

## Changing the way you search

If you're going to search for one thing after another (such as when you're leaving for work on Monday morning and you're looking for your keys and your wallet and your umbrella), it may be worthwhile to change the way Find works by using the Options menu. Yes, folks, just when you thought that WordPerfect couldn't have any more menus, here's another one. The Find and Replace Text dialog box has its own little menu bar.

### If you have no idea in which direction sanity lies

You can make WordPerfect search the entire document by clicking on Options on the Find and Replace Text dialog box's menu and then looking at the choices it presents. Choose Wrap at Beg./End of Document. That way, whether you choose Find Next or Find Prev, WordPerfect ignores the beginning or end of the document and continues the search until it gets back to where it started.

If you prefer, you can choose <u>B</u>egin Find at Top of Document from the <u>O</u>ptions menu and then click on <u>F</u>ind Next in the Find and Replace Text dialog box.

### If you have a darn good idea where sanity lies, but you still can't find it

You can make WordPerfect search selected text. With the Find and Replace Text dialog box still on-screen, select the area to search. Then choose <u>L</u>imit Find Within Selection (from the <u>O</u>ptions menu) before clicking on the <u>F</u>ind Next or Find <u>P</u>rev button in the dialog box.

### If you don't know where you are with respect to sanity

Try choosing the <u>O</u>ptions command from the Find and Replace Text dialog box's menu bar and then choosing <u>B</u>egin Find at Top of Document.

To return to your document, click on the <u>C</u>lose button. The word that was found remains selected, and your cursor is right there.

After you return to the document, you may want to return to where you were before you began the Find procedure. Choose the <u>E</u>dit⇨<u>G</u>o To command (or press Ctrl+G), and click on Last Position in the <u>P</u>osition list.

You can select, in your document, the text for which you want to look before you use the <u>E</u>dit command. When you do that, the text appears automatically in the <u>F</u>ind box as the text to search for.

## Searching for sanity and finding insanity

Finding the wrong text — such as finding the word *insanity* when you're searching for *sanity* — is a common problem, and it is quite treatable. Your therapy is on the Find and Replace Text dialog box's menu bar. We prescribe clicking on <u>M</u>atch and then on <u>W</u>hole Word. (The command otherwise assumes that you are just looking for a set of characters, even within a word.) The phrase Whole Word appears below the <u>F</u>ind text box to remind you.

Certain things you select in the Find and Replace Text dialog box, such as <u>W</u>hole Word mode, are "sticky," which means that they stay "clicked" until you change them or until you close the dialog box. You see a check mark next to these items if they are "on."

The capability to find a set of characters, even within words, is a useful feature. If you're searching a document for discussions of *reliability,* for example, you may also want to find *unreliability, reliable,* or *unreliable.* You can find any of these words by entering **reliab** (with <u>W</u>hole Word off ) as your search text.

## Getting picky about what you find

Most of the time, you don't much care what kind of *sanity* you find. Anything will do: *Sanity, SANITY, sanity, sanIty,* or ᴿᴬᴺᴵᵀʸ. Obligingly, the Edit⇨Find and Replace command normally ignores the fine points, such as what's uppercase and what's lowercase.

If you are picky about which typeface, size, style, or case you want, don't give up — just put a Match to it. That is, you use the Match command on the Find and Replace Text dialog box's menu bar. When you choose Match and then Case, Find pays attention to the uppercase or lowercase letters you type in the Find box, and it finds only versions of your text that are identically typed. WordPerfect reminds you about this feature by displaying Case Sensitive below the Find text box.

When you choose Match and then Font, WordPerfect displays the Match Font dialog box, which allows you to look for *sanity* in Helvetica, **boldly,** if you want. Check off what you want by pointing and clicking. Click on OK when you finish.

If you are among the WordPerfect secret-code cognoscenti, be aware that you can also find codes. You can look for specific codes, such as Lft Mar and Bot Mar, by choosing Match⇨Codes from the menu in the Find and Replace Text dialog box. If you would rather type a specific code, choose Type⇨Specific Codes from the menu in the Find and Replace Text dialog box.

# Finding Doctor Livingst[*]

In your search for *sanity,* you might seek *Doctor Livingstone.* Or was it Doctor Livingstein? Livingston? Livingstern? Oh, dear — how ever can we find him if we can't spell his name?

Never fear: WordPerfect goes with you into the untamed wilderness of your text to find the good Doctor What's-His-Name. You must, however, arm yourself with certain weapons, called *wildcard codes,* before you venture into the wild. You can include these special codes in the text you type in the Find box.

Be warned: These codes are not for the timid. But they are very useful, even for novices.

# Looking for Mr. Goodchar

The first wildcard code is [?] (pronounced [?]). This code stands for any single character, space, or tab in your Find text. (Don't get carried away yet, though — you cannot create this code simply by typing the three characters. You must use a special dialog box, which we discuss in a minute.)

This section explains how these funky wildcard codes work, as shown in this list of examples:

- **Livingst[?]n:** Finds *Livingston* or *Livingsten* but not *Livingstein* (too many characters between the *t* and the *n*). This code finds the better part of *Livingstone*, too — all except the last *e*. If you don't want any part of *Livingstone* or *Livingstonberg*, choose Match and then Whole Word from the Find and Replace Text dialog-box menu.

- **Livingst[?][?]n:** Finds *Livingstein* and *Livingstern* but not *Livingston* (too few characters; you told WordPerfect to look for exactly two characters between *t* and *n*).

- **Livingst[?]n[?]:** Finds *Livingstine* and *Livingston,* with a comma after it, because [?] can also mean punctuation. This code does not find *Livingston* , with a space (however unusual that might be), because the [?] code has to represent something and, as far as WordPerfect is concerned, a space isn't the right kind of something.

Terrific thing, this [?] code. But if you cannot type it, how the heck do you use it? (This question gets into the mysterious codes topic, which is best left alone for the most part — at least until Chapter 10.) To use the [?] code, follow these Mysterious Instructions:

1. **Begin typing text in the Find box.**

2. **When you get to the place where you want the [?] code, choose Match⇨ Codes from the Find and Replace Text dialog-box menu.**

   Up pops the Codes dialog box, displaying a list of all kinds of weird names, such as BotMar. Also in this list is your friend [?]. But it's wearing its formal name, which is ? (One Char).

3. **Click on the down arrow on the scroll bar to the right of the code list until you find what you're looking for: (One Char), or just type ? and WordPerfect will jet you right to it.**

4. **Double-click on ? (One Char) (or click on Insert after you click on the code).**

   WordPerfect displays ? (One Char) in the Find box for you.

   At this point, you can insert additional [?] codes, if you need them. If you don't need any more of them, click on Close. If you need more but want to type a few more letters first, click on the Find text box again to continue typing. The Code dialog box remains on-screen. Click on Close when you finish. Whew!

Notice that [?] is actually [? (One Char)] in your Find box in the Find and Replace Text dialog box. We use the short form here because it's hard as heck to see how things work when we use the full name.

# Looking for Stars

Back to the original problem: It looks as though the [?] code just isn't powerful enough to allow us to search for all the variants of *Livingstone* in one fell swoop. This situation calls for the elephant gun of wildcard codes: the [*] code. This code represents any group of characters, but *only in a word.* The [*] code stops matching characters when it gets to a space. For example, you may presume that "Livingst[*] I" will match "Livingston, I" but not "Livingston — I." You can find it in the same Codes dialog box in which you found [*]. The formal name of [?] is * [Many Char], and it's at the top of the list in the Codes dialog box.

This list shows some examples:

✔ **Livingst**[*]**n:** Finds *Livingstein, Livingston,* and *Livingstern,* but will not find *Livingstone* if you have Match⇨Whole Word checked. Nor will it find "Livingsti is quite well; good of you to ask, John."

✔ **Livingst**[*]**:** Finds the good doctor no matter how he spells the last syllable.

As with the [?] code, the formal name [* [Many Char]] is used, not [*]; we use the abbreviation in this book for simplicity's sake.

# Finding and Replacing Text

If your forthcoming best-seller *The Search for Sanity* just isn't working out, don't go crazy. Just replace *sanity* with *chocolate,* for example, and see how it hangs together.

To accomplish this literary feat, use the Edit⇨Find and Replace command, known to its friends as F2. Good gracious — it's the same command we've been using! This bold act displays the very same Find and Replace Text dialog box.

In the normal scheme of things, replacing *sanity* with *chocolate* is simple. Follow these steps:

1. **Choose Edit⇨Find and Replace from the menu bar (or press F2).**

2. **Type the text that you want WordPerfect to find and replace (sanity, for example) in the Find box.**

   As before, if you select *sanity* in your document before issuing the command, the word appears automatically in your Find text box.

3. **Click on the Replace With box and type the replacement word or phrase** (chocolate, **for example).**

4. **Click on either Find Next or Find Prev.**

   WordPerfect goes in search of your search text (*sanity,* for example). If it finds *sanity,* WordPerfect highlights it; if WordPerfect doesn't find it, it tells you so.

5. **If your text has been found, you can click on Replace to replace it.**

   The ever-eager Replace goes in search of any additional instances of your search text.

6. **If your text hasn't been found, search in the other direction; click on Find Prev rather than Find Next.**

   As before, you can search the entire document by choosing Wrap at Beg./ End of Document or Begin Find at Top of Document from the Options menu.

This list shows some general tips for replacing text:

✔ The commands in the Type, Match, and Options menus work the same way as they do for finding text.

✔ Replace⇨Case and Replace⇨Font are the commands for getting picky about replacement text — for example, if you want to replace *sanity* with *chocolate* in Helvetica (not to be confused with chocolate in Helvetia, which is also very good).

✔ To replace every instance of the Find text in your document, click on Replace All rather than Replace. Be careful, though: Unless you turn on Whole Word mode (from the Match menu), you can end up replacing not only *sanity* with *chocolate,* but also *insanity* with *inchocolate,* which is not nearly as nice a situation as it sounds.

✔ To delete every instance of the text in the Find box, first put a space in front of the text in the Find box; then put nothing at all (not even a space) in the Replace With text box. This step makes sure that you don't end up with two spaces where the deleted word used to be.

✔ To replace only a limited number of instances of your Find text, choose Options and then Limit Number of Changes.

You can also find and replace text in headers, footers, footnotes, captions, and all those other nooks and crannies in your document. Just move to the Find box and click on Options, Include Headers, Footers, and so on in Find.

# *Finding and Replacing All Forms of a Word*

Here's a cool feature: WordPerfect can search for not only a specific word but also *all forms of that word.* When we say "all forms," we mean plurals, past tenses — that kind of thing. If you write a short story about skiing in Vermont, for example, and later decide to change the setting to Bermuda, you can replace all forms of the word *ski* with the equivalent forms of the word *surf*. *Skiing* becomes *surfing*, *skied* becomes *surfed* — the whole shebang.

To tell WordPerfect to find or replace all forms of a word, choose Type⇨Word Forms from the menu bar in the Find and Replace Text dialog box. WordPerfect tells you that it will now look for word forms by displaying Word Forms of below the Find and Replace With boxes.

To search for all forms of a word, type the simplest form (singular, present tense) of the word you want to search for (such as *ski*) in the Find box, and click on the Find Next or Find Prev button. WordPerfect finds the next occurrence of the word in any of its forms. Cool!

To replace all forms of one word with the matching forms of another word, type the simplest forms of the two words (such as *ski* and *surf*) in the Find and Replace With boxes and then click on the Find Next or Find Prev button. WordPerfect finds the first occurrence of the word you are looking for; displays the word in the Find box; and displays, in the Replace With box, the word with which it plans to replace the original word. If WordPerfect found *skied,* for example, it displays surfed in the Replace With box. If you want to make the change, click on the Replace button; if not, click on the Find Next or Find Prev button again. Either way, WordPerfect searches for the next occurrence of the word.

Using the Replace All button when you replace word forms is a bad idea. Maybe we're just suspicious of fancy technology, but WordPerfect may not be absolutely right about each and every word form it finds. You can get into trouble if the word you are searching for has other meanings, if it can be used both as a verb and a noun or if it can be used in noun phrases. (Do you really want WordPerfect to change *ski poles* to *surf poles,* for example?) It's a good idea to eyeball the replacements WordPerfect suggests as they go by.

## *Finding and Replacing Codes*

If you really, really want to find and replace codes, it's okay, but you don't fit *our* definition of a dummy! Because you're so smart, we just say that you can find the codes you want in the same place you find the wildcard codes: in the Match⇨Codes dialog box. 'Nuff said. For more information, see Chapter 11.

## *Typing Misspelled Words*

You can't. Well, the folks at WordPerfect haven't taken it quite that far yet, but they're getting there. As you type along, you may notice that some of your

---

## Fun facts about finding

The quickest way to find or replace text is to press F2.

You can leave the Find and Replace Text dialog box displayed while you work on your document, which can be helpful if you do a great deal of editing.

If you're looking for whole words, turn on the Match⇨Whole Word option. Otherwise, you will find *insanity* while searching for *sanity* (and maybe replace it, too!).

WordPerfect searches in only one direction from your cursor. To search the entire document, either search both ways manually or turn on either Begin Find at Top of Document or Wrap at Beg./End of Document from the Options menu.

You can limit your search to a selected block of text in your document, but you should make the selection *after* the Find and Replace Text dialog box is on-screen. Text selected beforehand is automatically assumed to be the Find text.

---

words have a dotted red underline. As you do your work, WordPerfect looks over your shoulder, and it feels compelled to point out words it cannot find in its dictionary. And WordPerfect usually has a suggestion about what you may mean instead of what you typed.

To find out what WordPerfect thinks you should have typed, right-click on the underlined word. WordPerfect displays a list of suggested words, along with a few other options. You can add this word to your dictionary, skip it in this document, or open the full-fledged spelling checker, which we talk about in a minute.

If the word you want is in the list, you're in luck — just click on it, and WordPerfect automagically replaces what you typed with the correct word. If the word is not in the list, you have another choice. You can tell WordPerfect that what you typed really *is* a word and should be considered to be one from now on. We use this feature for words such as *Intranet* (a word that relates to using the Internet privately within a company) that we type frequently and are tired of having WordPerfect warn us about.

If the word you typed really isn't a word, but you'll be using it a lot in this document anyway, you may want to tell WordPerfect to ignore it. You may want WordPerfect to ignore product names, company names, and town names that you are using in just one document. You may get tired of seeing *SoVerNet* (the Southern Vermont Internet provider) underlined as you write your review of rural Internet service companies. On the other hand, when you're done with this study, you'll probably never write about those companies again. If so, add *SoVerNet* to the word list for this document by clicking on the Skip in This Document menu option when you right-click on *SoVerNet*.

You may see other words underlined as well, usually when there are two of them in a row. Every once in a while, you'll be forced to write something awkward, such as "I had had a thought that that might be a good good idea." WordPerfect would really rather that you didn't do this, and it tells you so by underlining the repeated words. There's not much you can do about that situation, other than tell WordPerfect to stop looking over your shoulder (see the following sidebar).

# Flying the Spell Checker Yourself

WordPerfect's Spell-As-You-Go feature is kind of like flying the spell checker on autopilot: It looks around your document while you're doing something else and finds the misspelled words. You can, if you want, fly the spell checker by hand. Take a reality check here, however. Although one of the great joys of today's word processing is that you no longer really have to be able to spell, you shouldn't get too excited. WordPerfect doesn't know how to spell either.

What WordPerfect *does* know how to do is check a word against a list to see whether it's there. This list of words is called a *dictionary,* even though it's not really a dictionary (it doesn't have any definitions). Well, sort of. We used to say that you wouldn't find the definition of *omphaloskepsis* anywhere in WordPerfect's dictionary, but being ever attentive to our word-processing needs, the folks at WordPerfect added this vital word. But they still won't tell you what it means.

TIP

---

## Stop looking over my shoulder!

You can stop WordPerfect from looking over your shoulder and correcting your spelling. Just choose Tools⇨Spell-As-You-Go from the menu bar (or press Ctrl+Alt+F1). That's all there is to WordPerfect's Spell-As-You-Go feature — which is another terrific *...For Dummies* feature, because it does what it does and you don't have to worry about it much. But beware! You may decide that your file is all ready to print just because it doesn't have any dotted red underlines in it. We wish we could tell you that we've never cent files to the printer with there wrong words in them, but as you can probably sell from his sentence, WordPerfect can't tell whether you used the *write* word in your document, only whether the words you did use are spelled correctly. (WordPerfect does have a feature that purports to do this, in the form of the Grammatik grammar checker, but we've never found it to be very useful; it found *none* of the word errors in the preceding sentence, for example.)

---

# *Spell checking your entire document*

To check the spelling of words in your entire document, follow these steps:

1. **Display the Spell Checker dialog box.**

   Any of the following actions activates the Spell Checker dialog box:

   - Click on Tools⇨Spell Check on the main menu bar.
   - Press Ctrl+F1.
   - Click on the book-with-a-red-check-mark-on-it button on the Toolbar.
   - Click the right mouse button with your cursor located anywhere in the text area of your document; then click on Spell Check on the QuickMenu that appears.

   The Spell Checker dialog box, shown in Figure 5-2, is displayed, and the spelling check begins.

   It doesn't matter where you're working in the document — the Spell Checker checks the whole thing, from top to bottom. You can change this arrangement by changing the selection in the Check section of the Spell Checker dialog box; choose To End of Document if you want to check starting from where you are now. If (when?) the Spell Checker finds a word that's not in its dictionary, it assumes that the word is spelled wrong. The Spell Checker then highlights the word in your document and displays it after Not Found in the dialog box (refer to Figure 5-2).

   In the example, the Spell Checker cannot find the name of this world-famous publisher in its dictionary. It helpfully lists in the Replacements window a variety of suggestions for replacement. None of these suggestions would satisfy the company's CEO, however.

   This sort of thing happens often: You use a person or company name that WordPerfect never heard of, and WordPerfect flags it as misspelled. When that happens, just skip the word, as described in Step 2.

2. **Skip or replace the highlighted word in your document.**

   If the highlighted word is okay, as in the example, you have two options (or three, if you count adding the word to the dictionary, which is covered in the next section):

   - Click on the Skip Once button. This action means "Don't worry about it — get on with the spell checking!"
   - Click on Skip Always. This action means the same thing, but it adds "And don't bother me again about this word!" (until the next time you use the Spell Checker).

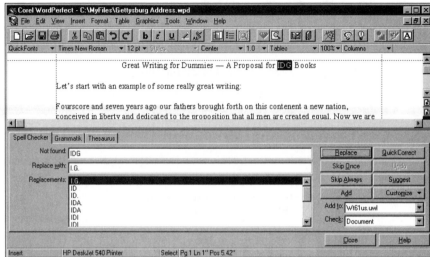

**Figure 5-2:**
The Spell
Checker
dialog box.

If you believe that the highlighted word is indeed misspelled, you have three options:

- If you know the correct spelling, just double-click on the Replace With box, type the correct word, and click on the Replace button.

- If the Spell Checker displays the correct spelling in the Replace With box, click on Replace.

- If you're not sure of the correct spelling, scroll through the Replacements box. If you find the correct spelling, double-click on it.

**3. Repeat the preceding steps for every misspelled word.**

WordPerfect continues until every word has been checked. When the spell check is complete, WordPerfect tells you so and asks you whether you want to close the Spell Checker. Click on Yes, and the Spell Checker closes. If you click on No, you can leave the Spell Checker box on-screen while you work on your document as usual. If the box is in the way, you can drag it around just as you would a toolbar (refer to Chapter 2). You can always click on Close to get rid of it.

## Dealing with real words that WordPerfect doesn't know

Perhaps the WordPerfect Spell Checker can be forgiven for not knowing names, such as *Margy*. But it's still annoying to have to repeatedly skip names and other real words that are unknown to the WordPerfect dictionary. The solution is to add these words to the Spell Checker's dictionary so that it skips them every time you use the Spell Checker.

WordPerfect has many dictionaries. It checks at least the following two dictionaries whenever you run the Spell Checker:

✔ A main dictionary of official, genuine English (or other-language) words

✔ A supplementary dictionary of anything else you consider to be a word

The Spell Checker can also check additional supplementary dictionaries, such as document dictionaries and special-purpose, or topical, dictionaries.

Document dictionaries are specific to each individual document. A short story might have a document dictionary that contains the names of the characters in the story, for example. Perhaps a character does not appear in subsequent stories because of a gruesome death by editing. Therefore, you want WordPerfect to consider the name to be okay in this document; if it appears in any other document, however, it should be flagged.

---

## Making and unmaking mistakes in your supplemental dictionary

It's easy to go tripping merrily through your document, clicking on A̲dd for every word the Spell Checker flags. Such glibness eventually causes you to add a word such as *klockwurst* to the dictionary. (The word was supposed to have been *knockwurst,* but you typed it just before quitting time, and you were looking at the clock.) Now *klockwurst* is considered to be a genuine word, so the Spell Checker ignores any subsequent *klockwurst*s.

To correct this situation, you must go deeper into the labyrinthine depths of the Spell Checker than a novice normally goes. Walk this way, please:

1. **Click on in the Spell Checker dialog box.**

2. **Click on User Word Lists. . . on the Customize menu.**

   The User Word List Editor dialog box appears.

3. **Click on the entry you want to edit in the Word List.**

   Usually, you see Document Word List and wt61us.uwl here.

4. **Scroll down the Word List until you see klockwurst (or whatever your mistake was); then click on the Delete button.**

   The word is gone, gone, gone.

5. **Find your way back to the Spell Checker dialog box by clicking on the Close button.**

The document dictionary is a useful beast. It can contain all the words that are perfectly fine in the current document but that would be incorrect in other documents. To add words to the document dictionary rather than to the supplemental dictionary, click on the Add T̲o option in the Spell Checker dialog box. A dictionary menu appears. Click on Document Word List. Thereafter, whenever you click on the A̲dd button, the highlighted word goes into the document dictionary.

Spell checking is not magic, although the name probably sounds promising if you're a wizard!

You also can create optional special dictionaries. You might write about several topics, for example, each with its own particular jargon. The word *e-mail,* for example, may be intentional when you are writing for programmers, but it probably would be a typo if you were writing for gardeners.

Keep things simple — just add words to the basic supplemental dictionary. To add words to the dictionary, start the Spell Checker as you normally do. (What? You forgot how already? Refer to the preceding section for details.)

When the Spell Checker highlights a word you consider to be okay, click on the A<u>d</u>d button in the Spell Checker dialog box. This step adds the word to the supplemental dictionary; as far as the Spell Checker is concerned, the word is a real word now. The Spell Checker will never bring it up again and will sincerely regret having brought it up in the first place.

The remainder of this section provides a few other factoids about spell-checking.

To check less than your entire document, click on Chec<u>k</u> in the Spell Checker dialog box; then choose <u>W</u>ord, Sente<u>n</u>ce, <u>P</u>aragraph, <u>P</u>age, To <u>E</u>nd of Document, or <u>S</u>elected Text. You can also check a specified number of pages from the current insertion point by choosing <u>N</u>umber of Pages. Whatever you check remains selected until you put the Spell Checker away again.

*Sí usted queria escribir en español* or some other language from Afrikaans to Ukrainian, choose Cust<u>o</u>mize⇨<u>L</u>anguage . . . and then select a language from the list that appears. But be warned: You must *have* the language dictionary for the language you want to spell-check; otherwise, sooner or later, WordPerfect will give you a tart message informing you that you don't. You can ignore the message, but WordPerfect still won't check the spelling. *¡Que bueno!*

The Spell Checker not only checks spelling but also points out common problems, such as duplicated words, words that contain numbers, and strange capitalization. You can turn these features off if they get in the way. Just click on Cust<u>o</u>mize in the Spell Checker dialog box to see a list of what is turned on or off. Click on a feature to change its on-or-off status.

# Chapter 6

# Fooling with Blocks of Text

. . . . . . . . . . . . . . . . . . . . . . . . . . . . . . . . . . . . . . . . . .

## In This Chapter

▶ Building basic blocks

▶ Selecting text with the mouse

▶ Selecting text with the keyboard

▶ Selecting text with the Find command

▶ Extending a selection

▶ Deleting, moving, and copying selected text

▶ Copying and pasting with the Clipboard

▶ Cutting and pasting with the Clipboard

. . . . . . . . . . . . . . . . . . . . . . . . . . . . . . . . . . . . . . . . . .

*E*ver since the first Egyptian hacked his papyrus scroll of *Pyramids For Dummies* into pages, the idea of blocks of text has progressed inexorably. The sentence. The paragraph. The page. The chapter. The volume. The CD. And now WordPerfect text selection both embraces and transcends these classic ways of dividing text into blocks, allowing you to handle any lump of text.

Text selection enables you to choose precisely what you want to delete, capitalize, italicize, spell check, or otherwise word-process. Think of the power — you can surgically excise tedious text, rejuvenate a lackluster paragraph with screaming 26-point type, selectively subdue injudicious jargon with grammar- or spell-checking, and eliminate annoying alliteration.

Like most Windows-based applications, WordPerfect gives you 60 quadjillion ways to select text and about as many things to do with it after it's selected. We stick to the simplest methods, from which you can get the general idea and go on.

## Basic Blocks

In WordPerfect, a *block* is a chunk of text in your document. Unlike the letter blocks your toddler friends play with, WordPerfect blocks can include a bunch of letters, words, lines, and even pages.

The WordPerfect program understands that humans are fond of blocks — not just arbitrarily defined blocks from "here" to "there," but also certain everyday blocks, such as sentences, words, and paragraphs. This list shows the main blocks of text that WordPerfect understands:

- Arbitrary blocks (as in "Begin with this word over here and end with that word over yonder")
- Individual words
- Sentences
- Paragraphs
- Pages

Like an overly fastidious nanny, WordPerfect allows you to play with only one block at a time. You cannot select a paragraph here, a paragraph there, and three words over there. Select a block. Have your way with it. Select another block. Do stuff to it. And so on.

# Selecting Text with Your Mouse

For most people, the overall best and simplest way to select a block of text is with your buddy, the mouse.

## The point-and-shoot approach

To select an arbitrary block of text (from any point to any other point), just follow these steps:

1. **Put the mouse pointer at the beginning of the stuff you want to select.**

2. **Hold down the mouse button, and drag the mouse pointer to the end of what you want to select.**

   Text is highlighted as you go, as shown in Figure 6-1.

3. **Release the mouse button.**

   The selected text remains highlighted, and you can do stuff to it (see the section "Doing Stuff with Selected Text," later in this chapter).

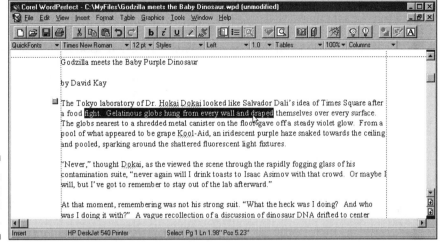

**Figure 6-1:**
Selecting
(highlighting)
text.

# Take my word for it

Take a close look at Figure 6-1. You'll see that the highlight starts at the word *fight* and ends at the word *draped*. We did *not* ever-so-carefully position the mouse right before *fight* and drag it ever-so-carefully just to the end of the word *draped*. Instead, we put the mouse pointer somewhere on the word *fight* and dragged the mouse until the word *draped* was highlighted. If you try this yourself, you'll find that you can't select just a portion of the word *draped* (or any other word, for that matter). As soon as the mouse pointer hits a word, the whole word is highlighted.

Is this good or bad? It's up to you. This business about selecting words automatically is new in WordPerfect 7. The folks at WordPerfect added this feature because many people found it hard to drag over exactly the selection they wanted, and most of them wanted to select whole words anyway.

We find this feature to be incredibly annoying. Maybe it's because we have steady hands (we kicked the caffeine habit), or maybe we're just picky about what we select. Whatever. But if you also find automatic word selection to be annoying, you can turn it off.

To do so, choose Edit➪Preferences. . . . In the Preferences dialog box, double-click on Environment. Almost at the bottom of the Environment Preferences dialog box, you'll see a check box labeled Automatically Select Words. If you clear this check box and click on OK and then Close, you'll be able to select any characters you want to with the mouse, just as you could in previous versions of WordPerfect.

If you're new to this sort of marking procedure, it can look weird. Here are a couple of tips:

✔ If the text you want covers several lines, don't bother to drag the mouse pointer to the end of the line and then back to the beginning of the next line, and so on. This method wastes effort and looks funny. Like driving in Rome, after you begin, you just have to close your eyes and go. Move boldly and directly toward your destination.

✔ You can go backward as well as forward (and up as well as down) — it makes no difference — but you cannot expand the selection in both directions. The place where you begin must be either a beginning or end point.

That's the simple way to select text. Now here are some faster ways to select words, sentences, and paragraphs:

✔ **To select a word:** Double-click on the word (position the mouse pointer anywhere within the word and then double-click the left mouse button).

✔ **To select a group of words:** Double-click on the first word in the group, and hold down the mouse button on the second click. Drag the edge of the highlight (in either direction) to the other end of the group you want to select. This method works even if you turned off automatic word selection (see the "Take my word for it" sidebar, earlier in this chapter). If you complete this maneuver successfully, you are eligible to receive your advanced mouse driver's license.

✔ **To select a sentence:** Triple-click on the sentence (move the mouse pointer anywhere in the sentence and triple-click the mouse button — it's similar to a double click, but with one more click). The WordPerfect idea of a sentence is anything that ends with a period and has a space before the next character. Therefore, the sentence "i write like e. e. cummings." contains three sentences, as far as WordPerfect is concerned.

If you find triple-clicks to be a bit daunting, you can use another convenient way to select a sentence: Click in the left margin, next to the sentence.

✔ **To select a group of sentences:** This procedure is similar to selecting a group of words. Do the triple-click described in the preceding item (like the samba, but faster), and hold down the mouse button on the last click. Then drag the highlight where you want it.

If you like the click-in-the-margin approach to selecting sentences, you can select a bunch of sentences by clicking in the margin and then dragging the mouse pointer up or down.

✔ **To select a paragraph:** Quadruple-click on the paragraph (move the mouse pointer anywhere within the paragraph and click four times in succession). Yes, the latté consumption in WordPerfect's engineering department must be at record levels if those people believe that you can quadruple-click without stuttering, but there it is: Four quick clicks of the mouse button nabs you a paragraph.

If you drink only decaf (such as New England hazelnut–acorn blend — our favorite), you may find the Alternative Paragraph Selection Method to be easier. Move your mouse pointer to the left of the paragraph (where the mouse pointer turns into an arrow), and double-click.

✔ **To select a group of paragraphs:** You guessed it: Hold down the mouse button on the fourth click and drag. Or click twice in the left margin and drag.

What about selecting a page? Logically, this procedure should consist of five clicks, but even the highly wired WordPerfect engineers decided that five clicks was beyond their motor skills. Instead, to select a page, try the QuickMenu approach, described in the following section.

## *The QuickMenu approach*

You can select sentences, paragraphs, and pages by using the QuickMenu. First, click anywhere within the sentence, paragraph, or page you want to select. Then move your mouse pointer to the left margin (where the shadow cursor goes away and the mouse pointer tipped to the left turns into a mouse pointer tipped to the right). With a quick click of the right mouse button, you get the QuickMenu shown in Figure 6-2.

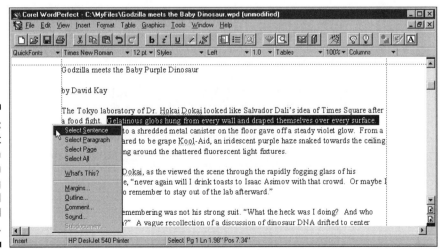

**Figure 6-2:**
The Left
Margin
QuickMenu
for selecting
text and
other cool
stuff.

The bottom of this QuickMenu has lots of really cool stuff, such as Sound and Subdocument. Don't play with that stuff now; show some restraint. This is serious business.

Now you get a chance to Select a Sentence, Paragraph, Page, or the ever-abundant All. Just click (with the left mouse button) on the menu option you want.

Notice that the menu has no word option. You have to point and shoot with the mouse to select a word or group of words.

## *The menu-bar approach*

You can also select a sentence, paragraph, page, or the entire document by using the main menu. Just as you do with the QuickMenu, you begin by clicking anywhere within the text you want. Then you choose the Edit⇨Select command, which has most of the same options as the QuickMenu.

# *Selecting Text with the Keyboard*

Some of us are still a little dubious about this business of taking our hands off the keyboard to use the mouse. We would just as soon use the keyboard, thank you.

Fortunately, many alternatives are available for the rodent-averse among us, whom we prefer to call Speedy Typists. All these alternatives involve the navigation keys.

The *navigation keys* are the arrow keys and the associated pad of keys that have such useful-looking names as Home and End. If you use the keyboard for selecting text, first read the section "Using the Keyboard, Staying Close to Home," in Chapter 3.

Finished reading Chapter 3? Okay, now you're briefed and ready for the highly complex secret of selecting text with the navigation keys:

Hold down the Shift key, and press the navigation keys.

That's it — really. To be painstakingly specific, these steps show you what to do:

1. **Position the cursor at the beginning or end of the text you want to select.**

   (Click the mouse at that position or press the navigation keys to move the cursor.)

2. **Hold down the Shift key.**

3. **While you hold down the Shift key, press the navigation keys to stretch the selection area to the other end of the text.**

   The selected text is highlighted, and you can do stuff to it (see the section "Doing Stuff with Selected Text" later in this chapter).

The following table shows you how to select text from where the cursor is positioned:

| To Select Text Up to This Position | Press |
|---|---|
| Next character | Shift+→ |
| Preceding character | Shift+← |
| Beginning of next word | Shift+Ctrl+→ |
| Beginning of current word | Shift+Ctrl+← |
| Same position, down one line | Shift+↓ |
| Same position, up one line | Shift+↑ |
| End of line | Shift+End |
| Beginning of line | Shift+Home |
| Beginning of next paragraph | Shift+Ctrl+↓ |
| Beginning of current paragraph | Shift+Ctrl+↑ |
| End of document | Shift+Ctrl+End |
| Beginning of document | Shift+Ctrl+Home |
| Bottom of screen | Shift+PgDn |
| Top of screen | Shift+PgUp |
| End of street | Accelerator pedal |
| Beginning of tape | Rewind button |

# Selecting Text with the Find Command

If you know which text you want to select (such as the words *herring fondue*) but don't want to waste time searching your document for them, use the Find command.

You can access the Find command by choosing Edit➪Find and Replace from the menu bar or pressing the F2 function key. Chapter 5 discusses in detail how to use Find, but the following steps provide the essence:

1. **Choose Edit➪Find and Replace or press F2.**

   The Find and Replace Text dialog box appears.

2. **Type the text you want to find (herring fondue, for example).**

   The text goes in the box labeled Find.

3. **Press Enter or click on Find Next to search down through your document, or click on Find Prev to search up through your document.**

   Whatever you are searching for gets selected (if it exists), and then you can do stuff to it.

4. **Press Esc or click on Close to make the Find and Replace Text dialog box go away.**

   Or you can leave it displayed, if you find it to be useful or decorative.

# Selecting Text with Your Nose and a Pickle

This approach to selecting text is rather unorthodox; it involves thinly sliced pickle spears and breathing through your mouth for a while. This method is not recommended for novices and is best reserved for cold and allergy seasons, when its decongestant effect is most welcome.

# Extending Selections

Suppose that you just finished carefully selecting text. With sudden shock, you see that you really should have selected more. You are consumed by regret and self-recrimination. Ah, how much like life itself is word processing. Unlike life, however, WordPerfect gladly allows you to select more text — or less, for that matter. You don't even have to do it over again; simply extend your selection.

To extend a selection you have already made (or a selection that the Edit⇨ Find and Replace command made for you), follow these steps:

1. **Hold down the Shift key.**

2. **With the mouse pointer anywhere in the selected text, hold down the left mouse button.**

   The endpoint of the selection shrinks back to the point where you clicked, and you can drag it back and forth with the mouse.

To extend a selection you made by using the keyboard, follow these steps:

1. **Hold down the Shift key.**

2. **Press any of the navigation keys to move the endpoint — just as you did to make the original selection.**

You can also extend any existing selection by using a special feature of the Find command, as shown in these steps:

1. **Choose Edit⇨Find and Replace or press F2 to display the Find and Replace Text dialog box.**

2. **Type your search text in the Find box.**

3. **Click on Action in the Find and Replace Text dialog box, and choose Extend Selection from its menu.**

   This feature stays on until you turn it off again or close the dialog box.

4. **Click on the Find Next or Find Prev button in the dialog box.**

   WordPerfect extends your selection, up to and including the text you told it to find.

Notice that WordPerfect doesn't allow you to change the original starting point of a selection; you can move only the end that you moved the first time.

# Doing Stuff with Selected Text

This section might as well be called "Doing Stuff with Molecules," for the breadth of discussion it opens. This list shows a few of the things you can change after you select text:

✔ Font

✔ Font size

✔ Font style

✔ Capitalization

✔ Paragraph layout

✔ Position

✔ Orientation

✔ Color

You can also delete, cut, copy, paste, move, replace, search, spell check, grammar check, or typeset the text; turn it into a bulleted or numbered list; or convert it to a subdocument. Because these topics are covered in most of the other chapters in this book, don't look for them here; check out those topics in the index or table of contents.

In this section, we cover just a few fundamentals, such as deleting, moving, cutting, copying, and pasting text.

## Deleting text

The fastest, easiest, and (depending on how you feel about the document at hand) perhaps most useful thing you can do with selected text is delete it.

After you select text, just press the Delete key (or the Backspace key). The text goes away, never to return. It doesn't utterly, completely go away, however; it passes on to the next dimension, from which you can recall it with the Undo or Undelete command (refer to Chapter 4).

## Moving text

Another simple, useful task is moving text. Just select what you want to move; then click and drag the highlighted text where you want it.

As you perform this procedure, the mouse pointer has a shadowed rectangle added to it. The mouse pointer moves to indicate where your text will go (or wherever your final destination may take you, as they say in the airline business). This pointer movement helps, because the icon can go virtually anywhere on the page, although the text can go only where text ought to go.

When you release the mouse button, the move is complete.

## Copying text

You can copy text by using almost exactly the same technique you use to move it. To copy, hold down the Ctrl key while you drag. A second copy of the selected text is placed in the new location. The original selected text stays put, just where it was.

# The Windows Clipboard

Before we progress to cutting, pasting, and all those other functions that once were well within the capability of kindergartners but that now (thanks to the so-called magic of computers) take $2,000 worth of hardware and software and a library of books whose titles loudly proclaim your Dummyhood, in screaming yellow and black, to all who pass your office — whack! Ouch! Thanks, we needed that. Let's see, where were we?

Oh, yes. Before we go on to cutting and pasting, we should stop to appreciate how Windows has simplified, amplified, and utterly transmogrified our lives by providing a way to cut and paste text and other electronic stuff within and between Windows programs.

A special place within Windows, called the *Clipboard,* can carry selected text, graphics, spreadsheets, and other useful stuff from any Windows-based program to any other one. The Clipboard is just as useful within a Windows-based program as it is between programs. Within WordPerfect, it's used to copy, cut, and paste.

The Clipboard is not really a visible thing in WordPerfect; no cute little Clipboard icon moves around. It's just a sort of hidden storage area. Windows 95 has an adorable little Clipboard viewer, though; you can run it to see what's in the Clipboard. From the Start menu, choose Programs⇨Accessories⇨Clipbook Viewer.

In this chapter, we talk only about using the Clipboard within WordPerfect. Keep in mind, however, that you can also use it to carry text, charts, graphs, pictures, or even — in these days of multimedia — rude noises into and out of WordPerfect (see Chapter 25).

# Copying and pasting with the Clipboard

Suppose that you are writing a contract for Dingelhausen-Schneitzenbaum Furniture Prefabrication Co. and you are oddly averse to typing Dingelhausen-Schneitzenbaum Furniture Prefabrication Co. more than once. Copying and pasting saves your fingers and your sanity by allowing you to make multiple copies of Dingelhausen-Schneitzenbaum Furniture Prefabrication Co. all over your contract. (Guess which feature was useful in writing this paragraph?)

To copy some text, follow these steps:

1. **Select the text.**

2. **Press Ctrl+C or choose Edit⇨Copy.**

3. **Click on where you want the new copy.**

4. **Press Ctrl+V or choose Edit⇨Paste.**

Here's some advice for former DOS users: In Windows, unlike in DOS, Ctrl+C no longer yanks the computer by its toenails to say "knock it off" when it misbehaves.

When you press Ctrl+C, WordPerfect copies your selection to the Windows Clipboard. The text stays in the Clipboard, so you can paste as many copies as you want. If you were to switch to a Windows-based spreadsheet program, you probably could copy Dingelhausen-Schneitzenbaum Furniture Prefabrication Co. there too.

WordPerfect is smart about including spaces after periods and commas when you cut or paste words and phrases. You may notice that it removes extra spaces after a comma and inserts a space after a period. Way cool!

## Maximum occupancy: 1

The Windows Clipboard can contain only one thing at a time. If you copy or cut out something new, the old contents of the Clipboard are wiped out.

## Copying between documents with the Clipboard

The Clipboard is particularly useful for copying between documents. Because WordPerfect allows you to have more than one document open at a time, you can copy text in document A and paste it in document B. See Chapter 14 for more information about having more than one document open at a time.

# *Cutting and pasting with the Clipboard*

Cutting and pasting isn't much different from copying and pasting. The only difference is that the original selection gets deleted as soon as you cut it.

To cut and paste some text, follow these steps:

1. **Select the text.**

2. **Press Ctrl+X or choose Edit⇨Cut.**

   The selected text vanishes, but a copy is kept in the Clipboard.

3. **Click at the location where you want to paste the text.**

4. **Press Ctrl+V or choose Edit⇨Paste.**

Just as you do with copying and pasting, you can paste as many copies as you want. (Dingelhausen-Schneitzenbaum Furniture Prefabrication Co. Dingelhausen-Schneitzenbaum Furniture Prefabrication Co.)

As with copying, if you cut something new, it replaces the old stuff in the Clipboard.

## Keyboard skills to last a lifetime

The keyboard commands that are used for cutting, copying, and pasting in WordPerfect (Ctrl+X, Ctrl+C, and Ctrl+V, respectively) are used in many other Windows-based programs. For this reason, it's slightly to your advantage to learn and use these commands rather than the WordPerfect menu commands. True, the keyboard names are not particularly mnemonic. We keep track of them by remembering that the X, C, and V keys form a little row on the bottom row of the keyboard in this order: cut, copy, and paste.

## A handy list of helpful keystrokes

- Double-click to select a word.

- Triple-click to select a sentence.

- Quadruple-click to select a paragraph.

  (As an alternative, you can select a para-graph from a QuickMenu by clicking the right mouse button while the mouse pointer is in the left margin.)

- Press Ctrl+C to copy selected text.

- Press Ctrl+X to cut selected text.

- Press Ctrl+V to paste selected text.

  (As an alternative, you can copy, cut, and paste from a QuickMenu by selecting text and then clicking the right mouse button while the mouse pointer is in the text area.)

Copying or cutting new stuff wipes out the old stuff on the Clipboard.

## *Using the QuickMenu approach to Clipboarding*

If you have trouble remembering Ctrl+C, Ctrl+X, and Ctrl+V, or where the Copy, Cut, and Paste commands are on the Edit menu, the QuickMenu is just your cup of (instant) tea. To order from the QuickMenu, follow these steps:

1. **Select something.**

2. **Click the right mouse button.**

   Your mouse pointer must be somewhere in the text area — not on a menu or in the margins.

   A QuickMenu appears.

3. **Choose Cut, Copy, or Paste from the QuickMenu.**

If you choose Delete from the QuickMenu, WordPerfect deletes the selected text without copying it to the Clipboard first.

# Part II
# Prettying Up
# Your Text

# In this part . . .

So far, so good. If you are comfortable with the techniques discussed in Part I (or if you skipped over them completely), you can make documents, edit them, save them, spell-check them, and print them. More or less.

But how do they look? Stand back a little and ask yourself, "Am I getting my money's worth from this program? Do these documents look like a million bucks?" (Or at least as much as you paid for your computer and WordPerfect.)

If the answer is No, this part of the book is for you. We talk about how to jazz up, tighten up, and spruce up your documents, including how to use different typefaces, control your margins, set the spacing between paragraphs, and all that good stuff. After all, you don't want your carefully worded documents to come out looking as though you typed them on your old Selectric!

# Chapter 7

# Charming Characters

. . . . . . . . . . . . . . . . . . . . . . . . . . . . . . . . . . . . . . . .

### In This Chapter

▶ Making text boldface

▶ Underlining text

▶ Using italics

▶ Making text bigger or smaller

▶ Using different fonts

▶ Getting text back to normal

▶ Copying character formatting

▶ Changing capitalization

. . . . . . . . . . . . . . . . . . . . . . . . . . . . . . . . . . . . . . . .

*W*ordPerfect allows you to control the way individual characters look — not where they are on the page, but their size and shape. By "characters," we mean the letters, numbers, and punctuation that make up your text. (We are not talking about people like the strange guy next door who has 47 cats and sings opera while gardening.) In addition to using underlining, boldface, and italics to add emphasis to your text, you can choose different typefaces and type sizes. In fact, the range of choices can be overwhelming.

The good news about WordPerfect is that you can see all these special effects right on-screen. Unlike old-fashioned word processors (the ones that ran under DOS), newer versions of WordPerfect draw each character (with help from Windows) and can draw them in all their formatted splendor.

The bad news is that it is easy to get carried away with character formatting. Nothing is more amateurish, or harder to read, than a letter or memo that uses five typefaces on one page — readers spend all their **time** *shading* their eyes from the ***glare*** of all that SNAZZY formatting and don't have time to <u>absorb</u> the import of the text. So watch out when you're formatting text. Use a little restraint, people!

# Emphasizing Text with Boldface, Italics, and Underlining

We'll start with the easiest way to add emphasis to your text. **Boldface,** *italics,* and underlining are three methods of making a word or phrase stand out and make itself known. These methods are called *text styles* in WordPerfect-ese.

All you have to do is follow these steps to add boldface, underlining, or italics to your text (not all three at the same time, please!):

1. **Select the text that you want to emphasize.**

   Chapter 6 shows you ways to select text.

2. **Click on the Bold, Italic, or Underline button on the Toolbar.**

   If you haven't guessed, these buttons have the bold **B,** italic *I,* and underlined U on them. Alternatively, press Ctrl+B for bold, Ctrl+I for italics, or Ctrl+U for underlining. (Hey, even we can remember *these* key combinations!)

   WordPerfect displays the selected text in the font style that you chose. Done!

When you use these text styles, WordPerfect inserts secret formatting codes before and after the formatted text. The first code turns the formatting on, and the second code turns it off. The names of these secret codes are Bold, Italc, and Und. (Like we always say, why make these code names readable when you can make them cryptic and hard to spell?) To see, move, and delete these secret formatting codes, see Chapter 10.

## Formatting as you type

You can also add text styles to your text as you type it. If you are about to type a word that you want to emphasize, follow these steps:

1. **Click on the Bold, Italic, or Underline button on the Toolbar, or press Ctrl+B, Ctrl+I, or Ctrl+U.**

   This step turns the formatting on, so that whatever you type is formatted this way.

2. **Type the text that you want to emphasize.**

   It appears with the formatting that you chose.

**3. Turn off the formatting by clicking on the same button or pressing the same key that you used in Step 1.**

You can tell when one of these formats is turned on by looking at the Bold, Italic, and Underline buttons on the Toolbar. If the buttons appear to be pressed in, the format is on wherever the cursor is or on whatever text is selected.

## Is this part formatted?

What happens if you select a bunch of text, and some of the text is already formatted? Suppose that you select a sentence that contains one italicized word. When you select the sentence, the Italic button does *not* appear to be pressed in, because the whole selection (sentence) isn't italics. If you click on the Italic button while the sentence is selected, WordPerfect italicizes the entire sentence; if you click on the button again, WordPerfect unitalicizes the entire sentence.

If you want to get rid of all boldface, italics, and underlining in a bunch of text, select the text and then click on each of the Bold, Italic, and Underline buttons twice. The first click formats the entire selection; the second click unformats the entire selection.

## Yikes! Getting rid of formatting

If you have gone a little overboard with formatting, WordPerfect can turn it off again. Follow these steps:

**1. Select the text that you want to unformat.**

**2. Look at the Toolbar.**

If all the text that you selected is formatted, the relevant text-style button looks as though it is pressed in.

If all the text that you selected is bold, for example, the Bold button looks as though it's pressed in.

**3. Click on the pressed button.**

This step releases the button so that it isn't pressed in anymore, and the formatting should disappear. If one click doesn't do the trick, click on the button again.

Here's an alternative to Step 3: Press the equivalent key combination (Ctrl+B, Ctrl+I, or Ctrl+U) to remove the formatting for the selected text.

You can use more than one type of formatting at the same time. You can make text both ***bold and italic,*** for example. Just click on both the Bold and Italics buttons (one at a time, please) on the Toolbar, or press Ctrl+B and then Ctrl+I; ditto to turn the formatting off.

# *Making Text Larger or Smaller*

Sometimes, you want to make your text big, big, big. For a headline or the title of a report, you may want to make a nice, big, centered title. We discuss centering in the next chapter, but for now, these steps show how to make the text big:

1. **Select the text for which you want to change the size.**

   You usually select an entire line when you change font size, because a line with letters of different sizes usually looks strange.

2. **Click on the Font Size button on the Power Bar.**

   It's the button that says something like `12 pt.`

   A little menu of font sizes drops down from the button, showing the available sizes. The sizes that are listed depend on which fonts Windows 95 knows about. (We talk about fonts later in this chapter.)

3. **Pick a size by clicking on it.**

You can also set text back to its original size. Select it again, click on the Font Size button again, and select the same size that you used for the surrounding text.

What size is the text that you're already using? The second and third buttons from the left on the Power Bar show the font and font size.

Depending on which font you are using, text looks larger or smaller. For example, 10-point Arial looks much larger than 10-point Times New Roman does. Luckily, you can see how things look on-screen and make adjustments as necessary. (For those of you who think that Arial is the Little Mermaid, we talk about fonts in the following section.)

Only rare situations call for type that's fewer than 7 points high. Have pity on us aging readers and don't make your type too small.

If you plan to fax your document, make the text a little larger than usual — maybe 11 points. Faxes always look grainy, so they are much more readable if the type is large.

When you change the font size of some text, WordPerfect inserts secret codes, named (amazingly enough) `Font Size.`

## What are these sizes measured in?

Text sizes are measured in *points* — an old-fashioned term that predates not only word processors and computers but also typewriters. Most normal text is either 10 or 12 points high. There are 72 points to an inch, so 12-point text is ⅙ inch high ($^{12}/_{72}$). If you want to make a title, make it 14 or 18 points.

Don't ask us why they are called points; the *Encyclopedia Britannica* probably knows.

# Fonts of Wisdom

OK, OK — bad pun. We won't let it happen again. Anyway, it's time to talk about the heart of character formatting: the font, which is a fancy word for *typeface*. (Or is it the other way around?) A *font* is a set of shapes for letters, numbers, and punctuation. The text that you are reading at this moment, for example, is printed in a font called Cheltenham. The headlines are printed in the Cascade font.

When WordPerfect starts, it usually displays and prints everything in a fairly nice-looking font called something like Times New Roman. This font is based on the typeface that *The Times of London* designed eons ago for its newspaper design.

You can vastly improve the appearance of your documents by using a nicer-looking font. The following two sections show you how.

## Changing the font for some text

To change the font in which some text appears, follow these steps:

1. **Select the text for which you want to change the font.**

2. **Click on the Font button on the Power Bar (the one that currently says something like** `Times New Roman`**).**

   This button is usually the second from the left. A list of available fonts drops down from the button.

3. **Choose a font from the list.**

   Poof — the selected text changes to the new font. The Power Bar may not show it immediately, but if you move the cursor to the section of text that you just formatted, the Power Bar shows the font and font size in which that text is displayed.

## Not just another pretty face

You can install lots of fonts for use with Windows 95 and WordPerfect. Some fonts have little doohickeys (called *serifs*) at the ends of the lines that make up the letters; look at the tops of the capital letters. These fonts are called, not surprisingly, *serif fonts.* Other fonts don't have these little lines and are called *sans-serif fonts* (it makes perfect sense in French). In some fonts, all the letters are the same width (*fixed-space fonts*); in others, such as the one that you are reading, some letters are wider than others (they are called *proportionally spaced fonts*).

The most popular fonts for PCs are Times Roman (a serif font that looks like an uglier version of the body text in this book), Helvetica (a modern-looking sans-serif font), and Courier (which looks like the type on an old-fashioned typewriter). Because some font names are trademarks, however, your versions of these fonts may have other names. Times Roman may be called Tms Roman or Times New Roman; and Helvetica may be named Arial or Swiss (it makes perfect sense in Latin).

When you change the font for some text, WordPerfect inserts two secret formatting codes, one at the beginning and the other at the end of the text that you formatted. The first code changes the font; the second one changes it back. All very logical. Even the name of the code is logical: Font.

To choose both the font and font size, you can select the text to be formatted and then click on the QuickFonts button on the Power Bar (the leftmost button). You see a short list of popular fonts and sizes, such as Times New Roman at 12 or 14 points, in regular, bold, or italics. This button allows you to set both the font and size, but you don't get many choices.

## Changing the font for the rest of the document

If you want to change fonts part of the way through a document, you can tell WordPerfect that from this point forward, another font should appear. Follow these steps:

1. **Move your cursor to the location at which you want to use a new font.**

   If you want all the pages starting with page 2 to use a different font, for example, move your cursor to the top of page 2.

2. **Click on the Font button on the Power Bar.**

   A list of available fonts drops down from the button.

**3. Choose a font from the list.**

The font name in the status bar changes to the new font, and the text that comes after the cursor changes to the new font.

Choosing a font from the Font list may not change the font for the entire remaining part of the document. Your action inserts a secret code that tells WordPerfect to change the font at this point, and this change stays in effect until the next secret font-change code, if another one is in the document. (See Chapter 10 to learn how to find and eliminate any secret formatting codes that you don't want.)

You can use the same method to select a font at the beginning of the document by moving your cursor to the top of the document and then clicking on the Font Face button. But a better way exists, as described in the following section.

# The Master Control Panel for Character Formats

So far, you have seen three facets of character formatting: text styles (boldface, italics, and underlining), font sizes, and fonts. Wouldn't it be nice to see and change them in one unified display — a place in which you can set all three types of formatting at one time?

Done. We have said the magic word. Such a thing exists: the Font dialog box (shown in Figure 7-1). The easiest way to see it is to press the F9 key.

**Figure 7-1:**
One simple dialog box shows all your character formatting.

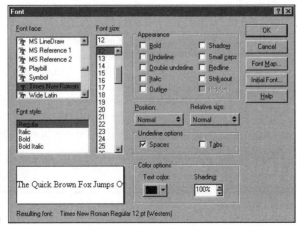

If you're not in a hurry, you can choose Format⇨Font from the menu bar. Another slow way to display this dialog box is to use the text QuickMenu. Position the mouse pointer anywhere in your text, click the right mouse button to display the QuickMenu, and choose Font from it.

TECHNICAL STUFF

# Where do fonts live?

Windows 95 includes a built-in font handler called *TrueType*. TrueType keeps track of which fonts are available to you. It is in charge of both *screen fonts* (the characters that Windows 95 and WordPerfect display on-screen) and *printer fonts* (the characters that your printer prints). After all, if you want WordPerfect to show you on-screen exactly how your document will look when it's printed, the fonts must match. TrueType also provides *scalable fonts,* which means that you can use its fonts in almost any point size.

Before TrueType, other font-handling programs were available, most notably a program named Adobe Type Manager (ATM, for short). Windows 95 runs TrueType automatically.

Each font is a collection of information about the size and shape of every single letter, number, and punctuation mark on the keyboard, in addition to some international characters that don't appear on any key. With TrueType, this information is stored in disk files (with the extension ttf) in your windows\fonts directory. TrueType fonts that are designed for use with older versions of Windows store additional information about the font in a file that has the extension fot. Many fonts have a font file for the normal font, a file for the font that's boldface, one for the font that's italic, one for the font that's underlined, one for the font that's bold *and* italicized — you name it. These font files can take up a lot of space on your disk but less than they did with Windows

3.1. We have 87 fonts installed (a lot, admittedly), and they take up 5MB of disk space.

When you look at the list of available fonts displayed by the Font button (or the Font dialog box, described later in this chapter), you can tell which fonts are which. TrueType fonts are listed with a little double-T logo before the name.

Fonts can live in one other place: in your printer. All printers know how to print at least one font by themselves — usually, ugly old Courier. Some printers come with several built-in fonts, and some have dozens. On WordPerfect's font list, printer fonts appear with a little picture of a printer before the name (it's supposed to be a printer, but it looks more like a tiny TV set with static on the screen). But what do you see on-screen when you use a font that lives in your printer? Windows 95 does its best to select a screen font that looks like your printer font, although the match may not be perfect.

What should you do if you need fonts that don't appear in the font list? What if your boss requires reports to be in Letter Gothic, which you have never heard of? You can buy additional fonts, usually in groups with such cutesy names as fontpaks. You may want to think about bribing a computer guru into helping you buy a package of fonts that are compatible with Windows 95 and installing them on your system.

# Using the options in the Font dialog box

This big mother of a dialog box contains all the character formatting that you have seen so far and more. This section describes the types of formatting that you can do with it.

To select the font (typeface), choose a font from the Font face list, which is the same list of fonts that you get by clicking on the Font button on the Power Bar.

In the lower-left corner of the Font dialog box, a box contains sample text about that quick brown fox that jumps over the lazy dog. (Are these folks original!) As you choose character formats in the dialog box, WordPerfect formats this text accordingly so that you can see how your text will look.

To set the font size (in points), choose a size from the Font size list, which is the same list of sizes that you get when you click on the Font Size button on the Power Bar.

If you want boldfaced, italicized, or underlined characters, first select the font from the Font face list. Then look at the Font style list, which shows you the combinations of bold, italics, and underlining WordPerfect can display and print in a high-quality manner. For these combinations, Windows 95 stores letter shapes in a font file (refer to the sidebar titled "Where do fonts live?" for technical information about this subject). If you see the combination that you want, choose it. If not, look over in the Appearance section of the dialog box, and click on the Bold, Underline, or Italic options there so that little Xs appear in the boxes for the options that you want.

Even though Windows 95 may not know the proper shapes of letters in these font styles, it is willing to try to fake it. Windows fakes boldface by adding some extra ink; it fakes italics by slanting everything forward; and it fakes underlining by (what else?) drawing a line. The quality is substandard for typeface aficionados, but it's probably fine for everyone else.

If you want to use additional font styles that we haven't talked about yet, check out the other options in the Appearance section of the dialog box. You can choose Double underline, Outline, Shadow, Small caps, Redline, Strikeout, and Hidden; see Table 7-1 for samples of all these styles. (Table 7-1 doesn't show hidden text, because hidden text is invisible when printed.)

| Table 7-1 | Font Styles and Examples |
|---|---|
| *Character Format* | *Sample Text* |
| Boldface | This **coffee** tastes like sludge! |
| Underline | This <u>coffee</u> tastes like sludge! |
| Double underline | This <u>coffee</u> tastes like sludge! |

*(continued)*

**Table 7-1** *(continued)*

| Character Format | Sample Text |
|---|---|
| Italic | This *coffee* tastes like sludge! |
| Outline | This coffee tastes like sludge! |
| Shadow | This **coffee** tastes like sludge! |
| Small caps | This COFFEE tastes like sludge! |
| Redline | This coffee tastes like sludge! |
| Strikeout | This ~~coffee~~ tastes like sludge! |

Scientific types who want to create a subscript or superscript should use the Position setting. Click on the setting button, which usually is Normal. WordPerfect displays a small pop-up list of your choices: Superscript, Normal, and Subscript. Click on your choice. The Position setting then displays the choice you made.

If you are underlining words and you have strong opinions about underlining spaces and tabs, you can tell WordPerfect so by using underline options in the Font dialog box. You can select Spaces, Tabs, or neither. Normally, only Spaces is selected, but you can change this setting by clicking on the boxes for these options.

After you select just the right formatting, click on OK or press Enter to exit the Font dialog box. In the following section, we tell you what text you just formatted.

If you want to forget the whole thing, click on Cancel or press Esc to escape from the Font dialog box with your text unscathed.

When you use the Font dialog box, WordPerfect sticks the appropriate secret formatting codes into your document. To get rid of them, you may have to refer to Chapter 10.

## *Knowing when to use the Font dialog box*

You can use this colossus of a dialog box to format text. This list shows you the two ways that you can use it:

✔ To format text that you have already typed, select the text and then use the Font dialog box. WordPerfect inserts two secret formatting codes, one at the beginning of the selection, to turn formatting on; and the other at the end of the selection, to return formatting to normal.

✔ To format the rest of the text in the document, position your cursor at the point where you want the font to change and then use the Font dialog box. WordPerfect inserts just one formatting code, at your cursor location.

# *Formatting the entire document*

What if you want to tell WordPerfect which font to use for the entire document, from soup to nuts? Every document has a *document initial font,* which is the font that WordPerfect uses for all text except where you specifically tell it otherwise. WordPerfect uses this font not only for the regular text in the document, but also for page headers and footers (described in Chapter 9) and for footnotes.

To set the document initial font, you use the Document Initial Font dialog box as described in the following text. It doesn't matter where your cursor is when you perform this little operation; make sure, however, that no text is selected. Then follow these steps:

1. **Choose Format⇨Document⇨Initial Font from the menu bar.**

   That is, choose Format from the menu bar, choose Document from the Format menu, and then choose Initial Font from the submenu. (Whew!) Alternatively, you can press F9 to display the Font dialog box and then click on the Initial Font button.

   WordPerfect displays the Document Initial Font dialog box, as shown in Figure 7-2.

**Figure 7-2:**
Telling
WordPerfect
the font to
use for the
entire
document.

2. **Select the Font face, Font size, and Font style.**

   The settings in this dialog box look and act like the ones on the left side of the Font dialog box.

3. **Click on OK or press Enter to exit the dialog box.**

   WordPerfect changes the font for all the text in the document, except where you formatted a section of text by using the Font dialog box or the Font and Font Size buttons on the Power Bar.

# *Copying Character Formatting*

After you have formatted some text the way you want it, you can tell WordPerfect to format some other text the same way. (Very useful!) WordPerfect calls this feature QuickFormat. These steps show you how to use it:

1. **Move the cursor into the middle of some text that is nicely formatted.**

2. **To turn QuickFormat on, choose the Format⇨QuickFormat command.**

   Alternatively, your Toolbar may include a button called QuickFormat (with a picture of a paint roller and the letters Ab). If so, click on it. Yet another way to turn QuickFormat on is to use a QuickMenu. (This discussion is getting a little too Quick for us.) With the mouse pointer pointing to your text, click the *right* mouse button to display the QuickMenu; then choose QuickFormat from it.

   You see the QuickFormat dialog box, shown in Figure 7-3.

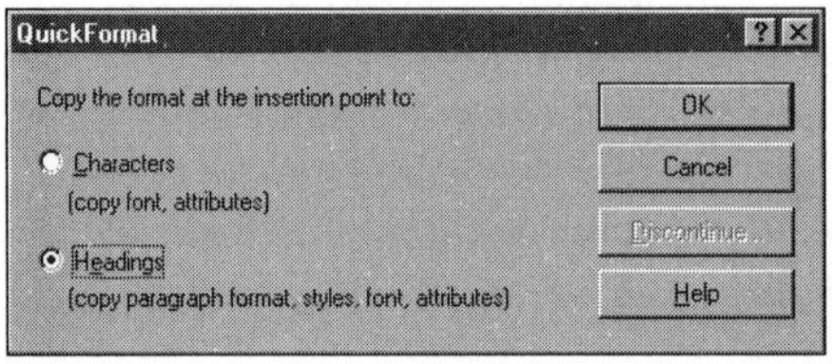

**Figure 7-3:**
How do
you want
WordPerfect
to copy your
formatting?

3. **Choose between copying only the formatting of the characters right where the cursor is (Characters) and copying paragraph formatting, too (Headings); then click on OK.**

   For a description of paragraph formatting, see Chapter 8. For now, choose Characters.

   The mouse pointer turns into the strangest-looking gizmo we have ever seen: a little paintbrush (for character formatting) or I-beam insertion point with a little paint roller next to it (for paragraph formatting). We guess WordPerfect wants to suggest that it will "paint over" any text with the new format.

4. **Select the text to which you want to copy the formatting.**

   As soon as you select the text, WordPerfect QuickFormats it instantly. Very speedy!

   The mouse pointer still has that strange shape. How the heck do you turn this thing off?

**5. To turn QuickFormat off, choose Format⇨QuickFormat again.**

Alternatively, just type something; click on the QuickFormat button on the Toolbar; or use the QuickMenu gambit described in Step 2. In any event, the cursor returns to its normal pointy self.

You can use QuickFormat to get rid of formatting, too. Select some unformatted text, choose Format⇨QuickFormat, and select some text that you wish that you hadn't formatted. WordPerfect removes the formatting from the text.

If you choose the Headings option in the QuickFormat dialog box, WordPerfect remembers that you copied paragraph formatting from one heading to another, and it considers the two headings to be karmically linked. If you later change the formatting of the original heading, WordPerfect changes the formatting of the other header, too — spooky! To unlink headings that have been linked by QuickFormatting so that you can format one without changing the format of the other, click on the Discontinue button in the QuickFormat dialog box.

# Changing Capitalization

dON'T yOU hATE iT wHEN yOU pRESS tHE cAPS lOCK kEY bY mISTAKE? We do. It's easy to type merrily along, hardly looking at the screen, until you see what you have done. Oops! In this situation, WordPerfect is your kind, thoughtful friend; it can fix the capitalization of text that you have already typed. Technology to the rescue!

To change some text into all capital letters, all small letters, or even All Small Letters Except For The First Letter Of Each Word, follow these steps:

**1. Select the text that you want to fool with.**

**2. Choose the Edit⇨Convert Case command.**

WordPerfect gives you three choices: Lowercase, Uppercase, and Initial Capitals. Cool!

**3. Choose one.**

WordPerfect changes the text as requested. The text remains selected, in case you want to do anything else with it.

You can use these commands only if you have selected some text; otherwise, they are unavailable and appear in gray on the menu.

The Initial Capitals option isn't smart enough to know exactly which words to capitalize in a title or a name. After you use this option, you probably will have to go back and make a few changes, to uncapitalize (smallize?) the first letters of prepositions, articles, and all those other types of words that you learned about in third grade.

# Chapter 8

# Sexy Sentences
# and Pretty Paragraphs

*I*n Chapter 7, you found out how to use all kinds of spiffy-looking character formatting so that your documents look much more professional. But wait — what about fooling around with margins, centering, indenting, and line spacing? That's what this chapter is all about.

Margins and spacing are extremely important, because they can make your documents look much longer or shorter than they really are. Suppose that you are a student who has an assignment to write a 10-page paper. With schedules and priorities being what they are, however, not to mention movies and pizza bashes, you have had time to write only seven pages.

Not a problem. Widen those margins. Pad that line spacing. Add a little white space to your prose. You can inflate it like a hot-air balloon. (We are not suggesting any similarity to your prose, of course.)

We can also address the opposite problem: packing it in. What if your boss reads only one-page memos, but you have a great deal of detail to include? Word processing to the rescue! Shave those margins, tighten that spacing, and maybe even shrink the font size a tad. You can squash everything in. If the whole thing still doesn't fit, remove all the adjectives and adverbs; that's what we do.

This chapter shows you how to mess around with margins, tabs, and justification, which WordPerfect calls the *line formatting* of your text. It also explains how to control the space between lines and paragraphs and how to indent the beginning of paragraphs — the *paragraph formatting*.

# Using the Ruler Bar

The first thing you need to do is display the WordPerfect ruler bar, if it is not already on-screen. If you don't see a horizontal strip just below the Power Bar, marked off in inches (or centimeters, for you jet-setters), choose View⤳ Toolbars/Ruler from the drop-down menu. You see the Toolbars dialog box, shown in Figure 8-1.

**Figure 8-1:**
Which bars
do you
frequent?

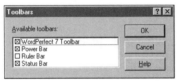

This dialog box allows you to choose which toolbars you want to see in the WordPerfect window. If you decide that you never use the Power Bar, for example, you can remove it from your screen by clicking on the box for that bar so that it doesn't contain an *X*. To see the ruler bar, click on the little box for the ruler bar and then click on OK. The ruler bar appears (see Figure 8-2).

**Figure 8-2:**
The ruler
bar shows
all your
margins
and tabs as little
triangles.

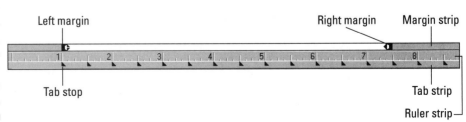

The ruler bar shows you the margins and tabs that are in effect in your document at the point where your cursor is located. When you change settings on the ruler bar, WordPerfect inserts the appropriate codes in your document. No information is really *stored* in, on, or around the ruler bar; it's just a nice graphical display of the state of your document. When you open another document, the stuff on the ruler bar changes to reflect the settings in the new document.

You can use the same View⇨Toolbars/Ruler command to get rid of the ruler bar later, when you finish with it.

For those who have their hands glued to the keyboard (and who also have memories like elephants), another way to display or remove the ruler bar is to press Alt+Shift+F3.

## What are all those little triangles?

The ruler bar packs a great deal of information about margins and tabs into a small space. It is made up of the following three gray strips:

- ✔ **The margin strip:** A thin strip above the ruler that shows you the margins. The rounded ends of the lighter part of this strip show the positions of the left and right margins. The dark-gray parts at the left and right ends of this strip are outside the margins. Just within the margins are little triangles that show the position of paragraph format margins, which are separate margins that you can set for each paragraph. (You probably won't need them; instead, see "Changing margins for a paragraph or two" later in this chapter.)

- ✔ **The ruler:** Marked off in eighths of inches. You can tell WordPerfect to display the ruler bar all the time.

- ✔ **The tab strip:** A gray strip below the ruler, which contains little triangles that point in various directions. The triangles show the positions of your tab stops. A *tab stop* is the position across the line where the cursor moves when you press the Tab key.

## What's the ruler bar for?

The ruler bar shows you the margin and tab settings that are in effect wherever your cursor is right now (not your mouse pointer, which is the pointy arrow thing, but your cursor, which is the blinking vertical line). You can set the margins, tabs, and other line formats at the beginning of your document, and you can change them partway through a document. If you want to include a long quotation in an article that you are writing, for example, you can indent only the paragraphs that make up the quotation.

In addition to showing you the current positions of margins and tabs, the ruler bar can change them — that is, you can use the mouse to drag the little gizmos and triangles around on-screen. In the rest of this chapter, we usually tell you (at least) two ways to perform each formatting task: one by using a menu or pressing a key, and the other by using the ruler bar. You can decide which method you prefer; WordPerfect doesn't care which one you use.

# Setting Margins

As you may recall from high-school typing class, the left, right, top, and bottom margins control how much blank space to leave along the edges of the paper. Normally, everything you type appears within these margins. The purpose of margins, of course, is to provide white space in which your reader can doodle while staring off into space. WordPerfect usually sets the left, right, top, and bottom margins to 1 inch, which is quite generous. You may want to make the margins smaller, to discourage excessive doodling.

## Dragging the margin lines

WordPerfect 7 shows where your left, right, top, and bottom margins are by using blue dotted lines, called *guidelines*. You can change your margins by dragging the guidelines around on-screen. Follow these steps:

**1. Move your cursor to the tippy-top of the document.**

If you want to change the margins for the whole document, it's important to start at the top. To change the bottom margin, move to the bottom of the first page of the document.

**2. Move your mouse pointer to the guideline for the margin you want to move.**

When your pointer is on the guideline, it turns into a line with arrows pointing in the two directions in which you can drag the guideline.

**3. Drag the guideline where you want it.**

Not to belabor the point here, but you can drag the left or right margin guidelines left or right, and you can drag the top or bottom margin guidelines up or down.

When you change the left margin, the top end of the guideline may refuse to move. Don't worry; WordPerfect is just being obstinate. The margin will look fine.

Call us old-fashioned, but by the time we're finished with that little maneuver, it's time for lunch. We would rather just use a nice, safe dialog box, as you'll learn in the following section. But feel free to suit yourself.

## *Using the Margins dialog box*

These steps show how to set the margins in your document by using a dialog box, if you don't like dragging things with the mouse:

1. **Move your cursor to the tippy-top of the document.**

   The quickest way to do this is to press Ctrl+Home.

2. **Choose Format⇨Margins or press Ctrl+F8.**

   This step displays the Margins dialog box, as shown in Figure 8-3.

**Figure 8-3:**
Setting the margins for your document.

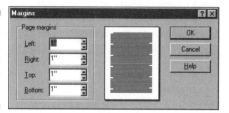

3. **Enter measurements in the Left, Right, Top, and Bottom boxes.**

   You can type numbers, or you can click on the little up- or down-pointing triangle buttons to the right of each box to increase or decrease the numbers by a 10th of an inch per click. As you change the measurements, WordPerfect changes the margins on the little page diagram in the dialog box so that you can see the effect you will achieve.

4. **To change the margins to the measurements you entered, press Enter or click on OK.**

   If you'd rather forget the whole thing, press Esc or click on Cancel.

Another way to see the Margins dialog box is to move the mouse pointer to the margin strip or the ruler strip on the ruler bar, click the right mouse button to display the ruler bar QuickMenu, and choose Margins from it.

Aha! One more way to see the Margins dialog box: Double-click on the margin strip on the ruler bar. That's it. No more ways.

When you set the margins, WordPerfect inserts invisible, secret formatting codes that contain the new margin information. The names of the codes are Lft Mar and Rgt Mar. (WordPerfect code names are always cryptic and strange; otherwise, they wouldn't be exciting and secret.) See Chapter 10 to learn how to see these secret codes and delete them, if necessary.

## Changing the margins for the rest of the document

You can change the margins partway through your document, which is useful if your document contains more than one distinct part (such as an executive summary followed by a detailed proposal). You can use different margins for the different parts of the document. (OK, we're reaching for an example here, but it sounds plausible.)

To change the margins for the rest of the document, follow these steps:

1. **Move the cursor to the position where you want the margins to change.**

   This position is usually at the top of a page, but it doesn't have to be.

2. **Display the Margins dialog box.**

   That is, choose Format⇨Margins or press Ctrl+F8.

3. **Fill in the margin measurements you want to use.**

4. **Click on OK or press Enter.**

   The dialog box goes away.

These steps show how to do the same thing with the mouse and the guidelines:

1. **Move the mouse pointer to the point in the document where you want the margins to change.**

   To change the top or bottom margin, go to the first page on which you want to have the new margin, and use the top or bottom margin guideline on that page.

2. **Use the mouse to drag the guideline to the position where you want the new margin.**

   When you release the mouse button, WordPerfect sets the margin for the rest of the document to the position you chose. If you change the left or right margin, the guideline gets a kink in it, showing where it changes to the new position (see Figure 8-4).

**Figure 8-4:**
The margin
guideline
acquires a
kink when
you change
the margin
in the
middle
of the
document.

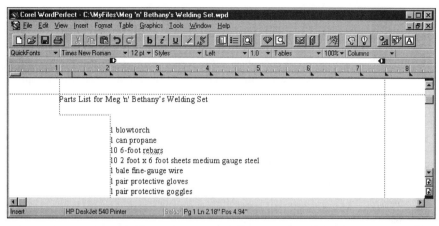

If you changed the left or right margin, WordPerfect changes that margin beginning with the line that your cursor is on. See Chapter 9 for more information about page formatting, including top and bottom margins.

## Changing margins for a paragraph or two

Indent

When you use paragraph formatting, you can specify special margins for one or two paragraphs. If you include long quotations in your text to impress people with your erudition, you may want the quotations to be indented more than the rest of your prose. WordPerfect provides three separate features for accomplishing this task, but we figure that you probably have more urgent things to do than learn all of them.

Our favorite way to change the margins for one or more paragraphs is to indent them, as shown in these steps:

1. **Move your cursor to the beginning of the paragraph you want to indent.**

2. **Choose Format⇨Paragraph⇨Indent or press F7.**

   If your Toolbar has a button called Indent (with a picture of a lined piece of paper and an arrow pointing to its left margin), you can click on that button instead.

   WordPerfect inserts an invisible, secret indent code, and the left margin of the paragraph moves to the right by one tab stop. (You can read more about tab stops later in this chapter.)

WordPerfect also provides the following useful variations:

- ✔ If you want to indent both the left and right margins for a paragraph, choose Format⇨Paragraph⇨Double Indent (or press Ctrl+Shift+F7).

- ✔ If you want to create a hanging indent, WordPerfect can do that, too. In a *hanging indent,* the first line of the paragraph is not indented, but the rest of the lines are. Choose Format⇨Paragraph⇨Hanging Indent (or press Ctrl+F7) at the beginning of the paragraph.

- ✔ If you want to indent several paragraphs, you can select the paragraphs and press F7. WordPerfect inserts a secret indent code for each one.

- ✔ An indent code indents the paragraph one tab stop. To control how far your paragraph is indented, you can move your tab stops; see "Playing with Tab Stops" later in this chapter.

WordPerfect, as usual, inserts a secret format code to record your request to indent the paragraph. The name of the regular code is (believe it or not) Hd Left Ind. The double-indent code is Hd Left/Right Ind (which has a certain logic to it). To achieve a hanging indent, WordPerfect inserts two codes: Hd Left Ind and Hd Back Tab. See Chapter 10 to learn how to see and delete these secret codes.

# Hitting the QuickSpot

A cute feature of WordPerfect 7 is the QuickSpot, a little button that appears in the left margin of the paragraph that the mouse pointer (not the cursor) is nearest (see Figure 8-5). The button, which is called the QuickSpot in Corel's marketing literature, is named Edit Paragraph if you point to it with the cursor. Clicking on this button selects the current paragraph and displays a window full of ways that you can format the paragraph. Figure 8-6 shows the menu.

You can use the Paragraph window to indent a paragraph, as follows:

1. **Move the mouse pointer into the paragraph that you want to indent; then click on the QuickSpot (the Edit Paragraph QuickSpot, to be precise) that appears in the left margin.**

   You see the Paragraph quick format box, shown in Figure 8-6. The first option is labeled Indent.

2. **Click on the Indent button, which says** None **with a down-pointing triangle at the right end.**

   The down-pointing triangle tells you that clicking on this button displays a list of options.

Edit Paragraph QuickSpot

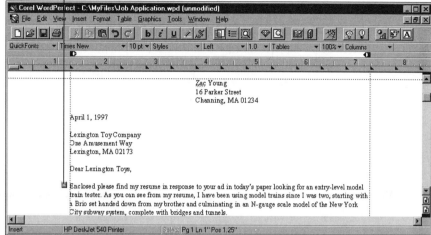

**Figure 8-5:**
The Edit
Paragraph
QuickSpot
appears to
the left
of the
paragraph
that the
mouse
pointer is in.

**Figure 8-6:**
Clicking on
the Edit
Paragraph
QuickSpot
displays a
bunch of
ways to
format the
paragraph.

### 3. Specify how you want to indent the paragraph.

Your choices are Indent, Double Indent, Hanging Indent, and Back Tab.

In the rest of this chapter, you'll see other ways to use the QuickSpot in the left margin to format paragraphs.

# *Centering Text*

**Center Text**

One of the most annoying typing tasks on a regular typewriter is centering text. Do you remember the bad ol' days, in which you had to count the number of letters in the line, press Tab to move over to the middle of the page, and then press Backspace to move backward half that number of times? The memory really makes you appreciate modern technology.

In WordPerfect, centering text is simplicity itself. With your cursor at the beginning of the line that you want to center, choose Format⇨Line⇨Center from the menu. Even simpler, just press Shift+F7. The line leaps to the center of the page.

You can center text that is more than one line long. To center several lines (a title and a subtitle, for example), you can select all the lines of text and then press Shift+F7 or choose Format⇨Line⇨Center.

You can even center a multiple-line paragraph. When you select the entire paragraph and press Shift+F7, all the lines in the paragraph are centered. The formatting looks a little funny, though, except on wedding invitations, graduation diplomas, and résumés.

Another way to center an entire paragraph is to click on the QuickSpot in the left margin of the paragraph, click on the Justification button, and choose Center from the menu that appears.

WordPerfect's secret formatting code to center a line is `Hd Center on Marg`. See Chapter 10 for details about formatting codes.

## Printing today's date

Everyone's favorite thing to print flush right is today's date at the beginning of a letter. WordPerfect can not only print the date at the right margin, but also provide the date. Follow these steps:

1. **Move your cursor to the beginning of the letter in which you want the date to appear.**

The location should be after your letterhead and before the address to which you are sending the letter.

2. **Press Alt+F7 to make the line flush right.**

3. **Press Ctrl+D to insert today's date.**

Wow! Betcha didn't know it would be that easy.

# Pushing Text Over to the Right Margin

The operation of pushing text over to the right margin, called *flush right* by typesetters, typing teachers, and small children who are undergoing potty training, is also a pain to do on a typewriter and extremely easy to do in WordPerfect.

If you want to make an entire line snuggle up to the right margin, follow these steps:

1. **Move your cursor to the beginning of the line.**

2. **Choose Format⇨Line⇨Flush Right or press Alt+F7.**

   The entire line leaps rightward.

To make an entire paragraph flush right, click on the QuickSpot in the left margin of the paragraph, click on the Justification button, and choose Right.

You can also move just the rightmost part of a line to the right margin. Suppose that your document must include a line that says *Draft* at the left margin and *Top Secret* at the right margin. Type all the text on one line and then follow these steps:

1. **Move your cursor to the beginning of the text that you want to make flush right.**

   For this example, you would position it just before the *T* in *Top Secret*.

2. **Choose Format⇨Line⇨Flush Right or press Alt+F7.**

   The text to the left of your cursor stays put, and the text to the right moves to the right margin.

WordPerfect's secret formatting code for flush right is `Hd Flush Right`. See Chapter 10 for details about secret codes.

# Changing the Justification

*Justification* is a serious-sounding word — one that makes us think about moral imperatives, rationales for our actions, and other philosophical stuff. What a disappointment when we learn that it has to do with sticking spaces into lines of text. Such is life.

In word processing and typesetting, as you may already know, justification deals with the moral problem of different lines of text being different lengths. If we could just write so that every line in a document had the same number of characters, we wouldn't have this problem. But no — we insist on making sense (with the possible exception of the contents of this book).

## Kinds of justification

Most people think that there are four ways to justify text, but WordPerfect has these five:

**Left Justification**

**Right Justification**

**Center Justification**

- ✔ **Left justification.** Text begins at the left margin and fills as much space as it takes up. Because different lines contain different text, the right edge of the text is uneven, or *ragged*. That's why this method is also called *ragged right*. Most of the text in this book uses left justification.

- ✔ **Right justification.** Works the same way as left justification, except that the lines are shoved over to the right margin (see the earlier discussion about flush-right margins). Now the left edge of the text is ragged, and the right edge is straight. (Wonder why nobody calls this *ragged left* or *straight right?*)

- ✔ **Center justification.** Usually used only for titles. This method centers each line on the page so that both the left and right edges of the text are uneven.

- ✔ **Full justification.** The trickiest type; both the left and right edges of the text are nice and straight. How do you manage this type if different amounts of text are on each line? The extra space is broken into little pieces and stuck in among the words in the line, so that all the lines are padded out to fill the space between the left and right margins. Magazines, newspapers, and books usually use full justification, which is also called *justified text.*

## Real versus fake justification

Old-fashioned word processing programs, such as the infamous original WordStar, performed a cheesy, fake kind of full justification: They just stuck extra spaces between the words. If a line didn't have much text, the gaps between words could become enormous. Modern word processing programs, such as WordPerfect, do a much suaver, sneakier job of distributing the extra white space along the line of text. WordPerfect breaks the white space into many tiny spaces and sticks them between the letters of each word, as well as between words. As you edit justified text, you can see WordPerfect shifting the letters slightly to adjust for the widths of the letters that you insert or delete.

✔ **"All" justification (as WordPerfect calls it).** Similar to full justification, only more so. In full justification, the lines at the end of paragraphs are exempt. If the last line of a paragraph contains a few words in it, for example, the text begins at the left margin and stops where it stops. But with "all" justification, WordPerfect justifies *all* the lines. No line is safe. If the last line of a paragraph contains a word or two on it, WordPerfect sticks *inches* of white space between each letter, if that is what it takes to stretch the line out to the right margin. We don't imagine that you will use this type of justification often; it looks downright weird.

## How to justify your text

To tell WordPerfect how to justify your text, follow these steps:

1. **Move your cursor into position.**

   To select the type of justification to use for the entire document, move your cursor to the beginning of the document. To set justification for the rest of a document, move your cursor to the point at which you want the justification to change. To justify only a paragraph or two, select the text that you want to justify.

2. **Choose Format⇨Justification.**

   WordPerfect comes back at you with another menu of options: the five types of justification.

3. **Choose one type of justification.**

   Alternatively, you can press one of these key combinations:

   - Ctrl+L for left justification
   - Ctrl+R for right justification
   - Ctrl+E for center justification
   - Ctrl+J for full justification

"All" justification has no key combination, which makes sense because it's hard to imagine that many people use it.

An easy way to justify a paragraph is to click on the QuickSpot in its left margin, click on the Justification button in the Paragraph window that appears, and then choose the type of justification to use.

Power Bar fans can also click on the Justification button on the Power Bar. This button usually says Left. To set the justification, click on the button. You see a menu of the five types of justification; choose one.

As usual, WordPerfect inserts secret codes to indicate the type of justification to use. If you selected some text, codes are stuck in at the beginning and end of the selection — one to change the justification, and the other to change it back. If no text was selected when you selected the type of justification, WordPerfect adds one code. The code in question is either `Just:Left`, `Just:Right`, `Just:Center`, `Just:Full`, or `Just:All`.

If you really want to fool around with the way that WordPerfect spaces the letters across the line, try the Format⇨Typesetting⇨Word/Letter Spacing command, which displays the Word/Letter Spacing dialog box. This technique is overkill if we ever saw it. You can control just how much white space WordPerfect can stick in among the letters to justify your text, suggest that WordPerfect crowd the letters together just a tad, or fiddle with the average amount of space between the words. If this is your cup of tea, go for it; we wouldn't dream of standing in your way.

# *To Hyphenate or Not to Hyphenate*

WordPerfect can hyphenate automatically, by deciding (sometimes rightly, occasionally wrongly) where to hyphenate words that are too long to fit on a line. Hyphenation is usually a good idea when you use full justification; otherwise, it looks dumb.

To tell WordPerfect to hyphenate words as necessary, follow these steps:

1. **Move your cursor to the beginning of the document.**

   Usually, you should use hyphenation on the entire document or not at all. Life is confusing enough as it is.

2. **Choose Format⇨Line⇨Hyphenation.**

   WordPerfect displays the Line Hyphenation dialog box. Ignore the cute little diagram, the percentages, and everything. No one we ever met ever wanted to change the parameters that a program uses when it does hyphenation. In fact, you can forget that you ever saw this box.

3. **Click on the little Hyphenation On box so that an *X* appears in it.**

4. **Click on OK or press Enter.**

   The dialog box vanishes.

At some point as you work on the document, WordPerfect decides that a word should be hyphenated, because it doesn't fit at the end of one line and is too long to move to the beginning of the next line. With no warning, you see the Position Hyphen dialog box, shown in Figure 8-7.

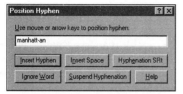

**Figure 8-7:**
Deciding
where to
split a word.

You have several options:

- Click on the Insert Hyphen button to insert the hyphen where WordPerfect suggests.

- Press the left- and right-arrow keys on the keyboard to move the hyphen to a better place to split the word and then click on Insert Hyphen.

- Decide that this long word should really be two separate words. Choose this option if you left out a space accidentally (which is our top-rated typo). Click on the Insert Space button.

- Decide that there is no good way to split the word in two and that the whole thing should be moved to the beginning of the next line. A classic example of this is the word *strength,* which has a bunch of letters but cannot be hyphenated. (Isn't it amazing how much trivia we authors can dredge up?) In this case, click on Ignore Word.

When WordPerfect hyphenates a word, it doesn't insert a plain old ordinary hyphen. No, indeed. If it did, and if you edited the paragraph some more so that the word was no longer at the right margin, WordPerfect would glue the word back together, but the hyphen would still show up. Every once in a while, you see this situation in a newspaper or magazine: a hyphen in the middle of a word where it doesn't belong. Now when you see it happen, you can sneer, "That word processor should have inserted a *soft hyphen!*"

WordPerfect *does* insert a soft hyphen, which looks just like a regular hyphen when the word is split in half at the margin but which disappears into the World of Secret Codes if the word is glued back together again. Totally cool.

## Playing with Tab Stops

In word processing, you use tabs and spaces a little differently than you do when you type on a typewriter. One reason is that WordPerfect is smarter than a typewriter; you can tell it to do such things as center text and flush it to the right without using a bunch of spaces or tabs. Another reason is that because most computer fonts are proportionally spaced (different letters are different widths; see Chapter 7), using spaces to line things up doesn't work very well. If you don't know what we mean, read on. What follows is a discussion of spaces, tabs, and tab stops.

## Stop! Tab!

A *tab stop* (did we say this already?) is a position across the line where tabs stop. Logical enough. When you press the Tab key, WordPerfect moves toward the right across the line until it gets to the next tab stop; then it stops. WordPerfect allows you to define a more-or-less-unlimited number of them across the line.

### Types of tab stops and other boring information

WordPerfect has a bunch of different kinds of tab stops. This subject is the kind of boring, petty stuff that you probably haven't thought about since high school, and we urge you to skip this section if you possibly can.

Still with us? OK, here goes. This sidebar describes the different types of tab stops, along with what happens when you press the Tab key to move to each type. Table 8-1 shows a live demonstration.

| *Left* | *Center* | *Right* | *Decimal* | *Dotted Right* |
|--------|----------|---------|-----------|----------------|
| Tom    | Jones    | Blue    | $150.00   | ........ Page 1 |
| Jo     | Bloggswirth | Greenish | 75.00  | ................. 2 |
| Sue    | Fish-Frei | Purple | 235.50    | ................. 3 |
| Mary   | Green    | Red     | 100.00    | ................. 4 |

✔ **Left or L.** What you type appears to the right of the tab-stop position. On your ruler bar, left tab stops are indicated by little black triangles that point down and to the left. ◣

✔ **Right or R.** What you type appears to the *left* of the tab-stop position. This tab stop doesn't sound too aptly named, does it? It's called a right tab stop because the text is flush right, or *right-aligned*, at the stop. On the ruler bar, the triangles for right tab stops point down and to the right. ◢

✔ **Center or C.** What you type appears centered on the tab-stop position. On the ruler bar, center tab stops are shown by little up-pointing triangles. ▲

✔ **Decimal or D.** This type of tab stop is designed for numbers that have decimal points, such as columns of dollar amounts. WordPerfect positions the text with the decimal point at the tab-stop position; columns of numbers look so much tidier if their decimal points line up vertically. If you type something that has no decimal point, WordPerfect right-aligns it. On the ruler bar, a decimal tab stop is indicated by an up-pointing triangle with a little dot in the middle. ▲

✔ **Dotted versions of the preceding four types.** You can tell WordPerfect to display a line of dots (also called a *dot leader*) that leads up to the entry. You see this kind of thing in the tables of contents of books such as this one. On the ruler bar, dotted tab stops are shown by triangles with dots below them.

---

## Put your tab codes in the right place!

Before setting your tab stops, you *must* move your cursor to the right place. We even tell you where the right place is!

If you want to set the tab stops for the entire document, move your cursor to the beginning of the document by pressing Ctrl+Home.

If you want to change the tab-stop positions partway through the document, you can do that, too. If your report contains two different tables,

for example, you may want to set the tab stops once at the beginning of the first table and again at the beginning of the second. Move your cursor to the place where you want the new tab-stop positions to take effect (at the beginning of a table, for example).

See "Setting up columnar tables" later in this chapter to learn where to set the tab stops for a table.

---

## *Setting tab stops*

As WordPerfect was delivered from the factory, your document probably contains tab stops every half-inch. How can you tell? Display the ruler bar, that's how! If you don't see it, choose View⊃Toolbars/Ruler, click on the ruler bar box in the dialog box that appears, and then click on OK. (Or just press Alt+Shift+F3.)

Just below the inch markings on the ruler, you see little black triangles that mark the positions of your tab stops. The ones that WordPerfect provides are, by default, left tab stops (the most commonly used type) and are symbolized by triangles that point down and to the left.

You may not want to have a tab stop every half-inch, and you may want to create tab stops of types other than left tab stops. If you are typing a list of names and phone numbers, for example, you may want just one tab stop at the position where you want the phone numbers to appear. Luckily, WordPerfect allows you to fool around with the tab stops at will.

When you change or create tab stops, WordPerfect inserts a secret code that contains the positions of *all* the tab stops that are in effect at that point. The tab-stop changes that you make take effect at that point and continue for the rest of the document or until they encounter the next secret tab-stop code. If you change your tab stops several times, with your cursor in different places, you can end up with a document that's littered with tab-stop codes, and your tab stops may change when you don't expect them to. If you think that this situation has occurred, move your cursor to the top of your document and then move down through the document line by line. Keep your eyes glued to the ruler bar. If you see the little triangles flittering around on it, you have lots of tab codes in your document. See Chapter 10 to learn how to see them and get rid of them.

The secret code that WordPerfect inserts when you change your tab stops is called Tab Set and is followed by the positions of all your tab stops.

You have (as always) two ways to position your tab stops: use commands or use the ruler bar. The command for setting tab stops, Format⇨Line⇨Tab Set, displays the Tab Set dialog box. This dialog box is horrific, terrifying, and downright scary-looking, and we refrain from reproducing it here for fear of chasing you away from word processing forever. We prefer that, rather than use it, you stick to the ruler bar method, which is a snap.

If you double-click on a tab-stop triangle on the ruler bar, WordPerfect thinks that it is doing you a favor by displaying the dreaded Tab Set dialog box. Don't panic — just click on the Cancel button or press Esc.

## Using the ruler bar to set tab stops

Fooling with tab stops by using the ruler bar is kind of fun. This section shows you all the moves.

To move an existing tab stop, follow these steps:

1. **Move to the place in your document where you want the modified tab stops to take effect.**

   This spot is usually at the beginning of the document or the beginning of a table.

2. **Click on the little triangle for the tab stop that you want to move.**

3. **Hold down the mouse button and drag the triangle along the ruler to its new position.**

   When you release the mouse button, WordPerfect moves the tab stop to the position where you left the triangle.

To move a bunch of tab stops at the same time, hold down the Shift key, drag the mouse across the tab stops that you want to move (to select them on the ruler bar), and then drag them to their new positions.

To get rid of a tab stop, follow these steps:

1. **Move to the place in your document where you want the change to take place.**

2. **Click on the triangle for the tab stop and drag it down off the ruler bar.**

   WordPerfect drops the tab stop in the Bit Bucket, which is the digital equivalent of the trash compactor. You never see the tab stop again.

If you move or delete a tab stop by mistake, choose Edit➪Undo or press Ctrl+Z to undo your change. You can also click on the Undo button on the Toolbar (the button with the U-turn arrow pointing to the left).

To get rid of all the existing tab stops, follow these steps:

1. **Right-click on a tab-stop marker on the ruler bar.**

   It doesn't matter which tab stop you choose. A QuickMenu appears.

2. **Choose Clear All Tabs from the QuickMenu.**

   Blammo — no more tab stops.

To create a new tab stop, follow these steps:

1. **First, tell WordPerfect which kind of tab stop you want to make.**

   (For the types that are available, refer to the sidebar titled "Types of tab stops and other boring information" earlier in this chapter.)

   You can tell what kind of tab stop WordPerfect thinks you want by looking at the QuickMenu for the ruler bar. Right-click on a tab stop to see the QuickMenu; one of the tab-stop types has a check mark next to it.

2. **If the tab-stop type isn't the one that you want, change it.**

   Choose the type of tab stop that you want from the QuickMenu.

   Now you are ready to create the tab stop. Get ready; this process is complex and painstaking.

3. **On the lower part of the ruler bar (where the triangles appear), point to the position where you want the tab stop, and . . . click.**

   That's all there is to it! WordPerfect creates the tab stop and the little triangle to go with it.

After you have your tab stops where you want them, you are ready to use them.

# Using Tabs, Spaces, and Indents

You must be thinking, "What's the big production about using tabs? Can't I just press the Tab key and be done with it?" Yes, you can do that, but your documents work better (that is, they look better and are easier to edit) if you use tabs wisely. This section looks at the ways in which you are likely to want to use tabs.

If you press the Tab key, and rather than inserting a tab, your cursor just slides below the existing characters to the next tab stop, you probably are in Typeover mode (refer to Chapter 4). Switch to Insert mode by pressing the Insert key.

## Indenting the first line of each paragraph

Indenting the first line of each paragraph is one of the all-time-favorite uses of tabs. If you want the first line of a paragraph to be indented, you can press the Tab key as you begin typing the paragraph. Or you can insert the tab later, after you type the paragraph. No big news here.

If you want to indent the first lines of a *bunch* of paragraphs, however, you can tell WordPerfect to do it automatically, without your having to stick a tab at the beginning of each one. These steps show you how:

1. **Select all the paragraphs for which you want to indent just the first line.**

   The paragraphs must be together, with no other paragraphs, titles, or whatever mixed in. (You can always select one group of paragraphs at a time and repeat these steps for each one.) If you want to indent the first line of every single paragraph in the document, don't select any text; instead, move the cursor to the beginning of the document. If you want to indent all the paragraphs starting partway through the document, move your cursor to the point where you want this formatting to begin. Whew!

2. **Choose Format⇨Paragraph⇨Format.**

   WordPerfect displays the Paragraph Format dialog box, as shown in Figure 8-8.

3. **In the First line indent box, enter the amount by which you want to indent each first line.**

   This amount is usually about half an inch.

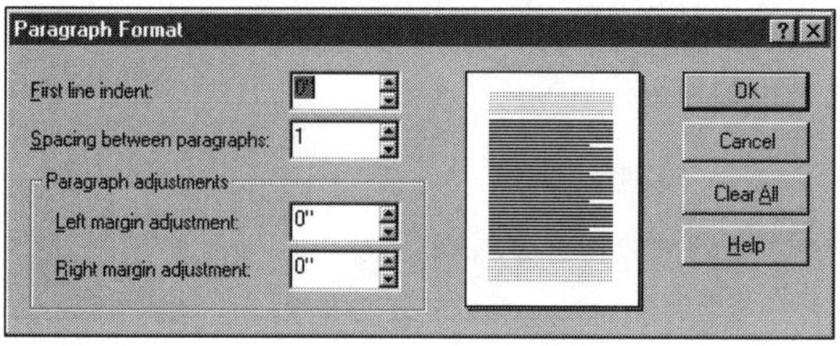

**Figure 8-8:**
Formatting a
bunch of
paragraphs
so that
their first
lines are
indented.

**4. Click on OK or press Enter.**

Voilà! WordPerfect adds that little bit of white space at the beginning of each paragraph, just the way your typing teacher taught you. Look, Ma—no tabs!

Another way to display the Paragraph Format dialog box is to right-click on the ruler strip of the ruler bar and then choose Paragraph Format from the QuickMenu that appears.

Whether you choose to use tabs or paragraph formatting, don't use spaces to indent paragraphs. In word processing circles, this method is considered to be tacky. The problem with spaces is that they are different widths, depending on which font you use (see Chapter 7 for information about fonts). Tap stops are always exactly the width that you see on the ruler bar.

The advantage of using tabs is that if you decide to indent your paragraphs by a different amount, all you have to do is slide that first tab stop over by a hair. Then all the tabs that depend on that tab stop move, too. When you perform this procedure, be sure that your cursor is in the right place: at the beginning of your document.

Whenever you use a tab to indent a line, you should have pressed Enter to end the preceding line. In other words, the line that you are indenting shouldn't begin as a result of WordPerfect's use of word wrap to fill the lines of a paragraph. Another way to say the same thing is that you should use a tab to indent only the first line of a paragraph. WordPerfect's word-wrap feature (described in Chapter 1) fills up the rest of the lines in your paragraph.

To indent *all* the lines in the paragraph, or all *except* the first line, refer to "Changing margins for a paragraph or two" earlier in this chapter. Never stick a tab at the beginning of each line of a paragraph. Yuck! Ptooey! If you do, when you edit the paragraph later, the tabs will be all over the place, and your paragraph will have unsightly gaps in all the wrong places. *Please* indent.

When you press the Tab key, WordPerfect inserts various secret codes, depending on the type of tab stop to which the tab moves. The codes are called `Left Tab`, `Right Tab`, `Center Tab`, `Dec Tab`, . . . `Left Tab`, . . . `Right Tab`, and so on.

## Setting up columnar tables

The other big reason to use tabs is to make a table (a bunch of columns side by side, such as a phone list). To make a table in WordPerfect, you can use WordPerfect's slick and snazzy tables feature, which is described in Chapter 15. But if you would rather do it the old-fashioned way, use tabs and follow these steps:

1. **Type your column headings.**

   Most tables have a line or two of headings at the top of the columns. Type the headings and separate them with tabs — just *one* tab between each column. Because you haven't set your tab stops yet, the spacing probably looks terrible. Stay calm.

2. **Move your cursor to the beginning of the line that contains the column headings (the first line, if there is more than one).**

3. **Set tab stops so that the column headings are spaced the way you want them.**

   You can always move the headings later, if the information doesn't fit in the columns the way you expect. Use only left, center, and right tab stops. Don't use decimal or dotted tab stops, because they make your column headings look downright odd.

4. **Move to the next line, where the information in the table will begin.**

   Now you are ready to type the information in the body of the table, as they say.

5. **Type one line of information and separate the columns with just *one* tab.**

   Perform this step no matter how lousy it looks; you learn how to fix it in a minute.

6. **Move back to the beginning of the line you just typed.**

7. **Set the tab stops for the table.**

   Use decimal tabs for numbers that have decimal points. Use dotted tab stops as you please. Slide the tab stops around on the ruler bar until everything is just right. But make sure that your cursor is at the beginning of that first line whenever you make a change.

When you get the first line of information the way you like it, you may want to go back and fix the spacing of the column headings. Just make sure that you put your cursor at the beginning of the first line of column headings.

**8. Type the rest of the table.**

Insert just one tab between columns. Everything should line up perfectly.

**9. At the end of the table, put the tab stops back the way they were.**

If you want to go back to the WordPerfect default — a left tab stop every half-inch — you may want to brave the Tab Set dialog box. Move your cursor to the first line after the table, and display the Tab Set dialog box by choosing Format➪Line➪Tab Set (or by choosing Tab Set from the ruler bar QuickMenu). Click on the Default button, which sets the tabs to the WordPerfect defaults. Then click on OK quickly, before this dialog box does something to your brain.

If you want to see where your tabs are and make sure that no spaces sneaked in, choose View➪Show ¶ or press Ctrl+Shift+F3. Suddenly, the document fills with little gizmos. The spaces turn into little dots, the Enters (carriage returns) turn into paragraph symbols, and the tabs — there they are! — appear as right arrows. If this display gives you a headache (as it does us), turn it off by choosing the same command, which is now called Hide ¶, or by pressing the same keys. If you want to see your tabs and Enters but not all those blasted dots in your spaces, you can use this wacky command to control exactly what WordPerfect shows; see Chapter 20 to learn how to customize which gizmos appear.

## *Tabbing backward*

We know that tabbing backward sounds like a bizarre idea, but it's not the only one in the world of word processing. A *back tab* allows you to tab backward to the preceding tab stop. WordPerfect sometimes uses back tabs without telling you. If you use the method for creating a hanging indent that was described earlier in this chapter, WordPerfect indents the entire paragraph one tab stop and then enters a back-tab code to back up to the margin so that the first line isn't indented. Mercifully, WordPerfect performs this procedure automatically and spares you the gory details.

You can use back tabs yourself, although why on earth you would want to escapes us. To insert a back tab, press Shift+Tab. If you want to type some text, such as *aaa,* on top of some other text, such as *bbb,* type **aaa**, press Shift+Tab to back up, and then type **bbb**. Looks just peachy, doesn't it?

We brought the subject up only to warn you in case you press Shift+Tab by mistake. If you see text stomping on other text, a back-tab code may be lurking in your document. See Chapter 10 to learn how to find and exterminate it.

If you press Shift+Tab and your cursor just slides below the existing characters to the preceding tab stop, rather than inserting a back tab, you probably are in Typeover mode (refer to Chapter 4). Switch to Insert mode by pressing the Insert key.

# Changing the Line Spacing

**Line Spacing**

If the stuff that you write is sent to an editor (as ours is — pity the poor woman!), you probably have to double-space your text to leave lots of room for making corrections, expressing confusion, and doing some general doodling. WordPerfect has, as usual, two ways to change line spacing.

If your Power Bar is displayed, follow these steps:

1. **Move your cursor to the point at which you want the line spacing to change.**

   To change it for the entire document, move to the beginning of the document by pressing Ctrl+Home. To change the line spacing for a paragraph or two (for a long quotation, for example), select the text that you want to change.

2. **Click on the Line Spacing button on the Power Bar and hold down the mouse button.**

   The Line Spacing button usually says 1.0 (which tells you that the current line spacing is 1.0, or regular ol' single spacing).

   A little menu of line-spacing options appears, those options being 1.0, 1.5, 2.0, and Other.

3. **Choose your new line spacing.**

   If you want single, single-and-a-half, or double spacing, choose 1.0, 1.5, or 2.0, respectively, by sliding the mouse pointer down to your choice and releasing the mouse button. If you choose Other from this little menu, go directly to Step 3 in the following series of steps.

If you don't see the Power Bar or don't feel like using it (hey, we all have days like that), follow these steps:

1. **Move your cursor as described in Step 1 of the preceding series of steps.**

2. **Choose Format⇨Line⇨Spacing.**

   Alternatively, you can double-click on the Line Spacing button on the Power Bar. (Oops! We forgot that you're not using the Power Bar.)

   WordPerfect displays the Line Spacing dialog box, as shown in Figure 8-9.

**Figure 8-9:**
Double-
spacing
your
document to
make it look
longer.

### 3. Enter a number in the Spacing box.

Enter **2** to get double-spaced text, for example. You can also enter fractions. To add just a little space between the lines, you can enter **1.1** or **1.2**.
Click on the little arrows at the right end of the Spacing box to increase or
decrease the number in the box a tad.

### 4. Click on OK or press Enter to dismiss the dialog box (Shoo!).

WordPerfect does your bidding and adds the vertical space that you
requested.

When you change the line spacing, WordPerfect inserts a Ln Spacing secret
code.

# Changing the Spacing between Paragraphs

You can tell WordPerfect to leave extra space between the paragraphs in your
document and not add any between the lines of the paragraph. This capability
results in text that looks sort of like this book does — an effect that we prefer
over first-line indenting. Take that, Miss Perpetua! (She was our high-school
typing teacher.)

This procedure involves paragraph formatting and the use of the Paragraph
Format dialog box, which you saw earlier in this chapter (refer to Figure 8-8).
Follow these steps:

### 1. Move your cursor to the beginning of the document by pressing Ctrl+Home.

(Assuming that you want to use this kind of thing for the entire document,
that is.)

### 2. Choose Format➪Paragraph➪Format.

WordPerfect displays the Paragraph Format dialog box.

3. **In the <u>S</u>pacing between paragraphs box, enter the line spacing that you want.**

   Entering **1** means that you want no extra space. We recommend entering **1.5**, which adds a blank half-line between each paragraph — enough to separate the paragraphs visually. (Don't we sound like we know what we're talking about?)

4. **Click on OK or press Enter to leave the dialog box.**

Changing the paragraph spacing inserts a secret `Para Spacing` code into your document.

# Chapter 9

# Perfect Pages and Dashing Documents

● ● ● ● ● ● ● ● ● ● ● ● ● ● ● ● ● ● ● ● ● ● ● ● ● ● ● ● ● ● ● ● ● ● ● ● ● ● ● ● ● ● ● ● ● ●

## In This Chapter

▶ Setting the page size

▶ Adjusting the top and bottom margins

▶ Starting a new page

▶ Keeping text together

▶ Centering a page from top to bottom

▶ Looking at different views of your document

▶ Numbering pages

▶ Adding headers and footers

● ● ● ● ● ● ● ● ● ● ● ● ● ● ● ● ● ● ● ● ● ● ● ● ● ● ● ● ● ● ● ● ● ● ● ● ● ● ● ● ● ● ● ● ● ●

*I*n earlier chapters, we talk about making your characters look just right, fooling with margins and indentation, and other heady stuff. Now for the Larger Picture: formatting your document as a whole. This chapter explains how to tell WordPerfect what size of paper you plan to print your masterpiece on; where to begin new pages; and what (if anything) to print at the top and bottom of each page, such as page numbers. This kind of formatting separates the — men from the boys? women from the girls? toads from the water buffaloes? — pros from the amateurs in the world of word processing.

## *Setting the Page Size*

Page Size

WordPerfect wants to know everything about your document. In particular, it wants to know which kind of paper you plan to print it on (letterhead? envelopes? labels?). It doesn't care what your paper looks like; it cannot tell embossed rag stationery with gold-leaf edges from cheapo copying paper; it just wants to know the paper's size.

If you don't mention anything about paper, WordPerfect probably assumes that you're going to use the usual: letter-size paper that you stick in the printer in the usual way. If you plan to print on the paper sideways (known as *landscape orientation*), however, or if you plan to use legal-size paper, envelopes, or whatever, you had better tell WordPerfect about it. Otherwise, you may run into trouble with your margins (as described later in this chapter).

To tell WordPerfect about the size of the paper on which you plan to print your document, follow these steps:

1. **Move your cursor to the beginning of the document by pressing Ctrl+Home.**

   Because paper size is something that usually applies to the entire document, set the cursor right at the beginning.

2. **Choose Format⇨Page⇨Page Size.**

   WordPerfect displays the Page Size dialog box, shown in Figure 9-1.

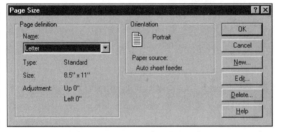

**Figure 9-1:** Choosing the kind of paper on which to print.

You see the Name box, which contains page definitions. To see a list of page sizes, click on the arrow to the right of the Name box, which probably is Letter. The exact list depends on the kind of printer that you use, because different printers can accept different paper sizes. Our list consists of the ones shown here:

- A4 (European paper, a tad bigger than American letter size)

- A4 Landscape (same thing as A4, but sideways)

- Envelope #10 (a regular business envelope, inserted into the printer sideways)

- Envelope C5 (another envelope size)

- Envelope DL (yet another envelope size)

- Legal (legal-size paper, which is longer than letter-size)

- Legal Landscape (same thing as legal, but sideways)

- Letter (our favorite)

- Letter Landscape (same thing as letter, but sideways)

3. **To use a different paper size, click on the arrow to display the list and then select the page size that you want to use.**

   The page size that appears in the Na<u>m</u>e box is the one that you are currently using for this document. Below the list, you can see the details of what WordPerfect knows about this kind of paper. A little diagram gives you the general idea.

4. **Click on the OK button.**

For details about how to print on envelopes and mailing labels, see Chapter 18.

If the list of available paper sizes looks odd, make sure that the correct printer is selected (see Chapter 22).

Use landscape printing for documents that are too wide to fit on the paper the regular way, especially for columnar tables that have numerous columns. Also, people always "ooh" and "ahh" when you produce a document printed sideways on the page, which is another good reason to use it.

When you set the paper size, WordPerfect inserts a secret `Paper Sz/Typ` code into your document (yes, another inspired code name!). To learn more about these codes, including how to delete them, see Chapter 10.

# An art lesson: Portraits and landscapes

We interrupt this book for a brief lesson on art — specifically, on the shapes of paintings.

As you have noticed from your extensive experience in art galleries, pictures of people tend to be taller than they are wide, to make room to include a complete hat-to-collar *portrait.* Pictures of places tend to be wider than they are tall, so that they can include more *landscape* and less sky.

The many art lovers among the computer scientists of the world decided to use this situation as the basis for naming the way that we print on paper. If you hold the paper so that it is taller than it is wide and then print lines of text that run across the short way, it is called *portrait orientation.* This orientation is the normal, everyday way to use paper. If, on the other hand, you turn the paper sideways so that it is wider than it is tall and then print on it accordingly, you have *landscape orientation.* Toddlers usually use paper this way, in our experience.

# *Adjusting the Top and Bottom Margins*

**Top and Bottom margins**

After WordPerfect knows the size of your paper, it has opinions about your margins. Unless you tell it otherwise, WordPerfect assumes that you want 1-inch margins all the way around the page, measuring from the edge of the paper. We generally find this measurement to be a little too airy and spacious for our tastes, and we usually change them — unless we are getting paid to write by the page, of course.

To change the left or right margin, refer to Chapter 8, which explains how to use the ruler bar, guidelines, or Margins dialog box for this task.

To change the top or bottom margin, follow these steps:

1. **Move your cursor to the point at which you want the new margins to take effect.**

   To change the top or bottom margin for the entire document, move to the beginning of the document by pressing Ctrl+Home. To change the margin beginning at a page other than page 1, move to the top of that page.

2. **Display the Margins dialog box by choosing Format⇨Margins or pressing Ctrl+F8.**

   If you get the urge, you can even display it by double-clicking on the part of the ruler bar that shows the margins. If you want to see a picture of this dialog box, flip back to Figure 8-3. But you don't have to; it's just a dialog box with entries for Left, Right, Top, and Bottom margins.

3. **Fill in the measurements for the top and bottom margins.**

   Alternatively, you can click on the little arrows next to the measurements to increase or decrease them a little at a time.

   The little page diagram changes to show you how the page will look, more or less. If you are using draft view (described later in this chapter), you don't notice a difference, except that the page breaks move.

   As an alternative, you can put your cursor where the changes should take effect and then change the top and/or bottom margins by clicking on and dragging the guidelines.

When you change the top or bottom margin, WordPerfect inserts a secret `Top Mar` or `Bot Mar` code into the text at the top of the current page. See Chapter 10 to learn how to fool with these codes.

# *Starting a New Page*

If you have typed any significant amount of text in WordPerfect, you probably have noticed that every so often, it suddenly introduces a huge gap between one line and the next. This gap is WordPerfect's way of telling you that you just filled one page and are starting at the top of the next page — a sort of digital equivalent of ripping the paper out of the typewriter and sticking a new sheet under the platen.

WordPerfect keeps track of where on the page each line appears. You can see your position on the page by looking at the status bar, where it says Ln (short, we guess, for Line), followed by a measurement in inches (or maybe centimeters). This spot is your position from the top edge of the paper.

But what if you don't want to fill a page before starting the next one? You can insert a secret code (not another one!) that tells WordPerfect to skip to the top of the next page, regardless of whether this one is full. This feature is called a *page break*. The page breaks that WordPerfect sticks in when pages are full are called *soft page breaks*. If you want to put a break in yourself, it's called a *hard page break*. (Read Chapter 10 to learn about the difference between hard and soft codes.)

To insert a hard page break, just press Ctrl+Enter. Poof! Your cursor dashes down to the top of a new page. If you were in the middle of the line, the part of the line after your cursor moves down to the new page with you.

To get rid of a hard page break, move your cursor to the top of the page *after* the page break, and press the Backspace key. This step backs you up, and with luck, it deletes the page-break code in the process. Alternatively, you can move your cursor to the last character *before* the page break and press the Delete key — same idea. If this step doesn't work, see Chapter 10.

You may be tempted to begin a new page by pressing Enter over and over until your page is full of carriage returns and you arrive at the top of the next page. We hate to be judgmental, but in our humble opinion, this action is *wrong, wrong, wrong.* Here's why: If you edit the earlier part of your document so that it gets just a teeny bit shorter, everything shifts up a tad. Now you have too few carriage returns to fill the page, and the text begins at the bottom of the preceding page rather than on a new page — not the effect that you want. Take our advice: Insert a hard page break instead. It's so much less work!

The name of the secret hard-page-break code is HPg, in case you were wondering. The soft page breaks that WordPerfect adds are named HRt-SPg or SRt-SPg, depending on whether the page break occurs between paragraphs or in the middle of a paragraph.

# Keeping Text Together

You have complete control over where hard page breaks occur, because you put them in yourself. But WordPerfect sticks in soft page breaks whenever it decides that no more lines can fit on a page. Sometimes, it chooses singularly bad spots to begin a new page — in fact, we suspect malice at those times. A technical term was created for lousy positioning of page breaks: *bad breaks.* (We always thought that it was a skiing term.)

## Avoiding broken homes (widows and orphans)

It looks lousy when a paragraph begins on the last line of a page so that only one line of the paragraph appears before the page break. This traditional typesetting no-no has a traditional name: widow (or is it orphan?). Our dictionary informs us that this line is called an *orphan*. A *widow* occurs when the last line of a paragraph appears at the top of a page all by itself. (At your next backyard picnic, amaze your friends by conducting a pop quiz to see who knows the difference.)

Luckily, you don't have to know about this stuff or even think about it, because WordPerfect does your worrying for you. Follow these steps to avoid the dreaded social disease of bad breaks:

1. **Move your cursor to the beginning of the document by pressing Ctrl+Home.**

   The following command and the resulting secret code apply to the entire document.

2. **Choose Format⇨Page⇨Keep Text Together.**

   WordPerfect displays the Keep Text Together dialog box, as shown in Figure 9-2.

   The dialog box contains three settings that have to do with positioning page breaks, and we discuss all three in this chapter. Our immediate concern, however, is those widows and orphans.

3. **Click on the little box by the instructions Prevent the First and Last Lines of Paragraphs from Being Separated Across Pages so that it contains a little check mark.**

   This check box is in the Widow/Orphan section of the dialog box.

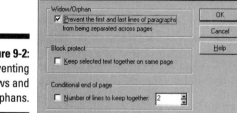

**Figure 9-2:**
Preventing
widows and
orphans.

**4. Click on OK or press Enter to leave the dialog box.**

Now WordPerfect avoids leaving widows and orphans alone at the top and bottom of pages. Instead, it moves page breaks up or down a line as necessary. The pages won't be completely full, but that's the price you pay for family cohesion.

When you follow the preceding steps, WordPerfect creates a `Wid/Orph:On` code in your document. Chapter 10 describes how to see and delete this code if necessary.

## *Keeping your act together*

Your document may contain information that should not be split over a page break. A columnar table looks crummy if it is split up, for example, unless it is longer than one page. You can select part of your document and tell WordPerfect, "Let no page break enter here!" Follow these steps:

**1. Select the text that you want to keep together.**

Refer to Chapter 6 to learn how to select text, if you don't already know. For tables, be sure to include any headings or titles.

**2. Choose Format⇨Page⇨Keep Text Together.**

WordPerfect displays the Keep Text Together dialog box (refer to Figure 9-2).

**3. Click on the Keep Selected Text Together on Same Page box so that it contains a check mark.**

This check box is in the Block protect section of the dialog box.

**4. Click on OK or press Enter.**

Block protect sounds like the maneuver that a 2-year-old uses when another kid comes to visit, but WordPerfect isn't talking about that kind of block. In earlier versions of WordPerfect, selecting text was always called "marking blocks," and doing anything with a bunch of text was called a "block operation." Now WordPerfect has adopted Windows-speak, which requires that you refer to a bunch of text as a "selection." It's another example of the Great March of Progress.

When you follow these steps, WordPerfect inserts two Block Pro codes into your document: one at the beginning of the selected text, and one at the end.

## *Keeping your head together*

Specifically, this heading means keeping your headings with the text that follows them. (You were thinking of the great Carole King hits of yesteryear, weren't you? Unless you're too young to remember them.) Leaving a heading stranded all alone at the bottom of the page while the text that follows the heading begins on the following page is considered tacky and gauche.

Unlike preventing widows and orphans, which you can do by issuing one command at the beginning of your document, you must issue a separate command for each heading that you want to keep with the text that follows it. (The solution to this annoying situation is to use styles to format your headings; jump to Chapter 11 if this subject interests you.)

To prevent WordPerfect from separating a head(ing) from its body, follow these steps:

1. **Move your cursor to the beginning of the line that contains the heading.**

2. **Choose Format⇨Page⇨Keep Text Together.**

   WordPerfect displays the Keep Text Together dialog box (refer to Figure 9-2). Look at the Conditional end of page section of the dialog box.

3. **Click on the little check box to the left of the title Number of Lines to Keep Together so that it contains a check mark.**

4. **Enter a number in the text box to the right of the title Number of Lines to Keep Together.**

   To keep the heading line and the first two lines of the text that follow it together, enter **3**. If you use a blank line to separate the heading from the text, you may want to enter **4**.

5. **Click on OK or press Enter to leave the dialog box.**

Now if the heading and the first few lines that follow cannot fit at the bottom of the page, WordPerfect moves the whole kit and kaboodle to the top of the next page.

When you follow these steps, WordPerfect inserts a `Cond1 EOP` (Conditional End of Page) code into your document. If you use styles to format headings, you can insert a `Cond1 EOP` code into the heading style to avoid headlessness throughout your document. (See Chapter 11 to learn more about styles.)

Don't use too many Block Protect and Conditional End of Page codes in your document, or WordPerfect will have a heck of a time finding *anywhere* to put page breaks. Cut it some slack!

# Centering a Page, Top to Bottom

**Center Page**

When you create a title page for a document, it's nice if the titles appear in the middle of the page, both up and down and left to right. Chapter 8 talks about how to center text between the left and right margins (oh, all right — move to the beginning of the line and press Shift+F7). The following steps show you how to center the titles top to bottom (of course, you can just press Enter a bunch of times above the titles, but why not let WordPerfect put your titles in exactly the right place?):

1. **Move your cursor to the top of the page that contains the text to be centered top to bottom.**

   In most cases, this page is the first page of your document.

2. **Choose Format⇨Page⇨Center.**

   WordPerfect displays the Center Page(s) dialog box, shown in Figure 9-3.

**Figure 9-3:**
Centering
titles on
a page.

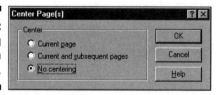

3. **To center this page, choose Current Page.**

4. **Click on OK or press Enter.**

   WordPerfect moves the text on the page up or down to its center.

You can tell the vertical position of the text on the page by looking at the `Ln` measurement on the status line.

To revoke centering on a page, move your cursor to the top of the page, choose Format⇨Page⇨Center to display the Center Page(s) dialog box, and choose No Centering.

When you center a page, WordPerfect quite sensibly inserts the secret `Cntr Cur Pg` code. Chapter 10 tells you how to see this magical code for yourself. (If you can deal with codes, double-click on the `Cntr Cur Pg` code to display the Center Page(s) dialog box so that you can change the setting.)

# Looking at Different Views of Your Document

WordPerfect can show your document from several angles, depending on how closely you want the view to resemble the printed page. This list shows the different views that you can choose:

- **Draft view.** Page breaks appear as horizontal lines across your document, and you cannot see top or bottom margins, extra space on a partially full page, headers, footers, or page numbers.

- **Page view.** WordPerfect shows how your page will look, including all margins, headers, and footers. Page breaks look like blank gaps between one page and the next.

- **Two-page view.** You can see two pages side by side, which is a lovely effect but totally illegible because the text is so small. Maybe if your computer screen were 3 feet across, you could read stuff in this view; except for a quick check of page formatting, however, it's relatively worthless.

To switch between these three views, choose View from the menu bar and then choose Draft, Page, or Two Page.

We bring up the subject of views because we are about to talk about page formatting that you can see only in page (and two-page) view: page numbers, headers, and footers.

A faster way to switch to draft view is to press Ctrl+F5. A quicker way to jump to page view is to swat Alt+F5. There is no fast way to see two-page view, and who would want to? For the most part, you can probably just work in page view. Why not see everything, after all?

# *Numbering Pages*

After you have a document with more than one page, you probably will want to number the pages. Few things are more annoying than a sheaf of pages with no page numbers that have gotten (or *may* have gotten) out of order. Don't look like a schnook; number your pages.

For some strange reason — probably some quirk of software history — WordPerfect has not one but *two* ways to number pages. (Why do we say this with surprise? WordPerfect *always* seems to have two ways to do everything.) The following list shows the two ways:

✔ Use the Format➪Page Numbering➪Select command to tell WordPerfect to begin numbering the pages. You can tell WordPerfect where the numbers should appear and also enter other text (such as today's date or the document title) to include with the page number.

✔ Use the Format➪Header/Footer command to define headers or footers, which can include page numbers.

It's difficult to tell the difference between these two approaches. Anyway, we talk about headers and footers in a minute. These steps show how to use the first method to number your pages:

1. **Move your cursor to the top of the page on which you want page numbers to begin.**

   If your classy-looking document has a cover page, for example, you can begin numbering on the next page.

2. **Choose Format➪Page Numbering➪Select.**

   WordPerfect displays the Select Page Numbering Format dialog box, shown in Figure 9-4.

3. **Tell WordPerfect where to print the page numbers.**

   Click on the little double arrow at the right end of the Position setting. You see these choices: No Page Numbering, Top Left, Top Center, Top Right, Top Outside Alternating, Top Inside Alternating, Bottom Left, Bottom Center, Bottom Right, Bottom Outside Alternating, and Bottom Inside Alternating. The alternating-top-and-bottom options do not mean that you and a friend have gotten your bikinis mixed up — they indicate that for outside alternating, the page number appears on the right side of odd-numbered pages and on the left side of even-numbered pages, and vice versa for inside alternating. This setting is just right for documents printed on both sides of the paper (this book, for example).

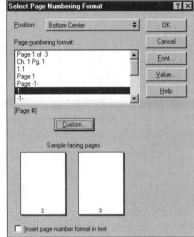

**Figure 9-4:**
Your pages
are
numbered!

Fortunately, you don't have to remember which numbering format is which. After you select a format, just check out the example of the page-numbering format at the bottom of the dialog box. Is this cute, or what?

**4. Choose the font for your page numbers.**

If you want the page number to appear in a different font, click on the Font button and then choose the font and font size from the dialog box that appears (which looks an awful lot like the Font dialog box described in Chapter 7). Then click on OK to return to the Page Numbering dialog box.

**5. Click on OK to bug out of this dialog box.**

Now WordPerfect prints page numbers on this page and on all the following pages in the document, even pages that you add later.

When you tell WordPerfect to number your pages, it adds a secret `Pg Num Pos` code at the top of the page. (See Chapter 10 for info about codes.)

## *For all you Roman-numeral fans*

You don't have to use boring, pedestrian Arabic numbers for your page numbers. You can use small Roman numerals to number the pages in the introduction of a report, for example. To tell WordPerfect which type of numbers to use (Roman or Arabic), follow these steps:

**1. Move your cursor to the top of the page on which you want the numbering to begin.**

2. **Choose Format⇨Page Numbering.**

3. **Scroll through the Page Numbering list until you find the lowercase Roman numeral.**

   The settings in this list start with regular old Arabic numbers, but there are zillions of choices; you decide how you want your page number to look by selecting one.

4. **If you can't find a format you like, click on the Custom button to display the Custom Page Numbering dialog box. In the box labeled Edit custom format and text setting, enter text until the sample looks the way you want your page numbers to look.**

   In this dialog box, you can add text to your page number so that it reads *Goofy Report, Page 1,* for example. Click on OK when you finish with the Custom Page Numbering dialog box.

5. **Click on OK to leave the Select Page Numbering Format dialog box and save your selection.**

You can even switch page-number styles part of the way through the document: Just move your cursor to the top of the page on which you want the style to change and then follow the preceding steps.

## Starting over again at 1

If you want to change your page numbering part of the way through a document, you can. If your report titled "Ten Thousand Uses for Chocolate" begins with an introduction, for example, you can restart the page numbering at 1 on the first page that follows the introduction. Follow these steps:

### Stop! Don't type that page number!

Untutored word-processing novices have been known to enter page numbers at the bottom of every page. A moment's thought tells you why this is a terrible, awful, yucky idea. If you insert a line at the bottom of each page and type the page number, what are you gonna do when an important update requires you to insert a few additional lines on page 1? Suddenly, all the page numbers that used to appear at the bottom of the pages slide down to print a few lines down from the top of the following pages. What a mess!

The moral of the story is "Never type page numbers as text." Always use either page numbering or headers or footers (described later in this chapter) to do it for you.

1. **Move your cursor to the top of the page on which you want to restart page numbering at 1.**

2. **Choose Fo_r_mat⇨Page _N_umbering⇨Value/Adjust . . .**

   WordPerfect displays the Value/Adjust Number dialog box. Absolutely, positively ignore all tabs in this dialog box except for Page, which should be the one that's selected.

3. **For the _S_et page number option, enter 1.**

4. **Make sure that the radio button next to Al_w_ays keep number the same is selected (has a dot in it).**

   This option ensures that the page that the cursor was on when you changed these settings will always be numbered 1.

   The _L_et number change as pages are added or deleted option does just that. If you add a page to the introduction, the page that you originally insisted should have the number 1 now has the number 2. This option is useful if you are inserting pages into a document from another source (graphs or figures, for example, although you can insert those into a WordPerfect document, too; see Chapter 15).

5. **Click on OK to leave the Adjust Number Value dialog box.**

# Adding Heads and Feets

Now that we have gone through all the gory details of page numbering, we admit that we usually don't use the Page Numbering dialog box to number our pages. We usually have lots of other things that we want to include at the top or bottom of each page, such as the title of the document, today's date, and notes that say *Draft* or *Confidential! Destroy Before Reading!* The easiest way to print all this stuff at the top or bottom of each page is to use headers and footers.

The cool thing about headers and footers is that they can contain almost anything — one line of text, an entire paragraph, or even a picture. Also, your document can contain two different headers (Header A and Header B) and two different footers (Footer A and Footer B, believe it or not), so you can print different headers and footers on the facing pages of documents that are printed on both sides of the page.

Header

## Making a header or footer

These steps show how to make a header or footer:

Footer

1. **Choose _V_iew⇨_P_age or press Alt+F5 to switch to page view, so that you can see the headers and footers that you create.**

   Headers and footers are invisible in draft view.

**2. Move to the beginning of your document by pressing Ctrl+Home.**

If you want headers and footers to begin part of the way through your document, move to the top of the first page on which you want the header or footer to appear.

**3. Choose Format⬄Header/Footer.**

You see the Headers/Footers dialog box, shown in Figure 9-5.

**Figure 9-5:**
Defining
heads and
feets.

**4. Choose the header or footer that you want to create.**

If you plan to use one header or footer for the entire document, choose Header A or Footer A. If you plan to use two headers or two footers (to number facing pages, for example), choose either A or B.

**5. Click on the Create button.**

This step tells WordPerfect to insert a new secret header or footer code into your document. WordPerfect adds a blank line at the top (for headers) or bottom (for footers) of the page; you can begin typing your header or footer in this line. Notice that headers and footers get their own guidelines — in a different color, even. You can drag all margins but the top margin of a header (you have to change the *page's* top margin) or the bottom margin of a footer (you have to change the *page's* bottom margin).

If you want to skip printing the header or footer on the first page of the document (a common technique), move to the beginning of the document anyway. You can tell WordPerfect to suppress printing the header and footer on the first page; this procedure is described later in this chapter.

Some grammar maniacs insist that headers and footers are more properly called *headings* and *footings.* Ignore them.

You can have several Header As, Header Bs, Footer As, or Footer Bs in your document. If you think that this arrangement would be confusing, you're right; don't use it.

You can create Header or Footer B before you create Header or Footer A; WordPerfect doesn't care. On the other hand, you may get confused. We stick with A if we are using only one header or footer. If you use two at a time, one prints over the other. Avoid this problem by defining one header or footer for odd pages and the other for even, as explained later in this chapter.

When you create a header or footer, WordPerfect inserts a secret code named Header A (or whichever header or footer you choose). The code also contains all the text that appears in the header or footer, including formatting. To see or delete this code, see Chapter 10.

## Typing the text in a header or footer

Now your job is to type the text that you want to appear in this header or footer. To help you, WordPerfect displays another little bar of buttons above your document. The Header/Footer feature bar is just below the Power Bar (if you have displayed the Power Bar); it's labeled in Figure 9-6.

This new line that WordPerfect adds for your header or footer is no ordinary new line — this line is in a special zone that contains the text for your header or footer. You cannot use the cursor-control keys to move between the header or footer zone and the rest of the document. You can use the mouse to click where you want to edit, however; this action enables you to switch between editing the regular document and your header or footer.

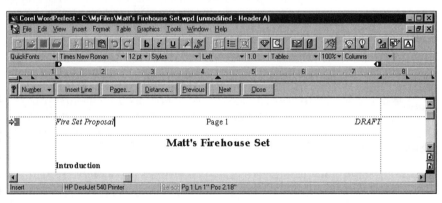

**Figure 9-6:**
Using the
Header/
Footer
feature bar.

When you are editing a header or footer, you can use the buttons in the Header/Footer feature bar. If you move your cursor to another part of your document, the feature bar stays on-screen, but all the buttons (except Close, used to remove the feature bar) are *grayed out,* which means that they go out of focus and do nothing if you click on them. If you move your cursor back to your header or footer, the feature-bar buttons come back into focus. Some of the buttons on the Toolbar and Power Bar, however, and some menu commands get fuzzy and unusable when you are editing a header or footer. You cannot use the New, Open, Save, and Print buttons on the Toolbar or their equivalent menu commands while you are editing a header or footer. *C'est la vie.*

To enter the text in your header or footer, follow these steps:

1. **Move your cursor to the header or footer zone, if it's not already there.**

   You can tell when you are editing a header or footer, because the buttons on the Header/Footer feature bar come into focus. You can also tell by looking at the title bar of the WordPerfect window. The title bar displays not only the name of the document that you are editing but also the name of the header or footer that you are working on ([ZUKESOUP.wpd - Header A], for example).

2. **Type the text.**

   You can control the font, font size, and text style in the usual ways (refer to Chapter 7). If you want the header or footer to be more than one line long, be our guest; just keep typing. Go ahead and press Enter at the end of the line if you want to include more than one paragraph.

   What about page numbers, you ask? Aha! It's time to use those cute buttons on the feature bar that WordPerfect insisted on using to clutter up your screen.

3. **To include the current page number in the header or footer, move your cursor to the place where you want the page number to appear, and click on the Number button on the feature bar.**

   A little menu drops down.

4. **Choose Page Number (as you probably have guessed).**

   If you close the Header/Footer feature bar and later want it back, choose Format⇨Header/Footer and then click on the Edit button in the Header/Footer dialog box.

5. **Choose Close from the Header/Footer feature bar to get back to the real world.**

When you type the text of your document, you don't have to leave room for the headers or footers. WordPerfect sticks them in at the top and bottom margins of the page and shoves the other text out of the way.

If you want to print the current date in the header or footer, see Chapter 25 or just press Ctrl+Shift+D.

If you want your header or footer to contain lines, boxes, or even pictures, see Chapter 15.

## The standard three-part header

If you want some text at the left margin, some text centered, and some text at the right margin, you can tell WordPerfect to center and right-align parts of your header. You can print the document title at the left margin, for example, the page number in the center of the header, and today's date at the right margin.

To make a header such as this one, type everything on one line, with nothing between the left part, the middle part, and the right part.

With your cursor just before the part of the line that you want to center, choose Format⇨Line⇨Center (or press Shift+F7). This step centers the rest of the line. Then move your cursor just before the text that you want to right-align, and choose Format⇨Line⇨Flush Right (or press Alt+F7). This step moves the rest of the line over to the right margin.

You can format the text in your headers and footers by using the same commands that you can use for text in the rest of your document. Commands that you cannot use appear grayed out in the WordPerfect menus, which is WordPerfect's subtle way of telling you that you cannot choose these commands.

If you cannot see your headers or footers, you are probably using draft view, in which they are invisible. Choose View⇨Page (or press Alt+F5) to switch to page view.

## *Controlling where headers and footers print*

After you create a header or footer and type its text, you can tell WordPerfect which pages to print it on. Click on the Pages button on the Header/Footer feature bar. WordPerfect displays the dialog box shown in Figure 9-7. Choose Odd Pages, Even Pages, or Every Page and then click on the OK button.

**Figure 9-7:**
Telling WordPerfect where to print headers and footers.

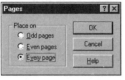

# *Don't print it here!*

You can tell WordPerfect not to print the header or footer that you just went to so much trouble to create. Why would you want to? We can think of these two good reasons:

- ✔ You don't want the header to print on the first page of your document. When you write a letter, for example, you may want all the pages except the first one to have a header that says *Joe Jones, Sept. 8, 1997, Page 2* (with the correct page number, naturally). Therefore, you want to suppress the header or footer for one page.

- ✔ Your document may have two or more sections, and you may want to use a header or footer for only the first section. You can discontinue the header or footer for the rest of the pages in the document.

To *suppress* the printing of a header or footer, you tell WordPerfect to skip printing on a particular page. To suppress a header or footer for one page, follow these steps:

1. **Move your cursor to the page on which you *don't* want to print the header or footer.**

2. **Choose Format➪Page➪Suppress.**

   WordPerfect displays the Suppress dialog box, shown in Figure 9-8.

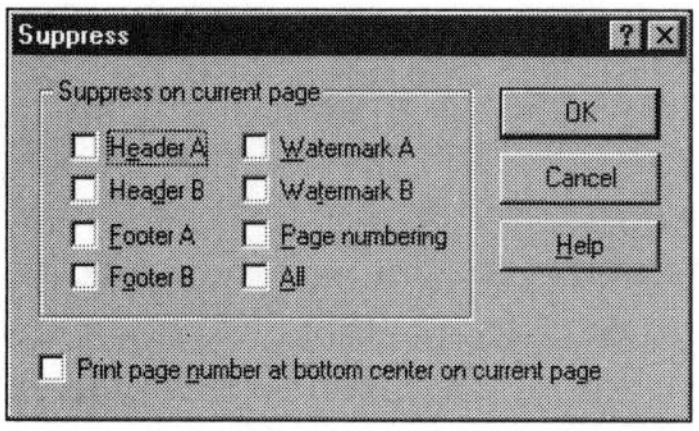

**Figure 9-8:**
Skipping
printing a
header or
footer on
one page.

3. **Choose the header or footer you don't want to print.**

   If you don't want any headers or footers or watermarks or *anything* on this page, check the All check box.

4. **Click on the OK button.**

   The headers or footers disappear from the page, only to reappear on the next page.

When you suppress the printing of a header or footer on a page, WordPerfect creates a secret code named Suppress at the top of the page.

## *Discontinuing headers and footers*

To *discontinue* printing a header or footer, you tell WordPerfect to stop printing this header or footer for good. Follow these steps:

1. **Move to the first page on which you *don't* want the header or footer to print.**

2. **Choose Format⇨Header/Footer.**

3. **Choose the header or footer that you want to discontinue.**

   If you want to discontinue all of them, you have to repeat these steps for each one. (Sigh.)

4. **Click on the <u>D</u>iscontinue button.**

   The dialog box disappears in a puff of bytes, and so does your header or footer from this page and all subsequent pages in the document.

When you discontinue a header or footer, WordPerfect inserts a secret code named End Header A (or whichever header or footer you chose). To see or delete this code, see Chapter 10.

After you discontinue a header or footer, you cannot turn it back on. To cancel discontinuing it (that is, to undo the preceding steps), you must delete the secret end code. If you just want to skip printing the header or footer for a page or three, suppress it on each page rather than discontinue it.

## *Getting rid of a header or footer*

If you change your mind about a header or footer, and you want to get rid of it for good, you can delete the contents of the header or footer. (You'll know that you've succeeded when the special guidelines go away.) You can also delete the secret code that defines the header or footer. Chapter 10 tells you how to find and exterminate codes that you no longer want.

## *Making the feature bar go away*

When you finish editing your header or footer, you may want to make the Header/Footer feature bar disappear so that its buttons don't distract you and so that you can see a little more of your document on-screen. To dismiss it from your sight, click on the <u>C</u>lose button.

If you want to see the feature bar again later so that you can do some more work on your headers or footers, just move your cursor anywhere on any page on which the header or footer prints; then choose Format⇨Header/Footer. Choose the header or footer you want to edit. Then click on the <u>E</u>dit button.

# Chapter 10

# The WordPerfect Secret Decoder Ring

· · · · · · · · · · · · · · · · · · · · · · · · · · · · · · · · · · · · · · · · · · · · · · · · · ·

## In This Chapter

▶ Knowing what secret formatting codes are

▶ Using character codes

▶ Dealing with character-formatting codes

▶ Undoing sentence and paragraph formatting

▶ Undoing page and document formatting

▶ Finding codes

▶ Replacing codes automagically

▶ Putting codes in their place

▶ Using mysterious codes

· · · · · · · · · · · · · · · · · · · · · · · · · · · · · · · · · · · · · · · · · · · · · · · · · ·

*A*fter you have worked on a WordPerfect document for a while, it may develop strange quirks and annoying tics. You may even suspect that your document is haunted and consider calling the local Byte Exorcist. WordPerfect has a simple reason for its mysterious behavior: So far, you haven't been able to see the Whole Picture.

As we allude to in preceding chapters, there is more to a WordPerfect document than meets the eye. To perform all its impressive formatting tricks, WordPerfect scatters hidden and powerful *codes,* or *formatting codes,* in your document. If these codes get discombobulated, your document can go haywire, too.

Ideally, you should never have to see these codes. After all, you don't care how WordPerfect does things — you just want them done. This is real life, however, and in real life, things go awry — horribly awry, at times. At these times, you must know how to roll up your sleeves, face those WordPerfect codes, and fix them. It's not really that bad; you won't even get your hands greasy.

# What Are Secret Formatting Codes?

WordPerfect codes are special objects that WordPerfect inserts into your document to turn special features on or off. The usual way to insert a code into your document is to choose a formatting command or click on a formatting button. WordPerfect saves the codes with your document.

WordPerfect has three types of codes: character codes, single codes, and paired codes. (We just made these terms up.) We describe each type of code in gory detail later in this chapter and tell you how to spot them and what they do. This list briefly describes the codes:

- **Character codes** represent special characters, such as Tab. Some codes represent keys on the keyboard, and others (such as Indent) don't.

- **Single codes** turn on a formatting feature. The Lft Marg and Rgt Marg codes, for example, set the left and right margins, beginning at the position of the code. The formatting that the code does remains in effect for the rest of the document or until WordPerfect runs across another occurrence of the same code.

- **Paired codes** come in pairs (you guessed that, we know). WordPerfect also calls these codes *revertible codes* — who knows where that little piece of jargon comes from? The first code in the pair turns a feature on, and the second one turns it off. Bold codes, for example, come in pairs: one to turn on boldface and the other to turn it off. The text between the two codes is in boldface.

# Seeing the Codes

This code business is all very exciting, you say. So where are all these codes that have been running around in my documents like cockroaches in the dark?

It's a good question with a simple answer: You can use the View⇨Reveal Codes command (or press Alt+F3) to see the codes in your document. Figure 10-1 shows the WordPerfect window with the Reveal Codes window at the bottom.

## Understanding the Reveal Codes window

The Reveal Codes window shows the same text that you see in the regular window. Because the Reveal Codes window usually cannot hold as much text as the regular window can, it shows the part that's right around the cursor position. The cursor appears as a red box; its location in the Reveal Codes window corresponds to its position in the regular window.

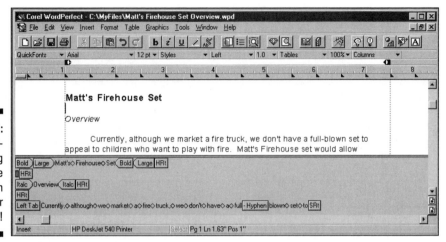

**Figure 10-1:**
Strange-
looking
codes are
lurking in
your
document!

It's a little hard to scroll up or down in the Reveal Codes window. You can press the navigation keys on your keyboard, such as PgUp and PgDn. Or you can move the cursor in the regular window and allow the Reveal Codes cursor to follow along.

Text in Reveal Codes is completely unformatted. Spaces appear as little diamonds, and codes look like little buttons. Character and single codes look like little rectangular buttons, and paired codes (such as the two Italc codes) have pointed ends, with the points of each pair pointing at each other.

You can type, edit, and perform all your normal WordPerfect activities while the Reveal Codes window is visible; some people like to leave it open all the time. (Of course, some people consider going to the dentist to be a recreational activity.)

You can control the colors that WordPerfect uses for the text and background of the Reveal Codes window, how much information is shown for each code, and some other arcane facets of the Reveal Codes window. Chapter 20 shows you how to customize this stuff. Watch out, though: This subject is getting into seriously nerdy activities, don't you think?

So what the heck do all those codes do? The rest of this chapter discusses the codes that you usually encounter and how to get rid of the ones that you no longer want.

## Click into the gap

You can reveal your codes by using the mouse and the scroll bar. You may have noticed (we didn't until we read the manual) a teeny-tiny gap between the top of the vertical scroll bar and the Power Bar, and a gap between the bottom of the vertical scroll bar and the status bar. What do you know?

It turns out that if you move your mouse pointer into one of these little gaps, the pointer turns into a double-headed arrow that points up and down. If you then click and drag with the mouse, the dividing line between the regular window and the Reveal Codes window appears, and you can drag it up and down to the position you want.

## *Adjusting the size of the windows*

A dividing line separates the regular window from the Reveal Codes window. Using the mouse, you can click on the line and drag it up or down.

## *Getting rid of the Reveal Codes window*

When you finish looking at your codes, you can make the Reveal Codes window go away. After all, seeing your codes leap around at the bottom of the screen is a little distracting. Use one of these methods to send the Reveal Codes window back into byte oblivion:

- ✔ Choose <u>V</u>iew⇨Reveal <u>C</u>odes again.
- ✔ Press Alt+F3.
- ✔ Click on the dividing line and drag it down to the status bar.
- ✔ Right-click anywhere in the Reveal Codes window and then choose <u>H</u>ide Reveal Codes from the QuickMenu that pops up.

# *Cracking the Codes*

Now that you know how to bring the secret WordPerfect formatting codes into the light of day, what can you do with them? Unlike cockroaches (which they otherwise resemble very closely), WordPerfect codes do not scurry away when they are brought to light. In the Reveal Codes window, you can examine them, modify them, and even delete them.

If you don't want to know about codes, skip the rest of this chapter. If you run into trouble with your document and it starts acting as though it has fleas, come back here to find out what's going on.

## A note to Microsoft Word users

If you have used Microsoft Word, you may wonder whether the WordPerfect View Reveal Codes command is similar to Word's View Codes command. In a couple of words: not really.

Microsoft Word doesn't use codes for formatting, so Word's View Codes feature doesn't show you anything about fonts, margins, page layout, and the like. Instead, Word's codes provide a way to include text that is under the control of the Word program — today's date, for example, which Word can update automatically. Some WordPerfect codes do this, too (see Chapter 25 to learn how to create a code that prints today's date), but most don't. As a result, Word's View Codes feature shows you many fewer codes; many documents contain no codes at all.

## *Looking at codes*

Some codes contain much more information than you might think. You may see a Header A code at the beginning of your document, for example; this code indicates that you have defined a header. To see more details about this code, place your cursor directly before the code. Suddenly, the code expands until it says Header A: Every Page, Chocolate in the Workplace. Many codes contain more information than meets the eye; place the cursor before a code to see just what it says.

## *Modifying codes*

To change a code, try double-clicking on it in the Reveal Codes window. This action tells WordPerfect that you want to do something to the code, and WordPerfect tries to guess what that something is. If you used a dialog box to insert the code in the first place, WordPerfect displays the same dialog box again. If you double-click on a Para Spacing code, for example, WordPerfect pops up the Paragraph Format dialog box, which displays the values that you specified when you created the code. (This feature is rather useful.) If you change the information in the dialog box and then choose OK, WordPerfect updates the code to match.

## *Deleting codes*

The position of each code is important, and codes that are in the wrong place can be a headache. If you see a code that seems to have wandered off into the woods, you can shoot it. Move your cursor before it and press Delete, or move the cursor just after it and press Backspace.

When the Reveal Codes window is not displayed, WordPerfect skips most codes when you press the Delete or Backspace keys so that you don't delete codes by accident. When the codes are revealed, however, WordPerfect figures that you can see what you are doing, and when you press Delete, it deletes the code to the right of the red cursor.

Save your document (press Ctrl+S) before you make any changes in codes because it's easy to make a horrendous mess with this code stuff. If you save your document before you goof up, you can just close the messy one (press Ctrl+F4) and reopen the original (press Ctrl+O).

Now that you know how to see and dispose of WordPerfect's secret codes, it's time to look at the different types of codes and what they do.

## Using the Open Style code

At the beginning of every document, you may notice a mysterious `Open Style` code. WordPerfect doesn't allow you to delete this code. This code tells WordPerfect that unless you insert codes to tell it otherwise, it should format the document by using the Initial Codes Style settings. What are the Initial Codes Style settings? We were wondering that ourselves. See Chapter 11 for more details; for now, just make a mental note that these settings include whatever you specify by using the Format➪Document➪Initial Font command (described in Chapter 7) and the Format➪Document➪Initial Codes Style, which we talk more about in Chapter 11.

---

### Hard- and soft-core codes

WordPerfect has two versions of many codes: one hard and one soft. This terminology has nothing to do with ripeness, materials used, or anything that we can't mention in a G-rated book such as this one. No, it has to do with how seriously WordPerfect takes them.

WordPerfect inserts a *soft code* itself and could just as well take it right back out. WordPerfect continually shuffles the codes around. When you edit the text in a paragraph, for example, WordPerfect changes SRt codes into spaces (and vice versa) as necessary so that the margins are correct. But WordPerfect never deletes a HRt code.

---

# Using Character Codes

The most common codes in every document are carriage-return (line-ending) codes, including the two in this list:

- ✔ **Soft return (**SRt**):** a carriage-return (line-ending) character that WordPerfect inserts automatically when you reach the right margin

- ✔ **Hard return (**HRt**):** a character that WordPerfect inserts automatically whenever you press the Enter key to signal the end of a paragraph

This list shows some other popular character codes:

- ✔ **Left tab.** The code is what you get when you press the Tab key and it moves to a left tab stop. (Chapter 8 discusses types of tab stops.) Right Tab, Center Tab, Dec Tab, . . . Left Tab, . . . Right Tab, . . . Center Tab, and . . . Dec Tab are the other types of tab-character codes that WordPerfect may insert, depending on the type of tab stop to which these tabs move.

- ✔ **Shift+Tab.** Pressing these keys inserts a Hd Back Tab code, used mainly in hanging indents (see Chapter 8).

- ✔ **Hard page break.** The HPg code represents the hard page break that you produce by pressing Ctrl+Enter (or choosing Insert⇨Page Break).

- ✔ **Soft page break.** When WordPerfect inserts a soft page break because a page has become full, it may use the SRt-SPg or HRt-SPg code (but don't worry about the difference between the two).

- ✔ **Automatic hyphenation.** Auto Hyphen EOL and TSRt: If you use WordPerfect's automatic-hyphenation feature (see Chapter 8), whenever WordPerfect decides to hyphenate a word at the right margin, it sticks in two codes. First, you see Auto Hyphen EOL (*EOL* is computerese for *end of line*); then you see TSRt (temporary soft return, maybe?).

You can delete any of these codes to get rid of the characters that they represent.

# Dealing with Character-Formatting Codes

Chapter 7 shows you how to format the characters in your documents seven ways from Sunday. When you use character formatting, WordPerfect creates a flurry of secret codes. Most of the codes are paired and mark the beginning and end of the text to be formatted. This list shows some of the character-formatting codes that you may see:

✔ **Boldface.** A pair of Bold codes enclose text in boldface.

✔ **Italics.** Likewise, Italc codes surround text in italics. (Can't those WordPerfect folks spell?)

✔ **Underlining.** Und codes appear around underlined text.

✔ **Font size.** A lone Font Size code changes the font size from its location to the end of the document or until you get to another Font Size code. A pair of Font Size codes can also enclose text that appears in a different size.

✔ **Fonts.** Likewise, one Font code (or a pair of Font codes) changes the font (typeface).

## Undoing character formatting

To undo character formatting, just blow away the formatting codes in the Reveal Codes window. For paired codes, you have to delete only one of them. When one of a pair of paired codes disappears, the other dies, too (from grief, we assume).

## Editing formatted text

After you format your text with character-formatting codes, editing can be a little tricky. If you format a heading in boldface, for example, when you add a word to the end of the heading, that word may not be boldface.

Why not? Because the new text was typed *after* the closing Bold code. Without using the Reveal Codes window, it is difficult to see whether your cursor is inside or outside a pair of formatting codes.

Some types of formatting are shown on the Toolbar and Power Bar. If your cursor is in bold text, for example, the Bold button appears to be pushed in. Likewise, the Font Face and Font Size buttons on the Power Bar tell you the font and size of the text where the cursor is. But to really be sure, you have to use the Reveal Codes window.

If you end with your formatting codes in the wrong place, you can delete them and create them again. Alternatively, you can use cut-and-paste commands (described in Chapter 6) to move the text around so that the codes are in the right places. This procedure looks weird when you do it, and it can be tricky, so be sure to save your document before trying this type of code acrobatics.

# Undoing Sentence and Paragraph Formatting

In Chapter 8, you fool around with the margins and tab stops in your document, as well as with some other things that affect entire paragraphs of text at a time. As you can imagine, WordPerfect inserts a secret code every time you use one of these formatting commands. This list shows some codes that you may encounter:

- ✔ **Tab Set:** Contains the settings for all the tabs that you can see on the Ruler Bar. Even if you change just one stop, the Tab Set code stores the positions of all of them. These codes belong at the beginnings of paragraphs — never in the middle of a line.

- ✔ **Hd Left Ind:** The indent character that you get when you press the F7 key.

- ✔ **Hd LeftRight Ind:** The double-indent character that you get when you press Ctrl+Shift+F7 key to indent from the left and right margins.

- ✔ **Hd Left Ind and Hd Back Tab:** Used for hanging indents. When you create a hanging indent, WordPerfect inserts two — count 'em, two — codes. First, it inserts a Hd Left Ind code so that all the lines of the paragraph are indented; then it inserts a Hd Back Tab code so that the first line of the paragraph is unindented. It's not elegant, but it works.

- ✔ **Hd Center on Marg:** Centers a line between the left and right margins.

- ✔ **Hd Flush Right:** Pushes your text to the right margin.

- ✔ **Hyph:** Indicates that you have turned on the hyphenation feature.

You may see the following codes by themselves or in pairs. If you see just one, it sets the formatting for the rest of the document or until you get to another of the same kind of code. If you see a pair of these codes, they set the formatting for the text enclosed by the pair. This list briefly describes the codes:

- ✔ **Lft Marg and Rgt Marg:** Set the left and right margins of your document, beginning at the position of the code; these codes belong at the beginning of a paragraph.

- ✔ **The Just family of codes:** Tells WordPerfect how to justify the text between the left and right margins.

- ✔ **Ln Spacing:** Sets the spacing between lines.

You can delete any of these codes to remove unwanted formatting from your document. When formatting codes come in pairs, you can delete just one of the pair; then they both disappear.

# *Undoing Page and Document Formatting*

Most codes that affect entire pages or the entire document appear at the beginning of a document, or at least at the top of the page. That arrangement makes them a little easier to find in the Reveal Codes window. To cancel the formatting controlled by these codes, just delete the code.

This list shows the codes created by the commands described in Chapter 9:

- ✔ **Paper Sz/Typ:** Sets the paper size and paper type for the document.

- ✔ **Top Mar and Bot Mar:** Set the top and bottom margins.

- ✔ **Cntr Cr Pg:** Centers the current page between the top and bottom margins.

- ✔ **Wid/Orph:** Tells WordPerfect how to deal with widows and orphans (at least with the types of widows and orphans described in Chapter 9).

- ✔ **Cond1 EOP (conditional end of page):** Tells WordPerfect to keep the next few lines together and not to split them with a page break.

- ✔ **Block Pro:** Encloses text that should not be split by a page break. This code should always come in pairs.

- ✔ **Pg Num Pos:** Tells WordPerfect where to print page numbers.

- ✔ **Header A, Header B, Footer A, and Footer B:** Defines what WordPerfect prints at the top and bottom of each page. When you discontinue headers, you get codes called Header A End, Header B End, Footer A End, and Footer B End. When you suppress the printing of headers or footers on a page, WordPerfect sticks a Suppress code at the top of the page.

# *Finding Codes*

The Reveal Codes window is not a model of readability; user-friendliness is not its middle name. (Heaven knows that it's a vast improvement over the Reveal Codes windows in earlier DOS-based versions of WordPerfect, which looked like a strange form of algebra crossed with some kind of circuit diagram.)

The main difficulty in using the Reveal Codes window is finding the code that you want. Because the line endings don't correspond with those in the regular window, it can be confusing to tell where you are.

Enter WordPerfect's Edit⇨Find and Replace command, which we describe in Chapter 5. In addition to using the Find and Replace Text dialog box to find text, you can use it to find codes.

You can tell WordPerfect to look for codes in two ways. Both of these methods can be useful:

- ✔ **Codes.** Tell WordPerfect the type of code to look for — a Lft Marg (left margin) code, for example. This method is useful when you want to know what the heck is going on with the margins in your document.

- ✔ **Specific codes.** Tell WordPerfect the exact code to look for (a Lft Marg code that sets the left margin to 0.5 inch, for example). This method is useful if you have decided to change all $1/2$-inch margins to $3/4$-inch margins, so you aren't interested in any other margin settings. You can also automatically replace all $1/2$-inch margin codes with $3/4$-inch margin codes; see "Finding specific codes" later in this chapter.

Because both methods call for using two dialog boxes at the same time, your screen may begin to look like a Dadaist painting. Give them a try, though, if you have the courage.

## *Finding all codes of one type*

To find all codes of one type in your document (all the Tab Set codes, for example, regardless of the tab-stop positions that they contain), follow these steps:

1. **Move your cursor to the beginning of the document or to the beginning of the part of the document that you want to search.**

2. **Choose Edit⇨Find and Replace or press F2.**

   You see the Find and Replace Text dialog box, shown in Figure 10-2. This dialog box has its own little menu bar (described in more detail in Chapter 5).

**Figure 10-2:**
Finding
codes
wherever
they may
lurk.

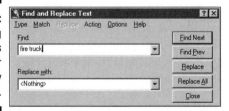

### 3. Choose <u>M</u>atch⇨<u>C</u>odes from this menu bar.

WordPerfect displays the Codes dialog box, shown in Figure 10-3. The Find <u>C</u>odes box lists all the secret codes that you can search for.

**Figure 10-3:**
Choosing
the code for
which to
search.

### 4. Choose the code that you want to search for.

Choose the Tab Set code, for example.

### 5. Click on the <u>I</u>nsert button in the Codes dialog box.

The code name appears in the F<u>i</u>nd box in the Find and Replace Text dialog box.

### 6. Click on the Close button in the Codes dialog box.

You have finished telling WordPerfect which code you want to look for.

### 7. Click on the <u>F</u>ind Next button in the Find and Replace Text dialog box.

WordPerfect looks for the code or codes that you specified and highlights the next occurrence in your document.

When you display the Find and Replace Text dialog box, its F<u>i</u>nd box contains text or codes — the last information that you searched for. The content of the F<u>i</u>nd box is selected, though, so as soon as you insert something new, that content replaces the former content. You can also just delete the information if you don't want to search for it again.

If WordPerfect cannot find your code, it displays a small dialog box that tells you so. Click on the OK button to make this dialog box go away.

For more information about using the Find and Replace Text dialog box, see Chapter 5.

To search backward through your document, click on the Find <u>P</u>rev button in the Find and Replace Text dialog box.

In the Find Codes list in the Codes dialog box, the first 16 codes have names that begin with punctuation, such as . . . Left Tab (a tab that moves to a left tab stop with dot leaders). After these codes, the codes are listed in alphabetical order.

To find a code in the Codes dialog box whose name begins with *T,* you can click on the Find Codes listing and press **T**. The list zooms down to the *T*s.

If you plan to continue looking for codes (or text) in your document, you can leave the Find and Replace Text dialog box open while you edit your document. This practice is faster than opening and closing the dialog box for each search, although it does clutter your screen. You can move the Find and Replace Text dialog box to an out-of-the-way part of your screen by clicking and dragging its title bar.

You can also leave the Codes dialog box open if you plan to look for different codes. Just skip clicking on its OK button until you finish with it.

You can search for a sequence of codes. WordPerfect uses the two codes Hd Left Ind and Hd Back Tab, for example, to create a hanging indent. To search for this combination of codes in this order, choose Hd Left Ind in the Codes dialog box, click on Insert, then choose Hd Back Tab from the list, and then click on the Insert button again. The two codes appear in the Find box. When you click on the Find Next button in the Find and Replace Text dialog box, WordPerfect looks for the sequence of codes.

You can also search for a mixture of codes and regular characters. If you want to search for a tab followed by an asterisk, for example, you can use the Codes dialog box to make [Tab (all)] appear in the Find box and then type an asterisk.

## Finding specific codes

WordPerfect has another way to look for codes that contain additional information. A *margin code* contains extra information, such as the size of the margin that you want. A Bold code, on the other hand, contains no other information. For codes that contain additional information, you can search for all codes that have a particular setting (all Font codes that set the font to 12-point Times New Roman, for example). Follow these steps:

1. **Move your cursor to the beginning of the document or to the beginning of the part of the document that you want to search.**

2. **Choose Edit➪Find and Replace or press F2.**

   WordPerfect displays the Find and Replace Text dialog box (refer to Figure 10-2).

3. **Choose** <u>T</u>ype⇨<u>S</u>pecific **Codes from the menu bar in the Find and Replace Text dialog box.**

    You see the Specific Codes dialog box.

4. **In the Specific Codes dialog box, choose the type of code for which you want to search.**

    WordPerfect lists only the types of codes that contain additional information. (To search for a code that isn't in this list, use the <u>M</u>atch⇨C<u>o</u>des command, described earlier.)

5. **Click on the OK button in the Specific Codes dialog box.**

    The Specific Codes dialog box goes away, and WordPerfect changes the Find and Replace Text dialog box to match the type of code that you are looking for. If you choose Font as the type of code for which to search, WordPerfect transforms the Find and Replace Text dialog box into a Find and Replace Font dialog box. The menu bar and buttons are unchanged, but rather than choose the text for which to search, WordPerfect allows you to enter the information that the code contains. The Find and Replace Font dialog box, for example, allows you to enter the font name and attribute.

6. **Go ahead and do it: Enter the settings of the code for which you want to search.**

    Choose Times New Roman for the font name, for example, and Italics for the style.

7. **Click on the** <u>F</u>ind **Next button to search for the next occurrence of the code.**

When you search for a specific code, you cannot search for a combination of codes and text or for a sequence of more than one code. (Bummer.)

If WordPerfect cannot find the code, it displays a dialog box that tells you so. Click on OK to make this dialog box go away. If you are sure that your code is in there somewhere, try using the <u>M</u>atch⇨C<u>o</u>des method described in the preceding section.

## *Knowing what to do after you find your code*

After you find the code that you are looking for, you can delete it by pressing the Delete key. If the code was created by means of a dialog box, you can modify it by double-clicking on the code in the Reveal Codes window.

It's a good idea to use the Reveal Codes window when you are finding codes so that you can see whether WordPerfect found the one you want.

# *Replacing Codes Automagically*

Here's a fairly common scenario: You formatted your document very tastefully with several fonts, including Tms Rmn. But you find out that the Times New Roman font looks much nicer when you print. What's the best way to change all those `Font` codes from `Tms Rmn` to `Times New Roman` without going nuts?

Like all decent word processors, WordPerfect has a find-and-replace command, which is described in Chapter 5. It swoops through your document, looking for the offending text and changing it to the proper text. The good news is that you can use it to look for and change WordPerfect's secret codes, too.

The bad news is that you cannot use the find-and-replace command to replace paired codes. You may have used pairs of `Bold` codes, for example, to make section headings in a report boldfaced and later decide to use italics instead. If you use the find-and-replace procedures described in the following section to replace all the `Bold On` codes (the ones at the beginning of the boldfaced heading) with `Ital On` codes, it just doesn't work.

Probably the best way to get around this whole business of finding and replacing codes is to use *styles,* which enable you to standardize the codes that you use for various parts of your document. Chapter 11 describes how to use styles.

Be sure to save your document before you use the find-and-replace feature. You never know what might go wrong. We guarantee enormous amounts of smugness if something goes wrong after you make a backup copy of your document.

## *Replacing specific codes with other codes*

Although WordPerfect's find-and-replace feature can be confusing and shouldn't be used with paired codes, it's great for replacing character codes and single codes. You can replace all the specific codes with other codes of the same type, such as changing all the `Font:Arial Regular` codes to `Font:Times New Roman Regular`. Follow these steps:

1. **Move to the beginning of your document by pressing Ctrl+Home.**

   If you want to replace the codes in only part of your document, move to the beginning of that part.

2. **Choose Edit⇨Find and Replace or press Ctrl+F.**

   WordPerfect displays the Find and Replace Text dialog box (refer to Figure 10-2). Like the Find Text dialog box, this dialog box has its own little menu bar (described in more detail in Chapter 5).

3. **With the cursor in the F̲ind part of the Find and Replace Text Box, choose T̲ype⇨S̲pecific Codes.**

   The Specific Codes dialog box appears.

4. **Choose the type of code that you want to replace.**

   Choose Font, for example.

5. **Click on the OK button to dismiss the dialog box.**

   WordPerfect transforms the Find and Replace Text dialog box into a dialog box that's more appropriate for the type of code that you are replacing (the Find and Replace Font dialog box, for example).

   Both the F̲ind and Replace W̲ith text boxes are transformed into boxes that are appropriate for the type of code with which you are working. If you are replacing Font codes, for example, WordPerfect displays settings for fonts and font styles.

6. **Choose the settings for the existing codes that you want to get rid of and for the new codes with which you want to replace them.**

   Choose Arial for the F̲ind Font setting, for example, and Times New Roman for the Replace W̲ith setting.

7. **To find the first instance of the code you're looking for, click on F̲ind Next.**

   Just tell WordPerfect to start looking; you won't have to tell it again.

8. **To replace the codes one by one, so that you can eyeball each occurrence before making the replacement, click on the R̲eplace button in the dialog box.**

   When you click on R̲eplace, WordPerfect replaces the code in the F̲ind box with the code in the Replace W̲ith box. To skip it, click on F̲ind Next. To replace this code and all the rest of the codes of this type in your document, go wild and click on Replace A̲ll.

9. **When you finish, click on C̲lose to make the Find and Replace dialog box go away.**

If you cannot see your codes, choose V̲iew⇨Reveal C̲odes in the WordPerfect window to open the Reveal Codes window.

## *Replacing codes with other codes*

So far, you have replaced WordPerfect codes with codes that are of the same type but that contain other settings. You can also replace one type of code with another — Hd Left Ind codes (indents) with Hd Left Tab codes (regular ol' tabs), for example. The following steps show you how:

1. **Move to the beginning of your document by pressing Ctrl+Home.**

   To replace the codes in only part of your document, move to the beginning of that part.

2. **Choose Edit⇨Find and Replace or press F2.**

   WordPerfect displays the Find and Replace Text dialog box (refer to Figure 10-2).

3. **With your cursor in the Find part of the dialog box, choose Match⇨Codes from the dialog box's menu.**

   You see the Codes dialog box (refer to Figure 10-3).

4. **Choose the type of code that you want to replace.**

   Choose Hd Left Ind, for example.

5. **Click on Insert to stick the codes into the Find box in the Find and Replace Text dialog box.**

6. **In the Find and Replace Text dialog box, move your cursor to the Replace With text box.**

7. **In the Codes dialog box, choose the code that you want to replace the old codes with.**

   Choose Hd Left Tab, for example.

8. **Click on Insert again to stick the codes into the Replace With box of the Find and Replace Text dialog box.**

   Now you have told WordPerfect what to look for and what to replace it with.

9. **Click on the Close button in the Codes dialog box.**

   You're finished inserting codes, and you probably want some of your screen back.

10. **Click on the Replace button in the Find and Replace Text dialog box to replace codes one at a time.**

    Or click on Replace All to go for the gold.

11. **Click on the Close button when you finish replacing codes.**

    You cannot use this method to insert codes that require additional information. You cannot replace all your Bold codes with Font codes, for example, because Font codes require additional information (the name and style of the font). It's just a WordPerfect limitation. Not that we can blame WordPerfect — this find-and-replace business is complicated enough as it is.

Using this method, you can replace combinations of codes and text with other combinations of code and text.

## Deleting all the codes

You can use the Find and Replace Text dialog box to get rid of all codes of one type in your document (all Font codes, for example). Use the preceding steps to tell WordPerfect which codes you want to find, but don't enter anything in the Replace With box. This action tells WordPerfect to replace these codes with nothing.

# Mysterious Codes

"What the heck is the !@#$% code? And who the #$%^&* put it in my document?" This cry has been heard throughout the land since WordPerfect first shipped back in the early '80s.

If you encounter a code that you have never seen and that isn't described in this chapter, stay calm; you can always delete it, after all. To find out what it is, place the cursor on top of it. A little yellow box pops up and gives you a hint. If the hint isn't enough, double-click on the code. In the dialog box that's displayed, you can click on the Help button in the dialog box or press the F1 key to get help in using this feature.

# Chapter 11
# Documents with Style

● ● ● ● ● ● ● ● ● ● ● ● ● ● ● ● ● ● ● ● ● ● ● ● ● ● ● ● ● ● ● ● ● ● ● ●

## In This Chapter

▶ How to create and apply a style

▶ How to use headings and other built-in styles

▶ How to use more built-in styles

▶ How to change styles with the Styles Editor

▶ How to turn styles off and chain styles

▶ How to reuse styles and get rid of them

● ● ● ● ● ● ● ● ● ● ● ● ● ● ● ● ● ● ● ● ● ● ● ● ● ● ● ● ● ● ● ● ● ● ● ●

*W*hen Og, the popular and celebrated mammoth hunter, trimmed his body with the colorful viscera of a woolly mammoth, the Og style caught the popular imagination. Anyone could simply walk into the local haberdashery, request an Og, and come out with all the necessary fine points taken care of. No need to specify all the details, such as the woven-tripe necklace, the bone in the hair, the brain-tanned bladder sporran — the word *Og* said it all. In the following year, when Og decided that the necklace should be sinew and not tripe, folks could still order an Og and be in style.

A more contemporary application of these named styles is text formatting. Text-formatting styles take advantage of the fact that most text formatting is repetitive. In this book, for example, all the level-1 headings are the same format, as are all the level-2 headings, the normal text, the captions, and so on. Rather than continually respecify for each block of text all the details of typeface, point size, indentation, justification, and the rest, why not call one collection of formats Heading 1, another Heading 2, and so on? That way, the only formatting that a block of text needs is a style name. Applying a named style is a heck of a lot simpler than accurately repeating the same half-dozen formatting commands over and over.

Another advantage is that after text is formatted by styles, any change in style definitions immediately takes effect throughout the document. An Og remains an Og; it just looks different.

# What Is a Style?

A WordPerfect *style* is a combination of various types of formatting, such as fonts and indentation — the kind of stuff that you typically do with the Format commands — assigned to a name. Then you can apply the style by name to text in your document that you want formatted that way.

Usually, you use a style for some simple combination of paragraph layout and font or font style, such as centered and bold. You can also use line, page, and document formatting, however. You can use anything, in fact, that changes the appearance of your document, from margins to page breaks.

After you use a style, any change in the definition of the style ripples through your document, changing appearances wherever you applied that style. This capability is way cool.

When you format text by using styles, however, a bit of a conflict occurs in places where you formatted the text directly by using the Format command or the function keys. WordPerfect resolves this conflict in favor of the directly formatted text. If you have indented a paragraph by using Format⇨Paragraph or F7, for example, and then you apply a paragraph style that is not indented, the indentation remains. Directly applied formatting can be tricky to remove, too, and often requires you to delete the secret codes discussed in Chapter 10. So if you use styles, be somewhat diligent about them. As much as possible, do not revert to your old, unprincipled ways of formatting your text directly by using the Format command.

# Creating and Applying a Style

The style stuff lurks at the bottom of the Format menu but is easier to access from the Select Styles button on the Power Bar. If you think that you already understand styles, just launch into the Format⇨Styles command (or press Alt+F8, or double-click on the Select styles button). Good luck.

The rest of us can choose an easier way: Do *not* launch into the Format⇨Styles command. Begin by formatting a bunch of text the way you want it, as an example. Then record that formatting as a style. This process is called *QuickStyle*. This section explains how to do it.

## Subtleties in style

You don't have to understand the subtle differences among styles right now (we explain them as we go), but it helps. WordPerfect has three fundamental types of styles:

Character     Affects selected text

Paragraph     Affects an entire paragraph

Document     Affects everything from the point where the style is applied

Do not confuse the *type of style* with the *type of formatting* that it can do. A *paragraph style* can contain fonts or font styles for all the text within the paragraph. A *document style* can contain fonts and paragraph-layout settings for all the paragraphs that follow it.

But wait! We said we were going to get in to the subtleties of style here, so here goes. There are two—count'em—two *kinds* of paragraph styles: Paragraph (paired) and Paragraph (paired-auto). And what, you ask, is the difference? Paragraph (paired) works as you might expect from the description we just gave: it formats the entire paragraph. Change the style and all the text formatted with that style changes.

Paragraph (paired-auto) styles are magic. *You don't have to change the style to change all the text formatted with the style.* It works like this: You change the format of some text that is formatted with the style and, presto!, *all the text in your document formatted with that style changes!* No need to fuss with editing the style; it just happens.

So which one do you use? We wouldn't presume to tell you. But the WordPerfect QuickStyle creates Paragraph (auto) styles, and we think they're awesomely cool.

## *QuickStyling a character style*

We begin this discussion with how to create a style for formatting selected characters. Suppose that you want foreign words in your document to be in bold and italic, so you want to create a style called foreign to format them.

These steps guide you through this process:

1. **Format some text in bold and italic as an example for WordPerfect.**

   Preferably, format some text to which you want to apply the style anyway. To format in bold and italic, select the text and then press Ctrl+B and Ctrl+I.

2. **Click on the Select Style button on the Power Bar and choose the QuickStyle button.**

   The QuickStyle dialog box appears, as shown in Figure 11-1.

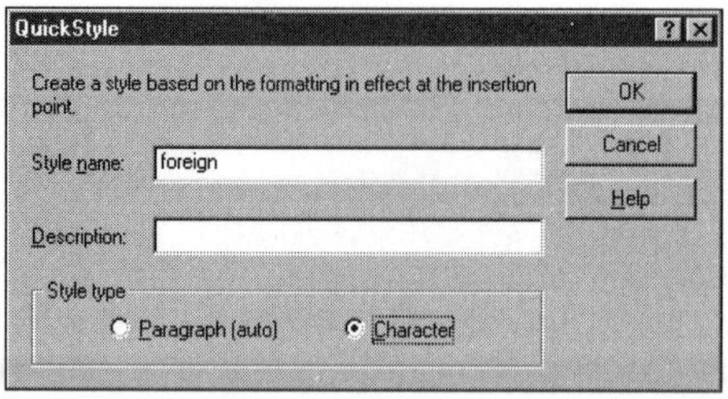

**Figure 11-1:**
The
QuickStyle
dialog box.

**QuickStyle**

Create a style based on the formatting in effect at the insertion point.

Style name: [foreign]

Description: [ ]

Style type
○ Paragraph (auto)    ● Character

OK
Cancel
Help

Another way to display the QuickStyle dialog box is to choose Format⇨Style (or press Alt+F8) and then click on the QuickStyle button.

3. **Make up a name for your style (such as foreign) and type it in the Style Name box, where your cursor awaits you.**

   Don't exceed 20 characters; WordPerfect doesn't allow more than that limit.

4. **If you want, type something in the Description box that describes the style's purpose.**

   You could type something such as **character formatting for foreign text.**

5. **In the Style Type section at the bottom of the dialog box, click on Character.**

   This step tells WordPerfect to create a character style. (Refer to the sidebar titled "Subtleties in style" for the three types of styles.)

6. **Click on the OK button.**

   The QuickStyle dialog box goes away. WordPerfect creates the style, and the Style List dialog box displays it.

   If you displayed the QuickStyle dialog box by using the QuickStyle button on the Style List dialog box, you'll see that dialog box again when you close the QuickStyle dialog box. Click on Apply.

That's it — you did it. You have created a style called foreign, which you now can apply by name to any selected text in your document.

## Applying a character style

To apply your character style, select some text and click on the Select Styles button on the Power Bar. This time, the style list contains your very own style. Click on it to apply it to your text.

# *QuickCreating a paragraph style*

Certain types of formatting do not belong in a character-formatting style. Paragraphy-type things such as indentation, for example, belong in a paragraph-formatting style. These things include stuff that you normally do with the Format⇨Paragraph command.

But wait — the nice thing about paragraph styles is that they can include both paragraph-type things and character-type formatting, such as boldface and font styles. (It doesn't work the other way; character styles cannot include paragraph stuff.) Unfortunately, WordPerfect's QuickStyle feature doesn't collect the paragraph information, such as indenting. But you can create a paragraph style with QuickStyle and edit it later.

To create a paragraph style, you perform the same steps as you do to create a character style, but when you get to the QuickStyle dialog box, make sure that the Style type is Paragraph (auto).

# *Applying a paragraph style*

Applying paragraph styles is much like applying character styles. Put your cursor in the paragraph that you want to style (because paragraph styles can apply only to whole paragraphs, you don't have to select text when you want to format just one paragraph). If you want to format multiple paragraphs, select them. Then click on the Select styles button on the Power Bar. When the style list appears, double-click on the style name to apply it to the selected paragraph(s).

If you applied a paragraph style and want to change it, there's a quick alternative to choosing Format⇨Styles from the menu bar. With your cursor in the styled paragraph, double-click on the second box from the left on the status bar at the bottom of the WordPerfect window. That's the "status" box, which displays the name of the current paragraph style and the Style List dialog box.

# *Creating a document style*

Sometimes, you want to create a style that applies beginning at a certain point and perhaps everything past it. This type of style is called a *document style,* and it is a little weird. Unlike character and paragraph styles, a document style has no predetermined point at which it ends. As a result, it generally continues until another one begins.

Document styles can include not only the formatting that you normally do with the Format⇨Document command, but also anything else that you do from the Format menu, including Font, Line, Paragraph, and Column commands. For that matter, styles can do darn near anything from the Insert, Tools, Graphics, and Table menus, including inserting page breaks, changing headers and footers, inserting dates, inserting graphics, or making quacking noises (if you go for that sort of thing and have laid out the bucks for sound).

Using a document style is a good way to set up the overall layout of a document, including the margins, the paragraph formatting for most paragraphs, and the font for most text.

You cannot create a document style by using the QuickStyle method, which we described earlier in this chapter. You must use the Create method. (You can use the same Create method for character and paragraph formatting, but it's more work, so why bother?)

To create a document style, follow these steps:

1. **Choose Format⇨Styles, double-click on the Styles button on the Power Bar, or press Alt+F8.**

   The Style List dialog box appears, as shown in Figure 11-2.

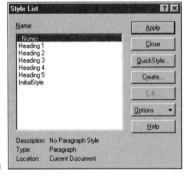

**Figure 11-2:**
The Style
List dialog
box.

2. **Click on Create.**

   Up pops the Styles Editor dialog box, shown in Figure 11-3.

3. **Click on Style name and type a descriptive name of no more than 20 characters.**

   You can also click and type a Description, if you want. (You do this step for character and paragraph styles in the preceding example, except that then you use the QuickStyle dialog box.)

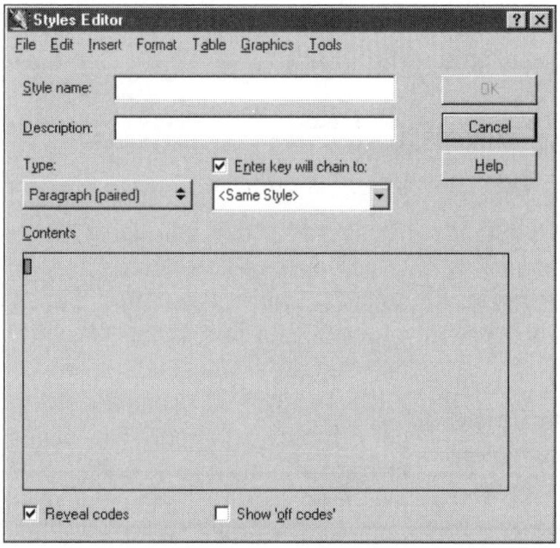

**Figure 11-3:**
The Styles
Editor dialog
box.

4. **Below the word *Type* is a button; click on it and then choose Document (Open) from the menu that pops up.**

   Certain things are grayed out in the dialog box so that you cannot use them. Don't worry; you don't want them.

5. **Now comes the fun part: Put in any formatting that you want by using the Styles Editor menu bar.**

   This bar duplicates commands from the main WordPerfect menu bar. Choose Format⇨Paragraph⇨Indent, for example, and then choose Format⇨Font and choose Bold in the Font dialog box. These layout features become part of your new document style. Codes are inserted into the Contents window as you give the commands that create them. (You may want to ignore what's going on in the Contents window of the dialog box unless you have read Chapter 10.)

6. **Click on OK when you finish.**

   You go back to the Style List dialog box.

7. **Click on Close.**

   Don't click on Apply unless your cursor is in the exact position at which you want this style to begin.

## Revealing your secret style codes

If you read Chapter 10 and understand the secret codes in WordPerfect, you should understand the bottom window of the Styles Editor box. It shows which codes are being encapsulated into the style, just as a Reveal Codes window does.

Moreover, you should understand why character and paragraph styles are denoted as (Closed) and document styles as (Open). *Closed* is another word for *paired* style codes; *open* means *single* style codes.

When WordPerfect applies a closed style (character or paragraph style) to your document, it uses pairs of codes to bracket the affected text. These codes use only the style name, which gives you complete freedom to edit the style definition without putting a bunch of screwy codes in your text. When WordPerfect applies an open style (document style), it uses single codes — again, using only the style name. Magically, these (unpaired) style codes can apply character formats such as bold text — and you remember (if you read Chapter 10) that bold text requires a paired code. Works anyway — go figure.

## *Applying a document style*

To apply a document style, first position your cursor where you want the style to begin (probably before a paragraph). If your style includes any insertions, such as page breaks, they also go here.

# *Built-In Styles*

Before you go on to changing styles, we should introduce the built-in styles, called Heading 1 through Heading 5 and InitialStyle. Unsurprisingly, Headings are styles for your headings and subheadings. Their definitions are preset, for convenience, because headings are what most people use styles for most of the time. To see them, click on the Select Styles button on the Power Bar.

## *Heading styles*

Heading styles (Heading 1 through Heading 5) do nice things, such as make your headings all bold or italic and enter them in the table of contents (if you ask WordPerfect to create a table of contents). They are nicely specified styles, fortunately, because changing them often requires you to understand (ugh!) secret codes.

Apply Heading styles as you would apply any other paragraph style: With your cursor in the paragraph to be formatted, click on the Select Style button on the Power Bar and choose the heading style that you want. After you apply these styles, you may want to use them to create a table of contents. If you do, take a look at Chapter 18; hidden in the section on "Reports and Other Big Documents" is a subsection on creating a table of contents!

## The initial style

The other built-in style, InitialStyle, specifies the way that your text looks when you create a new document, before you do anything to change its appearance. You don't have to apply the InitialStyle; it happens automatically at the beginning of your document. Unless you apply other styles, all the text in your document is formatted according to InitialStyle.

InitialStyle is, in fact, the central place where your choices are recorded when you use either the Format⇨Document⇨Initial Font command (described in Chapters 7 and 18) or the Format⇨Document⇨Initial Codes Style command (mentioned in Chapter 10).

If you want to add or change something in InitialStyle or a Heading style, check out the Styles Editor, described in "Changing Styles with the Styles Editor" later in this chapter.

If you want to remove something, you have to deal with secret codes (refer to Chapter 10). If you're not up to reading Chapter 10 in its entirety, you can also try a little guesswork while you are using the Styles Editor.

## More built-in styles

WordPerfect comes with a grab bag of predefined styles that you can use. They are not normally in the Style List, but you can bring them in by following these steps:

1. **Choose Format⇨Styles from the menu bar.**

2. **Click on the Options button, and choose Setup from the list that drops down.**

   The Style Setup dialog box appears.

3. **Click on the System Styles check box.**

**4. Click on OK.**

You can then choose among a few dozen useful styles in the Name box. As you do with any style, you double-click on the style name to apply it to the currently selected text (for character styles) or to the place where the cursor is (for paragraph or document styles).

# Changing Styles with the Styles Editor

Modifying styles requires that you learn something about secret codes. Fortunately, the task is worthwhile. Nothing is so satisfying as having every paragraph in your document hooked up to a style, so that you can change the formatting of whole swathes of documents at will through the Styles Editor. (We *can* think of one or two things that are more satisfying, but you can't do them with your computer.)

The process of editing styles is a little more complicated that creating them (if you use QuickStyle) or applying them. It takes you into the territory of menu commands and — touch wood — the dreaded codes. But it's worth it.

As you edit styles, you come across two dialog boxes: Style List and Styles Editor. Tables 11-1 and 11-2 give you details on the options in each dialog box.

| Table 11-1 | Style List Options |
|---|---|
| **Option** | **What It Does** |
| Name | Displays the name of every style defined in the current document |
| Apply | Applies the highlighted style to (a) the highlighted text if the style is a character style, (b) the highlighted paragraphs or the paragraph that the cursor is in if the style is a paragraph style, or (c) the rest of the document if the style is a document style |
| Close | Closes the dialog box |
| QuickStyle | Displays the QuickStyle dialog box and creates a style with the same format as the text at the cursor location |
| Create | Displays a blank Styles Editor dialog box to allow you to create a new style |
| Edit. . . | Displays the Styles Editor dialog box for the style highlighted in the Style List's Name box |
| Options | Provides further options for styles: Setup, Copy, Delete, Reset, Retrieve, and Save As |
| Help | Displays a WordPerfect help screen for styles |

| Table 11-2 | Styles Editor Options |
|---|---|
| *Option* | *What It Does* |
| Styles Editor Menu bar | These are formatting options for the style. (They allow you to insert codes to format your text. The most-often-used formatting commands are in the Format menu. To apply character formatting from this dialog box, for example, choose Format➪Font from its menu bar to display the Font dialog box. |
| Type: | Lets you control what type of style this is. See the sidebar "Subtleties in style" near the beginning of this chapter for the details. |
| Enter Key Will Chain To | Tells WordPerfect what the style of the next paragraph should be. |
| Contents | Shows you all the secret codes WordPerfect uses to make the style happen. (See Chapter 10 if you haven't already). If the style has any regular text in it (such as "This begins our styled text:"), this text appears here as well. We don't know anyone who uses styles to include text like this, but if you pressed us, we could probably come up with an example. |
| Reveal Codes | When selected, displays formatting codes in the Contents box. You can turn this option off, but then the Contents box would only show you the regular text that's part of the style, and we just told you how useful we think that is. |
| Show 'Off Codes' | Allows you to insert codes that will take effect when the style ends.  Do yourself a favor: just don't. |

You can get to these dialog boxes in several ways. The most straightforward method is to use Alt+F8 or Format➪Styles to display the Style List dialog box and then go from there, but here are a couple of other ways:

- ✔ To display the Style List dialog box, double-click on the box on the status line that tells you the name of the style while the cursor is in styled text. (When the cursor is in unstyled text, this box tells you whether you are in Insert or Typeover mode, and double-clicking it will do nothing about styles.)
- ✔ Double-click on the Styles button on the Power Bar.
- ✔ To display the Style Editor dialog box for a particular style, display codes (Alt + F3) and then double-click on a style code.

The following steps show you how to modify a style:

**1. Choose Format➪Styles or press Alt+F8.**

WordPerfect displays the Styles List dialog box.

**2. Click on the style that you want to change (Heading 1, for example).**

**3. Click on the Edit button.**

The Styles Editor dialog box appears, such as the one shown in Figure 11-3 earlier in this chapter.

Now things get dicey. To add something, such as a specific font style, use the Styles Editor dialog box's menu bar. (This procedure is the same as the one described in "Creating and Applying a Style" earlier in this chapter.) Add italic style, for example, by choosing Format➪Font from the Styles Editor menu bar and then clicking on Italic in the Font dialog box.

To change something, such as changing boldface to underline, you probably have to use the secret codes. Look in the Contents window at the bottom of the Styles Editor dialog box for a box that contains a suggestive word, such as Bold. Try double-clicking on it. Something should happen, such as the appearance of a Font dialog box. When it does, you can make your change. Close this dialog box, whatever it is, and you change the secret code.

To delete something in the Contents window, such as the Very Large font style, click it and then drag it out of the Contents window and into the Real World (anywhere outside the Contents window), where scummy secret codes cannot survive.

If you make a mistake while you are modifying styles in the Styles Editor dialog box, the Undo command in the Styles Editor menu bar can help you. Just choose Edit➪Undo. If you accidentally delete a code, you can also use the Edit➪Undelete command.

# *Turning Styles Off and Chaining Styles*

Suppose that you applied a style, and you are merrily typing along, updating your résumé to include the phrase *Mastery of WordPerfect styles*. You finish a delightfully styled paragraph, press Enter, and bingo! — you start another similarly styled paragraph. This automatic spawning of a similarly styled paragraph is lovely, but what if you don't *want* another similarly styled paragraph?

Or suppose that you're typing a letter to Aunt May in a character style that uses the lovely ShelleyVolante font, and you want to turn it off to write a more legible note to nearsighted Uncle George. Do one of these two things:

- ✔ To turn off a paragraph style in the paragraph in which your cursor is located, click on the Select styles button on the Power Bar and then click on <None> in the list.

- ✔ If you have been typing along in a character style and now want to turn it off for the following text, press the right-arrow key on your keyboard. This step moves your cursor past the secret style-end code. When you type again, the style is no longer in effect.

Another solution is to end or change styles automatically when you create a new paragraph. How do you do this? The Highly Inquisitive Reader will have noticed in the Styles Editor a dialog-box thingy labeled E̲nter key will chain to. This particular thingy is what you're looking for. (To display the Styles Editor, press Alt+F8 and then click on the E̲dit button in the Style List dialog box.)

This feature really asks, "What do you want to happen when you're typing along in this style and you spawn a new paragraph by pressing Enter? Do you want the new text to continue in this style, or what?"

When you click the down-arrow button to the right of the associated box, you see that you have three possible answers to this nitpicking question:

- ✔ **<None>** means "turn off the styles altogether."

- ✔ **<Same Style>** means "begin a new paragraph in this same style."

- ✔ **Any of your own homegrown styles in the Style List** (not the system stuff, such as Heading 1) means "begin a new paragraph with this style." These *chaining styles* are useful when styles normally follow each other, such as introductory text after a heading.

This feature works only for paragraph or character styles. For document styles, this dialog-box thingy gets all gray and fuzzy, like a bad video copy of the closing scene of *Casablanca*. It means, "I'm off duty, Mac."

For character styles, you have one more option. Click on the box next to the E̲nter key will chain to thingy to remove the *X*. This way, pressing the Enter key means "keep going in this same style." The only way that this method differs from choosing <Same Style> is that <Same Style> turns off the style and then turns it on again. The difference is so subtle that you will never care unless you often deal with secret codes.

# Reusing Styles

Reusing work that you have already finished is always a smart idea, and styles help you reuse your formatting efforts.

You can reuse styles in either of two ways:

- Retrieve them from an existing document into a new document
- Save them in another file

Retrieving styles from another document is the lazy way to do it and, therefore, our favorite. Follow these steps:

1. **Choose Format⇨Styles.**

   You see the Style List dialog box.

2. **Click on the Options button.**

   Now you see the Options drop-down menu.

3. **Choose Retrieve.**

   The Retrieve Styles From dialog box appears.

4. **Type the name of the document from which you want to retrieve styles.**

   Or you can click on the file-folder icon to select the file from a list. (See Chapter 14 to learn how this method works.)

5. **If you want just the user styles or the system styles, click on the appropriate box in the Retrieve Styles From dialog box.**

   Normally, you get both. WordPerfect asks whether you want to override the current styles.

6. **Click on the OK button.**

   In all likelihood, you want to override the current styles.

7. **Click on Yes.**

To be Really Systematic and Organized, however, you should save your styles to a central location. This procedure allows you to control styles from a single point.

In one of the two approaches, you copy your styles to a document *template* that automatically brings in styles when you create a new document. (Chapter 16 describes templates and all the wonderful things that you can do with them.) The other method, in which you save your styles to a separate file, requires you to retrieve the styles from that file manually. This method has the advantage, however, of allowing you to save all your styles — styles for memos, for example — under a name such as memos.sty.

If most of what you create will use the same styles, copy your styles to the standard template, on which all documents are based. (This approach is also great for pack rats, who don't mind if every style that they ever create is stored in one place.)

To copy styles to the standard template, follow these steps:

1. **Choose Format⇨Styles.**

   You see the Style List dialog box.

2. **Click on a style that you want to copy.**

3. **Click on the Options button in the Style List dialog box.**

   The little Options menu pops up (or down).

4. **Click on Copy in the Options menu.**

   The Styles Copy dialog box appears.

5. **Click on Template in the Copy To area.**

6. **Repeat Steps 1–5 for each style that you want to copy.**

From now on, whenever you create a new document, these styles will be available.

In the other method — saving your styles to a file — click on Options, click on Save As, and then type a directory and filename. (Or you can click the file icon to use a dialog box for this procedure.) Give the file an extension that will remind you that styles are in the file, such as .sty.

To use these styles, just open your new document, choose Format⇨Styles, click on the Options button, and then choose Retrieve.

# Getting Rid of Styles

After a while, particularly if you're of the pack-rat persuasion and keep all your styles in the same place, you will want to delete a few of them. You cannot delete the built-in styles, however — only your own. These steps show you how:

1. **Choose Format⇨Styles.**

2. **Click on a style that you want to delete.**

3. **Click on the Options button in the Style List dialog box.**

   If the Delete option is grayed out, you're trying to delete a built-in style. Stop that.

**4. Click Delete in the menu that drops down.**

A dialog box appears, asking, in effect, whether you want to delete the style definition and take out all the codes for that style in your document (the Include Codes option), or whether you want to remove the definition and leave the formatting in place (the Leave Codes option).

**5. Choose either Include Codes or Leave Codes.**

**6. Click on OK and you're finished.**

# Part III
# Things You Can Do with Documents

"PUT DOWN 'CAUSES FOOT DAMAGE'."

## In this part . . .

1t is a little-known fact that when humans lived in the trees, they didn't have a word for *forest*. (Okay, so they didn't have a word for anything else either. Be that way.) The reason was that they couldn't (everyone say it together now) "see the forest for the trees." They couldn't, that is, until they had mastered the trees, climbed the mountains, and attained the perspective that enabled them to say, "Whoa — look at them forests!"

Likewise, all who master the world of mere words and ascend the heights of word processing eventually find themselves saying, "Whoa — look at them *documents*." (Grammar hasn't progressed much over the millenia.) Accordingly, this part of the book explores the printing, dressing up, moving around, and overall whipping into shape of your documents. Head 'em up and move 'em out!

We'll even tell you how to move 'em out on the World Wide Web! Welcome to electronic publishing.

# Chapter 12

# On Paper at Last: Printing Stuff

*E*veryone has heard about the Paperless Office of the Future. Remember when computers were new and everyone claimed that after we all started using computers, we could stop using paper? Lo and behold, look around your office. Do you see paper? There's twice as much paper as ever before — *that's* how much paper you see.

In real life, you usually will want to print your documents, and this chapter talks about how to do it. For details about creating and printing some popular documents, including mailing labels and envelopes, see Chapter 18.

## Ready to Print?

You have written and formatted your document, and it looks *maahvelous*. Now you're ready to see how it looks on paper. But before you can do so, you had better be sure that your printer is ready to help.

Make sure that the printer is plugged into both the wall and your computer. The connection to the wall provides power, and the cable to your computer provides a way for the information in your document to get from the computer into your printer.

Be sure that your printer has the appropriate ribbon, ink cartridge, or toner cartridge, depending on your printer — unless you are interested in printing your document in white on white. (See Chapter 22 to learn how to determine which type of printer you have.)

You need paper, as you may have guessed. Your printer may use individual sheets of typing paper or continuous-feed perforated paper. Whatever your printer likes to eat, make sure that your printer has paper.

You should also make sure that your printer is paying attention to what your computer has to say. Most printers can be either *on-line* or *off-line* (either listening to the computer or not listening, respectively). These printers have an on-line light that tells you whether the printer is on-line and an on-line button that you can press to switch between on-line and off-line. If your printer is off-line, it ignores any information that your computer sends to it; it's like being turned off.

If your printer uses sheets of paper, you may want to print drafts of documents on the other side of used paper. We keep a stack of paper with stuff on just one side and use it for everything except the final drafts of our documents.

Before WordPerfect 7 can print anything, Windows 95 must know all about your printer. When you (or someone) installed Windows 95 on your computer, you should have told Windows which printer (or printers) you have. Windows 95 shares this information with WordPerfect. If you're not sure whether Windows 95 knows about your printer, see Chapter 22, or read the book *Windows 95 For Dummies* (Andy Rathbone, IDG Books Worldwide, Inc.) or any of the other great Windows 95 books published by IDG Books. You use the Printers icon in the Control Panel program that comes with Windows 95 (click on the Start button; then choose Settings⇨Printers).

Chapter 22 contains more information about printing, including what to do if printing goes wrong, but start here with the basics.

---

## Where's the printer?

If your computer is connected to a network and you use a network printer, someone else is probably in charge of making sure that the printer is connected to all the right cables. You should still check to make sure that the printer has paper, however, because the guy in the next cubicle may have the annoying habit of printing 200-page reports without refilling the paper tray.

You may also want to talk to your network administrator to find out which type of printer you can use and how to tell Windows 95 about these printers, if it doesn't already know. Chapter 22 also talks about some of these things.

---

# *Printing the Entire Document*

WordPerfect gives you a good idea of what your document will look like when it's printed. If you use page view ( by choosing View⇨Page or by pressing Alt+F5), you can even see where your headers and footers appear, as well as the top and bottom margins of the pages. (Chapter 9 describes page view and the other views that WordPerfect provides.) But you cannot really get the total effect until you see your document on paper.

These steps show you how to print your document:

1. **Make sure that your printer is turned on, on-line, and ready to print.**

   Make sure that the right kind of paper is loaded — recycled paper for drafts and nice, new, blank paper for final versions, letterhead, or whatever. We always keep a stack of paper near our printer with embarrassing first drafts printed on one side, ready for less embarrassing second drafts to be printed on the other side.

2. **Save your document, just in case something dire happens while you are printing it.**

   Practice safe printing!

3. **Click on the Print button on the Toolbar.**

   This button looks like a sideways view of a pasta maker. Alternatively, you can choose File⇨Print or press F5. WordPerfect displays the large and imposing Print dialog box, shown in Figure 12-1.

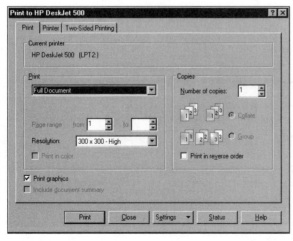

**Figure 12-1:**
Telling WordPerfect the who, what, where, when, and why of printing your document.

4. **Ignore all those interesting-looking settings, and just click on the Print button.**

WordPerfect informs you that it is preparing the document for printing. Other dialog boxes may flit across the screen as WordPerfect formats the document for printing. At long last, the printer starts to hum and begins to print. You may also notice a small printer icon on the Taskbar in the same box as the time; all this depends on how you have the Windows 95 Taskbar set up.

As soon as your cursor stops looking like The Sands of Time (a tiny hourglass) and returns to its normal shape, you can continue to use WordPerfect while your printer prints. You can open another document, edit the current document, or do whatever you want. It's probably not a good idea to either close your document or exit WordPerfect, however, because the chances of printing a document correctly on the first try are zero. We would bet dollars to doughnuts that you will see a large typo that was staring you in the face from the screen for the past half-hour but that became truly visible only on paper.

If the printer doesn't print anything, don't just print it again. Your document may still be wending its way through the bowels of Windows 95 on its way to the printer. It may have gotten stuck on its way (intestinal distress happens even to computers). Make sure that the printer is on and on-line. If nothing happens after a minute or two, see "Canceling a Print Job" near the end of this chapter.

If you are looking at the Print dialog box and decide not to print the document after all, just press the Esc key or click on the Close button in the dialog box (clicking on the X in the top-right corner of the dialog box works, too). No harm done, and no paper wasted.

Before printing the final draft of a document, you may want to consider checking its spelling. See Chapter 5 for complete instructions.

---

## Instant printing

If you press Ctrl+Shift+P, WordPerfect prints your entire document without showing you the Print dialog box. Slam! Bang! — the document goes directly to the printer. Be sure that you really want to print the whole thing before you press Ctrl+Shift+P. If you press Ctrl+Shift+P by mistake (how could you press that many keys by mistake?, you may ask), see "Canceling a Print Job" near the end of this chapter.

# Printing Part of a Document

When a document gets long (like some chapters in this book), you may not want to print the whole thing. What if you just printed a 30-page report, for example, and then find and correct a typo on page 17? Not to worry — you can print a single page, or any selection of text, for that matter.

## Printing selected text

To print a selection of text, follow these steps:

1. **Get the printer ready (turn it on, and so on).**

2. **Select the text that you want to print.**

   Refer to Chapter 6 to find out how to select text.

3. **Click on the Print button on the Toolbar.**

   Alternatively, press F5 or choose File⇨Print from the WordPerfect menu bar.

   The Print dialog box appears (refer to Figure 12-1).

   Notice that the first option in the <u>P</u>rint section of the dialog box says Selected Text. When you don't have text selected, the option says Full Document (unless you change it, of course).

4. **Click on the Print button.**

   WordPerfect prints the selected text.

## Printing a specific page

Follow these steps to print one page:

1. **Make sure that your printer is ready to print.**

2. **Place your cursor anywhere on the page that you want to print.**

3. **Click on the Print button on the Toolbar.**

   Alternatively, press F5 or choose <u>F</u>ile⇨<u>P</u>rint to display the Print dialog box.

4. **Choose Current Page in the <u>P</u>rint section.**

   The option you want is the first option below the word <u>P</u>rint. Click on the arrow at the right of <u>P</u>rint to see your options; then click on Current Page. From here on, we'll refer to that setting as the *print-selection setting*.

5. **Click on the Print button.**

## When your printer prints backward

Some printers print in such a way that you're always re-ordering multiple-page documents. What you really need to be able to do is print the last page first. Then, when the printer finished printing, everything would be in the right order. Fortunately, you can tell WordPerfect to do just that. Click on the Print in Reverse Order options in the Print dialog box.

## Printing a bunch of pages, but not all of them

To print a few pages, do the following:

**1. Make sure that your printer is all set to print.**

**2. Make a note of the page numbers that you want to print.**

It doesn't matter where the heck your cursor is.

**3. Click on the Print button on the Toolbar.**

Or press F5, or choose File⇨Print from the menu bar. Just get that Print dialog box on-screen.

**4. Click on the From option in the Page Range section and type the number of the first page that you want to print.**

You can also click the arrows to move the page number up or down.

**5. Click on the To option in the Page Range section and type the number of the last page that you want to print.**

Notice that the print-selection setting has changed to Multiple Pages.

**6. Click on the Print button.**

WordPerfect prints the pages that you specified and skips all the other pages.

## Printing random pages

The Page Range setting allows you to print contiguous pages in your document easily. If you want to print noncontiguous pages you can; you just have to perform an extra step. Change the print-selection setting to Advanced Multiple Pages and then click on the Edit button. The Advanced Multiple Pages dialog box appears. Use the P̲age(s)/label(s) option to specify the pages that you want to print; see Table 12-1 to find out how to specify a group of pages. Click on OK in the Advanced Multiple Pages dialog box and then click on Print in the Print dialog box to print the pages that you need.

| Table 12-1 | Print-Range Page Numbers |
|---|---|
| *Entry* | *Meaning* |
| all | Print all the pages in the document |
| x | Print page *x* |
| x,y,z | Print pages *x, y,* and *z* (separate page numbers with commas or spaces) |
| x-y | Print pages *x* through *y*, inclusive |
| x- | Print page *x* through the end of the document |
| -x | Starting at the beginning of the document, print through page *x* |
| x,y-z | Print page *x* and then pages *y* through *z* (you can include as many page ranges as you want, separated by commas or spaces) |

## Printing on both sides

It's cool to print documents on both sides of the paper, such as in a book. This method not only makes your document look terribly official, but also marks you as an Ecologically Sound Person, which is important in this day and age. If you want to print your document on both sides of the paper but your printer doesn't do that automatically, don't worry — you are not out of luck. Your Green reputation doesn't have to suffer.

In the Print dialog box, WordPerfect provides a whole tab full of printing settings for two-sided printing. Click on the Two-Sided Printing tab near the top of the Print dialog box to see the options shown in Figure 12-2.

This tab has the settings to use if your printer supports two-sided printing. Just choose Flip on Lo̲ng Edge or F̲lip on Short Edge. (If you're printing regular stuff, portrait-style, you want to choose Flip on Lo̲ng Edge.) You can also specify offset, which moves the printed part of the page to the left or right (depending on whether it's an even or odd page) to leave space for the document to be bound.

The options in the Two-Sided Printing tab of the Print dialog box apply only to the current session of WordPerfect. If you know that you always want to print a certain document on both sides, you can attach two-sided printing codes to a document by clicking on the D̲ocument Settings button.

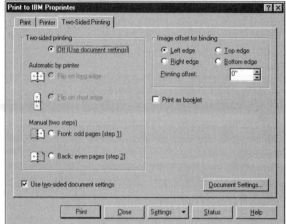

**Figure 12-2:**
WordPerfect
knows all
about
printing on
two sides of
the page.

If your printer doesn't know how to print on both sides, you can still do so. Use the Manual options near the bottom of the first column of settings in the Two-Sided Printing tab of the Print dialog box. Using these options, you can print all the Front (or odd) pages; then you can put the paper back in the printer, change the option to print the Back (or even) pages, and print again. Voilà — two-sided printing.

We want to point out something that we didn't figure out right away. The whole two-sided-printing part of this dialog box (the left half of the dialog box) consists of five radio buttons — which means that only one of the choices can be selected at a time. So to turn one off, select another one.

Here are the general steps for two-sided printing:

1. **Make sure that your printer is eager to print.**

   Also make sure that the paper you plan to use is blank on both sides.

2. **Click on the Print button on the Toolbar.**

   Alternatively, press F5 or choose File➪Print. You see the Print dialog box.

3. **Click the Two-Sided Printing tab.**

   WordPerfect displays the Two-Sided Printing options (refer to Figure 12-2).

4. **Change the settings as necessary.**

   If your printer know how to print on both sides of the page, just tell it whether to Flip on Long Edge or Flip on Short Edge. If you're not sure, try Flip on Long Edge first; it's probably what you want. If your printer doesn't know how to print on both sides, you can do it manually; choose Front: Odd Pages (Step 1).

**5. Click on the Print button.**

WordPerfect prints according to the settings that you changed.

If you're doing manual two-sided printing, you have a couple more steps to perform.

**6. Flip the paper over.**

After all the odd-numbered pages have been printed, put them back in the paper tray so that WordPerfect can print on the other side of the paper. Make sure that page 1 is printed-side-down and on top, so that WordPerfect prints page 2 on its back side. (You may have to turn each page over individually, not just flop the stack over.)

Also make sure that the paper is facing the right way, so that page 2 isn't upside-down and doesn't print on the *same* side of the paper as page 1. Because the exact orientation that you need depends on your printer, you may want to experiment with a short document.

**7. Repeat steps 1–5.**

This time, choose the Back: Even Pages (Step <u>2</u>) option in Step 4.

## Printing several copies

After you begin printing a document, you may want several copies. Hey, why not save yourself a trip to the copying machine?

To tell WordPerfect how many copies to print, follow these steps:

**1. Make sure that your printer is hot to print.**

**2. As usual, click on the Print button on the Toolbar.**

Also, you can press F5 or choose <u>F</u>ile⇨<u>P</u>rint to display the Print dialog box.

**3. In the <u>N</u>umber of Copies box, enter the number that you want.**

You can click on the little up- and down-arrow buttons to increase and decrease the numbers.

You can also tell WordPerfect how to print the multiple printouts: print a whole document before starting the next (C<u>o</u>llate), or print however many copies of page 1 you asked for before moving to page 2 (<u>G</u>roup).

**4. Click on the Print button.**

# *Printing a Document on Disk*

What if you want to print a document that isn't open? What if you wrote, saved, and printed a magnificent letter this morning, for example, and now you want to print an extra copy to show to your mother? You can open it first, admire it on-screen for a while, and then print it, but there's a faster way, as shown in these steps:

1. **Set your printer so that it's rarin' to print.**

   It doesn't matter where your cursor is or even which document is open.

2. **Click on the Print button on the Toolbar.**

   If you prefer, press F5 or choose File⇨Print. Either way, WordPerfect displays the Print dialog box.

3. **In the first box in the Print section of the dialog box (in the setting we called "print selection" earlier in this chapter), choose Document on Disk.**

4. **Click on the Edit button.**

   WordPerfect displays the Document on Disk dialog box, shown in Figure 12-3.

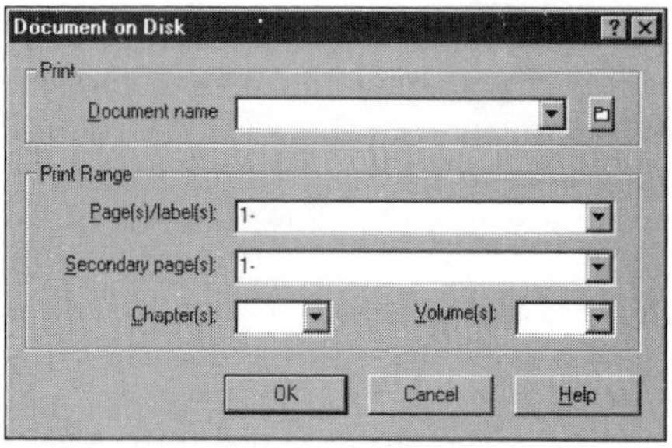

**Figure 12-3:**
Printing a
document
that isn't
open.

5. **In the Document Name box, enter the name of the document that you want to print.**

   If the document isn't in the current folder, you must enter its full path name. If you don't know what the heck we are talking about, or if you want to know how to use that cute little file-folder icon next to the Document Name box, see Chapter 14.

6. **Click on OK in the Document on Disk dialog box.**

7. **Click on the Print button in the Print dialog box.**

   WordPerfect prints the document without displaying it on-screen.

These steps are a good way to print a document you have already printed that doesn't need additional editing.

You can print only selected pages from the document on disk by entering page numbers in the Print Range boxes.

If the file doesn't exist, or if you type its name wrong (it can happen to anyone), WordPerfect displays the message that the file was not found. Click on the OK button to get rid of the message and try again. For help in finding files, see Chapter 14.

# Printing Several Documents

You can tell WordPerfect to print a bunch of documents, one right after the other. If you want to print 10 letters, for example, and each letter is in a separate file, opening each document, printing it, and then closing it is an annoying and slow process. A slightly less annoying and slow process is to print each file from disk, as described in the preceding section. The best way to do it would be to select the files you want to print and then print them all in a batch, and you can do just that.

This method is a great way to get lots of printing done in a hurry, but it's also an effective way to waste lots of paper, so be careful when you select the files to print. Follow these steps:

1. **Click on the Open button on the Toolbar.**

   Alternatively, you can press Ctrl+O or choose File⇨Open.

   WordPerfect displays the Open File dialog box.

   You can use any dialog box that allows you to select files. The Open File dialog box is our favorite, because if you click on OK by mistake, nothing bad happens.

2. **Select the files that you want to print.**

   If the files are listed together, click on the first filename and then Shift+click on the last one; WordPerfect highlights all the files from the first to the last. If the files aren't listed together, click on the first filename and then Ctrl+click on the other filenames; WordPerfect highlights the filenames that you choose but not the intervening filenames.

   Do yourself a favor: Click only on WordPerfect documents (ones that say WordPerfect 7 Document in the Type column). If you click on some other type of file, WordPerfect may (or may not) try to do you some big favor and try to print it, but you probably won't be pleased with the results.

3. **When you have selected the files that you want to print, right-click on one of the selected files.**

   WordPerfect displays a list of things that you can do with the files that you selected. We talk about most of them in Chapter 14.

> **4. Choose <u>P</u>rint from the little menu.**

If the files you want to print are in a different directory, go directly to Chapter 14 to find out how to find them. Information about the other things that you can do to files by right-clicking on them is also in Chapter 14.

# Canceling a Print Job

So far, printing has been pretty smooth sailing. Display a dialog box or two, click on the buttons, and presto — your document is on paper. Then one day, disaster strikes — you send your 150-page report to print while you are in the middle of reorganizing it. It's time to tell WordPerfect, "Stop printing! Never mind! I didn't mean it!"

## Who ya gonna call?

WordPerfect (like all Windows programs) prints by committee. When WordPerfect prints, it sends the information in your document to the Windows 95 Printer Folder. Windows 95 takes it from there. But WordPerfect keeps track of what is going on with Print Status and History, a program that comes with WordPerfect. With luck, you should never have to deal with the Printer Folder, but we'll show you two ways to stop a print job: by talking to WordPerfect and by talking to Windows 95.

If your computer and printer are connected to a network rather than directly to each other, you may have an additional step. Your document will get passed to the network print manager, which then sends it to the printer. A talk with your network administrator may be in order (accompanied by a few chocolate-chip cookies), so that you can learn how to cancel a print job after it's been sent to the network print manager.

While a document is printing, you probably will see a printer icon on the Taskbar. Double-clicking on this icon displays the Printer Folder. For more information about using the Windows 95 Printer Folder, see Chapter 22 or refer to *Windows 95 For Dummies*.

## WordPerfect, stop printing!

While your document is printing, you can tell Windows 95 and WordPerfect to forget the whole thing by following these steps:

1. **Click on the Print button on the Toolbar.**

   If you prefer, press F5 or choose File➪Print. Any of these methods displays the Print dialog box.

2. **Click on the Status button.**

   WordPerfect displays the Print Status and History window (see Figure 12-4), which shows you the status of your current and past print jobs in more detail than you could possibly want.

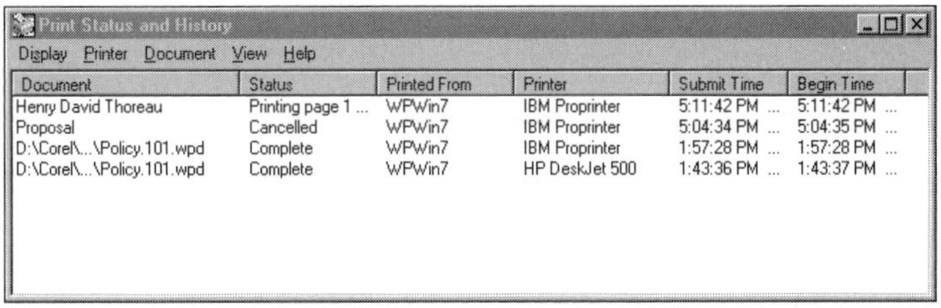

**Figure 12-4:**
The Print
Status and
History
window.

3. **To stop the document from printing, right-click on the document in question and choose Cancel Printing.**

   You can also select the document by clicking on it and then choosing Document➪Cancel Printing in the Print Status and History dialog box. The printing will stop, although maybe not quite immediately.

If you change your mind and decide that you don't want to cancel the print job, click on the Close button (the one with the X in the top right corner of the window) to make the Print Status and History window go away. You can also leave this window open, if you often want to check on the status of a print job. Notice that Print Status and History is a separate program and gets a separate button on your Taskbar.

## *Stop, stop, I say!*

You may prefer the direct route: going straight to the Windows 95 Printer Folder to stop your print job. Follow these steps:

1. **Look for the printer icon on the Taskbar, in the box that displays the time (or whatever information you asked for in that part of the Taskbar); then double-click on it.**

   You can also display the Printers folder directly from the Print Status and History window; choose Printer➪Open Printer. Alternatively, click on the Start button on the Windows 95 Taskbar, choose Settings➪Printers to see the Printers folder, and then double-click on the icon for your printer.

Windows 95 displays the Printers folder. The title bar is the name of your printer, and the jobs listed are jobs that are currently being printed or need to be printed.

2. **Cancel a print job by right-clicking on it and then choosing Document⇨Cancel Printing.**

The print job stops almost immediately.

# Chapter 13

# Juggling Documents on Your Screen

• • • • • • • • • • • • • • • • • • • • • • • • • • • • • • • • • • • • • • • • • • •

## In This Chapter

▶ Working on more than one document at the same time

▶ Sizing your windows

▶ Minimizing and maximizing your documents

▶ Closing documents

▶ Combining documents

▶ Knowing what to do if a file already exists

▶ Using foreign files

• • • • • • • • • • • • • • • • • • • • • • • • • • • • • • • • • • • • • • • • • • •

*I*magine living in New York City, in an apartment that has a powerful tele-scope. Using your telescope, you can look into the windows of your various neighbors. In one, you see an office worker typing away. In another, you see a warehouse. In a third, someone is washing the dishes. In the fourth — oops! Close the curtains!

In the same way, WordPerfect for Windows allows you to work on more than one document at the same time. As you open each document, WordPerfect creates a *window* to display it. You can open several documents at one time and view several windows simultaneously. Hey, this is what Windows is all about!

This chapter explains this multiwindowing stuff to you. You don't even need a telescope to do it. Using these techniques, you can improve your productivity by viewing and editing related documents at the same time, or you can turn your WordPerfect window into a big mess, as shown in Figure 13-1. The choice is yours.

While we are on the subject of opening documents, let's talk about how to open files that *don't* contain WordPerfect documents, such as documents created by other word-processing programs.

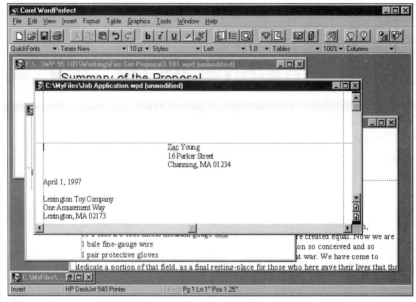

**Figure 13-1:**
Using
multiple
documents
can get out
of hand!

# How Can You Work on Two Documents at a Time?

To work on a document, as you know, you open it by using the File➪Open command (or clicking on the Open button on the Toolbar or pressing Ctrl+O). WordPerfect creates a window for the document; this window occupies the space between the Power Bar (if it is visible) at the top and the status bar at the bottom.

After you open a document, you can open *another* document. WordPerfect keeps the first document open but covers it with a second window that contains the second document.

## Switching between open documents

How do you get back to the first open document? Aha! The Window command on the menu bar is the solution. When you choose Window, you see a menu that contains three commands (Cascade, Tile Top to Bottom, and Tile Side by Side), followed by a numbered list of the documents you have open. To switch to another open document, just choose its name from the menu.

To switch documents without using the mouse, press Alt+W to open the Window menu. Find the number that precedes the name of the document you want, and press that number. You can also cycle through the open documents by pressing Ctrl+F6 or Ctrl+Shift+F6.

## Making baby documents

When you want to begin writing something new, you need a brand-spanking-new document with no text in it. No one ever told you how baby documents are made? It's about time you learned the Facts of Life.

To make a new document, click on the New Blank Document button on the Toolbar (it's the first button), or press Ctrl+N. WordPerfect names the new document something wild and crazy, such as Document2, and makes a window for it. You can give it a better name when you save it.

If you use the File⇨New command, WordPerfect asks you what kind of *template* you want to use. Forget about all that stuff for a while and click on Select to create a blank document by using WordPerfect's suggestions. See Chapter 16 to learn more about templates.

## Closing the curtains

When you finish working on a document, don't leave it lying around open. Each open document slows WordPerfect just a little. To close the window that contains a document, click on the document's close button (the X in the top right corner of the document window), choose File⇨Close, or press Ctrl+F4.

If the document you are closing has been changed since you last saved it, WordPerfect gives you the chance to save it before closing it, so that you don't lose your work. You can click on Yes (so that WordPerfect saves the document before closing it), No (so that WordPerfect closes it without saving your changes), or Cancel (so that WordPerfect abandons the idea of closing it).

In WordPerfect for DOS, you use the same key — the F7 key — to close a document and to exit WordPerfect. This situation has always been confusing, and WordPerfect for Windows has two separate commands: File⇨Close to close a document and File⇨Exit to leave WordPerfect.

Why did the friendly folks at WordPerfect choose Ctrl+F4 to be the magic keys to close a document? Why not Ctrl+C, for example? It turns out that most Windows programs use the Ctrl+F4 key combination to close windows, so WordPerfect went along with the standard. Besides, Windows programs usually use Ctrl+C for copying text to the Clipboard, and WordPerfect does too.

## *Working with multiple documents*

The most common reason for opening multiple documents is to refer to one document while you write another — or sometimes to rip off text from one document while you write another. WordPerfect makes this technique easy: You can use all of WordPerfect's cut-and-paste commands to move or copy text from one document to another.

If you wrote a truly stellar paragraph in one letter and want to use it in another letter, for example, follow these steps:

1. **Open both documents.**

   Use the usual File⇨Open command, or click on the Open button.

2. **In the original letter, select the paragraph.**

   Quadruple-click on it (if your fingers are dexterous enough), or double-click in the left margin next to the paragraph.

3. **Press Ctrl+C to copy the paragraph to the Clipboard.**

   Or choose Edit⇨Copy, or click on the Copy button on the Toolbar. Nothing seems to happen.

4. **Switch to the other document by using the Window command.**

   Or use the mouse to click on the other document, if you can see it.

5. **Move your cursor to the point where you want the paragraph to appear.**

6. **Press Ctrl+V to paste the paragraph there from the Clipboard.**

   If you prefer, you can choose Edit⇨Paste or click on the Paste button on the Toolbar.

After you get good at this kind of thing, it's amazing how much text you can recycle!

## *Maxing out*

You can keep opening additional documents until nine are open. Then WordPerfect puts its foot down and prevents you from opening any more by disabling the File⇨Open command and the Open and New Blank Document buttons on the Toolbar.

To open another document, you first must close one of your open documents. We have rarely found a situation in which we really had to refer to more than nine documents at the same time; maybe your brain cells have more capacity than ours do!

# *Windows within Windows*

It can be annoying to flip back and forth between two documents, copying information or just referring to what you have written. Sometimes it is more convenient to see both documents at the same time. Again, WordPerfect is happy to oblige.

## *Seeing lots of windows*

You can view multiple documents on-screen in these three ways:

- ✔ Choose <u>W</u>indow⇨<u>C</u>ascade. WordPerfect creates a little window for each document and stacks the windows like a deck of cards, as shown in Figure 13-2.

- ✔ Choose <u>W</u>indow⇨<u>T</u>ile Top to Bottom or <u>W</u>indow⇨Tile <u>S</u>ide by Side. Again, WordPerfect puts each document in a little window. This time, however, it fills the WordPerfect window with the documents like a game of dominoes (see Figure 13-3). Top-to-bottom tiling arranges the documents in wide horizontal strips; side-by-side tiling arranges the documents in skinny vertical strips. The top-to-bottom arrangement generally makes documents easier to read. If you have four or more documents open, WordPerfect simply arranges documents in a grid.

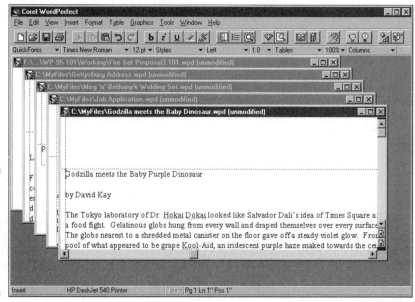

**Figure 13-2:**
Pick a
document,
any
document.
These are
cascaded.

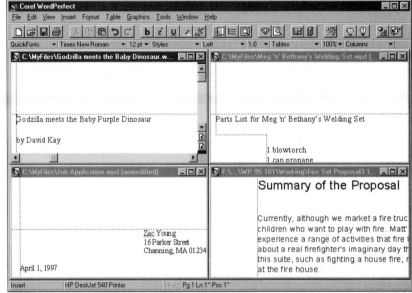

**Figure 13-3:**
Shuffle your
documents,
and lay them
end to end.

✔ If you maximize one document to fill the WordPerfect window, you see three little buttons at the right end of the menu bar. These buttons work only in the active document. The first is the Minimize button (it looks like a dash or a minimized document); the second is the document Restore button (it looks like two overlapping windows); and the third is the document Close button (it looks like an X). If you click on the Restore button, WordPerfect cascades or tiles your documents, using whichever command you used last.

If you minimize a document, it turns into a bar at the bottom of the WordPerfect window. (Minimize a document by clicking on the document's Minimize button, which looks like a dash.) When you arrange the open documents by using a Tile or Cascade command, the minimized window stays at the bottom of the screen. You can get it if you want, but it isn't taking up space.

Each document window has its own title bar that shows the filename of the document and that has its own little scroll bars. You can move around in each document by using the mouse and the cursor keys you read about in Chapter 3.

If you plan to look at several documents at a time, you may want to make your WordPerfect window as big as possible. To *maximize* it, click on the window's Maximize button — the middle of the three buttons at the right end of the title bar. It looks like one maximized window. (If the middle button looks like two overlapping windows, the button has turned into the Restore button; it does that when WordPerfect is already maximized.) Chapter 21 describes other things you can do with the WordPerfect window.

# I want that one!

When you can see multiple document windows, one of them is active. The *active* document window is the one with the highlighted title bar. It's usually on top of the other windows (no other windows obscure your view of it). The active window is the one you are editing, and your cursor is in it. The formatting commands you give affect the active window. Text that you type lands in the active window.

You can switch from one window to another by clicking anywhere in the window for the document you want to use, or you can use the <u>W</u>indow command described earlier in this chapter.

# Sizing your windows

It is extremely unlikely that either cascading or tiling your documents will produce document windows large enough for you to get any work done. You probably will have to move them around a little, perhaps making the window for the main document you are working on large and the other document windows small. No problem.

Each little document window has a border, and you can move these borders around at will, as shown in the following list:

- ✔ If you point to the left or right border of a window, the mouse pointer turns into a little left-and-right-pointing arrow. You can click and drag the window border to the left or right to resize it horizontally.

- ✔ When you point to the top or bottom border of a window, the mouse pointer turns into an up-and-down-pointing arrow, and you can drag the window border up or down to resize it vertically.

- ✔ When you point to a corner of a border, the mouse pointer turns into a diagonal  arrow, and you can drag the corner around in any direction. WordPerfect adjusts the borders accordingly.

You can also move the windows around by clicking and dragging their title bars. The process is similar to moving papers around on your desk, except that they never get coffee stains on them. You can waste most of your workday, in fact, by moving your windows around until you get them lined up just the way you want them.

## *Maximizing your documents*

All these windows, borders, and scroll bars on your screen can become distracting. When you want to get back to work and look at just one document, you can maximize it so that it takes up the entire WordPerfect window again.

To maximize a document, look at the right end of its title bar. Click on the middle of the three buttons (it looks like a maximized window). Poof! The other document windows are covered by this document.

## *Minimizing your documents*

If you click on the button with the dash at the bottom of it on the title bar of a document window, the window is minimized. That is, it gets really small and appears as a bar somewhere in the vicinity of the lower left corner of the WordPerfect window. (Refer to Figure 13-1 to see a minimized document.) No one we know ever minimizes a document on purpose, but it happens when you want to maximize your document window and you click on the wrong button. Double-click on the bar to open the document window again.

## *Saving all your open documents*

As you know, saving your open documents frequently is a good idea. Then, if all the air conditioners in the building kick in at the same time, the power dips, and your computer blips out, you don't lose your work.

If you have several documents open, you should save all of them. Many programs have a File➪Save All command, but WordPerfect seems to have forgotten it. Luckily, you can press the Save All key combination: Ctrl+Shift+S. This step saves all the open documents you have changed.

# *Combining Documents*

As you know, each WordPerfect document lives in its own cozy little file on your disk. But sometimes you want to break down the walls between your documents and get them together, throw a little party, or whatever.

One of your documents might contain a standard description of the product you sell — chocolate-belly futures, for example. Then you create a new document in which you begin a letter to a prospective client. You realize that you want to include the product description in your letter.

## Inserting one document into another one

No dirty jokes at this point, please. Let's just stick to word processing. Follow these steps:

1. **Move your cursor to the location where you want the text from the other file to appear.**

   Move the cursor to the point in your letter where you want, for example, to wax eloquent about chocolate-belly futures.

2. **Choose Insert⇨File.**

   WordPerfect displays the Insert File dialog box, which looks suspiciously like the Open File dialog box and half a dozen other dialog boxes that have to do with files.

3. **Choose the name of the file you want to insert into the current document.**

   Choose the file that contains the standard product description, for example.

4. **Click on Insert or double-click on the filename.**

   WordPerfect opens the file, sticks its contents into the current document right where your cursor is located, and shoves aside any text that comes after the cursor.

Another way to include information from one document in another is to open both documents and then use cut-and-paste commands to copy the information from one document to the other. The resulting combined document has the same name as the original document you opened.

You can insert more than one document into the current document. There is no limit, in fact, to the number of other documents you can stick into the current one. But watch out: Don't create enormous documents unless you have to. They can become slow and unwieldy.

WordPerfect doesn't keep track of where inserted text comes from. If you want the inserted text to change with its source document, you want *linked documents*. WordPerfect can do that; you have to use the File⇨Document⇨ Subdocument command, which we discuss in Chapter 18.

## Saving a chunk of text as a separate document

You can also do the reverse of inserting text — you can save part of the current document in a new, separate file. What if you write a letter that contains a terrific explanation of how to make vegetarian chili (your specialty)? Now you want to save your recipe in its own file, as shown in these steps:

1. **Select the text you want to save separately.**

   Chapter 6 shows you ways to select text.

2. **Choose your favorite way of issuing the Save command.**

   Choose File➪Save, click on the Save button on the Toolbar, or press Ctrl+S.

   WordPerfect notices that some text is selected and displays the Save dialog box, as shown in Figure 13-4.

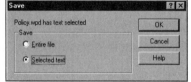

**Figure 13-4:**
Saving some text in its own file.

3. **To save the selected text in its own file, click on Selected Text and then choose OK.**

   WordPerfect displays the usual Save As dialog box so that you can tell it the filename you want to use for the selected text. You might call the selected text Chili Recipe.wpd, for example.

4. **Choose Save in the Save As dialog box to create the new document that contains the selected text.**

   The text you selected also remains in the original document — that is, WordPerfect saves a *copy* of it in the new file.

# What If the File Already Exists?

As you work in WordPerfect, opening and saving documents, you frequently type names for new files. The day will come when you type a name for a new file, little suspecting that you have *already* used that filename — probably for a document you have forgotten all about. According to the rules, you cannot have two files with the same name in the same directory.

What happens? WordPerfect asks you what the heck you want to do, that's what happens. You get to save the new file on the top of the old one, or you get to change your mind. A dialog box like the one shown in Figure 13-5 appears.

Figure 13-5:
Two files in
the same
place at the
same time?

You can click one of these two buttons:

✔ **Yes:** Means "Blow away the existing file with this name and replace it with the one I'm saving now." Show no mercy.

✔ **No:** Means "Wait! I chose the wrong filename! Give me another chance to enter the right one!"

# Using Foreign Files

I see a foreign document in your future. It is strong, handsome, and exotic. You will travel over water.

Oops! That's not the kind of foreign thing we are talking about. A foreign file is one that is not stored in WordPerfect 7 format.

You have several reasons to use foreign documents:

✔ You receive drafts of documents on disk from someone who uses Lotus WordPro.

✔ You want to give your documents on disk to someone who will edit them some more with Microsoft Word.

✔ You get data files (such as lists of names and addresses) from a database program such as Microsoft Access or Paradox.

WordPerfect can both read (open) and write (save) files in other formats, including the ones in this list:

| | |
|---|---|
| Lotus WordPro | Excel, Quattro Pro, and Lotus 1-2-3 |
| DisplayWrite | Earlier versions of WordPerfect |
| Microsoft Word | RFT (revisable-form text, an IBM standard) |
| MultiMate | RTF (rich-text format, a Windows standard) |
| OfficeWriter | Plain old ASCII text |

When you (or someone) installed WordPerfect on your computer, you (or someone) may have opted to conserve disk space by not installing all the conversion options that come with WordPerfect. If this is the case, your WordPerfect installation may choke on some of the preceding formats.

## Which format should I use?

If you want to read or create a file for one of the programs listed in the preceding section, you are in Fat City. Otherwise, see whether the other program can read or write RFT, RTF, or ASCII text files. If so, you should be able to communicate with WordPerfect.

ASCII text files contain nothing but regular old letters, numbers, spaces, and other punctuation — no formatting. They are called ASCII text files because they contain character codes defined by the American Standard Code for Information Interchange, or ASCII.

## Creating a foreign file

Creating a file in a format other than the regular old WordPerfect format is also called *exporting* a file. To export a WordPerfect document, follow these steps:

1. **Save the file in WordPerfect format.**

   In case you want to do more editing later, you can open this file and export it again.

2. **Choose File⇨Save As or press F3.**

   You see the dialog box shown in Figure 13-6. The As type option usually says WordPerfect 6.0/6.1 (*.wpd, *.wcm, *.wpt, *.frm, *.dat). This message is WordPerfect's way of saying that it plans to save the document in the usual WordPerfect 6.0/6.1 format and suggesting some commonly used file extensions.

3. **Click on the As type box, and select the format you want to use.**

   For many programs, such as Microsoft Word, several formats are listed. Use the scroll bar to see more formats. If you are not sure which one to use, choose a version that's a little older that the most up-to-date one. That choice gives you more latitude when you load a file, because newer versions of software can almost always handle the files created by older versions of the same software.

**Figure 13-6:**
Sending
your
WordPerfect
document
overseas.

4. **In the Name box, type a name and extension (a period, followed by as many as three letters) for the new file.**

   Don't type the wpd extension that is used for WordPerfect files. It's a good idea to use the file extension that is appropriate for the type of file you are creating (doc for Microsoft Word documents, for example, or sam for Lotus WordPro documents.) Look at the As type setting to see the extension that WordPerfect suggests. (We suggest reserving the extension wpd for WordPerfect files.)

5. **Choose Save.**

   WordPerfect flashes a little message that conversion is in progress while it saves the file.

Now you have created a foreign file right on your own disk.

## Reading a foreign file

Reading files in other formats, also called *importing* documents, is easy. Just use the same File⇨Open command you use to open a regular WordPerfect document, as shown in these steps:

1. **Choose File⇨Open from the menu, click on the Open button on the Toolbar, or press Ctrl+O.**

   You see the usual Open File dialog box.

# ASCII no questions, I'll tell you no lies

You can use WordPerfect to edit ASCII files. You might be called on someday to edit one of the special text files that tell DOS and Windows how to work, such as your autoexec.bat, config.sys, or win.ini file.

When you edit an ASCII file, you must be sure to save it again as an ASCII file, not as a WordPerfect document. Follow the directions in the next section for opening the text file in WordPerfect. Then edit it, but don't use any formatting or insert any special characters. Finally, save it as an ASCII text file just as you would any other foregin file (see the section "Creating a foreign file," earlier in this chapter).

For most ASCII-editing purposes, it is easier to use the Notepad program that comes with Windows. (It's in your Accessories program group.) Double-click on it to run it, use the File⇨Open command to open a text file, do your editing, use the File⇨Save command to save it, and choose File⇨Exit to leave.

**2. Choose the filename from the list, or type it in the Name box.**

If you don't see your foreign file listed in the Open dialog box, WordPerfect may deliberately be showing only its own WordPerfect format files. For the As type setting, choose All Files (*.*).

**3. Choose Open.**

Doesn't all this seem strangely familiar? These steps are the same ones you follow to open a WordPerfect document!

Aha! WordPerfect notices that something is amiss when it tries to open the file. It flashes the Convert File Format dialog box, shown in Figure 13-7. It even takes a stab at guessing the format of the file.

**Figure 13-7:**
What is this? Not a WordPerfect document!

| Convert File Format | ? X |
| --- | --- |
| File: H:\ALISON\AAJRNAL.DOC | OK |
| Convert file format from: | Cancel |
| MS Word for Windows 6.0/7.0 | Help |

**4. For the Convert File Format From setting, choose the format of the file.**

WordPerfect is usually correct about the format of the file. Probably all you have to do is go on to the next step.

5. **Choose OK.**

   WordPerfect displays its message that a conversion is in progress; then it opens (imports) the file.

6. **Save the file as a WordPerfect document by choosing File⇨Save As or pressing F3.**

7. **Enter a filename that ends with the WordPerfect extension (wpd), and choose WordPerfect 6.0/6.1 as the format.**

8. **Choose Save to save it.**

For tips on saving foreign files, see the following sidebar, "The name doesn't match the face."

---

## The name doesn't match the face

Here's one confusing thing: After you save a file in a foreign format, WordPerfect changes the document name on the title bar to the name of the foreign file. If you save the file again by using File⇨Save, Ctrl+S, or the Save button on the Toolbar, WordPerfect wonders which format you have in mind and displays the Save Format dialog box.

WordPerfect suggests that you save the file in regular WordPerfect format, in the format you last used, or in some other format. If you want to use the format you used last time, just tell it what you want. But if you want to save it in WordPerfect format now, you have a problem. We suggest that you just Cancel out of this dialog box and use the File⇨Save As command instead.

The reason is that if you choose WordPerfect format, WordPerfect does indeed save the document as a WordPerfect file. Unfortunately, it still uses the filename you typed when you exported the document. Suppose that you saved an important marketing report as Chocolate.wpd in WordPerfect format and then saved it as Chocolate.doc in Microsoft Word format. Now the filename that appears in the title bar is Chocolate.doc. You press Ctrl+S to save the document again, the Save Format dialog box appears, and you choose WordPerfect format. Now WordPerfect saves the report in a file named Chocolate.doc in WordPerfect format.

It's confusing if a file has the wrong type of extension for its contents; you (and WordPerfect) can get bollixed up this way. Watch out! You are better off using the File⇨Save As command (or pressing F3), which allows you to specify both the format and the filename.

## *Word processors versus food processors*

Although WordPerfect does a great job of importing and exporting files in many other formats, it isn't perfect. Not that this is WordPerfect's fault — the problem is that different word processors have different capabilities and do things in different ways. Sometimes files that have been imported or exported look as though they were put in a food processor for a few seconds by mistake.

When you are using a foreign file, look around it before you blithely edit or print it. The formatting may be fouled up. Fonts may change mysteriously. You may find extra line-ending characters (Enter keys) where they don't belong. Some cleanup may be in order.

### RTF: The Esperanto of file formats

If you must regularly use or provide foreign files, but they don't translate well, see whether your foreign buddy can export and import files as RTF, or Rich Text Format. RTF is a format designed especially for document exchange; it's sort of a universal language, such as Esperanto.

Not everybody speaks it (as is the case with Esperanto), but many word processors do, including WordPerfect and Microsoft Word for both the Macintosh and the PC. RTF keeps most of your formatting intact as long as both computers have similar fonts.

# Chapter 14
# Juggling Files on Your Disk

• • • • • • • • • • • • • • • • • • • • • • • • • • • • • • • • • • • • • • • • • • •

## In This Chapter

▶ Naming files

▶ Using directories

▶ Recognizing different kinds of files

▶ Copying, renaming, deleting, and moving files

▶ Finding a file with a forgotten name

• • • • • • • • • • • • • • • • • • • • • • • • • • • • • • • • • • • • • • • • • • •

Sorry, old-timers — gone are the days of keeping your documents on a nice thin 5-¼-inch disk, which you could conveniently stuff into a file folder. Oh, you can still do it that way, all right. It's just that the New and Improved Way of Doing Things is designed to keep everything on one big, humongous hard disk that is bolted into your computer, so that you cannot (without risking a hernia) grab it and run out if the house catches fire. (Maybe this is the reason why laptops are so popular.)

Anyway, this is the way things are now, so you may as well enjoy its benefits. Not that the situation is all bad: With everything on one disk, you're not continually shuffling floppy disks, writing labels for them, putting your coffee cup on them, or losing them. It's also easier to copy stuff from an old document to make a new one when everything is on one big disk. And thanks to Windows 95, which allows you to describe your documents with more than eight letters, you no longer have to remember whether your treatise on hermaphroditic mealworms is called HERMMEAL, MEALWORM, or WORMSEX.

Doing all this great stuff — doing darn near anything on the PC, in fact — requires a working knowledge of files and folders (or directories, for those of us who have been using WordPerfect under DOS and Windows for a long time). This knowledge includes what files are called; where they hang out; and how to reproduce them, change their names, find them, move them, or just kill them off. If you're already conversant with these topics, read "Finding a File with a Forgotten Name" later in this chapter; skim the rest of the chapter to learn how you can do these things without the Windows 95 Explorer; and then move along.

# *A File by Any Other Name*

Giving names to your files wasn't always much fun on the PC. In fact, Macintosh and UNIX users used to sneer at those of us who use Windows because, for perfectly ridiculous historical reasons, you couldn't give a file a name that is longer than eight characters (made up mostly of letters and numbers). Microsoft was listening; and it fixed this problem in Windows 95. (To be completely fair, there are still eight-character filenames lurking around inside your computer; see the next sidebar.)

This list shows the boring, detailed rules of naming files on a PC:

- Most filenames contain a period (.). What follows the period is called an *extension,* is usually three letters, and usually describes the type of the file. You supply the part that comes before the period — that's the *name* part. WordPerfect takes care of the extension (usually by adding wpd, frm, or dat to the end of the name that you give the file). When both parts are shown, the extension is separated from the filename by a period, as in the file called FILENAME.ext.

- You can use up to 255 characters in a filename; you'll probably want to use fewer.

- Uppercase and lowercase characters are identical, which is probably a good thing. Imagine trying to remember whether your document was MealWorm, MEALworm, or MeAlWOrm. In this book, we use capital letters for filenames, but you can type them by using either uppercase or lower-case letters. We don't care, and neither does Windows.

- You can use letters, numbers, spaces, and almost all punctuation characters in the name and extension. Rather than memorize which symbols are OK and which are no good, it is simpler to stick with letters, numbers, and spaces in your filenames.

The following examples of filenames (just the real name part, not the extension) are OK:

LETTER

Chapter 1 - First Draft

READ

But these filenames *aren't* OK:

- "Here's Johnny" (Quotes are some of the punctuation characters that you can't use in a filename.)

- \/:*?<>| (These are the rest of the punctuation characters that you can't use in a filename.)

## WHATIS~1. . . I mean, what is that ~ thingy?

There is no doubt in our minds that the capability to use long filenames is one of the nicest features of Windows 95. Sad to say, however, sooner or later you probably will find that inside Windows 95, there are still those cruddy eight-letter filenames that DOS and Windows (and WordPerfect 6.1) users have been struggling with for more than a decade. You may as well find out now. That way, when it comes up, you can say, "Oh, yeah, I read about that somewhere."

Here's the scoop: Although there are no human beings on the planet who have not heard of Windows 95, there is plenty of software that hasn't. Try to tell a program that was published in 1994 about one of those big long filenames, and it will boggle its little mind. Also, plenty of people are still using Windows 3.1, which doesn't understand those long filenames either. What to do?

For every file that you save, Windows 95 keeps *two* names: the long name, exactly as you typed it; and a short eight-letter version. The eight-letter version is made up of the first six letters of the long name, followed by a tilde (that's the ~ thingy), followed by a number, usually 1. That way, if you name files What's My Line and What's The Question, Windows 95 can call them What's~1 and What's~2, and not get them confused. When you share the files with someone who's using Windows 3.1, or when you open the files with a program written before the Windows 95 days, you'll have to call them by their eight-letter names.

How do you, a mere human, find out what the eight-letter name is? Well, there's no good way, really. If you're lucky, you'll never need to know it. If you're less lucky, the names that you use will be unique within the first eight letters, and you'll be able to take the first six letters of the filename and add ~1 to them. If you're really *un*lucky, you'll have to see a list of long names together with short names. Go buy a candy bar, and bribe your local nerd to show you a directory listing in MS-DOS.

# Using Folders

Like we said at the beginning of this chapter, when files lived on floppy disks, life was simple. Life is no longer so simple. So here's what we're gonna do: We're gonna talk about what folders are, why you would want to use them, and what folders you're likely to find lying around your computer. Then we'll talk about how to poke around and figure out what's on your computer. Finally, we'll talk about creating folders, moving files around between folders, and deleting files.

## What's a folder?

The price of having everything on a single hard disk is that it must be organized; otherwise, you can never find anything. To accomplish this organizational task, your hard disk is organized like a file cabinet. Within it are file folders (or folders), each of which may contain some files. The disk also has folders within folders. Each folder has a name that follows the same rules as a filename.

Without this organization, every file on your entire hard disk would have to have a different name. With it, you can have a file called MEALWORM, about mealworm reproduction, in the SEX folder, and another file, also named MEAL-WORM but about mealworm digestion, in the EATING folder (not to be confused with the RECIPES folder).

To help keep mealworms out of your recipes, in fact, you may want to keep these folders separate by putting them in their own folders, such as BIOLOGY and PERSONAL. This arrangement leads to a kind of hierarchy, as shown in Figure 14-1. In the figure, those little pictures of folders represent folders, and the folder labeled (C:) represents your hard disk.

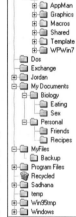

**Figure 14-1:**
A hierarchy
of
directories.

Even though we're talking about directories on the hard disk, called drive C, everything that we're discussing applies also to floppy disks (including those little 3-1/2-inch disks that are more crunchy than floppy), called drive A or drive B. You can certainly keep documents on these disks, if you want, and use directories, too. WordPerfect runs somewhat more slowly, though, when you use these floppy disks.

## *Exploring the folders in your computer*

Exploring the folders in your computer is actually a rather large topic. In fact, Andy Rathbone spends a whole chapter telling you everything about it in *Windows 95 For Dummies* (IDG Books; who else?). We're not going to do that here. What we *are* going to do is tell you just enough to get your files organized into different folders.

The topic is also large enough that Windows 95 has a program that does nothing but help you explore the folders on your computer. It's called, not surprisingly, the Explorer. We're not going to tell you about that, either. Instead, you may have noticed that the File⇨Open, File⇨Save As, and Insert⇨File commands all show you a dialog box that looks almost the same. This dialog box is sort of a mini-Explorer, and it's what we're talking about here.

Look at the Save As dialog box, shown in Figure 14-2. (The others are pretty much the same.)

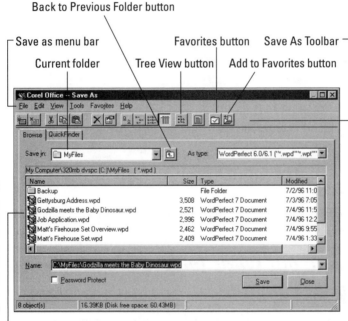

**Figure 14-2:**
File⇨Save As, the Swiss Army Knife of dialog boxes.

Like the WordPerfect screen, this box has several parts. Here are the most important ones:

✔ **Current folder.** This is the folder where WordPerfect will save your document unless you tell it otherwise.

✔ **Folder and file list.** These are the documents in the current folder and any folders that are in the current folder.

✔ **Back to the Previous Folder button.** Heck of a name, huh? Remember that folders can be inside folders that are inside folders, and so on, ad nauseum? This button figures out what folder the current folder is in, and makes *that* folder the current folder.

✔ **Tree View button.** Look at Figure 14-1 again. If you like this view of folders inside folders inside folders, you can see it on your own computer by clicking on this button. The folder and file list gets pushed over toward the right side of the Save As dialog box, and a hierarchical map of what's inside what is displayed on the left side. Now your dialog box looks like Figure 14-3.

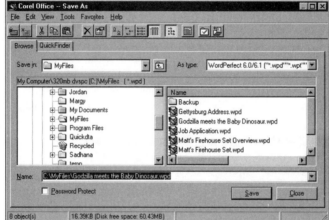

**Figure 14-3:**
The Save As dialog box with Tree View turned on.

OK, now that we've got the basics down, let's get to work using those folders!

## Finding out what folders are on your computer

The easiest way to find out what folders are on your computer is to click on the Tree View button. The list of files and folders in the Save As dialog box moves over to the right, and a diagram that represents the folders on your computer appears. Why, you may ask, is this called a tree? Well, most computer types don't spend a lot of time outdoors (too far from an electrical outlet), so they figured that anything that has a root and branches must be a tree. They seem to have ignored the fact that the root of this tree is at the top and the branches branch out downward.

Some people find this diagram of the folders and folders-within-folders completely bizarre ("Huh?" would be too kind a word to describe their reaction, but this is a family book). Other people find that it makes pretty good sense. Squint at this tree diagram for a while to see whether you get it; if you do, understanding what folders are around on your computer will be much easier. What's more, you'll be able to impress your coworkers.

You can use the scroll bar to move up and down this list of folders. You can even click on the Maximize button to make this box take up the whole screen. (Why not? There's a lot of stuff in there.) You should see MyFiles in this list, along with all the other folders that WordPerfect created when it was installed on your computer. Any folder with a plus sign (+) beside it has other folders inside it. To see what they are, click on the plus sign. The plus sign changes to a minus sign (–), and the folders inside that folder appear. Click on the minus sign, and they disappear. (They're still out there — just hidden.)

At the top of the list, you see a couple of things that act like folders but have different pictures. They represent your computer, your hard disk drive, your floppy drive, and perhaps other things. It doesn't really matter: If it has a plus sign or a minus sign next to it, it acts like a folder. If you are connected to a local-area network, you may see some other folderlike things toward the bottom of the list. They appear after the list of all your folders, and they probably are network disks — disks on some computer elsewhere in your company. You can use them like folders, too, if you've been given permission to do so. Grab some granola bars, find your network administrator, and get her to tell you whether there's anything interesting out there.

You may have noticed that as you clicked around the plus signs and minus signs in the tree view, nothing changed over in the file and folder list. But if you click on the *name* of a folder in the tree view, the file and folder list changes to show you what's in that folder.

WordPerfect creates some directories on your hard disk when it's installed. If you have used previous versions of WordPerfect, you may be familiar with the WPDOCS directory, which is where WordPerfect *used* to put your documents unless you said otherwise. Anyway, in Windows 95 with WordPerfect 7, things are different. Unless you tell it otherwise, WordPerfect saves all your documents in a folder called MyFiles. (For that reason, MyFiles is sometimes called the *default document folder.*) When WordPerfect was installed, it created MyFiles in the root of your disk drive, usually drive C.

You may also see a folder named Corel (unless you or your guru set things up otherwise, or unless you upgraded from WordPerfect 6.1 or WordPerfect 6.0). Everything else in the Corel folder (and all the folders inside it) are parts of the WordPerfect program (or other Corel programs that you may have on your computer). Don't mess with them.

You probably will not want to put all your documents in MyFiles, any more than you would want to put all your paper documents in the same file folder. It's easy to specify a different folder when you save your document. You can also change your default document folder. See "Expressing Your Preferences" in Chapter 20 for more information about changing the default document folder.

You may also find (as we did in Figure 14-1) that you have a folder named My Documents. Several Windows 95 programs use My Documents to store their documents. If you have My Documents, you'll definitely want to change your preferences; go to Chapter 20.

You can also create your own set of folders by using WordPerfect. Use them to organize your documents and other WordPerfect files. Just as with your paper files, the organization is up to you.

Finally, you may find that you have folders that aren't even on your own computer. If you're working in an office where computers are connected on a network, you may be able to store your documents on someone else's computer or on a central computer. Fortunately, doing this is just the same as using a folder on your own computer. In the following section, where we talk about exploring the folders in your computer, we'll also talk about finding folders on other computers.

Spend some time browsing around, looking for the folders on your computer; you never know what you might find. In case you've *really* lost some things, we'll talk about how to use the QuickFinder later in this chapter.

## *Creating folders*

This may sound intimidating, but it's not. Create a folder? No problem. First, you cut down a tree and grind it into pulp. Oops . . . I mean, first you grind up a bunch of discarded paper into pulp. . . .

Never mind — this is the clean electronic way. (Well, it's clean if you live a long way from the power plant and the plastics factory, but that's another issue.)

To create a folder, follow these steps:

1. **Choose File➪New➪Folder in the Save As dialog box.**

   If WordPerfect beeps when you click on File, you clicked on the wrong menu. Find the one that says Corel Office – Save As, and try again.

   A new folder, cleverly named New Folder, appears in the list of folders and files.

   Your folder is created inside the folder whose name is in the Save In portion of the dialog box. Because New Folder probably isn't the name that you had in mind, you can change it.

   The New Folder name should be highlighted, usually in white letters on a blue background. And if you look carefully, you'll see that the right end of the white-on-blue text is blinking.

2. **Type the folder name that you actually want to use and press Enter.**

Once you get the process down, it's not too bad. To actually save a document in that new folder, *now* you can double-click on the folder name. The new folder name appears in the Save In portion of the dialog box. Type the document name in the Name portion of the dialog box, and press Enter. Congratulations!

# Adding a folder to your Windows 95 list of Favorites (your favorite places)

Now that you know how to create a folder, and now that you know how to move around the tree view in the Save As dialog box, you're ready to keep track of your favorite folders. WordPerfect and Windows 95 actually work together to make this task pretty straightforward. Follow these steps:

1. **Move around the tree view until you see the folder that you want to add to your favorite places.**

   You can either create a new folder, as described in the preceding section, or find one that already exists on your computer.

2. **Click on the Add to Favorites button on the Save As toolbar.**

   Because this is Windows, there are at least two ways to do everything. In this case, you could also choose Favorites⇨Add from the Save As dialog box menu. Either way, you see a list of two choices: Add Favorite Folder and Add Favorite Item.

3. **Choose Add Favorite Folder.**

   The folder that you're in is added to your favorite places.

What? You don't see any difference? Come with me. . . .

# Looking at your favorite folders

You've probably figured out by now that there are *lots* of folders on your computer (and around it, if you are connected to a network). Most of the time, you don't care about most of them. Previous versions of WordPerfect had QuickLists to help you keep track of your favorite folders; back then, they were called directories. The folks at Microsoft thought this was a good idea, so they put something like it in Windows 95 itself: the Favorites folder.

To see what's in your Favorites folder, click on the Favorites button in the Save As dialog box. Presto — a list of documents and folders appears in the files and folders list. The folder that you just added should appear there as well. (If it doesn't, something quite untoward has happened; find your local computer whiz.)

What's in Favorites? Anything that you've added to your Favorites, using any other program in Windows 95. You get only one set of Favorites. This means that you may see Internet Shortcuts there (especially if you use the Microsoft Internet Explorer browser), documents saved by other programs, and who knows what else.

This is not as terrible as it may seem, because you can create folders inside your Favorites (see two sections ago), and you can add your own folders (see the preceding section). We don't actually spend much time in our Favorites, but we use it as a way to get to where we *really* want to be.

# Moving, Copying, Deleting, and Renaming Files

Now that you've mastered the basics of moving around among your folders, the rest (copying, renaming, and deleting) is pretty straightforward. After you've displayed the Corel Office Save As dialog box, you tell WordPerfect which file you are talking about by clicking on it (one time only, please) in the files and folders list. When WordPerfect knows what file you're talking about, the text appears in white on blue (or a similar tasteful scheme, depending on how you have your Windows 95 desktop set up). After you tell WordPerfect what file you're interested in, you can do something with it, as the following sections explain.

## Moving a file

If you want to move a file to another folder, you need to be able to see the folder. We don't think that this requirement is too unreasonable. But it is another reason why working in the tree view is useful — you can click on the file, as you just did, and then move around the tree view until you see the folder that you're interested in.

To move a file, follow these steps:

1. **Make sure that the Save As dialog box is displaying both the files and folders list and the tree view.**

   If all that you see is the files and folders portion of the dialog box, click on the Tree View button. (Refer to Figure 14-3 if you don't know where it is.)

2. **Select the file that you want to move.**

3. **Move around the tree view until you see the folder to which you want to move the file.**

Don't click on any of the folder names. If you do, the files and folders list will change, and you'll need to select your file again. Go back to Step 2 and do not collect $200.

If you need to, use the scroll bar to see folders that don't fit into the tree view right now. If you can't find the folder that you're looking for, it may be hidden inside another folder. Remember that you can open folders by clicking on the plus sign (+) right beside them. You can do all this without disturbing your file selection in the files and folders part of the dialog box.

4. **Click on the file that you want to move.**

5. **Move the file.**

*To move the file with the mouse,* drag it to the folder where you want it to go.

A quick refresher course, in case something has slipped your mind since Chapter 2: Click on the file in the files and folders part of the dialog box, but do not release the mouse button. While you are holding down the mouse button, move the mouse pointer over to the folder where you want the file to go. Notice that the mouse cursor has a little box attached to it now; it's dragging your document along with it. When the folder that you're interested in is highlighted, release the mouse button.

*To move the file with the keyboard,* choose Edit⇨Cut. Nothing happens. Don't panic. *Double-click* on the folder where you want the file to go. Then choose Edit⇨Paste. You see a message box, telling you that the file is being moved.

## Copying a file

Pardon us if we get a little brief here — copying a file is so much like moving a file that we don't want to put you to sleep by repeating everything. Just refer to "Moving a file" earlier in this chapter. Hold down the Ctrl key while you do the dragging. If you do things with the keyboard, choose Edit⇨Copy instead of Edit⇨Cut. The difference? The original file stays in the location from which you copied it and also appears in the new location.

## Deleting a file

This procedure is an example of how things actually got simpler in WordPerfect 7. Follow these instructions carefully; we assume that you've already selected the file that you want to delete.

To delete a file, follow these steps:

1. **Take a deep breath.**

2. **Press the Del key.**

   If you've already got your hand on the mouse, you can choose File➪Delete from the Save As dialog box menu.

   WordPerfect displays a dialog box, asking whether you're sure that you want to delete the file.

3. **Confirm that you *do* want to send the file to the Recycle Bin.**

4. **Cry in anguish as you realize that you just deleted the only copy of the project justification that funds your job.**

   Actually, there is a way back. Just to reassure you, we'll give you the quick tour. In the tree view, toward the end of the list of folders, is a folder named Recycle Bin. It has a cute little trash-can icon with a recycle symbol on it, but it is really a folder. Find your file in that folder, and use the procedure that we just talked about to move it back where it belongs.

## Renaming a file

The really alert reader (that's you, right?) will notice that we've already done something very similar to renaming a file. When you created a new folder, which WordPerfect so helpfully named New Folder, you renamed it as something more interesting. WordPerfect did you some favors to help you rename that folder. Here, we go over the whole process in gory detail. Follow these steps to rename a file:

1. **Click on the name of the file you want to change.**

   Actually, if you're following the instructions from the heading above, you've already done this. But remember, this can be a little tricky. *Do not* double-click on the file name.

   If you do double-click on the file by accident, WordPerfect will do one of two things: Either it will warn you that it is about to do something drastic to your file, in which case you should click on No to tell WordPerfect not to do whatever got in to its head. Or WordPerfect may just decide to open the file that you wanted to rename, in which case you should just close the file and try this renaming business again. In either case, before you try again, stop drinking so much coffee, and try to click on the name of the file again. You've got it right if the filename is highlighted, usually in white letters on a blue background.

2. **Click on the file's name again.**

   Again, don't double-click. If you're still having trouble with the caffeine habit, you can choose File➪Rename in the Save As dialog box menu. Either way, a box appears around the highlighted file name, and if you look carefully, you see that the right end of the white-on-blue text is blinking.

**3. Type the filename that you actually want to use and press the Enter key.**

I wouldn't exactly call that process painless, especially with the click-once-then-click-once-again business. (Dorothy, are you listening?) But once you've got it down, it's not too bad.

This brings up an interesting point: All this moving and copying and deleting and renaming works just the same for folders and for files. Select the folder in the file and folder list, search the tree view for the folder that you want to send it to, and have at it. Pretty nice. Your fingers never leave the keyboard, and you never leave WordPerfect.

# Path names

The directory structure shown in Figure 14-1 raises a question: When you want to talk to the computer about these files, how do you distinguish between files that have the same name (the Mealworm file in the SEX directory versus the one in the EATING directory)? One solution is path names, which tell your software how to navigate the hierarchy to get to the right place. A path name consists of the disk (written as A:, B:, C:, or D:, with C: usually representing the hard disk) and the directories, separated by a backslash (\).

A pathname to the SEX folder (directory) looks like this:

`C:\My Documents\Biology\Sex`

A pathname to the EATING folder looks like this:

`C:\My Documents\Biology\Eating`

If you want to be precise in telling your computer about a file, you can use the path name with the filename and its extension. The path name looks something like this line:

`C:\My Documents\Biology\
    Eating\Mealworm.wpd`

WordPerfect automatically puts the wpd extension on your document files.

You normally don't have to type things with a path name, because WordPerfect keeps track of the directory separately from the filename. Moreover, WordPerfect generally knows the correct file extension from the context, so you don't have to type it. Most of the time, all that you have to type is the filename. If you want to include the path, it doesn't hurt.

Even though you don't have to type path names, you often see them in WordPerfect. They tell you where WordPerfect is getting or putting files, in case you care. The most obvious example is the name of the file that you're working on, displayed in the title bar (the top line of the WordPerfect window).

# Kinds of Files

WordPerfect can, and does, use many different files. Some are its own, WordPerfecty kind of files. Others are of the import–export variety, such as spreadsheets, databases, graphics, and documents from other word processing programs. You have to be slightly aware of their differences to prevent confusion when, for example, a graphics file and a document file have the same name and are stored in the same directory.

For now, focus on three principal groups: documents, graphics, and templates.

You can usually tell a WordPerfect document file when you see it listed (as in a dialog box). It always has a three-letter wpd extension appended to the name and separated by a period (HiMom.wpd, for example), unless you deliberately gave the document a different extension when you created it (not a good idea). Documents from other word processing programs use other extensions.

Graphics files also generally have distinctive two- or three-letter extensions, but hundreds of variants exist. Some of the common ones are wpg (for WordPerfect Graphics), bmp (for Windows Bitmap), dib, wmf, tif, pcx, eps, and pgl. These extensions are used in the Graphics⇨Image command and elsewhere.

*Template files* are patterns for creating a new document. They typically store styles and standard text for a given type of document, such as a purchase order. WordPerfect supplies many templates, and you can create your own (refer to Chapter 17). Templates always have a wpt extension and are used principally in the File⇨New⇨Options⇨New Template command, which allows you to create a new file based on a template.

Most of the time, WordPerfect knows just which kind of file you want from the type of command you're giving, and it displays only the right sort of file. But considering all the settings that you can fool with, it's only a matter of time before you do something that makes WordPerfect throw up its hands and leave you to sort things out from the extensions.

# Making Backups

While we are talking about copying files, we should point out that you should make backup copies of your documents regularly. Just think how you would feel if you arrived at your office tomorrow and found that your computer — and all the files stored on its hard disk — had been destroyed by a freak ceiling cave-in or stolen by masked men. Not too good, right?

Because you probably have lots and lots of important files on your hard disk, including files that you created by using programs other than WordPerfect, it is a good idea to talk to a computer guru about a system for making daily backup copies of all your important files — on floppy disks or backup tapes, or to your local-area network.

In the meantime, take the precaution of copying your most prized WordPerfect documents to a floppy disk or to a network disk every day or so. You'll feel smug when you delete a file by accident and know that you have a backup copy!

To back up the files, you use the file-copying method described earlier. Specifically, follow these steps:

1. **Choose File⇨Save As from the WordPerfect menu bar.**

   You see the Save As dialog box.

2. **Double-click on the folder in which your files are located.**

   If you need to, click on the Tree View button so that you can browse around and find the folder that you're looking for. If you added your favorite folders to your favorite places, click on the Favorites button (refer to Figure 14-2) to look there for your folder.

3. **Select the files to copy.**

   Click on the name of a file that you're interested in. To select additional files, hold down the Ctrl key and click on each file that you want. To select a group of contiguous files, click on the top file, hold down the Shift key, and click on the bottom file.

4. **Move around the tree view until you see the folder to which you want to move the file.**

   Don't click on any of the folder names. If you do, the files and folders list will change, and you'll need to select your file again. Go back to Step 2 and do not collect $200.

   If you need to, use the scroll bar to see folders that don't fit into the tree view right now. If you can't find the folder that you're looking for, it may be hidden inside another folder. Remember that you can open folders by clicking on the plus sign (+) right beside them. You can do all this without disturbing your file selection in the files and folders part of the dialog box.

   Backups are most effective if they are not on the same computer as the original files. This means that you'll want to choose a network drive (listed in the Network Neighborhood folder, toward the end of the folder list) or a floppy disk drive (listed at the top of the folder list; make sure that you have a disk in the drive).

**5. Click on the file that you want to copy.**

If you selected more than one file, click on any one of the files that you selected.

**6.** *HOLD DOWN THE Ctrl KEY.*

This is important; it's what makes WordPerfect copy the files rather than move them.

**7. Move the file.**

*To move the file with the mouse,* drag it to the folder where you want it to go.

*To move the file with the keyboard,* choose Edit⇨Copy. Nothing happens. Don't panic. *Double-click* on the folder where you want the file to go. Then choose Edit⇨Paste. You see a message box, telling you that your files are being copied.

# *Finding a File with a Forgotten Name*

Boy, is WordPerfect ever glad that you want to know how to find your files. It has invested heavily in creating the Star Wars of file finding, the Saint Bernard of lost and stranded files, the veritable "Rescue 911" of technology-assisted document search and rescue. It's called QuickFinder, and you use it by clicking on the QuickFinder tab in the Save As and Open File dialog boxes. QuickFinder is so muscle-bound that we're not even going to try to describe everything that it can do; we're going to focus on how it helps you find a file.

QuickFinder finds files by looking for certain text. If you want to find a letter to Ms. Tannenwald, for example, but you cannot remember the name of the file, you just type **Tannenwald** in the right place in the QuickFinder.

QuickFinder then sounds the alarm; dispatches armies, navies, and air forces to execute your humble request; and comes marching back, proudly carrying in its teeth any and all files that have any hint of the word *Tannenwald* in them. This feature works for phrases and various word combinations, too.

Before we go any farther, we'll show you how to perform a simple single-word search. Follow these steps:

**1. Choose File⇨Open or File⇨Save As from the main menu bar.**

**2. Click on the QuickFinder tab in the dialog box that appears.**

The QuickFinder tab appears, as shown in Figure 14-4.

**3. Click on the Content box, and type a word that you want to search the files for (such as *Tannenwald,* in our example).**

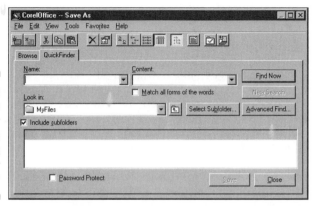

4. **Select the folder where you want the search to start.**

   The QuickFinder starts its search in the folder where it expects that you put your documents. It searches that folders and all the folders within it. If you want to start in a different folder, click on the Select Su_b_folder button. You see a list of folders, similar to the tree view that we talked about earlier. Select the folder where QuickFinder should start.

   *To search in a single directory:* Select the directory that you want to search in, as just described, but make sure that the Include S_u_bfolders check box is *not* checked.

   *To search an entire disk:* Click on the Select Su_b_folder button, and choose My Computer from the list of folders. (It's not really a folder, but we won't tell if you won't.) If you don't see My Computer on this list, keep clicking on the Back to Previous Folder button until you see it. It's the one with the folder and the hooked arrow on it, as shown in Figure 14-2 earlier in this chapter.

5. **To search for particular filenames or file types other than WordPerfect documents, edit the text in the _N_ame box.**

   Double-click in the box, and type a new partial filename or path. To search for Microsoft Word files, which have the extension doc, type **\*.DOC**. To search for Microsoft Word files that begin with the letter *P*, type **P\*.DOC**. The asterisk (\*) means *any group of characters.* Use a ? symbol to mean *any single character.*

6. **Click on the _F_ind Now button.**

   The F_i_nd Now button becomes the Stop F_i_nd button while QuickFinder searches. As QuickFinder finds files, it lists them in the list of documents.

Now you're finished. QuickFinder has found all the files that have your word in them. You can double click on one of these files if you selected the File⇨_O_pen command to see this dialog box, or you can just click on the _C_lose button in the Search Results dialog box and go about your business.

## *Searching for files by using more than one word*

Sometimes, a single word is not enough to specify the file that you want. As a real-estate lawyer, you may have written dozens of letters to Ms. Tannenwald, but only one that discusses her forest property. Likewise, you probably have dozens of letters to other clients who have forest property, but only one to Ms. Tannenwald. Neither *forest* nor *Tannenwald* alone is sufficient to find the correct file. You want the file that mentions both words.

To specify this sort of thing, you have to put special characters, called *operators,* between the words in your search line. For example, you can type this search phrase:

```
Tannenwald&forest
```

The & character means *and,* as in "Find me a document that has both *Tannenwald* and *forest.*" Some other useful operators that can be used in this position are shown in this list:

| | |
|---|---|
| \| (the vertical bar symbol) | Means *or,* as in "Find a document that has either word A or word B." The vertical bar can be darn near anywhere on your keyboard. Look around— it may be above the backslash symbol. |
| Space (the space character, not the word *space*) | Means the same thing as the *or* symbol, unless you tell QuickFinder that you're giving it a phrase (see the following section, "Searching for phrases"). |
| ! (the exclamation point) | Means *not,* as in "Find a document that has word A but not word B." |

## *Searching for phrases*

A final case in which a single word may not be enough is when you're looking for phrases. You cannot just type a phrase in the Content box; QuickFinder interprets it as a list of individual words and finds files that contain any of those words. (A space means the same as an *or* symbol in the normal mode of operation.)

To tell QuickFinder that you are typing a phrase, put it in quotation marks (the regular double marks). Then click on Find Now, and away you go.

# Chapter 15

# Dressing Your Document for Success

- - - - - - - - - - - - - - - - - - - - - - - - - - - - - - - - - - - - - - - - - - - - - - - - - -

### In This Chapter

▶ Columns

▶ Borders

▶ Graphics

▶ Text boxes

▶ Tables

- - - - - - - - - - - - - - - - - - - - - - - - - - - - - - - - - - - - - - - - - - - - - - - - - -

*T*he cool thing about today's word processors is that you can dress up a document in ways that only a designer, typesetter, or printer could do a few years ago. The trouble is, now that people (your boss, for example) know that normal people can do this kind of thing, they begin to expect it.

The other less-than-cool thing about today's word processors is that, in giving you all this wonderful stuff, "they" have gone absolutely overboard. WordPerfect, for all practical purposes, performs not only word processing but also drawing, charting, spreadsheet-like calculating, and elements of typesetting.

The problem for the average schmo is getting around all the fancy stuff to do the basic stuff. That's what you learn about here. We don't give you a course in spreadsheets or computer art; we just help you get started creating basic columns, tables, graphics, and stuff.

## Working with Columns

Columns are great for newsletters, newspapers, magazines, scripts, lists, and certain charts or tables. With newspaper and magazine documents, even if you don't print the document yourself, you can use columns and the correct character and paragraph formatting to determine approximately how long your article will be when it's printed.

WordPerfect can lay out columns in the following four styles (when was the last time we said that there was only *one* way to do something in WordPerfect?):

- ✔ **Newspaper:** Fills one column to the end of the page before beginning another column. Use this option for newsletters and long, incoherent, raving letters to the editor.

- ✔ **Balanced Newspaper:** Continuously shuffles your text to make sure that all columns are of more or less equal length. Use this style (which has nothing to do with a balanced editorial policy) when a document alternately uses a single column and multiple columns, such as when you have a long, multicolumn list in the middle of a regular document. You can also use it for ending the last page of a multicolumn newsletter before the end of the physical page.

- ✔ **Parallel:** Creates rows across your columns, and creates cells of text in a manner similar to a table. When you use this style, you create a row one cell at a time by inserting a hard column break when you want to begin writing the next cell to the right. This style is useful for scripts and contracts.

- ✔ **Parallel with Block Protect:** Similar to Parallel, but makes sure that automatic page breaks don't mess things up if your rows must continue on the next page.

If all these styles sound confusing, take heart. The WordPerfect Columns dialog box shows you neat pictures of what sort of columns are used for each option.

## Creating columns

To turn on columns in your document, follow these steps:

1. **Place your cursor where you want columns to begin.**

   If you want your entire document to appear in two newspaper columns except for the title at the top, for example, move your cursor to the first line after the title.

2. **Choose Format⇨Columns.**

   You can also use the Power Bar to turn on columns. Click on the button labeled Columns, and a menu drops down. To put your text in columns quickly, allowing WordPerfect to use the default column style (Balanced newspaper) and spacing, just click on the number of columns that you want and then skip to Step 5.

3. **Choose Define⇨Columns.**

   The Columns dialog box appears, as shown in Figure 15-1.

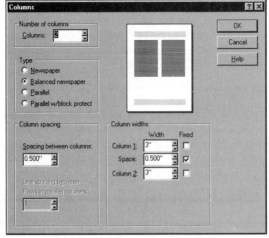

**Figure 15-1:**
Getting, like, totally columnar with the Columns dialog box.

**4. Choose the number of columns that you want.**

In the upper-left corner, in the Number of columns section, WordPerfect suggests two columns (unless you are working with text that is already in columns, in which case it shows you the current setting). Change this number by typing a number or by clicking on the up and down arrows next to the Columns box.

**5. Choose the type of columns that you want.**

In the Type section, choose one of the options (Balanced newspaper, for example) described in the preceding section.

**6. Adjust the column widths or spacing, if you want.**

In the Column widths section, WordPerfect suggests nice, even column widths with a half-inch space between them. It allows column widths to vary if you change the page margins, but it prevents the spacing between columns from changing — that is, it keeps the spacing "fixed."

To fix (or unfix) any column or space-between-columns dimension so that it doesn't vary, click on the box in the Fixed column to the right of the Width setting. To change widths, click on the Width box and edit the value by typing and deleting, or click on the adjoining up-and-down (increment and decrement) arrow buttons. Use the " symbol for inches or **mm** or **cm** for metric values.

If you want all the spaces between the columns to be the same size, you can adjust the intercolumn spacing in the Column spacing section. But be careful — if you change the value in this box, *all* the spaces between the columns (even ones that you changed by hand) will be set to the new column-spacing size.

If you made your columns look sort of like a table by using Parallel or Parallel with block protect, you can also specify the number of blank lines that WordPerfect leaves between rows. Click on the up-and-down arrow buttons in the small box with the long name (Line spacing between Rows in parallel columns) in the lower-left corner.

7. **Click on OK or press Enter when you finish (like we had to tell you that).**

To turn off columns at some point in your document, place your cursor where you want things to go back to normal. Then choose Format⇨Columns⇨Off from the main WordPerfect menu bar or Columns⇨Columns Off from the Power Bar.

## *Bad breaks and what to do about them*

There are good breaks, and there are bad breaks — column breaks, that is. WordPerfect decides where to break your columns depending on a lot of things, and it's different for different kinds of columns. But when your columns don't break where you want them to (or break where you don't want them to), you can regain some control by inserting hard column breaks.

To insert a hard column break, follow these steps:

1. **Place your cursor before the line (or word or character) where you want a column to begin.**

2. **Choose Format⇨Columns⇨Column Break, or choose Columns⇨Column Break from the Power Bar.**

Column breaks don't always do what you think they will do. It depends on which type of columns you have: newspaper, balanced newspaper, or one of the parallel styles. The following list shows the types of columns in the column-break story:

- **Newspaper.** Column breaks begin a new column in the way that you think that they should.

- **Balanced newspaper.** A column break begins a whole new block of balanced columns; it's almost like turning columns off and then on again. This style probably isn't what you have in mind if you're trying to fix the way that WordPerfect balanced your columns. So rather than use a column break to change the balance, try regular Newspaper columns, or try putting in blank lines where you want a column to end. It's tacky, but it works.

- **Parallel.** A column break moves you across your current row to the next column. It doesn't put you at the top of a new column, as you might expect. When you insert a column break at the end of the row, you're back in the left column, in a new row.

---

## Putting selected text in columns

Sometimes, you want to put a block of text in columns. You might put a long list of words, such as a packing list, into several columns to save space, for example.

Begin by highlighting the block of text that you want to columnate. (Columnarize? Columnify?) Next, issue the Format⇨Columns⇨Define command. In the Columns dialog box, choose

the style that you want. The Balanced newspaper style probably works best, unless you want to control where the columns break, in which case you use the Newspaper style. Then click on OK.

Using highlighted text in this way is equivalent to turning columns on before the block and off after it.

---

Column breaks are invisible no matter what you do, unless you use the Reveal Codes window (refer to Chapter 10), and who wants to do that? If you want to delete hard column breaks, have faith that they are located just before the first character in a column (or just before the current "cell" in a Parallel-type column). To delete hard column breaks, place your cursor before the first character in the column and then press the Backspace key. (Don't try to delete soft column breaks — the ones that WordPerfect puts in. Because they're soft, they just squish up and slither to safety.)

# *Working with Borders and Backgrounds*

For some reason, nothing looks as neat as text in a box. At least, that's what the folks at WordPerfect must believe, because their border features are yet another case of overkill for most of us common folks. WordPerfect allows you to choose among a dizzying array of tasteful (and not so tasteful) borders. You can fill the background of your document with subtle, interesting, or downright bizarre patterns.

Some of these features can be useful if you want to create some kind of fancy document — a certificate, for example. (See Chapter 18 for the particulars on creating certificates.) But unless you use them carefully, it's also easy to end up with an illegible mess.

## *Basic borders*

To put a snazzy border around part of your document, first select the area of your document that you're interested in making illegible — oops; we mean fancy. Choose Format⇨Border/Fill. Now you have to choose whether you are formatting pages, paragraphs, or columns. Choose Pages. The borders that you can apply are the same in each case, with a teeny-tiny exception for pages. Applying your borders to pages, paragraphs, or columns does pretty much what you might expect: You get borders down the whole side of your page, borders down the side of your paragraph (and that includes each paragraph in multiple columns), or borders down the side of the whole area that's in columns.

WordPerfect displays the Page (or Paragraph, or Columns) Border Fill dialog box (see Figure 15-2). That teeny-tiny difference that we mentioned about the Page Border Fill dialog box has to do with the button labeled Border Type. Right now, click on it and then choose Line. That way, everything will make sense. We talk about the Fancy option in "Some miscellaneous thoughts about borders" later in this chapter.

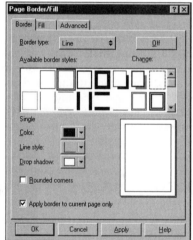

**Figure 15-2:**
The
Border/Fill
dialog box.

The folks at WordPerfect have wasted — er, we mean spent — a tremendous amount of time coming up with zillions of kinds of borders for your documents. You can scroll through the box labeled Available border styles and find the one that suits you best. When you see one that you like, click on it. If you don't find one that you like, you can set the color, line style, and shadow direction yourself, if you don't have anything better to do.

You're not quite done yet. In the lower-left corner of this box is a button labeled Apply borders to current page (or paragraph or column group) only. If you leave this box checked, that is exactly what WordPerfect does. But if you want to do a lot of damage quickly, *un*check this box. All the following pages (or paragraphs or column groups) will have this border.

If you liked borders, you'll love Phil. Phil is the guy who shows up when you click on the Fill tab of the Border/Fill dialog box. (We're not even going to talk about the Advanced tab; this *is* a . . .*For Dummies* book. . . .) Mostly, what this button does is make your text illegible by putting a pattern behind it. You may want to put a light-gray pattern behind something that you want to have stand out, but make sure that your printer and your copier are up to it; otherwise, you'll end up with a smudge instead of readable text.

Click on OK when you have what you like. When you see what you've done to your document, you may want to remove the borders and fills. Just click on the Off button in this dialog box.

## *Some miscellaneous thoughts about borders*

"But I'm not an artist!" you cry nervously. "What am I going to do with all these borders and backgrounds, other than make my documents totally illegible?" This section lists some things that you may want to do:

**Put a fancy border around your whole document.** Remember, we said that there was something different about the Page Border/Fill dialog box. If you leave the Border Type set to Fancy, you get some pretty neat borders that you can use for certificates and the like.

**Limit your borders to the paragraph, page, column, or whatever area your cursor is in.** In the Border/Fill dialog box, click on the box in the lower-left corner that says Apply border to current *whatever* only. Checking this box is an alternative to selecting an area of text before you issue the Border/Fill command.

**Put lines between columns.** Highlight your columns, and choose Format⇨Border/Fill⇨Columns. In the third row (click on the scroll bar that controls the Available border styles), over to the right, you see a vertical line. Click on it. Under the border style samples the name Column Between appears. If you don't see it, keep clicking around until it appears; it puts a line between your columns. In the next row down, sort of in the middle, you see a box with a line down the middle. This border is the Column All border; it puts borders around your whole set of columns, including lines between your columns. Very useful, but very obscure.

**Turn off borders.** Place your cursor where you want the borders to stop. In whichever border dialog box you're using (Paragraph, Page, or Columns), click on the Off button in the upper right corner.

**Don't use borders at all.** Use a horizontal or vertical line. For a horizontal line, press Enter to make a new paragraph, place your cursor there and then press Ctrl+F11, or choose Graphics⇨Horizontal Line. For a vertical line down the left side of your text, press Ctrl+Shift+F11 or choose Graphics⇨Vertical Line. To make a custom line, you're on your own; use the Graphics⇨Custom Line command.

# Working with Graphics

Michelangelo probably had fewer tools for painting the Sistine Chapel than WordPerfect has for creating graphics. For art's sake, that's probably a good thing. Otherwise, the descendants of Michelangelo would still be figuring out how many degrees to rotate whom and which color palette to use.

We asked the Assumption Fairy (the patron spirit of mathematicians) to grant us three Simplifying Assumptions about what you may want to do. Assume that the things that you want to do are limited to the ones in this list:

- ✔ Insert a picture, diagram, or chart that someone has created for you or that came with WordPerfect
- ✔ Create a simple picture or chart
- ✔ Size or position a graphic image, and possibly put a border around one

## Inserting existing graphics

Suppose that you already have a graphical file somewhere in your computer or on a floppy disk. This assumption is a pretty safe one to make, because WordPerfect gives you a bunch of graphical files. If you or your guru completed the standard installation procedure, those files are in your PC.

The simplest way to insert graphics is outlined in these steps:

**1. Put the graphics file on a disk in your PC (or on your network).**

If you're using one of the files that came with WordPerfect, no worries — it's already installed. If you're getting a graphics file from a friend or co-worker, you'll need to put it on your PC. The file can be either on a floppy disk or copied in a directory on your hard disk. The customary hard disk directory for it is C:\Corel\Office7\Graphics. If you don't know how to copy the file, weasel out of the job by subtly implying to the person who made the file that it's his or her responsibility. If that doesn't work, dig out the ol' cookie package and go get your PC guru.

**2. Place the cursor at the location in your document where you want to insert the graphic.**

Don't worry — you can always move it later.

**3. Choose Graphics⇨Image from the WordPerfect menu.**

Or click on the Image button on the Toolbar (the one with the diamond icon).

Either way, the Insert Image dialog box appears.

**4. Find the graphic file and select it.**

By default, WordPerfect shows you graphics files in the default graphics directory, which is usually C:\Corel\Office7\Graphics. If your file isn't there (because it's on a floppy disk, for example), see Chapter 14 for information about how to use the dialog box to tell WordPerfect where a file is located.

WordPerfect initially shows you only files in WordPerfect's own graphics format — files that have the extension .wpg. Alas, your file is probably not in that format. To see other types of files, click on the box labeled For type at the top right of the dialog box; then click on All Files (*.*). Alternatively, if you know which format your file is in (such as *.tif, for Tagged Image Format), click on that format.

**5. Double-click on the name of the graphic file that you want.**

If you're just experimenting with graphics, try one of the files that WordPerfect provides.

Several things have happened on your screen, as shown in Figure 15-3.

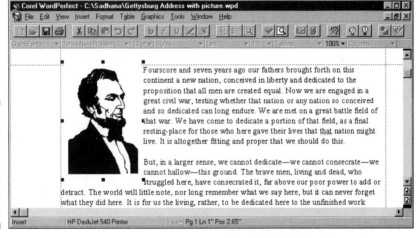

**Figure 15-3:**
A graphic of Abraham Lincoln adorns the Gettysburg Address.

- Miracle of miracles — the image (Abraham Lincoln, in Figure 15-3) has been inserted! The image has a frame and little black squares around it. The squares are for changing the size of the image, but hold that thought for a minute; we'll come back to it.

- Your mouse cursor, when it is on the image, is an arrow with four heads. This is a positioning tool. Hold that thought, too.

6. **If everything looks perfect — the image is the right size and in the right place — you can click anywhere outside the image to continue with your writing.**

   The funny frame goes away, and your mouse pointer goes back to normal.

## Positioning an image

The first trick is to put your image where you want it. Follow these steps:

1. **Move your mouse pointer into the image area.**

   It may be there already.

2. **If the pointer is not a four-headed arrow, click once (do *not* double-click).**

   Now your image should look like Figure 15-3, black squares and all.

   Incidentally, this image of Abe is available in C:\Corel\Office7\Graphics\ QuickArt\Premium.qad\Government\People\16 Abraham Lincoln. Make sure that you or whoever did your installation selected the option Graphics\QuickArt\Additional QuickArt (all 34 megabytes of it).

3. **Click and drag the image where you want it.**

   Text more or less flows around the image, more or less satisfactorily.

4. **When you finish, click in the text area again.**

If you're fussy, you can position the image more precisely by right-clicking on the image. This action brings up the Image QuickMenu; choose Position from this menu. In the Box Position dialog box that appears, enter the location (relative to the margins) where you want the box to appear. If you choose Paragraph or Character from the Attach Box To list, you can have the box move around your document as you edit your text.

## Sizing an image

Perhaps you'd like Old Abe to take up a little less of your page than he now does. The following steps show you how to *scale* your image (change its size and shape):

1. **Move the mouse pointer into the image area and click once to change it to a four-headed arrow.**

   Now WordPerfect knows that you want to scale the image.

2. **Position this new mouse pointer on one of the tiny squares around the image frame.**

You know that you have it right when the pointer changes to a two-headed arrow. The tiny squares around the image are *handles,* which you use to drag the sides or corners of the image to make it larger or smaller.

**3. Click and drag in either of the two directions indicated by the arrow.**

The edges of the image move with your mouse pointer.

**4. Release the mouse button when things look good.**

Keep in mind that the proportions that you see on-screen aren't exactly the ones that you'll see when you print. Print your document to check it.

You can also size the image to exact dimensions by right-clicking on the image and then choosing the Size command from the Image QuickMenu menu that pops up. In the Box Size dialog box, you can enter an exact height and width for your picture. This feature is useful, because it gives you the option of maintaining the proportions of your picture. When you are dragging the corners of your picture around, you can stretch it like Silly Putty, which works better for some pictures than for others.

If you want to keep the original height-to-width proportions of your picture, resize it by using the Box Size dialog box and then click on Maintain Proportions. If you click on Maintain Proportions for Height, you can change the width, and WordPerfect adjusts the height automagically. If you click on Maintain Proportions for Width, you can probably guess what happens. Click on the OK button when you're done.

## *Adding borders to graphics*

To fool with borders around your graphics (including charts and text boxes), you use basically the same overkill border system described earlier in this chapter, in the section "Working with Borders and Backgrounds." Like the other commands that we've been using to work on this picture, this one is available by right-clicking on the picture and then choosing Border/Fill from the QuickMenu.

## How to see where you're going

To make it easier to see where you're positioning an image, zoom out to full-page view before you begin positioning or sizing. Click outside the image area, somewhere in the text. Click on the Page/Zoom Full button on the Toolbar — the button with the magnifying-glass-and-page icon. Now start positioning and sizing.

When you finish positioning and sizing the image, click in the text somewhere and then click on the magnifying-glass button again.

The following steps show you how to put a border around your graphics image, chart, or text box:

1. **Click somewhere in your picture.**

   This click selects the image.

2. **Right-click on the picture.**

3. **Click on the Border/Fill button in the shortcut menu.**

   You see a dialog box that shows your options.

4. **Specify what you want.**

   For details, refer to "Working with Borders and Backgrounds" earlier in this chapter.

## Adding captions

It's virtually impossible to use regular document text to put a caption where you want it, such as below a picture. You have to use the special caption feature, as shown in these steps:

1. **Click on the graphic image you want to caption.**

   The image is selected.

2. **Click the right mouse button.**

   WordPerfect displays a QuickMenu.

3. **Choose Create Caption.**

   WordPerfect suggests a caption.

4. **If you don't like WordPerfect's suggestion, press the Backspace key.**

   This step deletes WordPerfect's suggested caption (Figure 1, or whatever). Alternatively, you can add your caption to the end of what WordPerfect suggests.

5. **Type your caption.**

   You can use any of the usual Format commands or formatting buttons, such as boldface or different type sizes.

You don't have to do anything special when you finish; just click somewhere else in the document. You can use the same procedure to edit the caption. When a caption already exists, the QuickMenu mentioned in Step 3 displays Edit Caption rather than Create Caption.

## The Edit Box

You can control everything about your picture boxes (and other boxes, for that matter) without having to right-click on them all the time. In the Graphics menu is the Edit Box command, which displays a box that is really more like a toolbar. This box has controls that affect the currently selected graphic — that is, the one that has the little black boxes around it. From this box, you can control everything we've talked about so far, and more.

Here are the things you can change with the Edit Box:

**Border:** Allows you to change the border just like any other border.

**Fill:** Allows you to make your text hard to read by spraying some pattern over it. Actually, this feature can be useful if you want to make the box gray, but as we said before, check the quality of your printer and copier; there's no point formatting something on your screen that you can't print or can't photocopy. You can also get some nice effects from the wash setting in this box, but only if you want to waste a certain amount of time.

**Wrap Text:** Tells WordPerfect how you want it to fit the text in your document around the graphic. Experiment with this option until you get the effect that you like.

**Attach To:** Tells WordPerfect how your box should move when you edit your text. Every box

in WordPerfect is attached to something: a page, a paragraph, or a character. That way, as you edit your document (adding and deleting text before the box), the box can move with the text that refers to it. Most often, you'll want to use boxes connected to paragraphs.

**Position:** Tells WordPerfect where the box should appear relative to the paragraph (or page or character).

**Box Styles:** Specifies what collection of characteristics your box should have. Refer to Chapter 11 for a description of how styles work. In this case, they are a collection of the things that describe the box (its border, fill, and so on).

**Caption:** As the name implies, allows you to add a caption to your box. (We talked about this option earlier in this section.)

**Content:** Describes what's in the box. You can edit the contents by clicking on the Edit button.

**Size:** Allows you to type an exact size for the box.

**Image Tools:** If your box contains a WPDraw object (that is, something that you drew or an image that you imported), you can do things to that image. Click on this button to find out what.

**Prev/Next:** Selects the previous or next graphics box in your document. That way, you can do the same set of things to the other boxes in your document without having to search for them.

## Creating your own graphics

For creating and modifying graphics, WordPerfect has a drawing program called WordPerfect Draw (or WP Draw, by its friends). So you're not Norman Rockwell — with WP Draw, you can still create your own home-style graphics and have them look . . . well, OK. Hey, at least you can't color outside the lines here.

You can fire up WP Draw in several ways. If you're editing an existing image that is already in your document, double-click on the image. If you're creating a new graphic from scratch, click on the Draw button on the Toolbar or choose Graphics⇨Draw.

There is a fairly long pause while WordPerfect fires up WP Draw. Figure 15-4 shows a map of the world from WordPerfect's supply of images. We'll annotate this map, although we could just as well be drawing in a blank box. (To insert a blank box, use the Graphics⇨Draw command.)

As you can with any image, you can enlarge or otherwise change the shape of this area by dragging any of the small black squares around its periphery. That bunch of oddly shaped stuff down the left side of the WordPerfect window is your very own set of drawing tools. If you place your mouse pointer on a tool, WP Draw describes what it does and tells you the tool's name, all in a little yellow tag. The basic idea is to select a tool by clicking on it and then go draw or edit something in the image by clicking (or clicking and dragging) your mouse.

Tool for drawing lines

Tool for drawing solid shapes

Tool for selection graphic objects

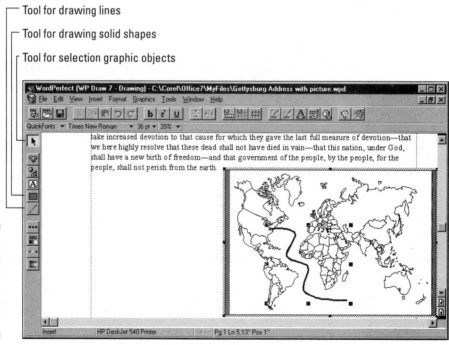

**Figure 15-4:**
Let's get
graphical
with
WordPerfect
Draw.

The following list describes what the tools do, from the top tool to the bottom one. Press the Esc key if you mess things up while you're drawing.

- **Select Object (arrow).** When you want to edit an object (line or shape) that you've drawn, click on this tool first and then click on the object. A set of black squares appears around the selected object in the drawing, as shown in the serpentine shape in Figure 15-4. When an object is selected, you can change its dimensions (drag the black squares), delete it (press the Delete key), move it (drag it), copy it (press Ctrl+C, press Ctrl+V, and then drag the shape), or change the color or style in which it is drawn (see the various Attributes tools, described later in this list).

- **Quick Art (diamond).** Click on this tool to insert an image into the drawing from an image file. This tool works like the Graphics⇨Image command described in "Inserting existing graphics," except that the image is inserted into the drawing, not directly into the document.

- **Data Chart (pie and bar chart).** Click on this tool to create a chart in the drawing. See the following section, "Using graphs and charts," for more information on WordPerfect's charting tool.

- **Text Object Tools (capital A).** This tool allows you to enter text in your drawing. Click on the tool and then click in the canvas area. After you release the mouse button, you can type text in the rectangle. To change the font, press F9 before you type.

- **Closed Object Tools (rectangle).** Click on this tool to select a tool for drawing various closed shapes. To draw the shape, click and drag in the drawing area and then release the mouse button. Initially, this tool draws rectangles. To change to another shape, click on this tool and hold down the mouse button; a selection of alternative shapes appears. Drag the red outline to select a new tool. (As you do so, those cute yellow tags describe the tool.)

- **Line Object Tools (diagonal line).** This tool works like the Closed Object Tools tool, but it gives you tools for drawing straight or curved lines. To draw a line, click once to mark the starting point; double-click to mark the ending point. If you want a series of connected straight lines or a complex curving line, you can mark intermediate points by clicking once for each point.

- **Line Attributes (dashed line).** Select an object that you have drawn, using the Select Object tool, and then click on this tool to view the different line widths and styles that you can apply to that shape. Click on a width or style to apply it to the shape. For additional line-attribute features, such as arrowheads, click instead on the Line button (the one with the pencil) on the Toolbar across the top of the WordPerfect window.

- **Fill Attributes (checkered and gray "tire marks").** This tool works like the Line Attributes tool but controls the pattern that fills a closed shape. For additional fill-attribute features, click instead on the Fill button (the button with the bucket) on the Toolbar.

✔ **Line Colors (colored line).** This tool works like the Line and Fill Attributes tools; it allows you to specify the color of the selected line (or outline of a shape).

✔ **Fill Colors (colored square).** This tool works like the other Attributes tools; it allows you to specify the color of the fill within a closed shape.

The menu bar across the top may look the same as ever, but if you were to click on many of the menus, you would find that their commands have changed. While you are working in the drawing area, WP Draw takes over the menu bar; it also changes the Toolbar and Power Bar. As soon as you click in the document text, everything reverts to normal.

Following are the most important commands and functions on the menu bar:

✔ **Edit.** The Undo command undoes actions. Edit Points allows you to change a shape by dragging points that define its perimeter.

✔ **View.** This menu provides drawing aids, such as gridlines and a ruler. Snap to Grid means that your shapes are determined in part by the gridlines. Zooming the drawing area is a good feature to use if your drawing gets big.

✔ **Graphics.** This menu is useful mostly for putting a selected object behind or in front of another object. Choose Order and then choose Front or Back. The menu is also useful for flipping objects left to right or upside-down: Choose Flip and then choose Left/Right or Top/Bottom.

Following are a few basic concepts that will make your drawing job easier:

✔ Everything you create is a graphic object that can be deleted, moved, duplicated, or otherwise changed independently from the rest of your drawing.

✔ Every graphic object you create has a bunch of properties that control its appearance in gory detail. You can (and should) right-click on your graphic objects to see what you can do to them.

✔ To do anything to an object, you must select it. To select it, first click on the Select Object tool (arrow); then click on the object. A frame appears, with handles around the edges for sizing and positioning. Sizing rules are the same as described in "Sizing an image" earlier in this chapter. To move an object, click anywhere inside the frame and drag.

✔ You should draw so that you fill the canvas area. Expand things and move them around, if necessary.

✔ Objects can overlap, with one apparently in front of another. You can change this arrangement by selecting one object and then choosing Graphics⇨Order.

✔ To delete an object, select it and then press the Delete key on your keyboard.

✔ Closed shapes are filled in by default and in a default color. To change this fill or make it go away, select an object and click on the Fill Attributes tool; choose None to remove the fill.

✔ To leave WP Draw, just click anywhere outside the drawing area (that is, in the text of your document). After a fairly long delay, the menu bar, Toolbar, and Power Bar are restored to their normal appearances. At this point, you may want to adjust the dimensions of your drawing. Click on the drawing to select it, and then click and drag any of the handles that appear around the drawing. You can also move the drawing while it is selected; click on it and drag it. If you decide that your drawing is too ugly for public viewing, just press the Delete key while the drawing is selected.

✔ To edit your drawing again, double-click on it.

## Using graphs and charts

Using the graph/chart tool, you can create a variety of data charts, including pie, bar, line, and other forms. No, that's not quite correct. Fill a gymnasium with economists, give them colored pens and rulers, lock the doors, and come back in 10 years. WordPerfect can do more graphing than these guys could do during that time. (If you had fed them, they might have had a fighting chance, of course, but why pass up such an opportunity?)

To create a chart in your document, you begin by clicking on the Chart button in the Toolbar or choosing Graphics⇨Chart. A chart obligingly appears in a panel in your document; and a separate window, called the *Datasheet,* gets splatted across the top of your document (see Figure 15-5). The Datasheet is a sort of spreadsheet or table where you put the data that you want to chart. WordPerfect draws the chart automatically from the data.

Mysteriously, a bar of drawing tools appears on the left side of the screen, but they are grayed out to indicate that you can't use them. The tools are present because, technically, when you create a chart in WordPerfect, you use WP Draw. Ignore them for now; later, you'll use them to change colors and line styles.

While you are using the WordPerfect charting feature, the menu bar, Toolbar, and Power Bar look different than they do when you're word processing. To exit the charting feature and return to the text of your document, just click any-where in the text. The menu bar, Toolbar, and Power Bar return to normal. To return to the charting feature, double-click on the chart.

WordPerfect starts you with a bar-chart example. You can easily change to another kind of chart, if you want, and then substitute your own data for the example data, as we discuss in a minute.

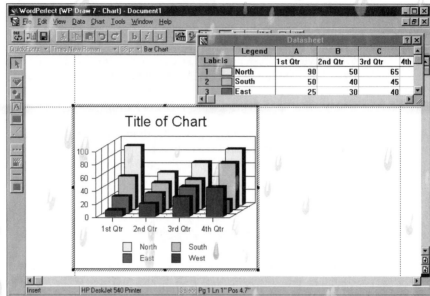

**Figure 15-5**:
WP Draw in
chart mode.

You can learn a lot about how WordPerfect charts data by examining the Datasheet and the chart. Notice that Labels (the top row of the Datasheet) places labels along the horizontal axis in the chart. Also notice that each row of data in the Datasheet has its own color, which matches the color of the data in the chart. Observe that the words in the Legend column (the leftmost column in the Datasheet) appear in the Legend box in the chart.

To make the sample chart into *your* chart, follow these steps:

1. **Change the chart to the type that you want.**

   Click on the Power Bar button that is initially labeled Bar Chart; then click on a chart type in the menu that drops down. If you want excitement in your life, you can also choose among screaming-color graphical representations of these variants by clicking on Gallery in this menu. Enjoy the riotous color of the chart gallery in the Data Chart Gallery that appears. Click on the Chart Type that you want, such as Line. Enjoy the colorful variants that are displayed. Click on one that you like; then click on the OK button in this dialog box.

2. **Delete the sample data.**

   Click on the title bar of the Datasheet window (which says Datasheet). Each little rectangle in the Datasheet that contains a word or number is a *cell.* Delete the values in individual cells by clicking on them, pressing the Delete key, and clicking in the Clear dialog box that appears. To delete a rectangular group of cells, click on the cell in the upper left corner of the data to be deleted; hold down the mouse button; and drag the mouse to extend the highlight to the lower right corner of the data. Release the mouse button and then press the Delete key on your keyboard. Click on OK again in the Clear dialog box.

3. **Click on individual cells and type your own data, legends, and labels.**

Expand the Datasheet window, if you need to, by clicking and dragging its edges.

4. **To put your own title on the chart, double-click on the title (which initially reads Title of Chart).**

In the Titles dialog box that appears, click in the text box that contains the words Title of Chart; change the text there; and then press the Enter key.

The Toolbar, Power Bar, and menu bar have selections that allow you to change the chart type (to, say, a line chart or pie chart), the style (3-D versus 2-D, for example), and other appearances. As always, if you position your mouse pointer on any button, WordPerfect displays the button's name and description. The first thing that you can try, if you want to change the way something looks in the graph, is to double-click on it. This works particularly well for things such as the *axis lines* (the horizontal and vertical lines that label the numbers in the graph). You get a dialog box with about a million options that allow you to control every aspect of the axis. Happy exploring!

There are more straightforward ways of changing one thing or another in the graph, in case you don't want to wrestle with each and every option. Here they are:

✔ **To change the chart type:** Click on the button on the Power Bar that is initially labeled Bar Chart (this is the Data Chart Types button). Click on any chart type listed in the menu that drops down. To choose among a visual selection of charts, click on Gallery in this menu.

✔ **To change from 3-D to 2-D:** Click on the button on the Toolbar that has a cube icon on it. (This is the 3-D Chart button.)

✔ **To change the line color and style, fill color and pattern, text color, or legend-box appearance:** Click on the line, bar, or text. Suddenly, those WP Draw tools on the left side of the screen come alive. Use them to change the line color and style, just as you would if you had drawn those lines yourself.

✔ **To change the font:** Click on the text and then on the Font Selection button (initially labeled Arial) on the Power Bar to choose a font; the Font Sizes button (initially labeled 48) to choose a size; or the **b**, *i*, and/or u button on the Toolbar to choose a style.

✔ **To change the axis range and intervals:** Choose Chart⇨Axis⇨X or Chart⇨Axis⇨Primary Y to display the Axis Options dialog box for the X or Y axis.

In general, you can change something in a chart by double-clicking on it. WordPerfect then presents a dialog box (of which there are dozens) that allows you to make the changes.

✔ **Sizing your chart:** There are, of course, two ways to change the size of your chart. This is WordPerfect, after all. What's more interesting is that the two ways are different. The *right* way to change the size of your chart is to drag the black handles while the chart is active (that is, while it has the hashed black and white stripe around it). This will encourage WP Draw to redraw your chart in the amount of space that you gave it. We talk about the wrong way after you're done working on the graph.

✔ **Changing how things look on your chart:** In general, you can change something in a chart by double-clicking on it. WordPerfect then presents a dialog box (of which there are dozens) that allows you to make the changes.

When you're all done, click anywhere in the text area of your document. After a rather long delay, your WordPerfect screen returns to normal. At this point, you may want to move your chart. Click on the chart to select it and then drag it around. You may also want to resize your chart by dragging the black handles at the corners — after all, it's a WP Draw thing, right? Resist this temptation. This is the wrong way to resize a chart. Although WordPerfect will resize the chart this way for you, instead of ending up with a nice-looking chart, you get a chart that looks as though you printed it on Silly Putty and stretched it out (which is sort of what you did). As we said a couple of paragraphs ago, select your chart by double-clicking on it and then resize it. If you decide that your chart is just too ugly to live, press the Delete key while the chart is selected.

# Working with Text Boxes

Suppose that you're reading a serious article — in *People* magazine, for example — about a celebrity ("Tom Hanks: Does He Really Hanker After Meg?"). In the corner of the page, bordered in fuschia, are two columns of text about some frivolous, annoying peripheral subject, such as "Tom Hanks and Cher: Separated at Birth?" Guess what? You, too, can make annoying sidebars such as this one in your document by using text boxes.

To create a text box, follow these steps:

1. **Choose Graphics⇨Text Box or click on the Text Box button on the Toolbar (it has the letter *A* on it).**

   Your mouse pointer changes to a hand holding a rectangle. When you click and drag this cursor diagonally, a dashed-line rectangle appears. This rectangle defines the location and size of your text box.

   If you don't see a hand-holding-a-rectangle pointer, but instead immediately see a text box, that's OK; just continue with Step 3.

**2. Click and drag to draw the text box.**

One of those frame gizmos appears, as it does when you insert graphics. This time the frame has thick bars at the top and bottom and no line connecting the handles (the little black squares). This frame is your text box. In the text box, a blinking cursor invites you to type text.

**3. Type the text that you want to box.**

You can format this text by using the Format commands, just as you would format any other text. You can even put text in columns. Don't try to use the Format commands to change the border of the text box, though; all you get are boxes within boxes.

Text is automatically centered between the top and bottom bars. If the text box is the wrong length or width, don't worry about it now; just type the text. You can change the box dimensions when you're done.

**4. To change the gory details of how the box looks, choose Graphics⇨Edit Box.**

We talked about the Edit Box in a sidebar earlier in this chapter. If you skipped it then, it's worth reading now; there's a lot of good stuff in that box.

**5. To leave the text box, click anywhere in the normal text of your document.**

At this point, you may want to adjust the dimensions of your text box. Click once on the text box to select it; then click and drag any of the handles that appear around the box. You can also move the text box while it is selected; click on it and drag it. If you decide that your sidebar is too annoying to live, just press the Delete key while the text box is selected.

To edit your boxed text, double-click on it.

# Working with Tables

When it comes to tables in WordPerfect, guess what? Yup — overkill again. WordPerfect is a word processor that swallowed a spreadsheet program. It can perform such tasks as automatically compute sums of columns and rows. It can, in fact, automatically compute the standard deviation of the arc tangent of the logarithm of the net present value of your mortgage, over multiple random variations of the interest rate.

Fortunately, for those of us who would just as soon leave spreadsheets to the accounting department, WordPerfect also does ordinary tables. It even makes them easy to create.

## Making tables with Table QuickCreate

The fastest way to create a table is to use the Table QuickCreate button on the Power Bar. Follow these steps:

1. **Click on the Power Bar button marked Table, and hold down the mouse button.**

   As you hold down the mouse button, a grid titled No Table appears. You can use this little grid to tell WordPerfect how big to make your table.

2. **Drag the mouse pointer down and to the right on the grid to highlight the number of rows and columns that you want.**

   The number of columns × rows appears above the grid (5 × 2 for a table with five columns and two rows, for example).

3. **Release the mouse button.**

   Your table is ready. Would Madame follow me? Walk this way, please.

To fill your table with goodies, simply click in a cell and type. You can use text, numbers, and even graphics, and you can format your text in the usual way by using the Format commands.

## Adding or deleting rows and columns

To make tables larger or smaller (that is, to increase or decrease the number of rows), you use the Table command on the main menu.

These steps show you how to add one or more rows or columns to your table:

1. **Click on any row or column that will adjoin your new row or column.**

   Click anywhere in the bottom row, for example, to add a new row to the bottom of your table.

2. **Choose Table⇨Insert.**

   The Insert Columns/Rows dialog box appears.

3. **In the Insert section of the dialog box, click on Columns (for columns) or Rows (for rows).**

   If you want more than one new row or column, type the number in the box next to Columns or Rows, or increment the number by clicking on the adjoining up- and down-arrow buttons.

4. **In the Placement section of the dialog box, click on Before if you want the row to go above (or the column to go to the left) of the cell that you selected in Step 1; otherwise, click on After.**

   To add a row to the bottom of your table, for example, click on After.

5. **Click on OK.**

To delete a row or column from your table, follow these steps:

1. **Click anywhere in the row or column that you want to delete.**

   For multiple rows or columns, click and drag to highlight them.

2. **Choose Table⇨Delete.**

   The Delete dialog box appears.

3. **In the Delete section, click on Columns or Rows.**

4. **Click on OK.**

To delete the entire table, begin by highlighting all the cells. Then, if you press the Delete key on your keyboard, the Delete Table dialog box appears. You can delete the whole table by clicking on Entire table. Or, if you prefer (and this is kind of a nice feature), you can delete only the table contents and leave the table framework behind by clicking on Table contents. Other weird options are available, too; ignore them. Then click on OK.

To delete the contents of a bunch of cells, highlight them and then press the Delete key. The Delete dialog box appears. Choose Cell contents, and click on OK.

## Changing column width

Changing individual column widths is simple. Click on the vertical line that divides the columns and drag it. The mouse pointer turns into a little horizontal-arrow gizmo, to tell you that you are moving a column divider. When you release the mouse button, the column divider moves over, so that the column on one side of the line gets wider and the other one gets narrower.

If you hold down the Ctrl key while you move the column divider, only the column to the left of the divider gets wider or narrower as you move the divider. The column to the *right* of the divider line stays the same size. All the columns to the right of the divider line just *move,* rather than get resized. This feature can be very handy.

Another convenient feature is WordPerfect's capability to set column width automatically to match the widest entry in the column.

Follow these steps:

**1. Click on a cell somewhere in the column you wish to resize.**

**2. Right-click to display a QuickMenu.**

**3. Choose Size Column to Fit.**

Changing the width of more than one column or the entire table is not hard, but it requires that you use a slightly intimidating dialog box. You can change other aspects of your table's appearance in this dialog box — such as left-right justification, alignment of numbers, column margins, table left-right justification on a page, and even text-style variations by column or row. But because SpeedFormat, discussed in the following section, does such a good job with all this, we won't go into it here.

Take a deep breath and follow these steps:

**1. To change the width of several columns, highlight the columns by clicking and dragging across them.**

**2. To change the column width of the entire table, click anywhere in the table.**

**3. Choose Table⇨Format or press Ctrl+F12.**

The Format dialog box appears.

The options across the top allow you to specify whether you want to format an individual cell, a column, a row, or the entire table.

**4. To change column width for the entire table, click on Table.**

**5. To change the column width for an individual column, click on Column.**

**6. Change the value in the Column Width box (the box marked Width).**

Click in the box and type a new number, or click on the increment–decrement arrow buttons. (If you cannot increase the width, the table may be set up to fill the width of the page.) If you fix a width by checking the Fixed width box, it cannot be changed by changes in the widths of page margins or of other columns.

**7. Click on OK or press Enter.**

## *Formatting with SpeedFormat*

Tables look best when certain rows or columns are specially formatted with bold or italics, or with colored shading. The fastest and coolest way to format your table is to use SpeedFormat. Follow these steps:

**1. Click anywhere within your table.**

**2. Choose Table⇨SpeedFormat.**

The SpeedFormat dialog box appears (see Figure 15-6), displaying a list of named table styles on the left side of the dialog box.

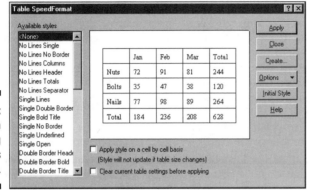

**Figure 15-6:**
Faster than a speeding format, it's SpeedFormat.

3. **Select a style in the A̲vailable Styles list.**

   SpeedFormat shows you an example of how that style looks. The example in the dialog box is just that — an example. SpeedFormat does not actually enter things into your table for you, typing titles or creating totals; it just formats the table with various fonts, row and column widths, alignments, and borders. You take care of actually typing stuff.

4. **Click on the A̲pply button.**

   (Or click on the C̲lose button if you decide not to use SpeedFormat after all.)

   SpeedFormat applies your chosen table style to your table.

If you later insert rows or columns into the table, WordPerfect automatically formats them in the same style. If you insert a column after a totals column, for example, WordPerfect formats the original totals column as an ordinary data column, and the new column takes the appearance of the original totals column. If you prefer that SpeedFormat leave its cotton-pickin' hands off your new rows or columns, click on the check box marked Apply s̲tyle on a cell by cell basis when you choose your style in the SpeedFormat dialog box.

You can use the same style consistently throughout this document and all subsequent ones by having WordPerfect use the style whenever you create a new table. In the SpeedFormat dialog box, choose a style, click on the I̲nitial Style button, and then click on Y̲es in the query box that appears. Click on C̲lose or A̲pply to close the SpeedFormat dialog box. (Remember — just because WordPerfect now uses this style by default, you're not stuck with it. You can always change to a different style. Simply repeat this procedure, using a new style.)

You can also create your own named style. Format your table the way you want it by using normal text formatting (such as italics or different fonts), or start with one of SpeedFormat's named styles and then modify it. Then, with your cursor anywhere within the table, display the SpeedFormat dialog box by choosing Table➪SpeedFormat. Click on the Create button; the Create Table Style dialog box that appears. Type a name for your style, and click on OK or press Enter when you're done. Your style now appears in the Available Styles list of the SpeedFormat dialog box.

## Dealing with incredibly complex spreadsheet-like tables

Spreadsheet-like tables don't have to be incredibly complex, but they can certainly get that way. Tables become like spreadsheet programs when they begin to calculate values automatically. To see how this process occurs in WordPerfect, we focus on a simple example of summing rows and columns. For more complicated stuff, use QuattroPro, which was included on your WordPerfect CD-ROM. You'll find a fine description in *WordPerfect Suite 7 For Dummies,* by Julie Adair King (IDG Books Worldwide, Inc.).

First, however, this list explains some basics for creating a spreadsheet-like table:

- Every cell in a table has a reference name that describes its row and column position. Rows use single letters, beginning with *A* in the top row. Columns use numbers, beginning with 1 in the left column. The top-left cell, therefore, is A1, and so on. Users of Lotus 1-2-3 and other spreadsheet programs should feel right at home.

- The calculations are based on formulas that are entered (in a special, invisible way) in the cell in which you want the answer to appear. To add cells A1 and B1 and put the answer in C1, for example, the formula A1+B1 must be specially stuffed into cell C1. We talk more about this subject in a minute.

Look at the simple budget shown in Figure 15-7. It has sums of columns and even a little division and subtraction to calculate the percentage change from year to year.

It's pretty hard to tell that formulas, not numbers, are entered in the total rows and right column. The only way to tell, in fact, is to turn on the Formula Bar. To turn on the Formula Bar, which allows you to enter or see formulas, choose Table➪Formula Bar. (Click on the Formula Bar's Close button to make the bar go away.)

The white box on the left side of the bar shows you which table WordPerfect thinks you're in (such as A, B, or C, which WordPerfect uses to keep track of tables) and in which cell your cursor is located. In Figure 15-7, that location is Table A, cell C14 — the sum of the FY96-97 expenses.

The WordPerfect Formula bar

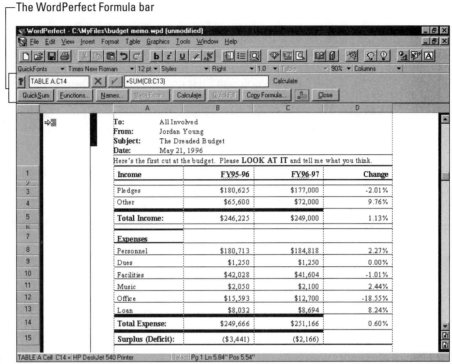

The other white box shows you the formula in this cell: SUM(C8:C13). The colon means "through," so this formula means "Sum cells C8 through C13." (Does this look like a spreadsheet formula, or what?)

To create this formula, click in the box and type the formula, or click on the QuickSum button. If you type the formula, click on the adjoining check-mark button to test the formula and insert it into the cell.

The QuickSum button is kind of magical. It inserts a formula for the sum of cells either above or to the left of the cell in which you're putting the formula. QuickSum is pretty intelligent about doing this correctly (it's not at all a dim sum), but sometimes, it guesses wrong about what you want.

Try it. If the QuickSum button guesses wrong, you can always edit the formula in the formula box. (Don't forget to click on the check-mark button when you finish.)

Values must already be in the cells for the QuickSum button to work. Put the values in first and then use the QuickSum button.

To get your numbers to look as pretty as ours do in Figure 15-7, with dollar signs and stuff, click in a cell that you want to format and then choose Table⇨Numeric Format or press Alt+F12. The Properties for Table Numeric

Format dialog box appears (catchy name, huh?). This dialog box allows you to format an individual cell or a column or the entire table. Rather than fool with the details of how to format your numbers, WordPerfect has defined some number types such as fixed-decimal-point numbers, scientific, currency, and accounting. Choose the number type you want and trust that WordPerfect will make your numbers look right. If it doesn't, you can always specify a different number type. In the Numeric Format dialog box, specify whether you want to format the Cell that your cursor is in, the Column, or the entire Table. Click on a selection in the Available types section (check out the example in the Preview section) and then click on the OK button.

To perform multiplication and other simple calculations, such as computing the percentage change year to year, you can use these symbols in your formulas:

- ✔ * (Multiply)
- ✔ / (Divide)
- ✔ + (Plus)
- ✔ – (Minus)

You can access other formulas by clicking on the Functions button in the formula bar, but hey — use QuattroPro itself. This stuff is pretty heady for a mere word processing program to be doing.

# Chapter 16

# Using Templates

## In This Chapter

▶ Learning about templates

▶ Using the templates that come with WordPerfect

▶ Making your own template

▶ Editing a template

*C*onfess — you have been plagiarizing, haven't you? Plagiarizing yourself, that is.

Nearly everyone who writes much, especially for business, ends up stealing from documents that have already been written to make new ones. Who wants to go to all the hassle of laying out a business letter to fit properly on the letterhead, for example, every time she writes a new letter? No, thanks. So what do you do? You probably begin with an older letter, change the name and address, and delete the text. The problem is trying to keep the formatting, text, and graphics that you want to keep and still replace other text.

Templates can help you solve this problem in a better way. Templates are among those ideas, such as frozen pie crusts, that can be a real convenience — but mostly only as long as somebody else makes them. If you have to make them yourself, be sure that you make a large amount of pie, or else it's not worth the effort.

## What Are Templates?

*Templates* are prototypes for different types of documents. WordPerfect includes many templates that are predesigned; you can also design and use your own. Templates are sort of like blank forms. They don't necessarily contain text, though. A template can contain only a collection of the particular fonts and format styles for a particular type of document, or it can contain all the text of your boilerplate contract.

Whenever you create a new document, WordPerfect uses a template. The blank document that you see when you start WordPerfect is (unknown to you) based on a template called standard. If you create a new document by clicking on the New Blank Document button on the Toolbar (the one that looks like a blank page with the corner turned down), WordPerfect again uses that standard template. If you start a new document by choosing File⇨New, however, WordPerfect explicitly asks you what template you want to use.

If you don't care for WordPerfect's prebuilt templates, you can create your own. You may want a template for letters that specifies, for example, that the font will be 10-point Times Roman. A template for product announcements may use 14-point Helvetica for titles and 12-point type for other text. A template for a newsletter, however, may also contain title text, a logo graphic, and three-column formatting, in addition to specified fonts.

For most practical purposes, though, you cannot do much more with a template than you can do by creating an ordinary document as a prototype, reusing it (opening it and changing the text) every time you want to write a similar document, and being careful to use Save As to save your new documents with new names. If the template stuff is too weird for you, just use this method.

## Using Templates

Talking about using templates is like talking about using air; it's not like you have much choice in the matter. All documents use templates. As we mentioned earlier in this chapter, you use something called the standard template every time you create a new document. There's not much in the standard template — at least, not much as it comes out of the box from WordPerfect (you can change it, though). Mostly, the standard template contains the initial paragraph,

---

### A trick if you decide not to create your own templates

If you make up an ordinary document that you reuse instead of a template, you can tell WordPerfect not to allow you to write on top of it. That way, when you customize the document and forget to use Save As, and use the Save command instead, WordPerfect complains that you are not allowed to write on your prototype document. Those of us who are a little absentminded find this reminder to be very useful.

Create your document and save it normally. Then choose File⇨Save As, find your file in the dialog box, and highlight it. Then choose File⇨Properties from the Save As dialog box menu. At the bottom of the dialog box that appears is a section labeled Attributes. Click on the Read-Only attribute; then click on OK. In the future, if you try to save on top of this file, WordPerfect complains. If you find that you want to modify the document, just deselect the Read-Only attribute before you try to save it.

character, and page formatting that WordPerfect uses for your documents. If you're having to change your fonts and other formatting every time you create a new document, you probably should edit the standard template; see "Editing or Deleting Templates" later in this chapter.

To use any template other than the standard one, use the File⇨New command. Follow these steps:

**1. Choose File⇨New.**

The New Document dialog box appears, as shown in Figure 16-1.

**Figure 16-1:**
The New
Document
dialog box
asks you to
choose a
template.

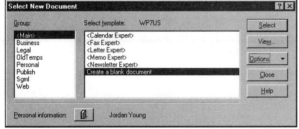

**2. Choose a template group from the Group list.**

WordPerfect has lots of templates for different purposes, such as business or legal documents and envelopes. Click on one of these groups, and the templates in that group are displayed in the big box on the right (the Select Template list).

**3. In the Select Template list, click on the template that you want to use.**

If you're not sure which template you want, you can get a rough idea of what each one looks like. Click once on a template name to highlight it and then click on the View button. A special View window appears, displaying a crude image of the template. (Don't be put off by its appearance; the template actually looks much better than that.) To peek at another template without putting away the View window, click once on that template's name. To put away the viewer, click on the Close button (that's the *X* in the top-right corner) in the View window's title bar.

**4. Click on the OK button.**

As Figure 16-1 shows, many templates other than the standard one usually are listed in the New Document dialog box. These templates came with WordPerfect; read the following section before you try to use them.

## Where do templates live?

The directory that is usually used for templates (both WordPerfect's and your own) is C:\Corel\Office7\Template. You can change this directory by choosing the Edit⇨Preferences⇨File command (see Chapter 20).

# Templates That Come with WordPerfect

WordPerfect supplies a bunch of templates that, like supermarket frozen-pie crusts, can be conveniently filled in with anything that you want as you use them.

These templates, shown in the following list, include fairly useful stuff:

| | |
|---|---|
| Signs | Invoices |
| Résumés | Memo forms |
| Legal forms | Press releases |

These templates also serve as examples of the clever things that you can do in WordPerfect. Just keep in mind that professional templatologists made these templates, so don't get carried away trying to do this stuff; it takes a long time to get some of the tricks they use to work correctly.

WordPerfect also has more sophisticated templates called *Experts,* which, by asking you to make certain choices, help you build custom documents step by step. The Experts in WordPerfect 7 include:

| | |
|---|---|
| Calendar | Fax |
| Letters | Memos |
| Newsletters | |

Some strange and wondrous things happen when you use a template. For many of the templates, a program of some sort begins to run when you select the template. This program is typically rather slow, so you may have to wait a while. In ordinary, non-Expert templates, this program is called a *macro.* (You may notice some mention of various macros on the status bar at the bottom of the WordPerfect window; you also may notice a WordPerfect Macro Facility icon at the bottom of your PC screen.) In Expert templates, the program is a Corel Office *QuickTask.* The program's job is to prompt you for certain information that is filled in automatically.

TIP

## "I can't edit the dang text!"

There's a good reason why you cannot edit some of the text that templates create. To prevent edits in certain areas, the clever people who made these templates put the text in a cell in a table and locked it. To determine whether that's your problem, look at the Power Bar and see whether the button that controls tables is grayed out. If it is, you are in a table, and the text may be locked.

To unlock the text, put your cursor inside the table by moving the mouse pointer into a cell and clicking the (left) mouse button.

Once you're in the table, choose Table⇨Format. This step displays the Format dialog box for tables. Click on the Table tab at the top. At the bottom of the dialog box, click on the box labeled Disable Cell Locks so that it shows a check mark. Then click on the OK button and wait. You should now be able to edit the text anywhere in the table.

Some templates require personal information. It's not that WordPerfect is nosy; it's just that some documents, such as fax cover sheets, normally display personal data, such as your name and address. The first time you use one of these templates, WordPerfect announces that it's about to allow you to personalize your templates. When you see this announcement, click on OK (not that you have much choice). Fill out the Enter Your Personal Information dialog box that appears next and click on OK there. WordPerfect stores this information for future use.

WordPerfect may also display a variety of other dialog boxes, depending on which template you choose. These boxes request information that is filled in for just this particular instance of template use. The newsletter templates, for example, request an issue number (for the issue of the newsletter) and a date. The dialog boxes typically also have a button (Personal Info) that allows you to change the personal information.

If you cancel out of any of these information-gathering dialog boxes (or press the Esc key), you have to fill in information yourself. There's usually no trick to this; just highlight the stuff in brackets ([ ] or < >) and type new text. If you have trouble deleting or changing something, it may be locked in a table (refer to the sidebar titled "I can't edit the dang text!").

The Power Bar may change. The designer of the template has the option to change this bar to suit the nature of the template. If a table has spreadsheet-like calculations, for example, there may be a Calc Doc button that updates the calculations.

# Creating Templates

Although it's pretty tricky to create the sort of interactive templates that WordPerfect offers, in which WordPerfect asks questions and fills in the blanks, making simple templates that are like prototype documents is pretty easy. One way to create a template is to begin with a document. Suppose that you want to make a template for business letters that will go on your preprinted corporate letterhead. You have to position the text so that it doesn't overprint the logo and has the correct margins.

Go ahead and write a document in the normal way. Fool with the layout until you get it right. (Chapter 18 has some tips on how to lay out various documents.) Press Ctrl+Shift+F3 to display the paragraph marks if they're not visible. Choose View⇨Page so that you can see exactly what you're doing. Set up the margins. If you want, set up styles for each type of paragraph or character format (refer to Chapter 11 for information about styles).

This list shows a few tips for creating a template from a document:

- ✔ When you finish creating the document, replace with little notes any text that you don't want to appear every time — perhaps in brackets, such as [Addressee's Name] and [Addressee's Company]. In WordPerfect's built-in templates, these bracketed notes are filled in automatically; that doesn't happen in your templates unless you create your templates by editing one of WordPerfect's templates (see the following section).

- ✔ So that you don't change the font when you replace text with notes, don't delete the existing text; just highlight the text and start typing replacement text over it.

- ✔ Don't change items that should always appear — your name below the signature area and the *Dear* in the salutation of a business-letter template, for example.

Finally, choose the File⇨Save As command to save the document as a template. Make sure that you save it in the template folder, not in the document folder. The easiest way to do this is to click in the Filename box and type C:\Corel\Office7\Template\ followed by the name of your new template, followed by the extension WPT (for *WordPerfect template*). (If your WordPerfect was installed somewhere else, you may need to search around for the Office7\Template folder; try using the Tree View button described in Chapter 14.) Now your template's filename appears in the New Document dialog box whenever you start a new document with File⇨New.

For information on adding a description to your template, see the following section. That section also gives you an alternative for creating your own template.

## It's not magic

The document that you get when you use a template is not a special document, even though it may look really cool. It's an ordinary WordPerfect document made up of text, tables, borders, and the like. It looks cool only because an official Very Clever Person created the template.

You can change the document, add stuff to it, delete stuff, and so on. But remember that you're changing just the document, not the template. To learn how to change the template, see the last section of this chapter, "Editing or Deleting Templates."

# *Editing or Deleting Templates*

Though templates may be analogous to the fill-your-own frozen pie crust in the supermarket, the ingredients of templates — unlike those of frozen pie crust — can be changed. (Anybody for a whole-wheat template?) Editing a template is a good way to create your own custom template.

To change a template, you have to open it first. Use the File⇨New command, as shown in these steps:

1. **Choose File⇨New.**

   The dialog box shown in Figure 16-1 appears.

2. **Choose a template group from the Group list, and click on the template that you want to edit in the Select Template box.**

   If you want to edit an existing template, check the description of the template in the middle of the dialog box. If you're still not sure which template you want, click on the View button in the New Document dialog box to produce a View window. Then click on any template filename to view that template. To close the View window, click on the Close button (the *X*) on the title bar.

3. **Click on the Options button and choose Edit Template from the drop-down menu.**

   Notice also the Delete Template option and the New Template option. Delete Template does what you think it does: deletes the highlighted template. New Template is just another way to begin making your own template. If you choose New Template, just type and format your template as you would any other document.

**4. Edit the template.**

Editing a template is just like editing a document, unless you try to use the advanced features, such as macros and objects. Anything that you change, including styles and any text that you add, appears in new documents that you create by using this template. Documents that you previously created by using this template, however, are not affected by these changes.

The easiest way to create a template that gets filled in automatically is to use an existing WordPerfect template that fills in the sort of information you want, such as [Addressee's Name]. Edit the template, retain the bracketed text as placeholders for the information to be filled in, and save the template under a new name. Text that is inside angle brackets (like <this>) is replaced with the personal data that you enter during customization. Bracketed information (like [this]) is requested by the Autofill macro whenever the template is used. You shouldn't change the text in the brackets because WordPerfect will be looking for that specific text, but you can move the bracketed items around.

If you're editing a WordPerfect template and run into trouble editing some text, it may be because the text is locked in a table. Refer to the sidebar titled "I can't edit the dang text!" earlier in this chapter.

Notice the new bar of buttons (oh, goody). For the most part, these buttons enable you to do vastly complicated things that we don't even want to think about.

**5. Click on the Exit Template button.**

WordPerfect asks whether you want to save the changes in your file. Click on Yes unless you have just been practicing your template skills and don't want to keep your work (or if you really messed up the template and don't want to save the changes).

# Chapter 17
# Creating Your Own Junk Mail

. . . . . . . . . . . . . . . . . . . . . . . . . . . . . . . . . . . . . . . . . . . . . .

## In This Chapter

▶ Generating tons of letters fast

▶ Creating a data file

▶ Creating a form file

▶ Merging your files

▶ Printing your data file

▶ Printing envelopes

. . . . . . . . . . . . . . . . . . . . . . . . . . . . . . . . . . . . . . . . . . . . . .

**D**on't you just *love* getting junk mail? Doesn't it warm your heart to know that some direct-mail marketing executive thinks enough of your buying (or donating) power to send you a cleverly personalized letter? Yes, JOHN, we know that you and the entire SMITH household really enjoy getting heaps of junk mail.

Seriously, though, there are times when what you really want to do is create junk mail. Perhaps you don't want to create the same kind of junk mail that gets sent to JOHN SMITH, but you want to use the same tools.

"What on earth are you thinking of?" you may ask. Think about the following situations:

✔ You receive a list of names or items or part numbers from someone. The other person went to all the trouble of putting the information in a computer file, maybe even in a WordPerfect document. Your job is to send a letter to each person, print a label for each item, or print a sheet for each part number. This is a time to use WordPerfect's junk-mail feature.

✔ You're keeping a list of people, but you need to print the list three ways: alphabetically, by last name; as a set of mailing labels; and by the age of the oldest child.

What's up with these two examples? In the first, you want to create a bunch of documents (letters or whatever) that are similar, from information that you got for someone else. You only want to do it one time, but a lot of items are in the list. If there are more than about 10, you probably ought to be using the WordPerfect junk-mail feature.

In the second example, you keep a small or medium number of names (or whatever), and every so often, you have to create two, three, or more kinds of lists from those names. The WordPerfect junk-mail feature — which we may as well call by its right name, *merge* — allows you to keep *one* list; make all your address changes, product updates, or whatever, in *one* place; and still create two, three, or more kinds of printouts.

You should be thrilled to hear that WordPerfect can help you out. Thanks to some pretty good engineering, the folks at WordPerfect took what used to be a tedious, nerdy job and turned it into something that most human beings can actually do. As is true of many things that a powerful program such as WordPerfect can do, you have to figure out when to allow WordPerfect to pretend to be a database and when to use the database features of Corel WordPerfect Suite 7 (kind of like deciding when to use table arithmetic, as described in Chapter 16, and when to use a spreadsheet). If you think that you need to use the database parts of Corel WordPerfect Suite 7, see *WordPerfect Suite 7 For Dummies* by Julie King (IDG Books Worldwide, Inc.).

Even better, if you want to create letters (or envelopes or mailing labels) for an address list, WordPerfect comes with an Address Book program that helps keep addresses on file for you, and it hooks right into WordPerfect.

# How Does the Junk-Mail Feature Work?

To create personalized junk mail, you need two documents: a data file and a form file.

The *data file* contains the stuff that you plan to put in each of your documents; you must enter this stuff in a special format. WordPerfect helps you do this by displaying a dialog box for your data file that allows you to fill in the blanks. If your data file contains only names and addresses, see the sidebar, "WordPerfect's been reading your little black book," later in this chapter. But if you have other information about the people in your list — the amount that they owe you, the name of their firstborn sons, or any other information that you may want to include in a form letter — you'll want to create your own data file. The data file is, in effect, a mini-database. Each piece of information is called a field. All the information about one person is called a record.

The *form file* contains the form letter. In place of a name or address, the form file contains *merge codes* that tell WordPerfect to use information from the data file. One of the most useful aspects of data files and form files is the fact that a single data file can feed several different form files. That way, the same data can appear in several different printouts. When someone's address changes, you don't have to change it on the mailing label and the address list and the family-tree listing, for example.

When you perform the merge, you tell WordPerfect to create one copy of the form file for each person in the data file. You can send this combined file directly to the printer or store it as a new third document.

So far, so good. We'll step through the procedure for creating a data file and a form file and then show you how to merge them. The procedure is not that bad, really, although it is a bit of work to set up.

The WordPerfect merge feature is cool, but it's not worth using unless you want to send a bunch of letters. For two or three letters (or even four or five), it's not worth the effort. For small jobs, type one letter and print it; then edit the address and print it again; and so on.

# Creating a Data File

When you choose Tools➪Merge or press Shift+F9, WordPerfect displays the dialog box shown in Figure 17-1.

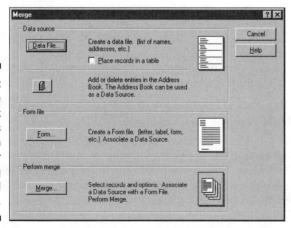

**Figure 17-1:** The Merge dialog box serves as Mission Control for creating personalized junk mail.

As you may have guessed, you click on the Data File button to create the data file. A little box just below the Data File button determines which of two formats your data file will be in:

- **Ugly** shows each piece of information in the data file on a separate line, with lots of weird-looking WordPerfect merge codes in various colors.
- **Tasteful** arranges the data-file information in a table, with one row of the table for each record and one column of the table for each field.

We show you pictures of these two formats a little later in this chapter. You should use whichever format you prefer, of course, but if you use the ugly method, you're nuts.

## Creating a data file

Now follow these steps to make a data file:

1. **Choose Tools⇨Merge.**

   You see the Merge dialog box (refer to Figure 17-1).

2. **If you want to create a tasteful (not ugly) data file, click on the Place Records in a Table check box so that a check mark appears in it.**

   Take our word for it: You want to create a tasteful data file.

3. **Click on the Data File button.**

   WordPerfect displays the Create Data File box. We talk about this box in a minute.

   WordPerfect *may* first display a box labeled Create Merge File. If so, you have two choices: Use file in active window and New Document Window. Unless you're converting an existing file, choose New Document Window. If you've already typed information that you want to merge into your junk mail, choose Use file in active window.

4. **Decide which pieces of information (fields) you want to store about each person (record).**

   If all you have are Name, Address, City, State, and ZIP fields, use the Address Book. Look at the upcoming sidebar, "WordPerfect's been reading your little black book." If you also have other information and want to create your own data file, you may want to have separate First Name and Last Name fields. Do this so that your letter can begin with *Dear Joe* and mention *the Bloggs family* later. Other fields can be something like the amount that each family donated last year in a church-donations letter or the child's name and the school's start date for a letter from a daycare center. Figure 17-2 shows the fields we use to send letters to your (hypothetical) day-care clients.

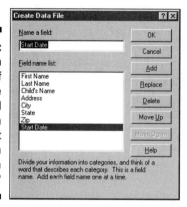

**Figure 17-2:**
Which
pieces of
intrusive
personal
information
do you want
to include in
your form
letters?

**5. Enter the names of the fields.**

For each field, type the name in the Name a field box. When you choose Add (or press Alt+A or the Enter key), the field name appears in the Field name list.

**6. Choose OK when you finish naming fields.**

WordPerfect does three things to prepare the data file for your use:

✔ First, WordPerfect puts information about your fields at the beginning of the document. If you choose the ugly method, you see special merge codes, which are visible even though you aren't using the Reveal Codes window. You can see FIELDNAMES and ENDRECORD codes at the top of the document window. If you choose the tasteful method, you see a table with one column for each field.

✔ Second, WordPerfect obscures your view of the document with a fill-in-the-blanks data-entry screen. (That's computerspeak for a dialog box that has blanks for each field that you created.) Figure 17-3 shows the Quick Data Entry dialog box that WordPerfect created for our hypothetical daycare center.

✔ Third, WordPerfect displays another row of buttons — in this case, the Merge feature bar. (Sounds like a swinging singles joint, doesn't it?) Figure 17-4 illustrates how boring the Merge feature bar really is.

Now your data file is ready to use.

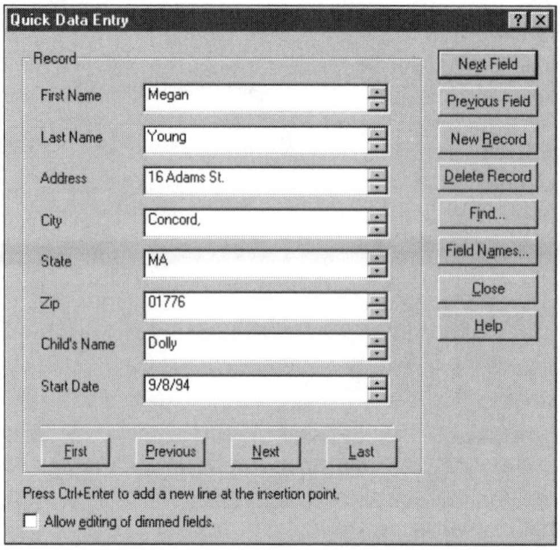

**Figure 17-3:**
WordPerfect's
Quick Data
Entry screen
for merge
data.

**Figure 17-4:**
The Merge
feature bar
as it
appears at
the top of
a merge
data file.

## Entering the data — at last

Before you can get WordPerfect to fill in the blanks and generate tons of letters, labels, address lists, or whatever, you have to tell it what to fill in the blanks with. Follow these steps:

**1. If the data file isn't already open, open it.**

If you just created the data file, it's still open.

**2. If the Quick Data Entry dialog box isn't visible, display it.**

Click on the Quick Entry button on the Merge feature bar, which is the row of buttons just above the top of your document. Refer to Figure 17-4.

**3. Fill in a value for each field to create one record.**

Click on the First button to see the first record. Wherever you are, you can fill in or review all the facts about one person (or record). To move down a field, press Tab, press Enter, or click on Next Field; to move up, press Shift+Tab.

**4. Click on New Record to start the next record (the next person).**

When you get to the last field in a record, pressing Enter is the equivalent of clicking on this button.

**5. When you finish entering all the facts (field data) about all the people (record data), click on Close.**

WordPerfect asks whether you want to save the changes to disk. Unless you have been typing names just to see your fingers move, answer Yes. WordPerfect then displays the Save Data File As dialog box so that you can enter the filename. (Oddly, WordPerfect displays this dialog box every time you add records; it doesn't assume that you want to continue to use the same filename. Go figure.)

**6. Enter a filename and choose OK.**

You can type just the name part, and WordPerfect uses the extension .DAT for your file. If you are updating an existing data file, WordPerfect becomes alarmed and warns you that a file already has that name. Of course, it does — it's the file that you are updating! When WordPerfect asks whether you want to replace it, choose Yes.

When you enter information in a data file, be sure to enter it as you want it to appear in your letters.

## Creating ugly data files

If you chose the ugly method, you can now see the fields, each on a separate line. Between one record and the next are an ENDRECORD merge code and a page break. At the end of each field is the word ENDFIELD (another merge code). Figure 17-5 shows a record or two in ugly format. To see more than one record at a time, choose View⇨Draft so that page breaks appear as double horizontal lines. Otherwise, with only one record per page, most of what you see is blank.

If you don't like your screen to be cluttered with these long merge codes, you can display them as little blobs. Click Options on the Merge feature bar (the button on the right). A menu that appears probably has a check mark before the Display Codes command, which indicates that right now, WordPerfect displays the names of merge codes in your document. If you choose Display As Markers, the code names are replaced by little red diamonds — much more tasteful.

If you choose Hide Codes, the code names disappear, but this idea usually is a bad one — in case you edit the records in the document, you should be able to verify that the ENDFIELD codes remain at the end of each field.

| | | | | | | |
|---|---|---|---|---|---|---|
| End Field | End Record | Merge Codes... | Quick Entry... | Merge... | Go to Form | Options ▼ |

FIELDNAMES(First Name;Last Name;Address;City;State;Zip;Child's Name;Start Date)
ENDRECORD

MeganENDFIELD ¶
YoungENDFIELD ¶
16 Adams StENDFIELD ¶
ConcordENDFIELD ¶
MAENDFIELD ¶
01776ENDFIELD ¶
DollyENDFIELD ¶
9/8/96ENDFIELD ¶
ENDRECORD

ChristopherENDFIELD ¶
LevineENDFIELD ¶
122 Mass. AveENDFIELD ¶
ActonENDFIELD ¶
MAENDFIELD ¶
01720ENDFIELD ¶
KatyENDFIELD ¶
9/10/96ENDFIELD ¶
ENDRECORD

**Figure 17-5:**
Records in a
data file,
with lots of
ugly merge
codes, as
seen in draft
mode.

## Creating tasteful data files

If you chose the tasteful method, you see a table like the one shown in Figure 17-6. For more information about using tables, refer to Chapter 15.

Corel WordPerfect - C:\MyFiles\Day Care List Table.dat (unmodified)

File  Edit  View  Insert  Format  Table  Graphics  Tools  Window  Help

QuickFonts ▼ Times New Roman ▼ 12 pt ▼ Styles ▼ Left ▼ 1.0 ▼ Table ▼ 100% ▼ Columns ▼

| | | | | | | |
|---|---|---|---|---|---|---|
| Row ▼ | Column ▼ | Merge Codes... | Quick Entry... | Merge... | Go to Form | Options ▼ |

| First Name | Last Name | Address | City | State | Zip | Child's Name | Start Date |
|---|---|---|---|---|---|---|---|
| Megan | Young | 16 Adams St. | Concord, | MA | 01776 | Dolly | 9/8/96 |
| Christopher | Levine | 122 Mass. Ave. | Acton, | MA | 01720 | Katy | 9/10/96 |

TABLE A Cell E1*    HP DeskJet 540 Printer    Select Pg 1 Ln 1.08" Pos 5.17"

**Figure 17-6:**
Records in a
data file in a
nice, neat
table.

## Making corrections

If your life is like our lives, sooner (rather than later), you'll have to fix up the addresses that you entered or delete the names of people whose children have decided not to attend the daycare center. You can edit the data file as though it were a normal document, but you have to be careful not to mess up the `ENDFIELD` and `ENDRECORD` merge codes. A better way to make all your corrections is to use the Quick Data Entry dialog box, which you display by clicking on the Quick Entry button on the Merge feature bar.

# WordPerfect's been reading your little black book

Well, if you typed the book on your PC, WordPerfect's been reading your little black book. WordPerfect has a million features. One feature allows WordPerfect to read directly from your address book (that is, the addresses you typed into Corel Address Book 7, a program that comes with WordPerfect). To make things more confusing, there's *another* address book that comes with Windows 95: Microsoft Exchange. WordPerfect can read from that address book, too.

To open the Address Book, choose Tools⊏>Address Book in WordPerfect, or click on the Toolbar button that looks like a book. A whole adventure in software begins in a window like the one shown in the figure.

The two tabs at the top of the white section indicate that there are two address books to look at. One (My Addresses) was created by WordPerfect for you to store your addresses in. The second (Frequent Contacts) is managed by WordPerfect. Ignore it (or if you really care, see *WordPerfect Suite 7 For Dummies*).

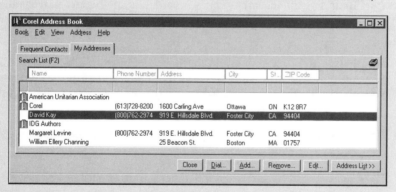

At the bottom of the Address Book window is a row of buttons. Click on the Add button, and Corel Address Book 7 asks whether you want to add a Person or an Organization. For merge, choose Person and click on OK. You see a form that allows you to fill in a lot of information about the person. Again, we won't go into the intricacies of this box. But for merge purposes, the person's name, organization, and address are the important information. (Actually, if you want to add Kid's Name and Start Date fields, you can. Click on the Custom button and hack your way through the wilderness yourself.) Click on OK when you finish, or click on New if you want to add another person. We show you how to use these entries in your merge documents in a minute.

You can get Corel Address Book 7 to look at your Microsoft Exchange addresses by choosing Edit⊏>Preferences from the Corel Address Book menu. If you have Microsoft Exchange installed on your computer, you can select it as your preferred profile; simply click on it and then click OK. The next time you start Address Book 7, you'll be looking at your Microsoft Exchange addresses. Aside from that, they work pretty much the same as the Corel Address Book 7 addresses.

That's all there is to using the Address Book to store your names and addresses. We highly recommend using it because it's created by WordPerfect and helps keep all your names well organized. You could do the same things yourself with a merge data document, but that would be more work.

While you are using the Quick Data Entry dialog box, you can do the following things:

- To find a record, click on the F̲ind button. (It doesn't matter which field your cursor is in when you do this; WordPerfect looks for the information in all the fields.) You see a Find Text dialog box that looks and works much like the familiar Find and Replace Text dialog box (refer to Chapter 5 if you don't recognize it).

- To move from record to record, click on the F̲irst, L̲ast, N̲ext, and P̲revious buttons near the bottom of the Quick Data Entry dialog box.

- To delete the record in the dialog box, click on the D̲elete Record button. But watch out — WordPerfect doesn't ask for any confirmation before blowing the record away. Click with care!

- To add more records, click on New R̲ecord.

- To update the information in a record, find the record, move your cursor to the field that you want to correct, and edit it.

When you finish using the Quick Data Entry dialog box, click on C̲lose. WordPerfect asks whether you want to save your work. Choose Y̲es. Choose the filename (probably the same filename that it has had all along) and reassure WordPerfect that you do want to replace the preceding version with the corrected version. Sheesh!

When you close the Quick Data Entry dialog box, the additions and corrections also appear in the document.

## Creating a Form File

After you create a list of recipients for your form letter, you can type the letter. The document that contains the form letter is called the *form file*.

A form file is a regular old WordPerfect document. But in place of the name and address at the top of the letter, you enter funky-looking merge codes, as shown in these steps:

1. **Choose T̲ools⇨M̲erge and click on the F̲orm button.**

   Unless the current document is blank, WordPerfect wants to know whether you want to create a new document to contain the form letter or whether you want to use the document that's on-screen.

2. **Choose N̲ew Document Window and then choose OK.**

   If you have already typed the letter, and if that letter is the current document, choose U̲se file in active window instead.

Either way, WordPerfect asks which data file will provide the data for this form letter. You create the form file by using the Create Form File dialog box shown in Figure 17-7.

**3. Enter the name of your data file and then choose OK.**

If you are using your Address Book as a data file, click the Associate an address book button. Right below that button, click Personal Address Book if you want to select a different address book (such as WordPerfect's My Addresses). You also can click on the little file-folder button at the right end of the box, which allows you to choose the filename and directory. If WordPerfect can't find your file, click on that button and browse around for the file. If you haven't created the data file yet, choose No Association.

WordPerfect opens a new document and displays the Merge feature bar just above it. When you are editing a form file, the merge bar contains different buttons than it does when you are working on a data file.

**Figure 17-7:**
Which document contains the names and addresses for this form letter?

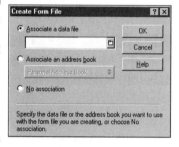

**4. Type any information that you want to appear before the date and the name of the addressee.**

Type the text for your letterhead, for example, if you'll be printing on blank paper. For a normal letter, the next thing that you want to see is today's date.

**5. Choose Date from the Merge feature bar.**

WordPerfect inserts a colorful DATE code into your document. When you merge this form file with a data file, today's date appears here.

**6. Press Enter to start a new line, and press Enter again to leave a space before the name and address.**

**7. Type any text that should appear before the first field, such as** Dear.

**8. Choose Insert Field from the Merge feature bar.**

WordPerfect displays the Insert Field Name or Number dialog box, shown in Figure 17-8. The dialog box lists all the fields that you defined in the data file that is associated with this form letter.

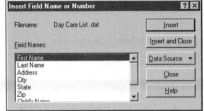

**Figure 17-8:**
Which
piece of
information
from the
data file do
you want
to use?

**9. Select the first field from the data file to appear in the form letter and then click on Insert.**

Select the First Name field, for example. WordPerfect inserts FIELD(First Name) in color. You're looking at a WordPerfect merge code, which displays each person's first name when you print the form letters. The dialog box is still visible, which is nice, because you have to use it a few more times.

**10. Type a space (to appear between the First Name and Last Name fields), select Last Name in the dialog box, and click on Insert again.**

Now codes for the First Name and Last Name fields appear in the form letter.

**11. Press Enter to start a new line.**

Continue in this vein by inserting codes and typing spaces, pressing Enter, or doing whatever between the codes, until you have laid out the entire address. Check out Figure 17-9 for an example.

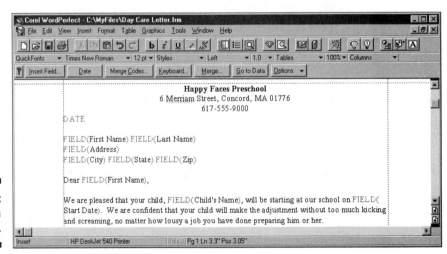

**Figure 17-9:**
Creating a
form file.

12. **Type your letter.**

You can use all the usual formats, fonts, and margins that you use in a normal letter. You can even include the contents of merge fields (JOHN, for example) in the body of the letter for that personalized touch.

13. **Save the document.**

Choose File➪Save As. It's best to type the filename and let WordPerfect worry about the three-letter extension. (The extension that WordPerfect uses is .FRM.)

You can create several form files for one data file. If your data file contains a list of people who owe you money, for example, you can make one form file that contains a polite letter requesting payment. A second form file can contain a letter using firmer language, and a third form file can contain the letter that tells your pal Vinnie whose legs to break.

When it comes time to print, you can print envelopes to go along with your letters. You can even print envelopes but no letters, but that's a little more complicated. We explain how to do both before the chapter's out.

What if you choose the wrong data file for this form letter? Or what if you create a new data file and want to use an existing form file? No problem. To associate a different data file with your form file, look on the Merge feature bar and choose Insert Field. Doing so displays the Insert Field Name or Number dialog box. Click Data Source and specify a new Data File or a new Address book and choose OK.

## Merging Your Files

After you have a data file and a form file, you're ready to merge. We know, folks, that this explanation is taking a while, but if you have a large number of letters to send, it's worth it. Here we go. Call the post office and tell them to stand back before you follow these steps:

1. **Choose Tools➪Merge and then click on the Merge button.**

WordPerfect displays the Perform Merge dialog box, shown in Figure 17-10.

2. **Enter the name of the form file.**

Click on the little button at the right end of the Form file box and choose Select File. WordPerfect allows you to select the filename and inserts the complete path name of the form file (C:\LETTERS\THREAT1.WPD, for example).

As soon as you enter the name of the form file, WordPerfect enters the name of the associated data file.

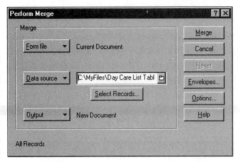

**Figure 17-10:**
Making junk
mail from a
data file and
a form file.

### 3. Tell WordPerfect where to put the resulting form letters.

Click on Output. We recommend the following choices:

- **<New Document>** (our favorite). WordPerfect makes a new document and sticks all the copies of your form letter in it for you to review before printing them.

- **<Printer>.** Choose this option to print the form letters without reviewing them. This choice is the "go for the gold" approach. You can waste a great deal of paper this way, however, if you have a typo in your form file.

### 4. Click on the Envelopes button.

WordPerfect gives you the option of tacking a bunch of envelopes to the end of your form letter. This option is useful if you plan to mail your letters. You should see the Envelope dialog box, similar to the one shown in Figure 18-1.

### 5. Type the return address or click on the button with the book on it to choose the address from your Address Book.

If you uncheck the Print Return Address check box, WordPerfect skips this part — useful if you have preprinted envelopes.

### 6. Click in the Mailing Addresses box and enter the merge codes to print addresses by using data in your data file.

Click on the Field button at the bottom of the dialog box to display the list of fields in data file. Select the first field from the data file to appear on the envelope (First Name, for example); then click on Insert. For this example, WordPerfect inserts FIELD(First Name).

### 7. Type a space (to appear between the First Name and Last Name fields); then click on Field, select Last Name, and click on Insert.

### 8. Press Enter to start a new line.

9. **Continue inserting codes and typing spaces, pressing Enter, or doing whatever between the codes until you have laid out the entire address.**

10. **Choose OK.**

    If you look carefully, you see that where the Perform Merge dialog box used to say All Records (as in Figure 17-11), it now says All Records; Envelope in the bottom-left corner. This means that every time you do a merge with this form file, WordPerfect adds envelopes to the end of the letters that it creates. If you change your mind, click on the Envelopes button again and select Cancel Envelope.

11. **Click on Merge.**

    WordPerfect makes one copy of your form file for each record in your data file and puts the results where you told it to put them.

    Figure 17-13 shows a letter to our hypothetical daycare center clients. All the letters are in this one new document, one per page. If you selected envelopes, all the envelopes come after all the letters.

12. **If your merged letters are in a new document, print the document.**

    If you added envelopes to your merge document, this step can be a little tricky unless you have a printer with a separate bin that you keep stocked with envelopes or a printer that is clever enough to ask for envelopes when it needs them. For the rest of us mortals, scan down through your document until you see the first envelope. Click on the envelope, and note the page number on the status bar (15, for example). Now print all the pages up to the first envelope (pages 1 through 14, in our example), put envelopes in the printer, and print pages 15 through 28, which are the envelopes.

You can look through the letters first to make sure that they look appropriately personal. You can even make changes in them so that they really are personalized. ("P.S. As you requested, we have added bars on the windows of our classrooms so that little Frederika will be sure to stick around.")

After you print your form letters, you can save the document that contains them or close it without saving it. After all, you can always create the letters again by repeating these merge steps.

# Printing Your Data File

If you want to print an address list of the people to whom you sent letters, you can print the data file. If your data file is in ugly format, it looks fairly stupid with all those merge codes in there. If your data file is in tasteful table format, it looks rather nice.

To hide the merge codes in ugly format, choose Options from the Merge feature bar and then choose Hide Codes.

---

## Creating envelopes without letters

Using the Perform Merge dialog box, you can create letters or letters with envelopes, but you can't create envelopes without letters. Don't ask us why. So here's how to do it:

Prepare your data file as you would normally. When it's done, prepare the form file just as you would for a letter. Then choose the Format⇨Envelope command to format your "letter" as an envelope. Insert the field codes just as you did for the envelopes when they were attached to your letter, but — and this is very important — click Append to Doc in the Envelopes dialog box. This option creates a form file that creates only envelopes.

When you perform the merge, make sure that the Perform Merge dialog box says All Records — not Envelopes — in the bottom-left corner. If it does, click on the Envelopes button in the Perform Merge dialog box, and cancel the automatic envelopes. Otherwise, you'll get two envelopes for each record.

# Chapter 18

# Recipes for Popular Documents

· · · · · · · · · · · · · · · · · · · · · · · · · · · · · · · · · · · · · · · · · · ·

*In This Chapter*

▶ Letters

▶ Memos

▶ Faxes

▶ Envelopes

▶ Mailing labels

▶ Booklets

▶ Books and other big documents

· · · · · · · · · · · · · · · · · · · · · · · · · · · · · · · · · · · · · · · · · · ·

*T*here's no point in reinventing the wheel. For years, the Great Minds of Word Processing have been contemplating the best ways to create many popular types of documents. This chapter contains recipes for whipping up crowd-pleasing documents in several standard styles.

If you frequently create documents in a standard format, you should think about creating a WordPerfect template that contains all the formatting (refer to Chapter 16).

## *Letters*

Every office has its own office style for letters, and we wouldn't presume to tell you how your letters should look. This section, however, offers some letter-writing tips.

## *Skipping space for the letterhead on stationery*

If you are printing on stationery, you have to leave a bunch of space at the top of the letter so that your text doesn't print on top of the letterhead. Use the following steps:

1. **Get out a ruler and measure how far down the page you want your letter to start.**

   That place is where you want the first piece of text (usually, the date) to appear.

2. **Make sure that guidelines are turned on and appear on your editing screen.**

   Use the View➪Guidelines command if you're not sure. Some of us like to have all the guidelines on all the time so that we can see what WordPerfect thinks it's doing to our documents.

3. **Click on the guideline at the top of the page and drag it down to where you want the first text to appear.**

   As you drag, a little yellow box appears, telling you exactly where your top margin is going to be. As soon as this box indicates that you've reached the correct position, release the mouse button.

This method works fine for one-page letters. But what if you are creating a letter that is two or more pages long? You don't want all that white space at the top of the second and subsequent pages; that would just waste space. No problem! As you're typing along, when you get to the top of the second page, simply drag the guideline back up to where you want it.

This is WordPerfect, so of course there are two ways to do everything. If you want to create a template (described in Chapter 16), you'll want WordPerfect to know that the spacing on the first page is different from the spacing on the second page.

To do so, use WordPerfect's Advance feature. With your cursor at the top of the first page, choose Format➪Typesetting➪Advance (don't ask us what advancing down the page has to do with typesetting). WordPerfect displays the Advance dialog box. For the Vertical Position option, choose From Top of Page, and fill in the Vertical Distance box with the number of inches (or centimeters) that you want to move down the page. When you choose OK, WordPerfect inserts an Advance code (VAdv, actually) that moves down to the position you specified.

## *Printing your own letterhead*

If you are too cheap to buy stationery (as we are), you can print your own as part of the letter. Using WordPerfect's many fonts, lines, boxes, and other effects, you can create a pretty snazzy letterhead; you can even include graphics. When you create a letterhead that you like, save it as a template (refer to Chapter 16) so that all your letters can include it automatically.

## *Dating your letter*

Be sure to make WordPerfect enter today's date rather than type it yourself; press Ctrl+D.

## *Numbering the pages*

For multiple-page letters, it is imperative that you number the pages. Use the page-numbering, headers, or footers feature (described in Chapter 8). Be sure to tell WordPerfect *not* to number the first page.

# *Memos*

Everything we said about letters goes for memos, too. If you don't use pre-printed memo paper, check out WordPerfect's ready-to-use templates (described in Chapter 16). Simply press Ctrl+T to start a new document.

The memo group includes four awesome memo formats, named Contemporary, Cosmopolitan, Traditional, and Trimline. You also have a Memo Expert that can help you design your own memo.

# *Faxes*

If you have a boring, old-fashioned fax machine into which you feed boring, old-fashioned pieces of paper, we don't have much to suggest. You may want to look at the four WordPerfect templates for faxes; these templates are very trendy and designerish. (See Chapter 16 for more information on templates in general.) Or use the Fax Expert; press Ctrl+T and choose the fax group of templates.

If your computer has a fax modem, however, you may be able to send faxes directly from WordPerfect without printing the fax on paper at all. Direct digital communication from your machine to somebody else's — very advanced.

## What do you need?

For this very advanced communication process to work, you need the following items:

- ✔ **A fax modem:** A gizmo that connects your computer to a phone line and pretends to be a fax machine. The fax modem can live inside your computer, or it can be a small box that sits next to the computer.

- ✔ **A fax program:** The software that makes the fax modem do its thing. Dealing with this software used to be a daunting proposition in and of itself, but because Windows 95 comes with fax software, all you need to do is to get it to work. (That's why you need the computer guru.)

  If you get another fax program, be sure to get one that works with Windows 95; the key phrase to look for is "installs as a Windows printer driver." In English, this phrase means that the fax program pretends to be a printer, so when you want to fax a WordPerfect document, you just tell WordPerfect to "print" the document on the fax/modem. Unbeknownst to WordPerfect, the document — far from being printed on paper — wings its way telephonically as a fax. Note that a great deal of the fax software that comes for free with fax modems does *not* work this way.

- ✔ **A phone line:** For your fax modem to talk on. This can be the same line that you use for your telephone *unless* you are in an office that has a fancy new digital phone. Don't plug your fax modem into a digital phone; the fax modem probably will break if you do. If your telephone says "ringer equivalence" on it, you're all set.

- ✔ **A computer guru:** To set everything up. Be sure to have not just one or two cookies but a whole bag of Mint Milanos up your sleeve.

## Just the fax, ma'am

After your computer has been rendered fax-capable, all you have to do to send a fax directly from WordPerfect is follow these steps:

1. **Create a document that contains your fax.**

   The WordPerfect document must contain everything you want to include in the fax. You cannot print the fax on your letterhead, for example; the document must contain your name and return address. Consider using one of WordPerfect's snazzy-looking templates (refer to Chapter 16).

Because the document is actually "printed" by your fax program, some fonts may not work. Your fax program cannot use fonts that exist only in WordPerfect. You may need to experiment by sending a fax or two to a friend to see whether the fonts that you use look right in faxes.

**2. Save the document.**

You can never be too careful.

**3. Press Ctrl+P to display the Print dialog box and then click on the Printer tab.**

WordPerfect displays the Printer tab, which contains a list of the printers (and things that pretend to be printers) that WordPerfect knows about. If your fax program or Microsoft Fax does not appear in the Name list, you need to select it. Click on the down-arrow button and select your fax program. If the program doesn't appear, your computer guru didn't do the job right.

**4. Click on the Print button in the Print dialog box.**

WordPerfect displays a message that it is preparing your document for printing, and the Print dialog box closes.

**5. Use your fax program's dialog boxes to enter the fax number to which the fax should be sent.**

Each fax program performs this procedure differently. Most programs offer a dizzying array of options, including cover sheets, annotations, and the capability to send the fax to an entire list of people. Enter the fax number to which you want to send the fax, and look for a button called something like Send.

Microsoft, ever helpful, has a Compose New Fax Wizard, which asks you to complete four screens of information before it sends your fax. You may want to use the Address Book (and within it, the Personal Address Book) to keep all your addresses in one place.

Also, be patient when you use Microsoft Fax. After WordPerfect says it's done printing your fax, you will see (and hear) a lot of whirring and clicking from your computer. Eventually, you get the Fax Wizard.

Your fax program should tell you when the fax has been sent, whether it has trouble getting through, and the hair and eye color of the person who receives it (just kidding). Our program displays a cute little picture of a fax machine with the paper rolling into it.

**6. After the fax is sent, select your regular printer again.**

Repeat Steps 3 and 4, but select your printer; otherwise, the next time you try to print a memo, it may get faxed.

## Signing your faxes

To include your signature on a fax, you need your signature in digital form, in a graphics file. Using a drawing program (such as WP Draw, described in Chapter 15, or Windows Paintbrush), you can attempt to write your signature. It may look more like your second-grader's signature, however.

Alternatively, you can find someone who has a scanner (you'd better have some more cookies on hand) and ask him or her to scan your signature, which will be converted to a graphics file. Bring along your signature written in black ink on a clean piece of white paper.

Either way, you end up with a file you can include in your document by using the Graphics⇨Image command (described in Chapter 15).

# Envelopes

After you write the world's most clear and cogent letter, you need an envelope to put it in. (We have stooped to using window envelopes because we are too lazy to print envelopes, but we suspect that you haven't fallen that far.) If your printer cannot accept envelopes (most printers can), skip this section.

The folks at WordPerfect created a command that formats a document (or one page of a document) as an envelope. We're talking *convenience.* Word processing takes a major step forward.

## Printing the address on the envelope

To print an address on a regular #10 envelope, follow these steps:

1. **If you have already written the letter that will go in the envelope, open that document.**

   If not, no big deal.

2. **Choose Format⇨Envelope.**

   WordPerfect displays the Envelope dialog box, shown in Figure 18-1. (It may instead tell you that no envelopes are defined for the current printer and ask whether you want to create one; if so, see the following section.) If the current document contains a letter in a fairly normal format, WordPerfect — get this — *finds* the name and address at the top of the letter and displays it in the Mailing Addresses box. This feature is really cool; you don't have to type the address again.

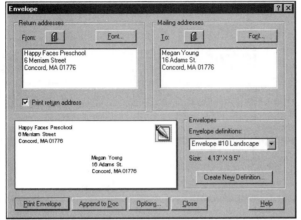

**Figure 18-1:**
Creating an
envelope.
(You don't
even have
to type the
address!)

**3. Enter your address in the Return Addresses box.**

If you have used this dialog box before, WordPerfect remembers the
address that you entered the last time — a nice touch.

**4. To print the envelope now, click on Print Envelope.**

Depending on how your printer works, you may be prompted (by a cute
little dialog box) to insert an envelope. (For some printers, you may have
to edit the paper definition, the paper size, and the orientation settings by
using the Format➪Page➪Paper Size command. Read the README file that
comes with WordPerfect and that is mentioned during installation.)

**5. To print an envelope as part of your document, click on Append to Doc.**

WordPerfect adds the envelope as a separate page at the end of your
document, along with all the formatting you need to make it print correctly. This feature is great when the current document is the letter that
goes inside the envelope. Whenever you print the letter, you print an
envelope, too.

## Tips for printing envelopes

When you choose the Format➪Envelope command, WordPerfect may demand
that you create an envelope definition. This is bad news; it means that
WordPerfect isn't familiar with printing envelopes on your type of printer. You
have to tell it the length and width of your envelopes, the margins — the works.
You may want to get some help for this task.

On most laser printers, you insert envelopes face up, with the right end of the envelope entering the printer first. You may have to do mechanical things to your printer, too; check the manual's "Envelopes" section. If your printer has a platen (most impact printers do), stick the envelope in upside down, with the front facing away from you so that it is right side up, facing toward you, after it comes up under the platen. Most inkjet printers have special envelope-feeding buttons; check your printer manual. Refer to Chapter 12 to learn how to tell which kind of printer you have.

Depending on your printer, WordPerfect may know how to print more than one size of envelope. In the Envelope dialog box, check out the Envelope Definitions setting. If you click on it, you may find that several sizes and shapes are available.

# Mailing Labels

Zillions of kinds of labels exist — sheets of mailing labels, continuous rolls of mailing labels, disk labels . . . you name it. This section shows you how to print addresses on them. Luckily, WordPerfect can handle an amazing variety of formats.

## Printing addresses on mailing labels

To print addresses on mailing labels, follow these steps:

1. **Begin with a new, blank document.**

2. **Tell WordPerfect which kind of labels you are using.**

   In technical jargon, you are providing a *label definition*. Choose Format⇨Labels to display the Labels dialog box, shown in Figure 18-2.

   WordPerfect already knows about an amazing variety of labels, including most of the ones manufactured by Avery. Most label definitions listed in the Labels section of the dialog box are identified only by their Avery part number. This number is useful, because most label manufacturers now include the equivalent Avery number on their packages.

3. **Choose the type of labels you have.**

   In case you're not sure which kind you have, WordPerfect displays a little diagram of the labels that you selected. Avery 5160 Address labels, for example, come in sheets of 3 across and 10 rows per page. The Label Details section of the dialog box describes the size and shape of the sheets and individual labels you selected.

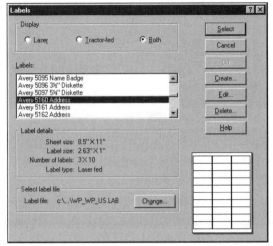

**Figure 18-2:**
Sheets,
rolls, or
stacks of
labels.

### 4. Click on Select.

The dialog box closes, and your document now looks truly weird. An area
the size of a label stays white (or whatever background color you use for
WordPerfect documents; see Chapter 20), and the rest of the page is
draped in shadow, as shown in Figure 18-3.

**Figure 18-3:**
Typing
addresses
for your
mailing
labels.

### 5. Type the addresses.

Or type whatever it is that you want to print on the labels. WordPerfect
allows you to enter only as much information as fits on a label.

To move to the next label, press Ctrl+Enter. After you enter a bunch of
labels, you can press Alt+PgUp and Alt+PgDn to move from label to label.
(If you cannot remember these arcane key combinations, just use your
mouse.)

6. **Save the document.**

7. **Print the labels.**

Put the labels in your printer. If you have a sheet-fed printer, be sure to insert the label sheet so that you print on the front, not on the back.

## *Selecting which addresses to print*

You don't have to print an entire page of labels at a time. To print selected labels, you can refer to them by number. WordPerfect thinks of each label as being a separate miniature page. On the status bar, in fact, the Pg number is the number of the label.

When you know which labels you want to print, choose File⇨Print and then choose Multiple Pages. When you click on Print, WordPerfect allows you to enter the print range in the Multiple Pages dialog box. In the Page(s) box, enter the number(s) of the label(s) that you want to print. Enter **3** to print the third label, for example; **5-12** to print a range of labels; **2,14,23** for several labels; or **15-** for all the rest of the labels, beginning at label 15.

## *Tips for printing labels*

You can use all the usual formatting for labels — choose a nice font, make the ZIP code boldface, or whatever.

WordPerfect's list of label definitions is awfully long. To make it shorter, choose Laser or Tractor-Fed in the Display section of the dialog box. WordPerfect lists only labels of that type. Then click on Print again.

If you have used WordPerfect's merge feature to enter a list of addresses for creating junk mail (refer to Chapter 17), you can print the same addresses on mailing labels. Create a new *form file* (the merge term for the document that contains the form letter), and choose Format⇨Labels to format it for labels. In the first mailing label, enter merge codes for the parts of the address. Then choose Tools⇨Merge to print the labels.

If you are using a type of label that WordPerfect doesn't know about, you can create your own label definitions. Choose Create in the Labels dialog box, and tell WordPerfect all about the size and arrangement of your labels.

## Printing bar codes

If you want to make the U.S. Postal Service happy (and who wouldn't?), you can print a USPS POSTNET bar code. (This code will impress your friends, too.) Choose Options in the Envelope dialog box, choose Include USPS POSTNET Bar Code, and then choose OK in the Envelope Options dialog box. Now a POSTNET Bar Code box appears in the Envelope dialog box, just below the mailing address. Type the U.S. ZIP code in this box. When you print the envelope, a tasteful row of little vertical lines appears above the address. Some machine at the post office must know what the lines mean.

# *Booklets*

A very common typing job is a pain in the neck with most word processors: a little booklet that consists of regular sheets of paper folded in half, like the one shown in Figure 18-4.

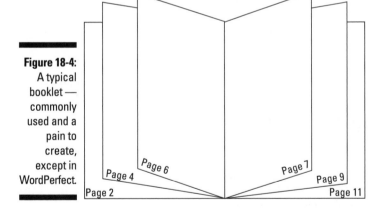

**Figure 18-4:**
A typical
booklet —
commonly
used and a
pain to
create,
except in
WordPerfect.

But wait — WordPerfect has a special booklet feature for making just this kind of document. This feature is a really cool one that makes us want to take back all the snide things that we've said about WordPerfect. (Almost all of them, anyway.)

## Creating a booklet document

These steps show you how to make a $5^1/2$- by $8^1/2$-inch booklet that consists of folded sheets:

1. **Type the text for your booklet.**

   Do all the character and line formatting that you plan to use, including fonts, boldface, and centering. Set up page numbering, headers, and footers as you want them.

2. **Save your document.**

   Whatever else happens, it would be a pain to have to type the text again!

   The next step is to tell WordPerfect to print sideways (landscape orientation) on the page and to print two pages of your booklet on each sheet of paper.

3. **Choose Format⇨Page⇨Page Size.**

   WordPerfect displays the Page Size dialog box.

   Make sure that your cursor is at the beginning of the document when you perform this step so that the formatting affects the entire document. (Press Ctrl+Home to get to the tippy-top.)

4. **From the Paper Definitions list, choose Letter Landscape (which is regular-size paper that prints sideways); then choose OK.**

   Europeans should choose A4 Landscape.

5. **Choose Format⇨Page⇨Subdivide Page.**

   WordPerfect displays the Subdivide Page dialog box, shown in Figure 18-5.

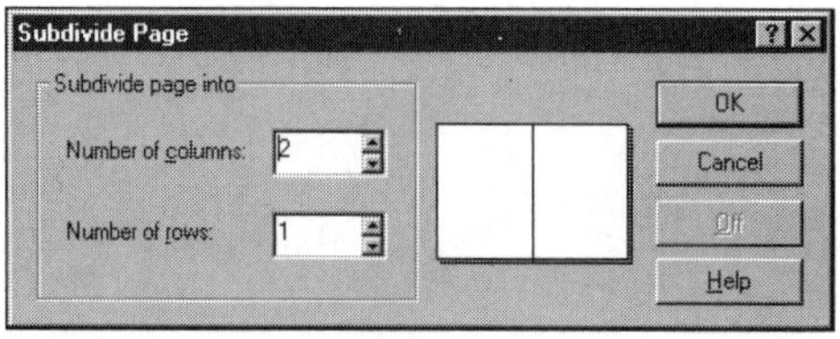

**Figure 18-5:**
How many booklet pages print on each piece of paper?

6. **Enter 2 in the Number of Columns box; then choose OK.**

   Your text moves around big-time.

   Subdividing a page into columns works like regular columns (described in Chapter 15), but WordPerfect knows that you want to treat the columns like separate pages. Way cool!

   If you don't see your text in two columns, choose View⇨Page.

**7. Set your margins.**

If you didn't set them before, you probably will want to set them now, to see how your text looks in these small pages. You may want to move your graphics, lines, boxes, and headings around a little.

**8. Create a front cover, if you want one.**

At the beginning of the document, enter the title or other material you want to appear on the cover. Press Ctrl+Enter to insert a page break between the cover text and the next page. You can center the cover text on the page by using the Format⇨Page⇨Center command.

Now your document looks like a booklet, with two pages per sheet of paper.

## Printing your booklet: the magic part

Now comes the really tricky part: telling WordPerfect to shuffle the pages so that they are in the right order when you fold your booklet in half. Luckily, WordPerfect does almost all the work. Just follow these steps:

**1. If your printer can print on both sides of the page (*duplex*), tell WordPerfect to print the booklet that way.**

Choose Format⇨Page⇨Binding/Duplex; then choose From Short Edge for the Duplexing setting. (If that doesn't work, try From Long Edge.)

**2. Choose File⇨Print, press F5, or click on the Print button on the Toolbar.**

WordPerfect displays the Print dialog box.

**3. Choose Options; choose Booklet Printing; then choose OK.**

This step tells WordPerfect to switch the order of the pages so that when the sheets of paper are folded, the booklet pages are in order.

**4. Back in the Print dialog box, choose Print.**

WordPerfect thinks about the job for a long time. A long, long time. After all, it is reshuffling the entire document. Many minutes later, your printer fires up and spews out the booklet.

## Tips for creating booklets

If your printer doesn't print duplex, WordPerfect prints half the pages and then prompts you to reinsert the pages so that it can print the remaining pages on the back. This procedure can get a little confusing, because you must be sure to insert the right page, the right way around, at the right time. We think that it's simpler to print everything on one side of blank sheets of paper and then photocopy them. After all, you probably want more than one copy anyway.

As usual, to insert a page break and move to the top of the next page, you press Ctrl+Enter. When you have subdivided your pages, you move to the next booklet page, not to the next sheet of paper. To move to the next or preceding booklet page, press Alt+PgUp or Alt+PgDn.

# Reports and Other Big Documents

These days, people use word processing programs for much more than writing letters. You may want to use WordPerfect to typeset a book, for example. This idea isn't as stupid as it sounds; WordPerfect can handle large documents, and it can even create tables of contents and indexes.

The secret is not to store the entire book (or report, or whatever) in one big document; instead, break it up into chapters or sections — one per document. Then create a master document to connect all the parts.

What's a master document? (We're glad you asked.) A *master document* is a WordPerfect document that contains secret codes that link it to other documents. These other documents are called *subdocuments*. When you are writing a book (to pick a wild hypothetical example), each subdocument might contain one chapter. The master document contains a secret code for each chapter document, in addition to introductory text, the table of contents, and the index.

To go about creating a really big document, such as a book or long report, create the subdocuments first. Then create the master document. Finally, set up the table of contents and the index. Don't worry; we step you through the process.

## Creating the master document and subdocuments

To create the master document and its subdocuments, get the text of the book organized. Follow these steps:

1. **Create a document for each chapter.**

   Because you want all the chapters to be formatted the same way, consider creating a template that contains the formatting (refer to Chapter 16). Don't worry about page numbering, headers, or footers in the subdocuments; those elements are controlled by the master document. Give the documents names such as Chapter1.wpd and Chapter2.wpd.

2. **Type the text in each chapter document, or copy it from existing documents.**

### 3. Create the master document.

Open a new document and then type the title page and other front matter. Skip the table of contents for now (we get to it in the following section). If the introduction and preface (or whatever) are short, you can include them in this document; if they are long, store each one in its own document, as you do chapters. Save the document with a name such as Book.wpd or Report.wpd.

### 4. For each chapter, create a secret code in the master document.

Move your cursor to the spot in the master document where you want the chapter to appear. If you want the chapter to begin on a new page, insert a page break by pressing Ctrl+Enter. Then choose File➪Document➪Subdocument. In the Include Subdocument dialog box, select the file name of the chapter, and click on Include. In our example, we included Chocolate - Chapter 1.wpd in our master document.

Not much happens at this point. If you are in page view, you see a little subdocument icon in the left margin of your master document. If you are in draft view, you see `Subdoc: Chocolate - Chapter 1.wpd` or whatever the filename of the subdocument is (it looks something like Figure 18-6). We prefer to work in draft view so that we can see the file names of our chapters all the time.

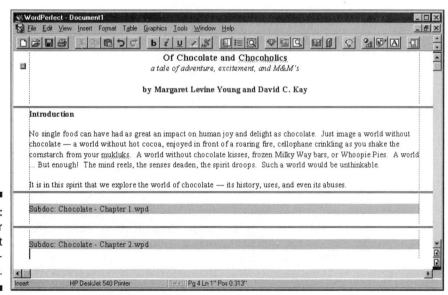

**Figure 18-6:** The master document and its sub-documents.

In page view, to find out which document the little subdocument icon refers to, click on it.

A faster way to issue the File⇨Document⇨Subdocument command is to use a QuickMenu. Right-click in the left margin of the document and then choose Subdocument from the QuickMenu.

## Expanding the master document

WordPerfect can display (and store) a master document in two ways: expanded or condensed. When a master document is *expanded,* WordPerfect retrieves the text of each subdocument and sticks it into the master document right where it belongs. When a master document is *condensed* — you guessed it — the text of each subdocument is stored in its separate file, and you see only subdocument icons.

To expand a master document, choose File⇨Document⇨Expand Master (or double-click on one of those subdocument icons). WordPerfect displays the Expand Master Document dialog box (see Figure 18-7), which lists all your sub-documents. To expand them all, choose OK. To skip expanding one, click on its little box so that no *X* appears in it.

**Figure 18-7:**
Expand, oh
master!

| Expand Master Document | ? X |
| --- | --- |
| Subdocuments: | OK |
| ⊠ chocolate - chapter 1.wpd | Cancel |
| ⊠ chocolate - chapter 2.wpd | Mark ▼ |
| | Help |

When you expand a master document, you still see the little subdocument icons. You see twice as many, in fact — they appear at the beginning and at the end of each subdocument, as shown in Figure 18-8.

When you are working on a master document, it's probably safest not to open any of its subdocuments in other windows. Early versions of WordPerfect for Windows get upset when you save a master document if any of its sub-documents are also open.

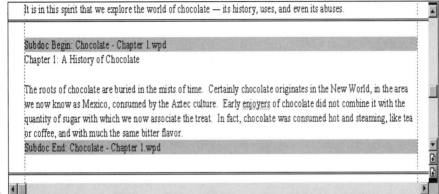

It is in this spirit that we explore the world of chocolate — its history, uses, and even its abuses.

Subdoc Begin: Chocolate - Chapter 1.wpd

Chapter 1: A History of Chocolate

The roots of chocolate are buried in the mists of time. Certainly chocolate originates in the New World, in the area we now know as Mexico, consumed by the Aztec culture. Early enjoyers of chocolate did not combine it with the quantity of sugar with which we now associate the treat. In fact, chocolate was consumed hot and steaming, like tea or coffee, and with much the same bitter flavor.

Subdoc End: Chocolate - Chapter 1.wpd

**Figure 18-8:**
Your sub-
documents
appear in
the master
document.

## Saving a master document

When you save a master document, WordPerfect wants to know two things about each of its subdocuments:

- ✔ Do you want to *save* the text of the subdocument back in the subdocument's file?
- ✔ Do you want to *condense* the subdocument so that only its icon appears in the master document?

You answer both of these pithy questions in the Condense/Save Subdocuments dialog box. When you want to save your master document, follow these steps:

**1. Choose File⇨Save, press Ctrl+S, or click on the Save button on the Toolbar.**

WordPerfect displays the Save dialog box.

If you haven't expanded your master document, or if you have condensed it (see Step 2), WordPerfect saves the document with no comment. If your master document is expanded, however, WordPerfect displays the message `Document is expanded. Condense?`

**2. Click on No to save the document as is.**

WordPerfect saves the master document with the text of all the expanded subdocuments, too. It *doesn't* save the text of the subdocuments back to the separate subdocument files. If you edited the text of your chapters in the master document, therefore, your edits are not saved in Chocolate - Chapter 1.wpd, Chocolate - Chapter 2.wpd, and so on — only in Chocolate.wpd.

*Or* click on Yes to save each subdocument in its own separate file.

WordPerfect displays the Condense/Save Subdocuments dialog box, shown in Figure 18-9. Each subdocument is listed twice: once so that you can condense it (remove the text from the master document) and once so that you can save it in its own file. We always leave all the boxes checked. Go for the gold, we say.

**Figure 18-9:**
Saving your book. Do you want to save each chapter back in its own file?

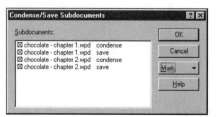

3. **Choose OK.**

WordPerfect saves and condenses as you indicated.

You can also condense a master document by choosing File⇨Document⇨ Condense Master.

## Editing a master document

After you have the master document set up, what do you do when you want to edit a chapter of your book? What if you get new information about early uses of chocolate among the Aztec nobility, for example, and you want to include it in Chapter 1?

You have these two choices:

- ✔ **Edit the chapter file.** In this case, make sure that your master document is condensed to ensure that the text of your chapter is stored in the subdocument file, not in the master document. Make your changes, and save the chapter file. The next time you open and expand the master document, the updated chapter appears.

- ✔ **Edit the master document.** In this case, make sure that your chapter file is closed. Open the master document and expand the subdocuments (or at least the one that you want to edit). Make your changes and save the master file.

This process can get rather confusing when you try to remember where the text of your chapters is *really* stored. We recommend that you always do your editing the same way and always store your master document the same way (either expanded or condensed).

## *Creating a table of contents*

"What good is a table without contents?" we always ask (when we're sitting down to dinner). WordPerfect can automatically generate a table of contents for your book (or any document) by using the headings in the file. These steps show you how:

1. **Open your master document and expand it.**

   You want to be able to see all your lovely chapters so that you can decide which ones should appear in your table of contents.

2. **Choose Tools⇨Generate⇨Table of Contents.**

   More lovely buttons appear, mostly named Mark (see Figure 18-10). This is (what else?) the Table of Contents feature bar.

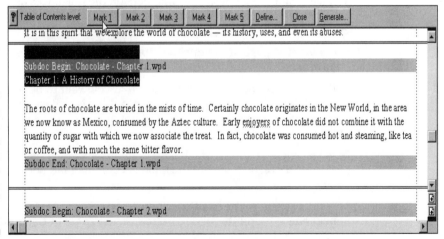

**Figure 18-10:** Marking the headings that you want to appear in your table of contents.

3. **Mark the lines of text (headings) that you want to use in the table of contents.**

   Your table of contents can have several levels (chapters and sections within chapters, for example). To mark each heading, select it and then click on the appropriate Mark button. Mark each chapter title by using Mark 1, for example.

When you perform this step, nothing seems to happen. WordPerfect inserts secret codes at the beginning and end of each selected heading (the `Mrk Txt ToC` code, if you were wondering).

4. **Create a new page where you want the table of contents to appear.**

   For most books, you want the table of contents to be on a page by itself, right after the title and copyright pages. Press Ctrl+Enter to insert a page break.

5. **Beginning with the first page of the master document, tell WordPerfect to number the pages with small Roman numerals.**

   Most books number the front matter (including the table of contents) with Roman numerals and then start the page numbers again with Arabic numerals at the beginning of the introduction or first chapter. You can do that, too. (Won't your document look just like a real book?)

   Move your cursor to the beginning of the master document and choose Format⇨Page Numbering⇨Select. Set the Position option to Alternating Top or Alternating Bottom so that the numbers appear on the right side of left pages and on the left side of right pages. Select one of the Roman-numeral options (iv, -iv-, IV, or -IV-). Then choose OK to finish page numbering.

   You may want to suppress page numbers on the title pages and some other front-matter pages. To do so, use the Format⇨Page⇨Suppress command.

6. **Go to the first page of the introduction or Chapter 1 and reset it to be page number 1.**

   With your cursor at the top of the page that you want to be page 1, choose Format⇨Page Numbering⇨Value/Adjust. Set the New Page Number option to 1, and set the Page Number Method option to 1,2,3. Then choose OK to finish page numbering.

   Now WordPerfect knows which page numbers should appear on every page. You are ready to create the table of contents (and not a moment too soon!)

7. **Move the cursor to the location where you want the table of contents to appear and click on the Define button on the Table of Contents bar.**

   WordPerfect displays the Define Table of Contents dialog box (see Figure 18-11).

8. **Tell WordPerfect the number of levels and which style to use for each level (whether to include page numbers and dot leaders); then choose OK.**

   WordPerfect inserts an invisible code and the text `<<Table of Contents will generate here>>`. Don't worry; WordPerfect does better than that in a minute.

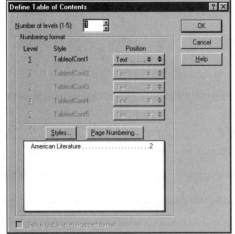

**Figure 18-11:**
What
contents do
you want in
your table?

9. **Click on the Generate button.**

   WordPerfect displays the Generate dialog box.

   The Generate button is at the right end of the Table of Contents feature bar; you may have to make your WordPerfect window wider to see it. Once again, you have the option to save your subdocuments. We always think that this is a good idea. You can also build hyperlinks, but don't worry about that now; we'll talk about hyperlinks in Chapter 19.

10. **Choose OK.**

   Some messages flash by. Then, poof — you have a table of contents.

No big deal, you may say; it would have been faster to copy the chapter titles by hand. But here's the nice thing: If you update your book and make chapters shorter or longer, when you click on the Generate button again, WordPerfect updates the table of contents and corrects the headings and page numbers.

When you finish fooling with the table of contents, click on the Close button on the Table of Contents bar. To get the bar back, you can always choose Tools⇨ Generate⇨Table of Contents.

## Creating an index

Creating an index is similar to creating a table of contents. You mark stuff in the text of the book, define the format of the index so that WordPerfect creates a secret index code, and then generate away. The difference is that the index always looks terrible the first time you generate it; you find typos and inconsistencies galore. Don't despair — just correct the entries in the text and keep generating the index until it looks right.

## *Inserting the index codes*

Follow these steps to add the secret index codes to your document:

**1. Open your master document, and expand it.**

**2. Choose Tools➪Generate➪Index.**

You see yet another bar: the index bar (see Figure 18-12).

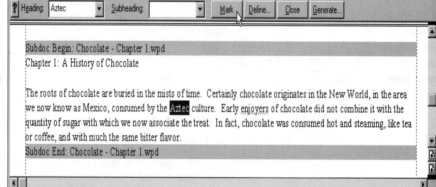

**Figure 18-12:**
Using the
index bar to
decide
which terms
to index.

**3. For each place in the text for which you want an index entry, create a secret index code.**

If the term to be indexed appears in the text, select it and then click on the Heading box on the index bar. The text appears in the box, and you can edit it, if necessary. To make this text an index entry, click on the Mark button.

A term that you want to include in the index may not appear in the text. For the sentence *The roots of chocolate are buried in the mists of time,* for example, you may want the index entry to be History. Just click the place in the text to which you want the index entry to refer, click on the Heading box, type the index entry (you may want to capitalize the first letter), and click on the Mark button.

**4. Create a new page at the end of your master document for the index.**

At the end of the document, press Ctrl+Enter to insert a page break. Type a title for the index, too.

**5. With your cursor on the new last page of your master document, click on the Define button on the Index bar.**

You see the Define Index dialog box, shown in Figure 18-13. We usually leave all the settings and options alone; the default settings make a perfectly nice-looking index.

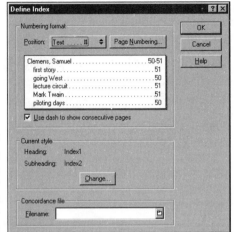

**6. Choose OK.**

WordPerfect inserts a secret index code and the text `Index will generate here.`

**7. Click on the Generate button to display the Generate dialog box.**

**8. Choose OK.**

WordPerfect merrily indexes away!

## Tips for making a good index

Be consistent in your index entries. We usually capitalize all entries (except subheadings), for example, and we use plurals of all nouns and gerunds of all verbs ("Cakes, making" and "Making cakes").

When you see typos in the index, don't correct them in the index; if you do, the next time you click on Generate, the changes will be blown away. Instead, you must laboriously find the index codes in the text and fix them. Use Reveal Codes view (described in Chapter 10) so that you can see the index codes. You can also use the Edit➪Find and Replace command to find them. When you move your cursor directly before the index code in Reveal Codes view, it looks like this:

```
Index: Milky Way bars.
```

You cannot edit the text of the index code; instead, delete it by pressing the Delete key. Then make a new index entry. What a pain! It's enough to make you think about chucking the whole thing and hiring a professional indexer.

To make index entries with subentries, enter text in both the Heading and Subheading boxes on the index bar before you click on the Mark button.

Creating a good index is trickier than you think. You must include all the terms that a reader is likely to look up, including synonyms that you might never use yourself. Refer to a good book on the subject, such as *The Chicago Manual of Style* (University of Chicago Press).

# Chapter 19

# Spinning Web Pages

· · · · · · · · · · · · · · · · · · · · · · · · · · · · · · · · · · · · · · · · · · ·

### In This Chapter

▶ What is all this Internet stuff, and what is it doing in my word processor?

▶ What is hypertext?

▶ Your own personal mini deskwide Web

▶ Ra! Ra! for the IntRAnet!

▶ The World Wide Web

▶ WordPerfect and HTML: Markups for free

▶ Creating your own Web pages

▶ Converting your documents to Web pages

· · · · · · · · · · · · · · · · · · · · · · · · · · · · · · · · · · · · · · · · · · ·

*O*ne of the little-known provisions of the U.S. Communications Reform Act of 1996 made it illegal to market any piece of software in the United States unless it could connect to the Internet. Thus we have Internet-enabled word processors, databases, spreadsheets, and toaster ovens.

Well, it's not actually a law, but it might as well be. Let's call it a trend. WordPerfect has not been immune to this trend. In this chapter, we explain what all this stuff is doing in WordPerfect. We also explain what Web pages are and how you can use them in your office. Then we get you started creating your own documents for display on the World Wide Web.

## What Is All This Internet Stuff, and What Is It Doing in My Word Processor?

Because it is so easy to connect computers together now, millions of them, large and small, are connected together—some via telephone, some via local-area networks within an office, and some via high-speed telephone links. Rather than try to keep all these computers rigidly organized, people have discovered that you can get a message from any computer to any other by asking a computer to pass the message to some computer that might know the recipient. *That's* the Internet: a whole bunch of computers playing whisper-down-the-lane.

For years, people used this network of computers very simply: All the small computers asked the big computers to do something for them. In 1990, Tim Berners-Lee at the European Particle Physics Laboratory (CERN) realized that the information could be anywhere, and he developed a way for any computer to ask (almost) any other computer connected to the Internet for some information. The way that he linked all that information was through hypertext. He called it the World Wide Web.

For more information, you might want to look at *Internet FAQs: Answers to the Most Frequently Asked Questions about the Internet* by Margaret Levine Young and John Levine ( published by IDG Books Worldwide, Inc.) or *The Internet For Dummies,* 3rd Edition, by John Levine, Carol Baroudi, and Margaret Levine Young ( published by IDG Books Worldwide, Inc.).

## *What is hypertext?*

*Hypertext* is just like regular text, really, except for one thing: When you click on certain words or phrases, you're magically transported to different text, either in the same document or in another document. The concept sounds very space-age, but it's simple. You can follow related ideas in a way that would be difficult if you had to skip around from page to page in a book, or from book to book.

You may be familiar with hypertext; in fact, you may have used it. Where? In the online help system that is used by almost all Windows programs. Back in Chapter 2, Figure 2-7 shows a sample WordPerfect Help screen. Those four phrases at the bottom are hypertext links to other parts of the Help system. When you click on one of those links, another screen of information appears. Jumping immediately to related information is useful in a help system. Imagine how much more convenient it might be if all the text didn't have to be on one computer (or even on one continent).

---

### Hyperwhat?

Everyone in the computer biz talks about hypertext. Every program has a hypertext help system. *The New York Times* has even reviewed hypertext novels. So where did hypertext come from? It turns out that it was the brainchild of a rather wild and wacky guy named Theodor H. Nelson. Beginning in the 1950s, he was thinking of wonderful ways for computers to make information available to everyone, and he was around when word processing was invented. ("Use a $1 million computer to do what!?")

Hypertext is part of a much bigger, not to mention grandiose, plan called Xanadu. Xanadu is designed to be a worldwide network of libraries with all their books online. All books are written, updated, and read interactively as hypertext (the setup is hard to describe). Read Ted's books — *Computer Lib* and *Literary Machines*, among others — for the full description.

# *Hypertext on the World Wide Web*

When you combine the Internet and hypertext, you get the World Wide Web. The Web actually looks like a regular word-processing document on your screen, except that some of the words are underlined.

What does any of this have to do with word processing and WordPerfect? Amid all the hype and all the fanfare about the World Wide Web, one fact is frequently overlooked: All those Web pages have to have something on them. The pages have to have *content*. And that content has to be written with some tool. The folks at WordPerfect already had a tool that could produce tables, boldface text, italics, outlines, and even hypertext links, so WordPerfect was reborn as a Web-page creator.

You probably didn't know that WordPerfect creates hypertext links. (If you did, it's not because *we* told you — at least, not yet!) Hypertext links in WordPerfect are called *bookmarks*.

# *Bookmarks*

Bookmarks within a single document work pretty much the way that the name implies — they allow you to mark a position in a document and go back to it quickly. Think about *Of Chocolate and Chocoholics*, which we discussed in the preceding chapter. Suppose that you had expanded it to a 500-page document with 30 chapters. If you were working on Chapter 23, "Ceremonial Uses of Chocolate," and wanted to check what you said about that topic in Chapter 1, "A History of Chocolate," you have several options (of course you do; this is WordPerfect):

- ✓ Press the PgUp key on your keyboard until you get to Chapter 1. This method will make your finger sore and will take a long time.

- ✓ Choose Edit➪Find and Replace to search for the text *A History of Chocolate*. The problem with this method is that WordPerfect stops at every occurrence of *A History of Chocolate* in the entire book up to this point. This method also will take a long time.

- ✓ Use a bookmark. After you set a bookmark on the text of *A History of Chocolate*, you can get back there any time by displaying the Go To dialog box and selecting the name of the bookmark. No matter how far away you are, WordPerfect takes you there as though you were on a magic carpet. After you check out what you want to see, you can use Go To to take you back to your last position in Chapter 23.

To create a bookmark, follow these steps:

1. **Highlight the text that you want to appear inside the bookmark.**

   For what you're doing here, it doesn't matter how much of your text you highlight.

2. **Choose Insert⇨Bookmark.**

   The Bookmark dialog box appears, as shown in Figure 19-1.

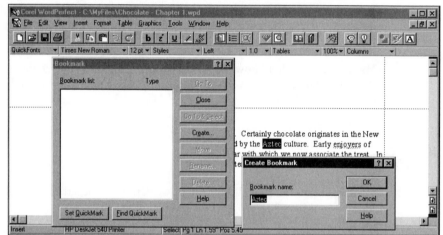

**Figure 19-1:**
Creating a
bookmark.

3. **Click on the Create button.**

   A little dialog box appears, and if you highlighted text, it suggests that text as the name for your bookmark. If you didn't highlight some text, type a name for your bookmark.

4. **Click on OK to create the bookmark.**

   Poof! Nothing happens. Well, the dialog boxes go away, but nothing looks different in your document. But now the fun begins!

Using hypertext links and bookmarks, you'll create a teeny-tiny version of the World Wide Web on your very own computer in the following sections.

# *Your Own Personal Mini Deskwide Web*

Consider Chapter 23, "Ceremonial Uses of Chocolate," in the tome that you are writing. In a traditional book, you might say something like "The first known ceremonial use of chocolate occurred in Aztec society long before the European discovery of America (see Chapter 1)." The reader then flips to Chapter 1 and skims it to see whether it says anything about Aztecs. This works fine on paper but is a little awkward on a computer screen, especially the flipping part.

As a result, word processing scientists have found a way to create document features that cannot even be put on paper: hypertext links. (Remember those four phrases from Figure 2-7? Be honest, now — did you really flip back to look at them? Of course not! What a pain in the neck. But you probably clicked on those little links in the Help system. And *that's* why hypertext is a good idea.) The following sections show how you can create those kinds of links yourself.

## *Creating a hypertext link to another WordPerfect document*

Hypertext links between WordPerfect documents allow you to explore hypertext without using communications or any of that complex foolishness. To get started, you can create hyperlinks from one WordPerfect document to another. Follow these steps:

1. **Create a bookmark at the place *to which* you want your reader to be able to jump.**

   In Figure 19-2, we created a bookmark on the word *Aztec* in the document Chocolate - Chapter 1.wpd.

2. **Open the document that contains the place *from which* you want your reader to be able to jump.**

   In this case, that's Chocolate - Chapter 23.wpd.

3. **Highlight the word(s) that you want the user to be able to click on.**

   In this case, choose a reference to the Aztecs at the beginning of Chapter 23.

4. **Choose Tools⇨Hypertext/Web Links.**

   WordPerfect displays yet another feature bar — this one for the care and feeding of hypertext links. We go over what the buttons do in a minute; for now, we concentrate on creating a link.

**5. Click on Create on the hypertext link bar.**

The Create Hypertext Link dialog box appears; Figure 19-2 shows what the hypertext bar and the Create Hypertext Link dialog box look like. In this box, you are telling WordPerfect what you want to have happen to the person who clicks on the link that you are creating. Again, we'll go over the choices in a minute; for now, we'll just create a link back to Chapter 1.

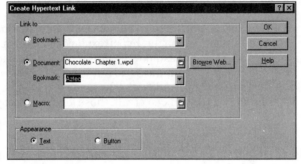

**Figure 19-2:**
Creating a
link to a
WordPerfect
bookmark.

**6. In the Document box, type the name of the document that you want to link to.**

In this case, it's Chocolate - Chapter 1.wpd. If you're lazy or can't remember, click on the little file-folder button. You see the WordPerfect standard file-browsing dialog box, and you can select the file there.

**7. In the Bookmark box, type the name of the bookmark you want WordPerfect to take the user to.**

In this case, it's Aztec. If you've forgotten the names of the bookmarks in the document that you just selected, you can click on the down arrow at the end of this box. You see a list of all the bookmarks in that document. You don't have to specify a bookmark. If you leave it out, WordPerfect just takes the user to the beginning of the document.

**8. Click on OK.**

This time, you actually see a change in your document. The word (or phrase, or character) that you highlighted is now underlined and green.

Do yourself a favor: save the document now. Also, if a button on the hypertext link feature bar says Activate (as one does in Figure 19-3), click on it. It changes to say Deactivate. If the button already says Deactivate, don't worry about it. Now, when the cursor passes over the underlined green word, it changes to a little hand with a pointing finger. Clicking while the cursor is a pointing hand takes you to the other end of your link.

Congratulations; you've created your own hypertext link. All there is to creating hypertext is creating lots and lots of these links.

## *Feature bars and dialog boxes that you'll use*

We promised you a rundown of the tools on the hypertext link feature bar. Here they are:

- **Perform.** Clicking on this button is the same as clicking on a link, though links don't work when they've been deactivated. The Perform button works regardless. Also, see Activate/Deactivate later in this list.

- **Back.** After you follow a link someplace, it's nice to be able to go back where you came from. Use this button to do so.

- **Previous.** This button finds the last hypertext link before your current position in your document.

- **Next.** You guessed it — this button finds the next hypertext link after your current position in the document.

- **Create/Delete.** This button changes, depending on whether your cursor is on a hypertext link. If your cursor is *not* on a hypertext link, clicking on this button displays the Create Hypertext Link dialog box. If your cursor *is* on a hypertext link, clicking on this button deletes the hypertext link.

- **Edit.** Clicking on this button displays the Create Hypertext Link dialog box, in case you want this link to go somewhere else.

- **Activate/Deactivate.** Links in a document can be a pain in the neck to edit. You may click on a link by mistake, thinking that you are going to select it, and type over it. Instead, WordPerfect displays the document to which the link points. That's not very useful. By clicking on Deactivate, you can turn off all the links in the document.

- **Bookmark.** Clicking on this button displays the Create Bookmark dialog box that we talked about earlier in this chapter.

- **Style.** Clicking on this button allows you to change the way that links are displayed. For more information, make sure that you understand Chapter 11.

- **Close.** In case you don't want this feature bar hanging around while you're doing real work, you can close it. By now, you've figured out that the only thing the Tools➪Hypertext/Web Links command does is to display this feature bar so you know how to get it back later.

We also promised that we'd talk a little more about the options in the Create Hypertext Link dialog box:

✔ **Bookmark.** This option allows you to create a hyperlink to somewhere else in the current document.

✔ **Browse Web.** We'll talk about this option in detail later in this chapter, when we talk about the World Wide Web.

✔ **Macro.** You can run a little WordPerfect program when people click on a hypertext link, but try not to think about that.

✔ **Appearance.** If you think that underlined words are too subtle, you can try displaying your links as buttons — the same kind that appear all over Windows.

Now you've got all the tools that you need to create hypertext documents.

# So What Do You Do With Your New-Found Ability to Create HyperText Documents?

Before you go public, it might be a good idea to use hypertext for your own documents or for documents that you're working on in your office. This is a good idea for several reasons:

✔ It gets you familiar with the pluses and minuses of hypertext.

✔ It gives you a chance to concentrate on the content of your hypertext without worrying so much about how artistic it is.

✔ In many cases, it's a good way to present information, so you might as well use it.

## Ra! Ra! for the IntRAnet!

Not long ago, *Intranet* was considered to be a typo. *Intranet* refers to documents connected by hypertext that are used within a company, as opposed to publicly — hence the Intra (for inside) as opposed to Inter (for between).

Although you can set up some nifty groups of documents on your own PC, complete with hypertext links, they're not very useful to anyone but you (or whoever's sitting in front of your computer). You could use the old sneaker net to distribute them to other people: copy the files to floppy disks and start running around the office, giving them to people. But every time you change something, you have to get back in the running shoes for a trip around the office.

If the all-powerful computer wizards in your organization have set up a local area-network, it may be much easier to "go live." Ask one of the gurus for a public place to put your documents. You need a place on the network where other people in your organization can look at things but not change them. You should be the only person who's allowed to change your documents.

After your network wizard assigns you such a place, you can sound tremendously knowledgeable. Tell your friends and co-workers that they can look at your magnum opus by opening a file called something like \\SharedPlace\ MarysStuff\Opus.wpd. This information is useful to them only if they have WordPerfect installed on their computers as well. Still, it's a good way to get started.

## *The World Wide Web*

What's the difference between a bunch of WordPerfect documents with hypertext links and the World Wide Web? We hinted at the answer in the preceding section. If you create a bunch of WordPerfect documents, only other people who have WordPerfect can use them. Because not everyone has WordPerfect (amazing, but true; we assume that everyone else will get with it sooner or later), this fact can limit your audience.

Remember that we said that computers communicating on the Internet are like a bunch of people playing whisper-down-the-lane. Well, if the computers are just whispering to one another, that's not much use to us humans in front of the screen. What would *my* computer have to tell *your* computer to get it to display a picture? Or what would *your* computer have to tell *my* computer so that when I click on a word in this document, my computer asks your computer for the text of the Gettysburg Address?

The answer is that computers (well, their users) have agreed on the HyperText Markup Language (HTML) as the way to ask one another to perform these tricks. HTML is the format of hypertext documents, including the links that ask for related documents. Unlike WordPerfect documents, which can be read only by WordPerfect and a few other word processing programs, many programs can display HTML documents. What are those programs called? Answer: *Web browsers,* such as Netscape Navigator and Internet Explorer. "Great," you say. "Another piece of software to buy and learn." Well, yes. But this news has a couple of good aspects.

## *Why use Netscape?*

You already have a copy of Netscape Navigator; it came with WordPerfect 7 as part of the AT&T WorldNet software on the CD-ROM. Even if you already use another Web browser or another Internet provider (the folks whom you call on the phone to connect to the Internet), or even if you connect to the Internet through the mystery of your corporate network, *you should install AT&T WorldNet Service if you plan to write Web pages with WordPerfect.* Why? Because WordPerfect has a strong bias toward using Netscape (which comes with AT&T WorldNet Service) for working on Web pages. (If you already have Netscape, you shouldn't need to install AT&T WorldNet Service.)

Another reason to install Netscape is that it's easy to learn to use Web browsers. A great book called *Dummies 101: The Internet For Windows 95 by* Young and Bender (published by IDG Books Worldwide, Inc.) shows you how to use AT&T WorldNet Service and the Netscape Web browser that comes with it.

Why do you need a Web browser when you have WordPerfect? WordPerfect can do everything to your text: tables, links, arithmetic, you name it. Web browsers cannot, however, display all that stuff. In fact, until recently, they couldn't even display tables of data. On the other hand, what Web browsers *can* do changes every week or so (no kidding). They are also acquiring extra features that allow them to do things that you may not care about. In short, Web browsers do less with fancy formatting of text but more with the talking-to-the-other-computer aspect.

Why do you need WordPerfect when you have a Web browser? Web browsers are not word processors or text editors. In fact, they have no tools to help you *create* the Web pages that they are so good at displaying. (Well, Netscape has a rudimentary editor, but it's nothing like WordPerfect.) The short of it is: Use WordPerfect to create your Web pages and Netscape Navigator to look at them.

Now you have all the pieces in place for spinning Web pages with WordPerfect: The Internet or Intranet connects the computers; they talk to one another, using HTML. When the HTML gets to your computer, Netscape displays it. And if you want to create some HTML, use WordPerfect. Start with creating a Web page.

## *WordPerfect and HTML: Markups for free*

HTML is a markup language (that's what the *ML* stands for). Remember what the Reveal Codes window looks like in WordPerfect? If you skipped Chapter 10, you have mercifully been spared WordPerfect's codes. But if you read that chapter, you know what a markup language is: All those codes that WordPerfect puts in your document tell WordPerfect how it should make your document look on-screen or on the printer. The codes are like the old symbols that editors used to use to mark up a manuscript before they sent it to the typesetter: Make this bold, print this in a big font, and so on.

When you select commands and format text in WordPerfect, you are putting in these secret markup codes. When WordPerfect displays your text on-screen (or the printer), it reads the markup code and makes the page look the way that it should. HTML, as the name implies, is a markup language, so the geniuses at WordPerfect concluded that it shouldn't be too hard to translate WordPerfect codes to HTML codes. Poof — WordPerfect becomes the world's fanciest HTML editor.

# Creating Your Own Web Pages

The easiest way to get WordPerfect to create an HTML document is to allow WordPerfect's Web Page Expert to guide you through the process, especially the first time. We'll also show you how to take an existing document and convert it to a Web page. In this example, you are building pages for DinoWorks, a company that makes life-size dinosaur skeletons for schools, museums, and families with little kids.

## The easy way: Ask the Expert

To get started with the Web Page Expert, follow these steps:

### 1. Choose File➪Internet Publisher.

It doesn't matter whether or not you have a document on-screen when you issue this command. You see the dialog box shown in Figure 19-3.

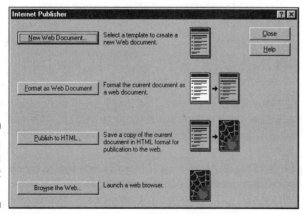

**Figure 19-3:**
WordPerfect's
Internet
Publisher.

**2. Click on New Web Document.**

Stop drooling over those other options; we get to them in an minute. If you're with the program, you see the Select New Web Document dialog box.

**3. Click on Web Page Expert and then on click Select**

Be patient. Be very patient. In fact, be very, very patient. First, a sample Web page appears as a document. Then the sample Web page grows to fill the screen. Finally, the Web Page Expert asks you for a new folder to put your Web page in.

You can tell by looking at this Web page that one size does not fit all where Web pages are concerned. The Web Page Expert is designed to help you put a "personal" Web page on the Net — one that talks about you and shares some aspect of your life that might be of interest to other people. If you're going to be using Web pages for work, this format probably does not apply to you. Still, bear with it the first time through so that you get familiar with all the parts of a Web page.

**4. Enter the name of the folder that you want to use for this Web page, or click on the folder button and select one; then click on Next >.**

The Expert asks you for the title of your Web page, your name, and your e-mail address. The reason for the title is clear enough: At this writing, more than 30 million pages exist on the World Wide Web. Try to make your title meaningful and unique.

Your name and e-mail address are there in case anyone actually wants to get in touch with you as a result of reading your Web page. You'll see a link on the Web page that allows people to send you mail with just one click.

**5. Enter the relevant information, and click on Next > when you're ready to go on.**

Web pages typically are divided into several sections. A main Web page, such as the one that the Expert helps you create, usually leads the reader to subtopics. This step of the Web Page Expert allows you to set up standard sections by clicking on Add. (We added a section titled My Professional Information, so Figure 19-4 may look different from your screen.) You can also choose to include or exclude any of your standard sections on a particular page by checking or unchecking their boxes in the Table of Contents.

**6. Select the table-of-contents entries that you want to use by checking or unchecking the boxes next to each one; then on click Next >.**

Now here's something that you can't normally do in WordPerfect. Web pages can have different color schemes and pictures (called *wallpaper*) behind the text on the page. Having a professional staff prepare all these

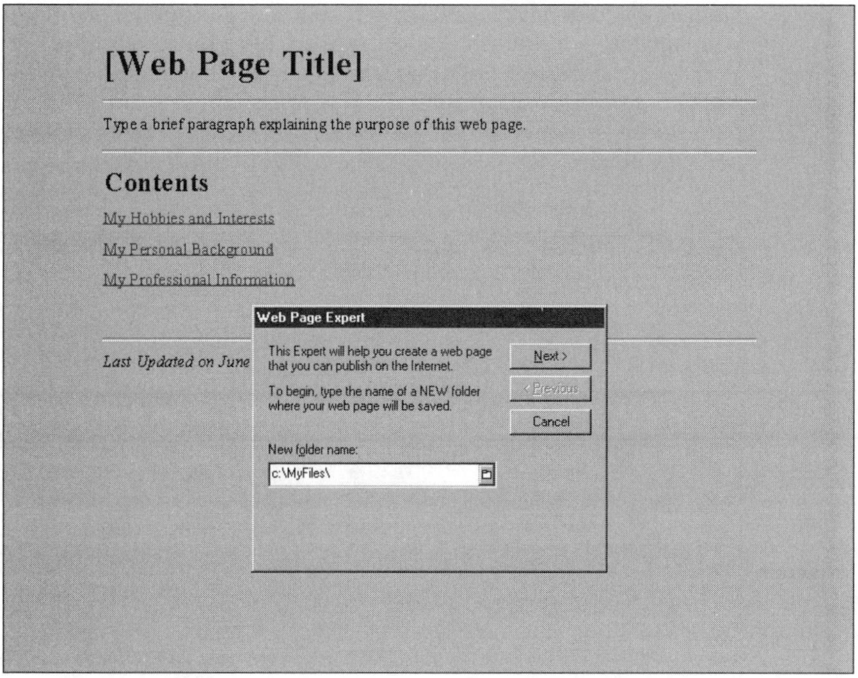

[Web Page Title]

Type a brief paragraph explaining the purpose of this web page.

**Contents**

My Hobbies and Interests

My Personal Background

My Professional Information

*Last Updated on June*

**Web Page Expert**

This Expert will help you create a web page that you can publish on the Internet.

To begin, type the name of a NEW folder where your web page will be saved.

New folder name:

c:\MyFiles\

Next >

< Previous

Cancel

**Figure 19-4:**
The Web Page Expert beginning to create a Web page.

color and background combinations for you comes in handy, if you can arrange it. Unless you are an artist, choosing Web-page colors is hard to do well. Surprisingly, most of the Background Wallpaper and Color Schemes that you can select are pretty good. WordPerfect shows you your selection as soon as you make it. You'll find that some combinations of color and background make your text almost impossible to read.

You can also specify a default alignment for your text: all lines to the left, centered, or to the right. Don't worry much about alignment; you can change it for any individual line.

7. **For your first time through, leave the Color Scheme and Background Wallpaper alone; just click on Next >.**

Surprise — you're all done.

8. **Click on Finished and OK when you are reminded to publish your Web page.**

We said earlier in the chapter that WordPerfect creates an HTML Web document by translating the WordPerfect codes to HTML codes. This Publish to HTML step is when that translation occurs. You will be reminded that all of WordPerfect's zillion formatting features are not available; click on OK.

Suddenly, you're back in familiar territory: the WordPerfect editing screen. All your familiar WordPerfect editing tools are here, and the blue underlined phrases are hypertext links that lead to other documents. Figure 19-5 shows what your page looks link after the Web Page Expert is through with it. This page doesn't say much about dinosaurs, but we can fix that problem. Start by adding a picture.

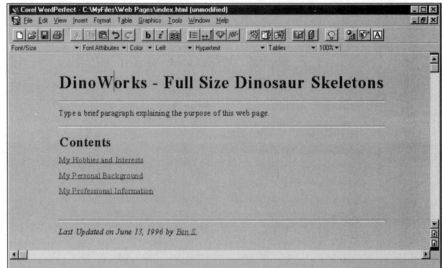

**Figure 19-5:**
A very basic
Web page
created by
the Expert.

# Adding a picture to a Web page

As you do with any WordPerfect document, you add a picture to a Web page by inserting the file that contains the picture into your document. Follow these steps:

1. **Press Ctrl+Home to move to the beginning of the document.**

   Many Web pages have pictures at the top to provide a little visual interest while the reader looks over the text.

2. **Choose Insert⇨File.**

3. **Select the file that contains the picture that you want to insert.**

   In this case, you have a tasteful picture of three dinosaur skeletons. It doesn't matter where on your computer the file that contains the picture is, relative to where your Web page is stored. You can browse all over the place (even to other computers) to find this file.

That's all there is to putting the picture in a Web document. Now you can use WordPerfect's normal picture-formatting commands to move the picture around. We happen to like our picture in the upper left corner of the page, with the text running down beside it. In case the procedure slipped your mind, see Chapter 15.

## Creating a link to another Web page

This will be a real Web page if we replace the references to the Web Expert's made-up pages with references to some real dinosaur pages. Start with links to pages that talk about our dinosaur models. We typed the text that is going to go on our page, so all we have to do is replace each of the three dinosaur names with a link to a page by the same name. Figure 19-6 illustrates the following steps which we used to do create some links on this page:

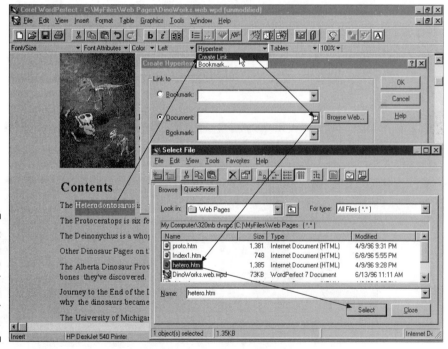

**Figure 19-6:**
Creating a link to another Web page on your computer.

1. **Highlight the text that the user should see as a link.**

   In this case, we used the dinosaur name Heterdontosarus.

2. **On the Internet Publisher Power Bar, click on Hypertext⇨Create Link.**

   As we mentioned earlier, this action displays the Create Hypertext Link dialog box.

**3. Click on the file folder to the right of <u>D</u>ocument:**

This displays the Select file dialog box and allows you to select a document on your computer as the destination of the link.

**4. Click on the file that contains the Web page (HTML) text.**

This file is probably a Web page that you created with the Internet Publisher and saved as an HTML file. At the end of this chapter, we talk about saving HTML files.

**5. Click on Select.**

The Select File dialog box goes away.

**6. Click on OK.**

The Create Hypertext Link dialog box goes away, and the word *Heterdontosarus* is underlined and highlighted in blue.

We did the same thing for our other dinosaur models. We also did two other things to make our Web page a little classier. We formatted the sentences that contain links as bullet items. (We used the Font/Size button, described in the section, "The HTML Menu Bar and Power Bar." And we formatted "Other Dinosaur Pages on the World Wide Web" as Heading 2 (the same way). That way, it matches the Contents created by the Web Page Expert. Our page now looks like Figure 19-7.

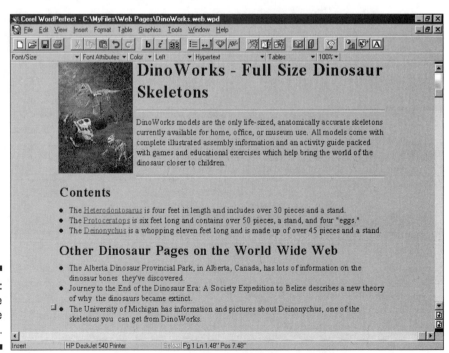

**Figure 19-7:**
A Web page with some formatting.

# Jumping into Netscape

Now comes the fun part: browsing the World Wide Web and seeing whether we can find some dinosaur sites. We'll spare you the wandering-around-in-the-wilderness part and jump directly to a couple of links. Figure 19-8 illustrates the following steps, which we used to create a link to a World Wide Web page.

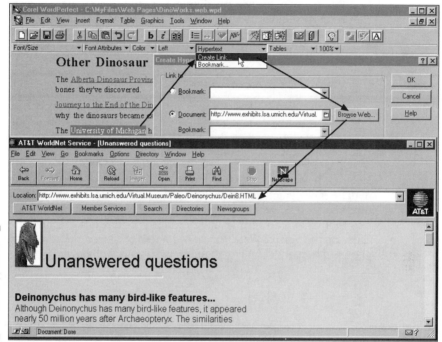

**Figure 19-8:**
Creating a
hypertext
link to a
World Wide
Web page.

1. **Highlight the text you want to be the link.**

   This is the same thing that you've done before.

2. **Choose Hypertext⇨Create Link from the Web Page Power Bar.**

   Again, this procedure is the same as before; the Create Hypertext link dialog box appears.

3. **Click on Browse Web.**

   Be patient. Eventually, Netscape Navigator appears on-screen, followed by some messages about dial-up networking (assuming that you're using dial-up networking to connect to the Internet). If you're all set up to get on the Internet and have done this before, it should look familiar. If you haven't, you have another project ahead of you. Get the cookies, and go find your local Internet wizard.

If everything works right, you see the Netscape Navigator. You can wander around the World Wide Web until you get to a page that you want to link to. To wander from page to page, click on links.

Depending on how your windows are set up, WordPerfect may disappear at this point, to be replaced by Netscape. If that happens, don't panic. When you're at the page that you want to link to, use the Windows 95 TaskBar to switch back to WordPerfect.

When you're back in WordPerfect, look at the <u>D</u>ocument box in the Create Hypertext Link dialog box. It should contain the address of the page that you're looking at. If it doesn't, highlight the address (in the Netscape window); press Ctrl+C to copy the address; and press Ctrl+V to paste it in the <u>D</u>ocument box.

**4. Click on OK to complete the link.**

The link is highlighted in blue, just like the links to WordPerfect documents. But when you look at this document on the World Wide Web, when your readers click on this link, they see the same Web page that you were looking at when you created the link.

Now you have something that looks like a WordPerfect document with a couple of differences (such as the background color). A close look also reveals that the menu bar and Power Bar have changed a little bit. Figure 19-9 illustrates the new toolbar and Power Bar, and describes the buttons that are different from those on the normal WordPerfect toolbar. We'll describe these buttons, because you need to use a couple of them to finish your Web page.

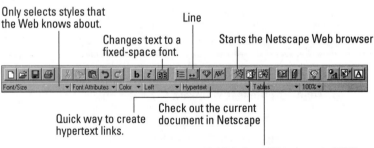

**Figure 19-9:**
The HTML menu bar and Power Bar.

Only selects styles that the Web knows about.

Line

Changes text to a fixed-space font.

Starts the Netscape Web browser

Quick way to create hypertext links.

Check out the current document in Netscape

Publish these Web pages in HTML

## *The HTML menu bar and Power Bar*

The following list describes seven items on the HTML menu bar and Power Bar that you should know about:

✔ **Font/Size.** Displays a list of the sizes and styles that Web pages understand. "Why," you ask, "can't I use all of WordPerfect's eight zillion features to format my text?" You can't, because some poor Web browser far, far away on some other computer may have no idea what you're talking about. Web browsers know how to do only what HTML tells them to do, and HTML has no way of saying, "Format the following text in a spiral, using ornamental pumpkins in small caps." Actually, *some* Web browsers know what to do with this, and others don't. So you're better off doing your formatting with the styles in the list that drops down when you click on Font/Size.

✔ **Fixed-space font.** Unless you're into typesetting, fixed-space text looks ugly. But if your Web page is about technical stuff, you may want to use it. Somewhere near the beginning, most computer books say, "Text that you should type to the program appears like this: `sample command`." We went to great pains not to do that in this book. But you may want to do it on your Web page. Again, as with the fonts and sizes, you can use WordPerfect's galaxy of features to do this, but the poor Web browser on the other end may not have a clue.

✔ **Hypertext.** Earlier in this chapter, you created your own hypertext links by using the Hypertext Feature bar, which you displayed by choosing Tools➪Hypertext/Web Links. This button takes you directly to the Create or Edit dialog box from the feature bar without having you display the feature bar. Pretty impressive, huh?

✔ **Line.** Web pages frequently have horizontal lines on them to separate different sections of the content. This design seems to make the pages easier for people to read. You'll notice that the Web Page Expert put some horizontal lines on your page; you may want to, too. Use this button to do so.

✔ **Start Netscape.** You don't need to use this button when you create a Web page, but we figured that if we explained the next two buttons and didn't explain this one, you'd wonder.

✔ **Check out the current document in Netscape.** We've been saying over and over that these pages will look different in the Web browser than they do in WordPerfect. Before you decide that you have your page just exactly the way you want it, you should see what it looks like in at least one browser. This button makes that very easy to do. Use it. (Unfortunately, they don't make it particularly easy to get back to WordPerfect when you've looked at your page. Click on the Corel WordPerfect button on the Windows 95 Taskbar.)

✔ **Publish these Web pages.** We'll talk more about this button later in this chapter, in "Saving and Publishing Your Web Pages."

# Creating Web Pages the Hard Way: Doing It Yourself from Scratch

A while ago, we said that we'd get to some of the other options in the File⇨Internet Publisher menu. Now's the time. If you look at Figure 19-4, choosing New Web Document⇨Create a Blank Web Document gives you a blank document screen with the characteristic Web gray background. Then, as with any word processing document, you're on your own.

You can do a lot of stuff in WordPerfect that you cannot do on a Web page. Columns immediately spring to mind, as one example. And that's another reason why there are Web browsers and word processors.

## Stuff you can do in WordPerfect that you can't do on a Web page

As you look at the WordPerfect menus while you edit a Web document, you'll notice that most of the commands in the Format menu have disappeared, because most of them can't be used on a Web page. Following are the features that really don't convert to a Web page, roughly in the order in which we think you might care about them:

- **Tabs.** Yes, that's tabs as in the Tab key — something so simple that you probably don't even think about it. We're sure that there are lots of technical reasons why tabs aren't in HTML as we know it today, but the fact remains that they aren't. If you used tabs to create a table, reformat the text to be a table. HTML can handle tables okay.

- **Margins (left or right).** Web pages take their margins from the size of the user's window.

- **Page numbering.** What's a page? Numbered relative to what? We're talking about hypertext here.

- **Columns.** WordPerfect will try to do something with columns, but you probably won't enjoy the results. Newer Web browsers are moving toward columns, but they're not part of the mainstream yet.

- **Headers and footers.** These elements don't apply to Web pages.

- **Indents.** Indents aren't critical to most documents and don't even exist in HTML documents.

- **Drop caps.** The absence of drop caps is a shame, because they can be nice-looking. WordPerfect turns them back in to regular text. If you still want to be artsy, replace drop caps with graphics.

- ✔ **Fill (shading behind text).** Use your page background for this.
- ✔ **Vertical lines.** Use tables again, if you can.
- ✔ **Watermarks.** Watermarks should be part of your page background.

## Stuff you can do on a Web page that you can't do in WordPerfect

Life is not totally unfair, however; you can do some things on a Web page that you can't do in a WordPerfect document. The only one that springs to mind is changing the color of the *background* of the page. If you chose Format➪Text/ Background, you see a new dialog box in WordPerfect. The bottom portion of this box, labeled Background Color/Wallpaper, allows you to choose a color for your page and a graphics file that contains the background wallpaper for your page. Try doing *that* in a regular WordPerfect document!

## Converting your documents to Web pages

One of the most useful things about the fact that WordPerfect can create Web documents is that you can use those documents on the World Wide Web. You probably already have a bunch of WordPerfect documents. Presto — instant content for your Web site. The only problem is that the documents are not formatted as Web pages, and they probably use all sorts of features that don't work on Web pages.

Once again, WordPerfect comes to the rescue. The Format as Web Document button on the Internet Publisher screen removes all the non-Web-page format-ting from your document. What you see on-screen is the result of this button's labors.

Depending on how much formatting you did in your document, you will be more or less pleased with the result. If your document looks totally destroyed, you have two options:

- ✔ You can reformat the document as a WordPerfect document, using only the features that work in Web documents.
- ✔ You can fix the Web version by hand.

The option that you choose depends on how you intend to maintain your document. If you want to keep both a WordPerfect version of your document (for printing on paper) and a Web version for people to look at, choose the first option. This option involves a little more work, but you have to keep the document up to date in only one place. Every time you change the WordPerfect version, you can convert it to a Web page again. You won't be able to make it a very fancy WordPerfect document, but maybe that's okay.

If you are converting your documents for use on the Web, fix the Web version by hand, which is just a matter of using the formatting features that are available. The better you make a document look as a Web document, the more it is going to differ from the original. That's okay, but it usually is hard to keep two versions of the same document up to date with one another.

You can also add to your document HTML features that WordPerfect has no idea about. Simply type the HTML codes in to your document, highlight them, and choose Format⇨Custom HTML. To do this, you have to know HTML. Go get a copy of *HTML For Dummies* by Ed Tittel and Steve James (published by IDG Books Worldwide, Inc.).

# Saving and Publishing Your Web Pages

There are three — count 'em, three — ways to save your Web pages in WordPerfect. This shouldn't surprise you, because there are a bunch of ways to do everything in WordPerfect. But in this case, the three ways do three different things, so it's important to know when to use which one.

## Saving your Web page as a WordPerfect document

Here's the confusing part: After you convert your WordPerfect document to a Web page, it is still a WordPerfect document. It's just a WordPerfect document with some magic stuff that tells WordPerfect that only the Web-page features work. Because the document is a WordPerfect document, you should save it as a .WPD file, which is exactly what WordPerfect does if you choose the File⇨Save As command. In fact, you'll notice that after you convert your document, it still has the same name. So if you're not careful, you'll end up saving the Web-page version (which, we assume, has lost a lot of formatting) right on top of your beautiful WordPerfect version. You won't even get a warning.

We don't think that this is a good idea. Our recommendation is that you put the word .WEB right before the .WPD so you'll know that this is a Web-page version of your file. Our document Chocolate - Chapter 1.WPD would become Chocolate - Chapter 1.WEB.WPD. If you do that, at least you'll know what's what. Save your Web pages with a .WEB.WPD extension if you expect to continue to work on them as time goes by. That way, you can still use WordPerfect editing features on them.

## *Saving your Web page as an HTML document*

You may want to use WordPerfect to edit your Web pages because you like WordPerfect (as we do, despite all our snide comments); because someone gave you some special WordPerfect tools to use on your documents, and you want to use them on your Web pages; or because your Web pages started as WordPerfect documents. You can even use Netscape to save a page off the Web and edit that page in WordPerfect. You can do these things because WordPerfect now has a filter for HTML. This filter is similar to the filters that allow WordPerfect to load and save documents from Lotus 1-2-3, Microsoft Excel, and Microsoft Word.

To save your document as an HTML file, choose File⇨Save As. In the As Type box of the Save As dialog box, select HTML (*.htm" "*.html). Your file will be saved with the extension .HTM. Save your Web pages this way if someone else is going to worry about getting them onto the World Wide Web or onto your corporate Intranet.

When you open your .HTM file, WordPerfect asks you what format you want your file to be converted from. It suggests HTML, which is, after all, the right answer. Go ahead and tell it okay. But it may be useful for you to know that an HTML file actually is just a text file. If you want to look at the file as a text file (and see all the HTML in it), tell WordPerfect to convert it from ANSI Windows Text format. The guts of your Web page will be revealed to you.

## *Publishing your Web page*

So what the heck is the difference between publishing a Web page and saving a Web page as an HTML file? If your Web page doesn't have any links to any other Web pages that you maintain, and if your Web page doesn't have any pictures in it, there is no difference. If both of these things are true, you have a pretty boring Web page. If they are not true of your Web page, publishing your Web page does you a couple of useful favors:

> ✔ **Publish creates a folder for your Web page.**
>
> Why do you want a folder for your Web page? Most Web pages actually are collections of Web documents. Remember when the Web Expert asked you what sections you wanted to include in your Web page? The Expert considered each of those sections to be a new Web page. Just to be helpful, it also created a little WordPerfect document for each of those sections. And it very confusingly gave those files .HTM tags, *even though they're WordPerfect files and should have .WPD tags.* Hey, it's software; it's not perfect. But you may find this arrangement confusing. (We did!)

✔ **Publish creates a subfolder for the images on your Web page.**

When you add an image to your Web page, the graphics file can be stored anywhere on your computer or on someone else's computer, if you're attached to a local-area network. This is not very handy for gathering all the pieces that you need for your Web page together in one place, so the Web publisher creates a single folder to put your images in.

✔ **Publish puts copies of the images on your pages in the subfolder that it made.**

In fact, it makes copies in .GIF format (don't ask, it's a kind of image that Web browsers can display for readers) or .JPEG format (same idea), and puts the copies in this folder. Thereafter, if you move the .HTM Web pages *and* the subfolder together, your Web pages still work.

All these facts make using the File➪Internet Publisher command a good idea. If you created your Web page with the Web Page Expert, you still have to open each of the subpage files as an .HTM file individually to save the files as HTML files instead of WordPerfect documents. You'll have to open them in WordPerfect and then save them as type HTM (as described earlier in this chapter). But that's OK; you probably want to edit them anyway.

## Putting your pages on the World Wide Web

We've talked a lot about preparing your pages for the World Wide Web, but we haven't actually said what you have to do to get your pages onto the World Wide Web. That's because it varies from location to location. In general, you have to find a computer that is always connected to the Internet (or the Intranet, if you're just interested in distributing information around your com-

pany). Then it's just a matter of putting your .HTM files in the right place.

In all likelihood, you are going to need a local computer-systems junkie to do this for you, because companies are (or should be) careful about how their computers connect to the rest of the world.

# Part IV
# Help Me, Rhonda!

"THE PHONE COMPANY BLAMES THE MANUFACTURER, WHO SAYS IT'S THE SOFTWARE COMPANY'S FAULT, WHO BLAMES IT ON OUR MOON BEING IN VENUS WITH SCORPIO RISING."

## In this part . . .

**I**s all going well with your word-processing experience? No? You've run into a snag? Well, you've come to the right place.

This part of the book solves a number of thorny problems, including dealing with Windows itself (which is sometimes unavoidable) and talking sense into your printer. You also learn how to make WordPerfect's behavior more socially acceptable. If you run into bug trouble, run (do not walk) to Chapter 23 for solutions to the most common WordPerfect problems.

# Chapter 20

# Training WordPerfect to Act Your Way

*Y*ou know how software can be — badly behaved, saving files in the wrong folders, displaying incomprehensible things on-screen, and being generally rude. It's time for some lessons in deportment. You can teach WordPerfect to behave more like the kind of gentleman or lady you like to be seen with.

It's pretty nifty that WordPerfect allows you to customize so much about the way it works. In this chapter, you find out how to display information about your documents, how to zoom in on the text of your document in close-up, how to control which buttons appear on the Power Bar and Toolbar, how to control where WordPerfect stores things (in which folders on your disk), and how to set other preferences.

If you are happy with WordPerfect just the way it is, you can skip this chapter. On the other hand, if you are really, *really* happy with WordPerfect, you may want to see a shrink. Leaving your WordPerfect settings alone is not such a bad idea. One advantage of this approach is that your WordPerfect will work just like everyone else's (unless they have customized *their* copies), so it is easier to get help from your WordPerfect-savvy friends.

# Seeing Information about Your Documents

You can enter information about your document in the Document Summary dialog box. To display this dialog box, choose File⇔Document⇔Properties. The spaces for all the kinds of stuff you might want to know about a document don't all fit in the dialog box, but you can use the little scroll bar to slide down to see the rest.

The information that you enter in the document summary is stored along with your document. You can view or edit it at any time.

What if you don't want to enter something in the Descriptive Type box? (What if you don't even have the faintest idea what a descriptive type might be? We don't.) What if you want to keep track of the document's version number instead? Wow — WordPerfect allows *you* to choose which blanks appear in the Document Summary dialog box. To change the facts included in all summaries that you create, click on the Configure button in the Document Summary dialog box. WordPerfect displays the Document Summary Configuration dialog box and allows you to choose among a long list of possible facts about a document, including Authorization, Checked By, Document Number, Project, Status, and Version Number. Does this sound official or what?

# Setting Your Favorite Font

Have you ever gotten annoyed at WordPerfect for always suggesting the same font whenever you create a new document? We have. Enough with Times New Roman, already — we're in the mood for Arial!

The following list provides some solutions to this problem:

- **Use templates.** Templates allow you to predefine all the styles you use for the kinds of documents that you usually create. You can make one template for letters, one for memos, and one for faxes, each with the proper fonts selected.

- **Tell WordPerfect the name of your favorite font.** WordPerfect then uses this font for all new documents unless you select another one.

For instructions about using the first approach, refer to Chapter 16, which is all about templates. These steps show you how to use the second approach:

1. **Choose Format⇔Document⇔Initial Font.**

   WordPerfect, ever ready to pop open another dialog box, displays the Document Initial Font dialog box.

**2. Choose your favorite font, size, and style.**

Show some restraint here — no one will be able to read your polished prose if you print it in Shelley Volante.

**3. Choose Set as printer initial font.**

Make sure that a check mark is in the little box by this option, at the bottom of the dialog box; otherwise, this step sets the font only for the current document.

**4. Click on OK or press Enter.**

You have just told WordPerfect to use your favorite font whenever you create a new document to be printed on the selected printer. Unless you use several different printers, you are all set.

If you use several printers, display the Print dialog box, click on the Printer tab, and choose a printer. Then click on the Initial Font button and set the font in the Printer Initial Font dialog box.

See Chapter 22 for more information about choosing printers. See Chapter 7 to find out how to change fonts within a document.

# Zooming Around in Your Documents

Maybe we're just getting old. Or the light bulb in the desk lamp may be getting dim. Or it may be our monitor — its phosphors are probably running down or something. Anyway, when we edit documents in 10-point type, we used to press our noses to the screen to read the teeny-tiny letters that WordPerfect uses. After a few visits to the chiropractor, we realized that something had to be done.

Then we found WordPerfect's Zoom feature. You can blow up the text on your screen as much as you want without changing its size on the printed page. These steps show you how:

**1. Choose View⇨Zoom.**

WordPerfect displays the Zoom dialog box.

**2. Choose one of the percentages listed in the dialog box.**

The larger the percentage, the bigger the text looks on-screen (as though you were sticking your face closer to it). If you don't like any of the options that WordPerfect offers, click on Other and enter the percentage you want (we like 120 percent).

**3. Choose OK.**

If you prefer the Power Bar to the menu bar, click on the Zoom button, which displays some percentage; then click on one of the selections in the list that drops down.

In addition to numerical percentages, the Zoom dialog box contains these four options:

- ✔ **Margin Width:** Blows up the text until it fills the window from side to side, with the left margin against the left edge of the window and the right margin against the right edge. This option automatically zooms the document to the maximum percentage that allows you to see the full width of your text.

- ✔ **Page Width:** Blows up the page until it fills the window from side to side, including the left and right margins. The left edge of the paper is just inside the left edge of the window, and the right edge is just inside the right edge. You see a little space between the edge of the paper and the edge of the window. This option always gives you a smaller zoom percentage than Margin Width does.

- ✔ **Full Page:** Blows up the page until it fills the window from top to bottom. The top edge of the paper is near the top edge of the window, and the bottom edge of the paper is near the bottom edge of the window. If you use normal paper in its normal orientation, so that the paper is taller than it is wide, Full Page produces a rather small (not to say unreadable) image, but it gives you the overall effect of the page.

- ✔ **Other:** Displays the Zoom dialog box, in which you can set any zoom percentage you want to use.

If you use zooming to increase the size of the text on-screen and you *still* cannot read it, save your document (or documents); then get a clean damp handkerchief and wipe all the dust off the front of your monitor. Something about the way that computer screens work creates static electricity that attracts dust from all over your house. There! Isn't that better?

You cannot use zooming when you are in two-page view (refer to Chapter 9). No one we know uses two-page view, so who cares?

One problem comes with using a large zoom percentage — that is, a zoom percentage bigger than what you get with Margin Width: Most documents get so wide that you cannot see an entire line of text. It is annoying to have to scroll left and right to read each line of the document. Here's an alternative: At the beginning of your document, switch to a large font size, such as 12 or 14 points. WordPerfect reformats the document (at least, up to the next font-size code) by using larger characters, and it wraps the text to fit within the margins. Now you can read it just fine. When you print it, on the other hand, the text is enormous. To fix it, delete the font-size code that you just added. (Refer to Chapter 10 to learn how to use the Reveal Codes window to delete a formatting code.)

# *Expressing Your Preferences*

The process of teaching WordPerfect how to behave is generally simple: You tell WordPerfect your preferences, and it whips into line. Wouldn't it be nice if everyone worked this way?

You tell WordPerfect what you want by using the Edit⇨Preferences command, which displays the Preferences dialog box, shown in Figure 20-1.

**Figure 20-1:**
Wow! A
dialog box
with lots of
little
pictures!

Instead of the dull, boring boxes and buttons you see in most dialog boxes, this one has nifty little icons for the different types of preferences that you can express.

- **Display:** What WordPerfect displays on-screen, including what the ruler bar includes; how the Reveal Codes windows looks; and whether you want to see symbols where your spaces, tabs, and returns are. We describe these settings in detail later.

- **Environment:** Miscellaneous stuff that didn't fit into any of the other categories of preferences.

- **Files:** Where WordPerfect stores your documents, templates, macros, and other files; and whether you want it to keep backups of your files. This stuff is described later in this chapter.

- **Summary:** How document summaries work, and when you want to see them (if ever).

- **Convert:** Some advanced settings that tell WordPerfect how to convert graphics files, ASCII delimited-text files, WordPerfect 4.2, DCA, and DisplayWrite documents.

- **Toolbar:** Which buttons you want to include; whether you want to see words, pictures, or both on the buttons; and where the Toolbar should appear. WordPerfect comes with a bunch of predefined Toolbars; you can make your own, if you prefer. We discuss this subject later in this chapter.

- ✔ **Power Bar:** Which buttons you want to include on the Power Bar, and which fonts and font sizes should appear when you use the Font and Font Size buttons (also described later in this chapter).

- ✔ **Status Bar:** Which information to display, in addition to the font and general appearance that you prefer. (Read on for more information.)

- ✔ **Menu Bar:** Which commands you want to list in each menu, believe it or not.

- ✔ **Keyboard:** What you want each key on the keyboard to do. (This subject is discussed later in this chapter, although we refuse to go into detail.)

Yikes! This list presents an unbelievable number of things to think about. The scary part is that you can control how all these things work. Does this give you a feeling of power? It gives us a feeling of stark terror — think of all the things that we might break!

To use the Preferences dialog box to express your preferences, double-click on the icon of your choice; it displays one or more dialog boxes. When you dismiss the dialog box(es), you return to the Preferences dialog box. When you finish fooling with WordPerfect's innards, click on the Close button in the Preferences dialog box or press the Esc key.

The rest of this chapter explains how to change some of the settings in the Preferences dialog box and why you would want to. Don't worry — you can always change them back.

Changing too many things at the same time is a bad idea. When you're fooling around with preferences, make one or two changes and then close all the dialog boxes. Look around in WordPerfect to see what you have done.

# Changing the Way WordPerfect Looks

As you have noticed, WordPerfect displays a zillion gizmos on-screen. These steps show some things that you may want to change and instructions for changing them. All these settings appear in the Display Preferences dialog box, which you display by following these steps:

**1. Choose Edit⇨Preferences to display the Preferences dialog box.**

**2. Double-click on the Display icon.**

You see the Display Preferences dialog box.

WordPerfect has so many categories of display settings that it displays a tab at the top of the dialog box for each type. If you choose Document, Symbols, View/Zoom, Reveal Codes, Ruler Bar, or Merge, the rest of the dialog box changes to show settings that pertain to that subject.

A quicker way to display the Display Preferences dialog box is to right-click on the scroll bar and then choose Preferences from the QuickMenu.

## Zooming

We always end up zooming in our documents a little, because the usual 100 percent display is a tad too small for us to read comfortably. How annoying to have to do this every time we open a document! Instead, you can tell WordPerfect once and for all what zoom percentage you want to use. While you are at it, you can tell WordPerfect which view you usually want to see: draft, page, or (ugh!) two-page.

Follow these steps to tell WordPerfect how you want to zoom:

1. **Choose Edit⇨Preferences.**

2. **Double-click on the Display icon.**

   WordPerfect shows you the Display Preferences dialog box.

3. **Click on the View/Zoom option at the top of the dialog box.**

   WordPerfect shows you two groups of settings: Default view and Default zoom.

4. **Choose a Default View (Draft, Page, or Two Page).**

5. **Choose a Default Zoom.**

   You see the same options listed earlier in this chapter.

6. **Click on OK and then click on the Close button to escape from the world of dialog boxes.**

When you close the Preferences dialog box, WordPerfect changes the zoom of the current window to the one that you just specified. Whenever you open a document or create a new one, WordPerfect uses this zoom percentage. You can still change the zoom for individual documents as necessary.

## Editing bars

Button, button, who's got the button? You do — that is, you can control which buttons you have on the Toolbar and the Power Bar.

WordPerfect comes with 15 predefined Toolbars — 15 sets of buttons that the folks at WordPerfect think are useful for different sorts of documents. The Generate Toolbar, for example, contains buttons for tasks that you perform in large documents, including generating tables of contents and indexes. The Font Toolbar contains buttons for selecting many text styles.

The following steps show you how to choose which Toolbar you see:

1. **Right-click anywhere on the Toolbar.**

   WordPerfect displays a list of defined Toolbars. The one that you see now has a check mark by its name.

2. **Choose one by clicking on it.**

   Poof — a new set of buttons appears.

The Toolbar that appears when you first install WordPerfect — which is the one we use in the figures in this book — is called WordPerfect 7.

If you use templates (described in Chapter 16), you can tell WordPerfect which Toolbar to use whenever you open a document by changing the Toolbar when you're defining the template. Then you can display buttons that are appropriate for the type of document that you are creating.

Although it has multiple Toolbars, WordPerfect comes with only one predefined Power Bar, so you cannot switch among Power Bars. But you *can* change the way that the Power Bar looks. These steps show you how to use the Power Bar Options dialog box:

1. **Choose Edit⇨Preferences.**

   You see the now-infamous Preferences dialog box.

2. **Double-click on the Power Bar icon.**

   The Power Bar Options dialog box appears. This dialog box allows you to change the appearance of the buttons (the font and type size, and whether or not a picture appears), but not which buttons are on the Power Bar. If you have edited the Power Bar and want the regular one back again, click on the Default button.

After you decide what you want the Power Bar to look like, you can treat it just like a regular Toolbar, even if you have it displaying buttons with text on them (which is the way it appears in WordPerfect if you don't change anything). So everything we say in the following text about Toolbars applies to the Power Bar, too.

You can define your own Toolbars — add buttons to do the things that you do most. Editing the bars is pretty cool; you can drag buttons off them and drag new buttons (from the Toolbar Editor dialog box) to them.

Remember, even though the Preferences dialog box contains different buttons for the Toolbar and Power Bar, you do all your adding, removing, and rearranging buttons from the Toolbar Preferences dialog box. To edit a Toolbar, follow these steps:

1. **Choose Edit⇨Preferences.**

2. **Double-click on the Toolbar icon.**

   The Toolbar Options dialog box appears.

3. **Click on the Edit button.**

   The Toolbar Editor dialog box appears, and the Toolbar looks a little funny.

   You can also get to the Toolbar Editor dialog box by right-clicking one of the bars and then choosing Edit from the QuickMenu.

4. **Choose a Feature Category.**

   Click on the box below Feature Categories, and select a category. These are the same categories that you see in the menu bar.

5. **Choose a feature from the Features box.**

   You can add a feature in two ways: click on the feature and then on the Add button to add the feature to the end of the bar that you're officially editing; or drag the feature to either bar (the suave approach). The dragging approach also allows you to specify where you want the button to be. If it isn't obvious, we prefer the dragging method.

You can edit your Toolbar and Power Bar to have buttons that issue any WordPerfect command, run a macro (a prerecorded series of keystrokes, which is a subject that we don't get into in this book), run another program (this is seriously cool Windows-type stuff), or type something from the keyboard. You can also create your own Toolbar from scratch by clicking on the Create button in the Toolbar Preferences dialog box.

If you want the regular old Toolbar back, right-click on the Toolbar and choose WordPerfect 7 from the QuickMenu. If you want the regular Power Bar back, display the Power Bar Options dialog box (right-click on the Power Bar and then choose Options from the QuickMenu, or choose Edit⇨Preferences and double-click on the Power Bar icon); then and click on the Default button.

---

## Choose your buttons with care

If you find that you never use a button on the Power Bar or Toolbar, get it out of there! There's no point in staring at something useless every day while it takes up valuable screen real estate. We never use the Cut, Copy, or Paste buttons, for example; it's faster to press Ctrl+X, Ctrl+C, and Ctrl+V. So we dragged those puppies off to oblivion.

On the other hand, if you use the same command a million times a day, add a button for it to the one of the bars. We like to add these buttons, for example:

✔ File⇨Close

✔ File⇨Exit

✔ View⇨Toolbars/Ruler⇨Ruler Bar

✔ View⇨Show ¶

When the Toolbar Editor dialog box is open, you can use some of the methods in this list to customize your bars:

- ✔ **To remove a button:** Click on the button and drag it off the bar into the document area. Your mouse pointer turns into a cute trash-bucket icon. Release the mouse button, and the button gets tossed away.

- ✔ **To move a button to a new location:** Drag it with your mouse.

- ✔ **To add a little space (called a *separator*) between two buttons:** Click on the picture in the Separator section of the dialog box and drag it to the spot on the bar where you want it to be. Separators don't mean a thing to WordPerfect, but they make your Toolbar easier to use by allowing you to separate your buttons into groups. For clarity, you can insert as many separators as you want; you can also put more than one separator between buttons.

When you're all done fooling around with the bars, click on OK in the Toolbar Editor dialog box; then click on OK or Close in any other dialog boxes to return to your document.

## Controlling the status bar

Status is important in our society. The status bar allows you to keep track of your status. Among other things, you can find out your exact position in the social strata of your document.

When you install WordPerfect, it displays the following information on the status bar:

- ✔ **General status:** Usually tells you whether you are in Insert or Typeover mode (refer to Chapter 4), but also displays different information

- ✔ **Printer:** Which printer is currently selected

- ✔ **Select on/off:** Whether text is selected

- ✔ **Combined position:** The page that your cursor is on and the exact location of the cursor on the page, both horizontally and vertically

Lots of other pieces of information would be useful to see, however, such as whether your Caps Lock key has been pressed accidentally.

To choose what you want to see on the status bar, use the Status Bar Preferences dialog box, as shown in these steps:

1. **Choose Edit➪Preferences.**

2. **Double-click on the Status Bar icon.**

   WordPerfect displays the Status Bar Preferences dialog box.

Alternatively, you can follow these steps:

1. **Right-click on the status bar.**

   WordPerfect displays a small QuickMenu of commands that pertain to the status bar.

2. **Choose Preferences from the QuickMenu.**

   The Status Bar Preferences dialog box appears.

The Status bar items list in the dialog box shows all the possible items that can appear on the status bar. An *X* marks an item that appears. To add an *X* or remove an existing one, click on the check box. You can add items, remove them, or switch them around by dragging them to a new position on the status bar. In addition, while this dialog box is open, you can change the size of an item on the status bar by using the mouse to drag its left or right edge.

When you finish, choose OK in the Status Bar Preferences dialog box and then click on the Close button in the Preferences dialog box, if you're finished with it, too.

This list shows the items that we like to keep track of on the status bar:

- ✔ Combined position (horizontal, vertical, and page number)
- ✔ General status (shows what's happening and usually shows whether WordPerfect is in Insert or Typeover mode; you can make this item much smaller than WordPerfect suggests)
- ✔ Caps Lock status (in case it's on by mistake)
- ✔ Num Lock status (ditto)

Many of the items on the status bar do things if you double-click on them. Try it!

## Displaying spaces, tabs, indents, and returns

It can be useful to see exactly which characters are in your text. After all, spaces, tabs, and indent characters all leave blank spaces in your text, but they behave very differently. If you want to be nosy about this stuff, you can ask WordPerfect to display little gizmos where your spaces, tabs, indents, and returns appear.

To see the characters in your text, follow these steps:

1. **Choose Edit⇨Preferences.**

2. **Double-click on the Display icon.**

   WordPerfect shows the Display Preferences dialog box.

3. **Click on the Symbols tab.**

   WordPerfect displays options for showing nonprinting symbols.

4. **If you want to see gizmos for these characters all the time, choose Show Symbols on New and Current Document.**

   You can always turn the symbols off if you get sick of them by choosing View⇨Show ¶.

5. **Remove the check marks next to items for which you don't want to see symbols.**

   To remove a check mark, click on the setting in the Symbols to Display list. It can get ridiculous, for example, if you display a special symbol for each and every space in your document. This is one symbol whose display we turn off.

6. **Choose the OK button and then click on the Close button in the Preferences dialog box.**

   Your document is suddenly littered with little arrows, paragraph marks, and other gizmos. (If you didn't choose Show symbols on new and current document in step 4, you must choose View⇨Show ¶ to get this effect.)

Alternatively, you can use the Reveal Codes window to see all of your codes — not just the spaces, tabs, indents, and returns. Refer to Chapter 10 for details.

## Changing your colors

Normally, WordPerfect displays your documents in a realistic but eye-tiring black-on-white color scheme. You may be glad to hear that you can change this scheme, especially if you have a laptop that has a monochrome or LCD display. This procedure is a way to make your WordPerfect window much more readable.

Changing screen colors requires talking to Windows 95. If you want to change the colors that are used in the document — not just in the menus, dialog boxes, or title bar — you have to change one WordPerfect setting, too. Follow these steps:

1. **If you don't want to change the colors of the document text, skip to Step 5.**

2. **Choose Edit⇨Preferences and then double-click on the Display icon.**

   WordPerfect displays the Display Preferences dialog box.

3. **In the Document section of the dialog box (click the Document tab), click Windows System Colors.**

This step tells WordPerfect to use the colors that Windows 95 suggests for the document text, rather than always use black on white. Make sure that a check mark appears in the box for this setting.

4. **Click on the OK button and then click on the Close button to exit all the dialog boxes.**

   The next step is to tell Windows 95 which colors you want to use.

5. **Click on the Windows 95 Start button and then choose Settings⇨Control Panel.**

   The Windows 95 Control Panel — a window with a bunch of icons in it — appears.

6. **Double-click on the Display icon.**

   Windows 95 displays the Display Properties dialog box, showing options for the Desktop Background.

7. **Click the Appearance tab at the top of the dialog box.**

   You see the Appearance settings, which are all about the colors that Windows 95 uses. At the top of the dialog box is a picture of how Windows 95 looks with its current colors. Below that picture is a list of color Schemes, which are predefined sets of colors that some color-blind person at Microsoft thought looked good.

8. **Choose a color scheme by clicking on the arrow at the right end of the Scheme box and choosing one from the list.**

   To show you what the color scheme looks like, the top of the dialog box shows two miniature windows with a miniature menu bar and menu. The part labeled Window Text corresponds to the document-text part of the WordPerfect window.

   Look at the color schemes to see which one you dislike the least.

   You can make your own Windows 95 color schemes, too: Click on an item in the picture of a miniature window (the name of the item that you clicked on appears in the Item section), and choose a color for it, using the Color list. If the situation and the screen get ugly, you can always click on Cancel.

9. **Choose OK to leave the Display Properties dialog box.**

   Poof — your screen colors change. If you hate them, go back to Step 6.

10. **Click on the Close button in the top-right corner of the Control Panel window.**

    The Control Panel goes away.

11. **Switch back to WordPerfect (if you need to) by clicking on the WordPerfect button on the Taskbar.**

You can spend all day getting your screen colors just right (and many people have). The key consideration is how your eyes feel at the end of the day.

# Where Does WordPerfect Put Your Files?

You have a hard disk, and heaven knows how many files are on it. Through the miracle of folders (described in Chapter 14), you don't have to look at all of them whenever you decide to pop open a document. The vast majority of files on your disk probably are program files, which you would just as soon never see.

## Telling WordPerfect about folders and backups

To tell WordPerfect where you want to store your documents in general (you can always choose different folders for some documents), as well as when to make automatic backups of your documents, follow these steps:

1. **Choose Edit⇨Preferences and then double-click on the Files icon.**

   WordPerfect displays the Files Preferences dialog box. The Document tab is selected, so the dialog box shows the settings that have to do with documents and backups.

2. **To indicate where you want your documents to go, enter a folder name in the Default document folder box.**

   This name must be a complete path name from the root folder of a disk drive, including the drive letter (such as C:). You can enter **C:\DOCS, C:\LETTERS,** or **C:\WPDOCS\MEMOS,** for example. You can use the little button with the file folder on it to find the folder that you want.

3. **To tell WordPerfect that you want all new documents to have the file extension .WPD, choose Use default extension on open and save.**

   WordPerfect suggests the extension .WPD, and we do, too. You can change it, though.

4. **To make a backup copy of your open documents at regular intervals, choose Timed document backup.**

   This step tells WordPerfect to save copies of all your open documents every so often. If the power goes out or you kick the computer's plug out of the outlet, this option is a godsend. To learn how to get these files back if you need them, see "Getting back your timed backups" later in this chapter.

   You can change the number of minutes in the box between Every and Minutes. This number specifies how often WordPerfect makes the backups.

5. **To prevent WordPerfect from accidentally replacing good files with bad ones, choose Original document backup.**

If this option is selected, every time you save a document, WordPerfect renames, rather than deletes, the old version. It renames these backup documents by using the file extension .BAK.

If you mess up a document irretrievably and then compound your error by saving it, this setting prevents WordPerfect from deleting the preceding version of the document. You can close the document without saving it and then open the .BAK version of the document.

6. **If you use templates, click on the Template tab at the top of the dialog box.**

You can change the folder in which WordPerfect looks for your templates (choose the D̲efault template folder option). See Chapter 16 for a description of using templates.

7. **If you use graphics or macros, click on the Graphic/Hyphen or Merge/ Macro tab to change the default folder.**

You probably are better off leaving them alone, though. Why mess with success?

8. **Click on the OK button and then click on the C̲lose button to get rid of all these dialog boxes.**

WordPerfect puts your changes into effect (invisibly).

## Getting back your timed backups

If WordPerfect (or Windows 95, or something else) crashes and you use timed backups as described in the preceding section, listen up. The next time you run WordPerfect, it notifies you if timed backup files are lying around. If you had several documents open, you may have several of those files.

WordPerfect displays a Timed Backup dialog box with the message that a Document1 backup file exists. (Unfortunately, WordPerfect doesn't remember the name of the file that this is a copy of, so it calls it Document1.)

You have these three choices:

✔ **O̲pen.** This option, which is your best choice, opens the backup file in WordPerfect. You can look at the file to determine whether you want it or whether it is an incomplete version of a document that you saved before the crash. You may want to open the copy that you saved in the regular way, compare it with the backup, and see which version you want to keep. If you want to save the file, choose File⇨S̲ave or File⇨Save A̲s to save it under a specific name in a specific folder. If you don't want to save the file, choose File⇨C̲lose.

✔ **Rename.** This option tells WordPerfect to store the backup files in an out-of-the-way place (usually in your \MyFiles\Backup folder) with a name that you specify.

✔ **Delete.** Choose this option if you're sure that you don't want the backup file. It's hard to imagine why you would want to choose this option, though. Why not open the backup file, just to be sure?

If you choose to open the file, or if you rename it and then open it, see whether it is the latest version of the document or whether you did some additional work on it after it was saved. Timed backups are usually made every 10 minutes, so you may have done 9 minutes' worth of editing since the backup was saved. You have to do that work again.

If more than one document was open when WordPerfect bit the dust, WordPerfect goes on to tell you that a Document2 backup file exists. Repeat the procedure ad nauseam.

# Some Cool Environment Settings

The environment settings are worth looking at — they allow you to tell WordPerfect how to select words, and (via one of our favorite features) they allow you to tell WordPerfect to open documents automatically. Figure 20-2 shows the environment settings that you can control.

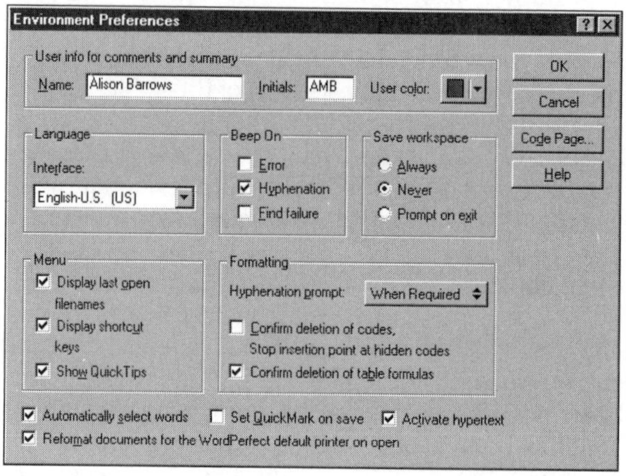

**Figure 20-2:** The settings in the Environment Preferences dialog box tell WordPerfect how to work.

# Finding where you left off

WordPerfect gives you two ways to easily find where you left off:

- ✔ Create a bookmark where your cursor is when you save a document
- ✔ Save the entire workspace, including multiple documents and cursor positions, which are restored the next time you open WordPerfect

To tell WordPerfect to create a special bookmark, called a *QuickMark,* at the spot where your cursor is when you save a document, follow these steps:

1. **Choose Edit⬄Preferences.**

2. **Double-click on the Environment icon.**

   The Environment Preferences dialog box appears (refer to Figure 20-2).

3. **Click on the Set QuickMark on Save check box.**

   This option sets a QuickMark each time you save a file.

To find your QuickMark the next time you open the document, simply press Ctrl + Q. Presto! You're right back where you were when you left off.

You can also use the Environment Preferences dialog box to save your workspace. WordPerfect has another nifty feature that opens WordPerfect to look exactly like it did when you exited. This feature allows you to have multiple documents open, with the cursor where you left it in each document when you exited.

To turn this feature on, follow these steps:

1. **Choose Edit⬄Preferences.**

2. **Double-click on the Environment icon.**

   The Environment Preferences dialog box appears.

3. **In the Save Workspace section, change the setting to Always.**

   If you prefer, you can set the Save Workspace setting to Prompt on Exit, which means that WordPerfect will ask you each time whether you want to save your workspace.

4. **Click on OK to close the dialog box.**

From now on, WordPerfect always opens the documents that you had open when you last closed WordPerfect. In each document, the cursor will be where it was when you closed WordPerfect.

## Controlling mouse selection

You may have noticed that WordPerfect assumes that when you're selecting text with the mouse, you want whole words. So the selection often jumps to include the whole word when you really wanted only part of it. For most of us most of the time, this feature is useful — but it may drive some of you bonkers. Here's how to turn it off:

1. **Choose Edit⇨Preferences.**

2. **Double-click on the Environment icon.**

3. **Clear the Automatically Select Words check box.**

4. **Click on OK.**

# Chapter 21

# Fun with Windows 95

. . . . . . . . . . . . . . . . . . . . . . . . . . . . . . . . . . . . . . . . . . . .

## In This Chapter

▶ Switching to other Windows programs

▶ Looking at the WordPerfect window again

▶ Making shortcuts to WordPerfect

. . . . . . . . . . . . . . . . . . . . . . . . . . . . . . . . . . . . . . . . . . . .

*I*t seems like an idiotic thing to point out, but while you are running WordPerfect 7 for Windows, you are also running Windows 95. You already know that this statement is true, but it occurred to us that there might be some things that you want Windows to do — WordPerfect doesn't do everything.

WordPerfect does lots of things that other word processing programs drop the ball on. Most other programs don't provide ways for you to delete, rename, or copy your files, for example. Instead, you must use the dreaded Windows 95 Explorer or My Computer. WordPerfect, however, thoughtfully allows you to do these thing by using the Open File or Save As dialog box (refer to Chapter 14).

This chapter describes tasks that you can perform with Windows 95, such as switching to other programs, changing the size and shape of the WordPerfect window, and running WordPerfect automatically.

If you are not technically inclined, feel free to skip this chapter; nothing here is absolutely necessary for your word-processing well-being. On the other hand, if you just love the stuff in this chapter and want to know more Windows 95 tricks, consider buying *Windows 95 For Dummies,* by Andy Rathbone (IDG Books Worldwide, Inc.), which is full of this kind of stuff.

# *Switching to Other Windows 95 Programs*

Windows 95 has several big selling points: the cute little buttons used for easy navigation between windows, use of the mouse, and lots of different typefaces shown on-screen. Another big advantage is its capability to run several programs at the same time.

At this very minute, for example, we are running WordPerfect, the Windows File Manager, a program for sending and receiving faxes, and a screen-capture program (for creating the pictures of WordPerfect dialog boxes that litter this book). Windows 95 can keep track of all the different activities going on in its brain and on its screen. (Sometimes, *we* have trouble with that task.)

Windows 95 has two reasonable and two ultra-unmemorable ways to switch from one Windows program to another, as shown in this list:

- ✔ **Click on a visible window.** If you can see part of a program on-screen, use your mouse to click on it. The program's window immediately comes to the front so that you can see the entire window.

- ✔ **Click a button on the Taskbar.** Unless you've done something special with it, the Windows 95 Taskbar is probably at the bottom of your screen, displaying a button for every program that you are running. Click on a program's button to view that window.

- ✔ **Press Alt+Esc.** Windows 95 switches to another one of the programs you are running. Every time you press this key combination, Windows switches to another one. By pressing Alt+Esc enough times, you cycle through all the programs that you are running and get back to the program that you started with. You can see which program you're switching to because that program's button on the Taskbar turns a lighter gray. If that program has an open window (that is, if you didn't use the Minimize button to make it shrink to the Taskbar), you'll see the program's window on-screen; otherwise, you just see its button on the Taskbar turn a lighter gray. In that case, you can press Enter to get the program's window back.

- ✔ **Press Alt+Tab.** When you press Alt+Tab and release it, you switch to another running program. When you press Alt+Tab and hold down the Alt key, a little window appears, displaying an icon for each program that is running. Keep holding down the Alt key and pressing Tab until you get to the program that you want. The line at the bottom of the box tells you what the program is, in case you don't recognize the icon.

We can never remember which of these totally forgettable key combinations does what, so we usually use Alt+Tab and hold down the Alt key to see the list of icons for our running programs.

# Revisiting the WordPerfect Window

In Chapter 1, you learn about all the parts of the WordPerfect window, which can be one of these three sizes:

- ✔ Itty-bitty, or *minimized* — that is, just a button on the Taskbar. The button bears the WordPerfect icon (a little picture of a fountain-pen nib), tells you that the button is for WordPerfect, and displays the name of the current document if one is open. (Not all of this information fits on the button, especially if you're running several programs.)

✔ Huge, or *maximized* — that is, it takes up the entire screen.

✔ Somewhere in between, or *in a window.*

This section describes some things that you can do with WordPerfect, depending on how big the program is on your screen.

## What you can do when WordPerfect is minimized

When WordPerfect is minimized, it appears as a button on the Taskbar, probably at the bottom of your screen somewhere. You can switch to it by using any of the methods described earlier in this chapter. When you switch to it, it grows to a more useful size (either maximized or in a window — whichever size it was when you minimized it).

You can exit WordPerfect by right-clicking on the WordPerfect button and then choosing Close from the little menu that appears. If you have been editing documents and haven't saved them, don't panic — WordPerfect asks whether you want to save each one and cleans things up properly before closing down.

You can also maximize WordPerfect. Right-click on the icon and then choose Maximize from the menu that appears.

## What you can do when WordPerfect is maximized

When WordPerfect is maximized, it takes up the entire screen. You cannot see any other programs, but you have lots of space to see your documents. You can minimize WordPerfect by clicking on the Minimize button. This button, which looks like a dash (or a button on the Taskbar), appears in the top-right corner of the screen at the right end of the title bar.

You can put WordPerfect in a window by clicking on the Restore button, which is just to the right of the Minimize button. The Restore button, which looks like two overlapping windows, becomes the Maximize button when WordPerfect is in a window.

You can switch to other programs by using the Taskbar or any of the keyboard methods described earlier in this chapter. (The mouse method doesn't work because you cannot see any other programs to click on them.)

## *What you can do when WordPerfect is in a window*

This section describes some of the things that you can do when WordPerfect is running in a window.

You can minimize WordPerfect by clicking on the Minimize button — the one at the right end of the title bar with the dash at the bottom. You can maximize WordPerfect by clicking on the Maximize button, which looks like a single window next to the Minimize button.

You can switch to other programs by using the Taskbar buttons or any of the other methods described earlier in this chapter.

You can change the size of the WordPerfect window by using the thin borders around the window. Move the mouse pointer to the border. When the pointer turns into a double-headed arrow, click and drag any of the sides or corners of the border to make the window bigger or smaller. You can move the window around on-screen by clicking and dragging the title bar.

We usually run WordPerfect in a window. We make the window the full height of the screen so that we can see as many lines of our documents as possible. We make the window just wide enough to show the full width of the document, from the left to right margin. This technique leaves some blank screen to the side of the WordPerfect window; in that space, we can see part of the Windows 95 Desktop, with its icons and those of any other programs that we may be using.

# *Having Fun with Windows 95*

Windows 95 is pretty easy to use, but it can be even easier. You can make WordPerfect very accessible. You can even tell Windows 95 to run WordPerfect every time you turn on the computer.

## *Menu madness*

You probably run WordPerfect by using the Windows 95 Start button (or a button on the Taskbar that starts WordPerfect). The Start button is the key to Windows 95; if you haven't got it figured out, you aren't going to get too far. When you click on the Start button, you see a menu of things that you can start. The important ones for you right now are Documents; Programs; Corel Office 7; and, of course, the Shut Down option, which you probably have been using on a regular basis.

If you use other Windows 95 programs, and especially if you upgraded from an earlier version of Windows, you probably use the <u>P</u>rograms option in the Start menu. <u>P</u>rograms lists programs and program groups in a treelike structure; you may have to go a ways before you can actually click on a program. But WordPerfect 7 doesn't get put in the <u>P</u>rograms part of the Start menu; it gets its own Start menu item.

You've probably been starting WordPerfect by clicking on the Start button, moving the highlight to Corel Office 7 (or Corel WordPerfect Suite 7), and then clicking on Corel WordPerfect 7. There are plenty of other ways to start WordPerfect, especially if there's a particular document you want to work on.

A different way to start WordPerfect is to choose a WordPerfect document from the <u>D</u>ocuments menu. Click on the Start button, select <u>D</u>ocuments, and click on a WordPerfect document. (You may notice that files that you wouldn't consider to be "documents" appear in this list; Windows 95 defines *documents* as files that the user creates with a program.) When you click on a WordPerfect document in the <u>D</u>ocuments menu, Windows 95 starts WordPerfect and opens the specified document.

## Customizing your Start menu

If it's not enough to have WordPerfect one level off the Start menu, you may want to create a Start menu item for WordPerfect. On the way, you'll create another shortcut for opening WordPerfect; you can decide which method you like best. Follow these steps:

1. **Double-click on the My Computer icon on the Windows 95 Desktop.**

   (If you can't see it, minimize all your applications until you can.)

   The My Computer window opens.

2. **Double-click on the drive where WordPerfect is installed.**

   This drive probably is C, but it might be something else. Try one, and if you don't see the Corel folder, close the window and try another.

3. **Double-click on the Corel folder.**

4. **Double-click on the Office7 folder.**

   You now see the folder that contains the Corel Office 7 programs and other files.

5. **Double-click on the Wpwin7 folder.**

   A window opens, displaying a few items including a file called Wpwin.exe, which is the WordPerfect program executable file. You can actually run WordPerfect by double-clicking on this icon, but we wouldn't call that a shortcut.

6. **Drag Wpwin.exe to the Windows 95 Desktop.**

   The Desktop is the part of your screen on which all you see is background. You may have fancy wallpaper, or your Desktop may be plain.

   An icon appears, with the label *Shortcut to Wpwin.exe.*

7. **Click on the icon twice, pausing between clicks.**

   Double-clicking on the icon would start WordPerfect, which you don't want to do yet. Clicking on the icon twice enables you to edit the label, which is what you want to do right now.

8. **Edit the label to make it a little less techie (maybe WordPerfect 7); then press Enter.**

9. **Click and drag the icon to the Start button.**

   That's it! When you click on the Start button, you see WordPerfect 7 (or whatever name you used for the icon label) in the initial menu. You can also drag the WordPerfect icon straight from My Computer to the Start button, but you end up with the name of the menu item being Wpwin7.

10. **Close all those My Computer windows.**

You now have two shortcuts for opening WordPerfect: an item in the Start menu and an icon on the Windows 95 Desktop. You can easily delete the icon on the Desktop: Click on it and then press Delete. Windows 95 asks whether you're sure. You're deleting only the icon — not anything that's integral to WordPerfect — so go ahead and delete it if you want to.

Deleting the item from the Start menu is quite a bit more complicated. You have to go into the Start menu and choose Settings⇨Taskbar. Click on the Start Menu Program tab in the Taskbar Properties dialog box, click on the Remove button, find the new item that you added at the bottom of the menu, select it, click on the Remove button, and close all the dialog boxes. See? You might as well just leave it there.

## Starting WordPerfect automagically

Windows 95 can start programs for you when you turn on your computer so that your favorite programs are already running when you get back from the coffee machine. These steps show you how:

1. **Click on the Start button and then choose Settings⇨Taskbar.**

   You see the Taskbar Properties dialog box.

2. **Click on the Start Menu Programs tab at the top of the dialog box.**

3. **Click on the Add button in the Customize Startup Menu section.**

   You see the Create Shortcut dialog box. Windows 95 needs to know the name of the file that runs WordPerfect.

4. **If you have a standard installation of WordPerfect, you can type** C:\Corel\Office7\Wpwin7\Wpwin.exe **in the box, but a safer way is to browse for the same file.**

   Click on the Browse button, which displays folders on the C drive. Look for the Corel folder and double-click on it. (If you can't find the Corel folder, you may need to look on another drive; click on the Up One Level button to choose another drive.) Double-click on the Office 7 folder; then double-click on the Wpwin7 folder. You should see the Wpwin.exe program. Click on it then click on Open. The file name now appears in the Command Line section.

5. **Click on Next in the Create Shortcut dialog box.**

   Windows 95 displays a tree structure of the entire Start menu. You need to find the StartUp folder (which is not to be confused with just plain Start).

6. **Scroll down the list, select StartUp, and click on Next.**

   Windows 95 takes you to the next step, in which you can select a title for the shortcut.

7. **Type** WordPerfect 7 **or something like that.**

   It doesn't matter what you type because you probably won't look at this menu item; it will work automatically. But it's a good idea to use a moderately appropriate name.

8. **Click on the Finish button.**

9. **Close the Taskbar Properties dialog box by clicking on OK.**

   The next time you start your computer, Windows 95 will start WordPerfect automagically.

# Chapter 22
# Solving Printing Problems

● ● ● ● ● ● ● ● ● ● ● ● ● ● ● ● ● ● ● ● ● ● ● ● ● ● ● ● ● ● ● ● ● ● ● ● ● ● ● ● ● ● ● ●

### In This Chapter

▶ Looking at types of printers

▶ Fixing jams

▶ Caring for and feeding your printer

▶ Selecting a printer to use

▶ Setting up a new printer

▶ Printing on a network

● ● ● ● ● ● ● ● ● ● ● ● ● ● ● ● ● ● ● ● ● ● ● ● ● ● ● ● ● ● ● ● ● ● ● ● ● ● ● ● ● ● ● ●

**A**fter enduring the technical complexities of formatting your document, you would think that getting it on paper would be easy. In Chapter 12, we talk about how to print an entire document or just parts of it, as well as how to cancel printing if something goes wrong. But if you have a problem with printing, you may have to learn how to fix it, such as unjamming the printer or using a different printer. We talk about these topics in this chapter.

# Goldilocks and the Three Printers

You probably don't care that there are three basic kinds of printers, but if something goes wrong, you may want to know. The three types of printers use different types of paper and ribbons (or the modern-day equivalent of ribbons), and you handle paper jams differently. Just in case, here's the lowdown. The three general types of printers you may find attached to your computer or network are *impact, inkjet,* and *laser.*

## Impact printers

The oldest (and slowest) kind of printer is the impact printer, which works by pressing an inked ribbon against the paper, like a typewriter. In fact, some early impact printers looked exactly like typewriters without keyboards.

Most modern impact printers are *dot-matrix printers*, which use a matrix (or grid) of tiny pins to press the ribbon against the page. By sticking out different sets of pins, the printer can form different letters.

## Inkjet printers

A better alternative is the inkjet printer, which squirts itty-bitty drops of ink on the page. Ink drops are quiet, and so are inkjet printers. By using very small drops and precise positioning, inkjet printers produce a fairly nice print quality and can print graphics and different fonts. You can get inkjet printers with multicolored ink cartridges so that you can print your documents in full color.

The advantages of these printers include their capability to use typewriter paper and their cost (fairly cheap). Their disadvantages are that they are relatively slow (although they're faster than impact printers) and that the ink can smear.

## Laser printers

The top of the line, printerwise, is the laser printer. Laser printers work like photocopiers, but rather than duplicate a paper original, they draw a picture or text on the copier drum.

Laser printers usually are more expensive than the other types of printers, and they are usually large (bigger than your computer), but they produce high-quality output quickly. Laser printers use sheets of paper, not continuous perforated stock, and can print different fonts and graphics. Some laser printers can print on both sides of the page and also can handle stacks of envelopes.

# Fixing Jams

In this age of advanced data processing, what the world needs is better paper processing. Rather than print nicely, our printer frequently crumples up its paper and smears ink all over it, like a recalcitrant 2-year-old. If the weather is a little humid, the paper curls and doesn't feed properly. If the air is dry and crisp, static electricity builds up, and sheets stick together. And just when the paper is moving along fine, it's time to print on checks, mailing labels, or envelopes.

When your printer mashes up its paper like a baker kneading bread, the first thing to do is to tell WordPerfect to stop printing. The sooner you can stop the printer from smearing any more ink around, the better. (Refer to Chapter 12 to learn how to cancel a print job.)

If you use a laser printer or print on a network printer, you may not have to tell WordPerfect to stop printing. After the paper in a laser printer jams, it stops by itself. Most laser printers and networks are even smart enough to reprint the page that jammed before they continue to print the rest of the document.

## *Stop that printer!*

After you tell WordPerfect to stop printing, the printer may struggle along for a while. Most printers contain an *internal buffer,* which is a temporary storage place for it to store the next page or so to be printed. Even after you tell your computer (or the network) to stop printing your document, the printer may continue for a page or so, printing the information in its buffer.

 There is no easy way to prevent a printer from printing the information in its internal buffer. Here's what *not* to do: *Don't turn the printer off and on.* On laser printers, this technique may let loose a bunch of smeary black toner dust that will get all over your hands and on the next 1,000 pages the printer prints. Instead, follow these steps:

1. **Push the printer's Stop or Off-Line button.**

   The printer's online light should go out. You have told the printer to stop printing as soon as it feels like it.

2. **Wait for the paper to stop moving.**

   Aha! It heard you.

3. **Turn the printer off.**

   Wait about 10 seconds to make sure that the printer's internal buffer forgets everything.

4. **Unjam the printer.**

   The following section discusses this highly technical topic.

5. **Turn the printer back on.**

   It should have forgotten about printing your document.

6. **If the printer isn't online, press its Online button.**

## *Clean up your mess!*

If you have an impact printer, the paper is probably wrapped around the platen 10 times at this point. While the printer is turned off, rewind the platen knob to eject all that paper.

If you are printing on sticky labels, *don't* rewind the platen to get them out. If you do, they might stick to your printer, right under the platen, and then you will have a devil of a time getting them out. Instead, pull gently on the labels to bring them out the front and move them forward so that the labels don't touch the platen.

If you have an inkjet printer, flip the top open and take out the paper. It's a piece of cake (but don't get any cake in the printer).

If you have a laser printer, pop open the lid and pull out all the shreds of paper inside. Be careful — some of the parts are hot. Then slam the lid shut.

# The Care and Feeding of Your Printer

Depending on which kind of printer you have, your printer likes different kinds of supplies to eat. No matter which kind of printer you have, it is a good idea to blow the dust out of it from time to time.

## Impact printers

Impact printers use ribbons. Always be sure to have an extra ribbon on hand because the one you are using will suddenly break or run out of ink on the final draft of your report.

You can get almost any kind of paper these days as continuous-feed, including labels, letterhead, invoices, and even envelopes. If you are looking for supplies, we recommend The Drawing Board in Dallas, Texas (800-527-9530). You can also get continuous-feed paper with perforations so fine that after the sheets of paper have been separated, you cannot tell that they were perforated. This type of paper is sometimes called *microperf.*

Amaze your friends with your prodigious vocabulary. What's the name for the strip of paper that runs down the side of continuous-feed paper — the strip with the little holes in it? Answer: *perfory.*

## Inkjet printers

Inkjet printers use little ink cartridges. The early cartridges contained ink that was water-soluble, so you could wash your document right off the paper — an interesting recycling idea, but not too hot for business correspondence. Newer cartridges have corrected this problem, and you can even get them in different ink colors. Color inkjet printers, of course, take special multicolor cartridges.

You can buy little bottles of ink with which you recharge your inkjet cartridges, but we haven't had terrific luck with them.

You can use regular photocopying paper in inkjet printers. The tiny drops of ink shot out by an inkjet printer look different on different types of paper because of differing absorbencies (sounds like a paper-towel commercial, doesn't it?). If you are unhappy with the print quality of your inkjet, try a different kind of paper. You can even get photographic-style paper from companies such as Kodak. In our experience, however, the quality of the print, though better, is far short of photographic. Depending on the paper you get, prices range from about half a penny a sheet (for a case of 100 percent recycled paper) to almost 75 cents a sheet for the photographic-style stuff.

After that, you have to buy the inkjet cartridge. They cost between $20 and $30 and print somewhere between 1,000 and 2,000 pages (depending on a bunch of factors). Cost per page: about two or three cents.

## *Laser printers*

Laser printers, like small photocopying machines, use *toner cartridges* to provide the black. Toner cartridges contain (not surprisingly) *toner,* which is a fine black dust that can get all over your clothes if you don't treat your laser printer with respect.

Your laser printer tells you that its cartridge is running out of toner by flashing a light on its panel, displaying a message, or changing an indicator on the side of the printer from green (full) to yellow (low) to red (empty).

To change the toner cartridge, pop open the lid of the printer, remove the cartridge (some slide out sideways), and insert the new one. Look on the cartridge box for additional instructions — you may have to pull a tab to release the packet of toner into the cartridge. You also may have to use a little cotton swab to clean the printer's *corona wire.* Doing so is a good idea because it allows your printer to make clearer copies. (While the printer is open, you may want to clean out the dust and cat hair, too.)

You can generally extend the life of an empty toner cartridge by taking it out of the printer, dancing vigorously (not too vigorously) with it to shake the toner around, and putting it back in the printer.

Rather than buy new toner cartridges all the time, you can have your cartridges refilled with toner dust. Look in the back of PC magazines to find services that refill cartridges. Each cartridge can be refilled only one time, however, and sometimes the print quality is not as good as that of the original. You can also recycle toner cartridges rather than send them to the dump; ask your supplier how to do it, or look for instructions in the box your new toner cartridge came in.

# *Choosing Which Printer to Use*

Enough about hardware — let's get back to software issues. If you have more than one printer attached to your computer (or to the network to which your computer is attached), how do you tell WordPerfect which one to use when printing?

WordPerfect gets its information about printers primarily from Windows 95. When you install Windows 95, you tell it which printer or printers you have, and it creates a printer driver for each one. A *printer driver* contains information about how this particular printer works, including which fonts it can print and how to tell it to use fancy type styles.

To see a list of the printer drivers installed on your computer for both Windows 95 and WordPerfect and to choose which one to use, follow these steps:

1. **Choose File Print.**

   The Print dialog box appears.

2. **Click on the Printer tab.**

   WordPerfect displays information about the current printer, including its name, in the Name box.

3. **Click on the arrow on the right side of the Name box.**

   A list of printers drops down. (Your list will almost certainly differ from ours.)

4. **To use a different printer, choose it from this list.**

   WordPerfect switches to the printer you selected.

5. **Click on Close in the Print dialog box (if you're done with it) or Print (if you're ready to print).**

The list of printer drivers may include drivers that aren't for real printers. The Envoy 7 driver shown in Figure 22-1, for example, is used for saving text to a formatted file; this file is read by Corel's Envoy program rather than printed on a printer. The WINFAX printer driver is used to send a document as a fax by using the WinFax Pro program from Delrina Software. (Chapter 18 explains how to format and print faxes.)

It's absolutely necessary to tell WordPerfect the correct printer to use. Every printer has its own weird, bizarre codes to tell it which fonts to use and when to print things in boldface or italics — not to mention codes that tell it how to print lines, boxes, and pictures.

# Setting up a New Printer

What if you get a new printer that's not listed on the Printer tab in the Print dialog box? Yikes — it's time to install a printer. This procedure is easier than it used to be, but you may want to identify a local computer wizard to call if you get into trouble.

Still with us? Ready to install your new printer? Here goes!

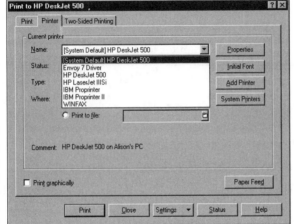

**Figure 22-1:**
Select a printer from the drop-down list.

# Telling Windows 95 about your new printer

There's a new breed of peripherals (a category that includes printers) that are called Plug-and-Play. These devices used to be called Plug-and-*Pray*, but rumor has it that they work better than they used to. What Plug-and-Play means to you is very easy setup of your new printer — turn off your computer, plug in the new printer, and turn everything back on. With luck, Windows 95 will find the new printer and ask you a couple of questions, and you're all set. (You have to have any disks that came with the new printer; you also must have your Windows 95 disks or CD-ROM on hand.)

Even if you don't have a Plug-and-Play printer, telling Windows 95 about it isn't so tough. But you do have to tell Windows about your printer so that WordPerfect and any other programs you use can print on it. To install the Windows printer driver, you use the Add Printer Wizard, which comes with Windows 95. You can awaken this wizard yourself (see the following section) or have WordPerfect awaken it for you (see the section after that).

To install a new Windows printer driver, you need your Windows 95 program disks, which make up the large stack of disks you (or someone) used to install Windows 95 in the first place (if you're lucky, rather than a pile of disks, you have a CD-ROM). The good news is that you don't have to use them all: Windows 95 knows which disk contains the driver you want.

You can run the Add Printer Wizard program from Windows or from WordPerfect; the effect is the same.

### Awakening the Add Printer Wizard yourself

To run the Add Printer Wizard program directly from Windows 95, follow these steps:

1. **Double-click on the My Computer icon on the Desktop.**

   The My Computer window opens, displaying icons for various parts of your computer.

2. **Double-click on the Printers folder icon.**

   You see the Printers folder, with an icon for each printer driver and an extra (Add Printer) for good measure.

3. **Double-click on the Add Printer icon.**

   The Add Printer Wizard begins. Follow the directions in the section after next to install the new printer.

4. **Close the My Computer window and the Printers folder window by clicking on their Close buttons (the X in the top right corner).**

   You don't have to do this right away, but it's a good idea to do so sooner or later.

### Awakening the Add Printer Wizard from WordPerfect

To run the Add Printer Wizard program from WordPerfect, follow these steps:

1. **In WordPerfect, choose File Print.**

   WordPerfect displays the Print dialog box.

2. **Click on the Printer tab.**

   You see printer settings.

3. **Click on the Add Printer button.**

   WordPerfect starts the Add Printer Wizard program.

4. **Follow the next set of instructions to install the driver.**

   Or simply follow the directions the Add Printer Wizard gives you; it's not called a wizard for nothing!

5. **Close the Print dialog box by clicking on the Close button.**

### *Advice for dealing with the Add Printer Wizard*

Whichever way you get there, you use the Add Printer Wizard to install the Windows 95 printer driver for your new printer, as shown in the following list of steps. (Be aware that because Windows 95 is pretty smart, it may skip steps or add steps, if necessary.) Click on the Next button when you're done with a dialog box, and click on the Back button if you want to change an earlier setting. Click on Cancel at any time if you want to forget the whole thing and find an expert to help you.

To install the printer driver, follow these steps:

1. **The Add Printer Wizard displays an introductory blurb; click on the Next button.**

   The printer wizard asks you how your printer is connected.

2. **Click on Local Printer and then click on the Next button.**

   If you're installing a Network Printer (a printer to be shared by several people on a local-area network), you probably need more help than we can give you here.

3. **Choose your printer manufacturer from the Manufacturers list; then choose your printer from the Printers list. If you have the printer driver on disk, also click on Have Disk and then tell Windows 95 which drive the disk is in.**

   If you have a disk with a printer driver, you should use it, even if you find your printer in the list. Chances are that the driver you got with the printer is more up-to-date.

4. **Click on the Next button.**

   Windows may take this opportunity to ask you for the Windows 95 disk that contains the printer driver.

   Alternatively (or next), Windows asks which port your printer is attached to.

5. **Select a port from the list.**

   The LPT ports are for parallel printers, and the COM ports are for serial printers. If you're not sure which one to use, accept the highlighted choice.

6. **Click on the Next button.**

7. **Type a new name for the printer in the Printer Name box, if you want.**

8. **If you are installing a printer you will use most of the time, click on Yes below the question** Do you want your Windows-based programs to use this printer as the default printer?

9. **Click on the Next button.**

   Windows 95 gives you the opportunity to print a test page.

10. **Click on Yes or No.**

**11. When you're done, click on the Finish button.**

Congratulations! You've installed a printer!

Now the new Windows 95 printer driver also appears in the list of printers in WordPerfect's Print dialog box (click on the Printer tab). To select your new printer, follow the instructions provided earlier in this chapter.

If your printer is a new type, the printer driver may not be in the list of Windows 95 printer drivers. Instead, a disk that contains the Windows 95 printer driver may come with the printer. If so, in step 3 in the preceding series, click on Have Disk. Windows 95 asks you to put the disk in the drive and tell it which drive you put the disk in (picky program, huh?).

# Printing on a Network

If you work in an office that has a computer network, the printer you use may not be in your office; it may not even be anywhere near your office. You may be able to quit going to the health club, in fact, because you'll get such a workout running up and down the stairs to the printer three floors above you to get your documents.

If you don't know where your network printer is, you may have to ask people in nearby cubicles or stand quietly in the center of the office and listen for the sound of printing (whirring and clicking, if it is a laser printer).

After you find the printer, you probably will want to find the document you printed. If you're lucky, no one else will have printed anything recently, and all the paper in the printer will be yours. More likely, however, lots of people will have printed things, and a pile of paper will be waiting for you on top of the printer.

Correct network etiquette requires that you sort through the pages, being careful to keep them in order. Pull out the documents that are yours without shuffling the pages or dropping the whole mess on the floor. If you cannot find your document, maybe someone else decided to drop it off at your office on her way to lunch. Or else someone decided that your document looked interesting and sneaked off with it.

Networks usually have their own print-management programs. You may want to ask your network administrator to show you how to cancel a print job after it is in the hands of the network, how to see the *queue* (the waiting line) of documents waiting to be printed, and which other printers on the network you can use.

# Chapter 23

# Don't Panic! Read This Chapter!

. . . . . . . . . . . . . . . . . . . . . . . . . . . . . . . . . . . . . . . . . . . . .

*In This Chapter*

▶ Where's WordPerfect?

▶ Where's my document?

▶ Where am I?

▶ The entire document is boldface!

▶ The screen looks weird!

▶ My document isn't printing!

▶ Yikes — I didn't mean to delete that!

▶ They can't open my document!

▶ WordPerfect's not listening to me!

▶ What do you mean, a Document1 Backup file exists?

. . . . . . . . . . . . . . . . . . . . . . . . . . . . . . . . . . . . . . . . . . . . .

As long as you have this trusty book by your side, nothing should go wrong while you are using WordPerfect. The IRS should never audit your tax returns, of course, and your toast should never burn.

So much for living in a perfect world. This chapter describes some things that just might, once in a while, perhaps, happen to you or to someone you know.

## "Where's WordPerfect?" (Part 1)

Hmm. . . I know it was here yesterday. Where is WordPerfect on the Start menu?

WordPerfect usually hangs out on the Start menu under the Corel Office 7 or Corel WordPerfect Suite 7 option. If it isn't there, have a look at Chapter 21 to find two ways to create shortcuts to WordPerfect.

If you always run WordPerfect when you use your computer, you may want to tell Windows 95 to run it automatically when Windows starts. See the section "Starting WordPerfect automagically" in Chapter 21.

It's possible that you can't even find the Taskbar — you (or someone else) may have told Windows 95 to hide it. Do you know on which edge of the screen the Taskbar usually appears? Just put your mouse pointer off the screen in that direction, and give it a second; the Taskbar should appear. If you don't remember which edge the Taskbar is usually on, try all four edges — slowly.

# "Where's WordPerfect?" (Part 2)

Another way for you to lose WordPerfect is for it to vanish before your very eyes. You are working away, and you click on something — probably something in the top right corner of the WordPerfect window. Blammo — without so much as a puff of smoke, the entire WordPerfect window disappears and takes your documents with it.

What probably happened is that you clicked on either the Minimize button or the Close button. The Minimize button is the leftmost button of the tiny buttons in the top right corner of the WordPerfect window. It has a little bar at the bottom of it. Clicking on this button freeze-dries WordPerfect into a button, which appears somewhere on the Taskbar.

If you see the WordPerfect button, click on it to bring WordPerfect back to life. Is it still breathing? Pulse steady? Whew!

The Close button is the rightmost of the three tiny buttons in the top right corner of the WordPerfect window; it has an X on it. It is just as easy to click on the Close button as it is to click on the Minimize button. But if WordPerfect disappeared without protest, you must have just saved your open documents before you closed things up by mistake. Also, if you closed the program by mistake, there's no WordPerfect button on the Taskbar. But that's okay: Simply run WordPerfect and reopen your documents; they should be in the list at the bottom of the File menu.

# "Where's My Document?" (Part 1)

Uh-oh. You want to open that important report so that you can do some more work on it, but there's no sign of it on your disk. Looks as though it ran off with that cute little memo you wrote yesterday. Call in the bloodhounds.

But first try looking around. You probably saved it with a different name or in a different directory. Try the things in this list:

✔ Click on the File menu, and see whether the document you want is at the bottom of the pull-down menu (it may be if you used it recently).

✔ Use the File⇨Open command, and look in the directory in which you thought you left it. Oh, yeah . . . you probably already tried this trick.

✔ While you are in the Open dialog box, look in some other directories you use.

✔ Consider the possibility that you used the wrong name when you saved the document. You never know when a brain spasm might strike.

✔ Use the QuickFinder tab in the Open dialog box. This feature can look in all the files on your hard disk (or in selected directories) and search for some text that you know is in your document. See the section "Finding a File with a Forgotten Name" in Chapter 14 for directions.

✔ Use the Windows 95 Find feature (it's on the Start menu).

# "Where's My Document?" (Part 2)

Here's another twist on losing a document. You open the document and work on it diligently. Then you click on something (you're not sure what), and zip — your document vanishes.

You may have minimized your document accidentally. As part of its capability to edit multiple documents at the same time, WordPerfect allows you to temporarily shrink your document to the size of a postage stamp while you work on other documents. It's hard to imagine a good use for this feature, but there it is — you minimize a document by clicking on the *document's* Minimize button, which is in the top right corner of the *document's* window. (Chapter 13 discusses how to see multiple documents in multiple document windows and other confusing topics.)

To find your lost document, click on Window on the WordPerfect menu bar. After the Cascade and two Tile commands, you see a list of the documents that are open. With luck, yours is one of them. Choose it, and voilà — it's back.

# "Where Am I?"

You click on something and find yourself in the unexplored reaches of your document. Where are you, and how do you get back to where you were?

Luckily, WordPerfect has a "go back to where I was a minute ago" command; it's in the Go To dialog box. Follow these steps to go back to where you were:

1. **Press Ctrl+G.**

   You see the Go To dialog box, which is described in Chapter 3.

2. **Click on Last Position in the <u>P</u>osition list.**

   This location is the "where I was a minute ago" place.

3. **Choose OK.**

   WordPerfect zips your cursor back to where it was just before the last search or Go To command.

If this technique doesn't work, try searching for a word or phrase that appears near where you were editing. Choose the <u>E</u>dit➪<u>F</u>ind and Replace command or press F2 to display the Find and Replace Text dialog box. (Chapter 5 describes searching in detail.)

# "The Entire Document Is Boldface!"

Or it's in italics or in a weird font. WordPerfect's character-formatting commands can get out of hand sometimes. The usual way to format some text (as explained in Chapter 7) is to select the text first and then do the formatting. This method tells WordPerfect to insert a secret code to start the special formatting at the beginning of the selected text and to insert another code at the end of the selected text to turn off the formatting.

If your codes get bollixed up, your carefully chosen formatting can be applied to your entire document rather than to just a small selection of text.

Use the Reveal Codes window (press Alt+F3) to check for the code or codes that turn on the formatting. (Chapter 10 explains how to use the Reveal Codes window.) When you find the offending code, delete it. Then try applying your formatting again.

# "The Screen Looks Weird!"

The WordPerfect screen usually looks weird, so it's nothing to worry about. If the screen looks even weirder than normal, this list shows some things you can try:

✔ Choose View➪Page or View➪Draft. Maybe WordPerfect has switched into the alternative reality of outline view.

✔ Choose View➪Zoom and choose a reasonable zoom size. (Chapter 20 describes zooming, for you zoom freaks.)

✔ Use the Reveal Codes window (press Alt+F3) to check for bizarre codes that may have arrived from outer space (refer to Chapter 10). If you see a code you don't like the looks of, delete it. (It's a good idea to save your document under a different name first.)

✔ Close your document, and open it again. Maybe it will feel better.

✔ Exit WordPerfect, and run it again. This step may exorcise the cooties that inhabited it.

✔ Exit Windows 95, and run it again. This step is necessary only when the situation is serious.

✔ Exit Windows 95, turn off your PC, and go out for a walk. Who knows — maybe your eyeballs flipped out and need a rest.

✔ Sell your computer, and go into another line of work, such as flower arranging.

# *"My Document Isn't Printing!"*

You click on the cute little Print button on the Toolbar or use some other method to tell WordPerfect that you want it to arrange some ink tastefully on some paper. Is this such an unreasonable thing to ask?

In the world of Windows 95, arranging ink certainly can be complicated. Chapter 12 describes the sometimes tortuous path your document can take from WordPerfect to your printer.

Here's the key thing: If the printer doesn't print anything, don't just try printing again. Your document may still be en route to the printer (especially if you used extensive formatting or graphics). If you issue another Print command, you probably will end up with two copies. Instead, figure out where your document got stuck.

This list shows some things to try when your document won't print:

✔ Make sure that the printer is on and on-line. For information about taking the shreds of jammed paper out of your printer (and even *finding* your printer), refer to Chapter 22.

✔ Tell WordPerfect to cancel printing the document so that you can start over. Display the WordPerfect Print Status and History window by pressing F5 and then clicking on the Status button. (See the section "WordPerfect, stop printing!" at the end of Chapter 12.)

✔ If you use a network, the problem undoubtedly can be blamed on it. Ask other computer users in your office whether they can print on the printer you want to use. You may have to talk to your network administrator. Ask such questions as "How can I tell whether my print job is in the queue?" and "Can you make sure that my system is attached to the right printer?" Who knows — the joke memo you just finished writing may be printing on the fancy printer in the executive suite!

✔ It is worth checking into silly, pedestrian problems, such as the printer cable falling out the back of either the printer or the computer. If the cable has detached itself, you should shut down WordPerfect, Windows 95, the computer, and the printer before reconnecting the cable. Electricity is your friend, but you may as well play it safe.

# *"Yikes! I Didn't Mean to Delete That!"*

The finger is quicker than the brain, especially when it is heading straight for a key that deletes something. In WordPerfect, like all powerful word-processing programs, blowing away hours or weeks of work is horrifyingly easy.

✔ If you have just deleted some text, you can bring it right back by pressing Ctrl+Shift+Z. This step, in fact, displays the Undelete dialog box, which allows you to bring back any of the last three things you deleted. (Choosing Edit⇨Undelete works too.)

✔ If you just deleted a picture or some other fancy-pants item in your document, pressing Ctrl+Shift+Z can undelete it, too.

✔ If you just deleted a code, try pressing Ctrl+Z (or choosing Edit⇨Undo).

If you just deleted an entire document by selecting it in the Open or Save As dialog box and then pressing Delete, you have a more serious problem. This list shows some approaches to take after you delete something accidentally:

✔ Display the Recycle Bin by double-clicking on the Recycle Bin icon on the Windows 95 Desktop; you may need to minimize your windows to be able to see it. Then undelete your document by right-clicking on it and choosing Restore from the menu that pops up. If the document isn't there, either you didn't delete it or you emptied the Recycle Bin (which you should do periodically) after you deleted it. *Now* you have a problem. See whether one of the following techniques will help.

✔ If you told WordPerfect to keep the previous version of your documents, you can retrieve the previous version and enter all the changes you made since you saved that version. This process is tedious but better than typing everything again. Chapter 20 explains how to tell WordPerfect to keep backups. Backups of your documents have the same names as the documents, but they use the file extension .BAK.

✔ If you told WordPerfect to make timed backups of documents you are editing, and if you were just editing the document you deleted, the timed backup may still be around. Choose File⇨Open, and go to your Windows 95 program directory (usually, C:\MyFiles\Backup; Chapter 14 explains how to move to a different directory). Look for a file named WP{WP}.BK1, and open it immediately. If it is the file you want, save it in another directory, and use another filename. If it isn't the file you want, try WP{WP}.BK2 and so on.

✔ In the worst case, dredge around in your wastepaper basket, and find the last version of the document you printed. Typing the document all over again is a tremendous waste of time, although we usually find that in the process, we improve it considerably. (Maybe we should have deleted all the files that contained the chapters of this book!)

# *"They Can't Open My Document!"*

You create a marvelous document and copy it to a floppy disk to give to your co-worker Fred. Fred also uses WordPerfect, so you figure that he should be able to open the file right up and edit it. (Not that it needs any editing, of course — your prose is too pristine and luminescent to be improved.)

Rather than oohs and ahhs, you hear gnashing and grinding of teeth emanating from Fred's office. "This WordPerfect document is no good," he reports. No good? That document is Pulitzer-prize material, you think. It turns out that Fred never even got to lay his eyes on your finest prose to date because his version of WordPerfect refused to open your document.

Here's an ugly truth about WordPerfect: Every version of WordPerfect stores documents in its own, slightly idiosyncratic format. Luckily, newer versions of WordPerfect can *always* read the formats of earlier versions. Beginning with version 6, WordPerfect for DOS and WordPerfect for Windows use the same format.

You can run into a problem if you give one of your WordPerfect documents to someone who uses an older, inferior version of WordPerfect, such as WordPerfect 5.1 or 5.2. To prevent problems, you can save your document in a format that one of these older programs can read.

To save your document in an older format, choose File⇨Save As. In the Save As dialog box, type a new filename so that you don't replace the version you saved in regular WPWin 6.1 format. In the As type box, choose WordPerfect 4.2, WordPerfect 5.0, or WordPerfect 5.1/5.2. Then choose OK.

Now you can give this new document — in a moldy old WordPerfect format — to your friend Fred and see what else he can find to complain about!

# *"WordPerfect's Not Listening to Me!"*

You try choosing a command from a menu. Nothing happens. You try clicking on a button on the Power Bar or Toolbar. Nothing. You click the right mouse button. No QuickMenu. Hmmm. WordPerfect must be deliberately and maliciously ignoring you. Maybe it's taking its afternoon siesta.

If you cannot get WordPerfect's attention, your first inclination may be to pound on the keyboard, shout at it, or slap it around. For technical reasons that are too complex to explain here, we recommend the shouting approach (assuming that you are responsible for paying for a broken keyboard and that you are not interested in breaking your hand on the side of the monitor).

After you get your frustrations out, follow these steps:

- ✔ Try talking to Windows 95. Try switching to another program by clicking on a button on the Taskbar. Or press Alt+Tab (holding down the Alt key) to see that window full of icons (described in Chapter 21) listing the programs that Windows 95 is running. If the window doesn't appear, Windows 95 is incommunicado. If the window does appear, try switching to another program and then switching back to WordPerfect. If you can switch to any other program, exit that program. Maybe it and WordPerfect are having an argument.

- ✔ Make sure that your mouse and keyboard cables are securely connected.

- ✔ If nothing else works, wait about five minutes. Maybe some part of your computer system is so busy doing something that it hasn't had a chance to respond to you. You never know.

- ✔ Press Ctrl+Alt+Delete, and see what Windows 95 has to say for itself. This key combination lists the programs that are running, and allows you to close them. (This is not the recommended method, but it's the right way to close a program if it's hung.) If you see, next to WordPerfect, the words `not responding`, you really do have a problem. See the steps later in this section to learn how to close WordPerfect by brute force.

If talking to Windows 95 doesn't help, even after five minutes, it's time for serious violence. Time to bash some bits! Unfortunately, this technique blows away WordPerfect and the documents you opened. With luck, you saved your documents recently or you use timed backups (refer to Chapter 20). If you can switch to other applications, close them now in the traditional way.

Follow these steps when WordPerfect is out to lunch:

1. **Hold down the Ctrl and Alt keys and then press the Delete key.**

   This infamous Three-Finger Salute kills programs in their tracks. It should kill only WordPerfect, but in some cases, it kills everything, including Windows 95.

   Windows 95 displays the Close Program dialog box, with a list of programs that are running. Chances are that next to WordPerfect are the words not responding.

2. **Make sure that WordPerfect is selected, and click on the End Task button.**

   You'll lose your most recent edits in WordPerfect.

   Windows 95 may suggest that you give the program some time to respond, but if you have already waited the suggested five minutes, another minute probably isn't going to result in a miraculous revival. Just close the darn thing.

3. **Restart Windows 95 (optional).**

   You don't have to restart Windows, but it's a good idea, especially if you've had to close more than one application by the brute-force method (or the same application more than once). Choose Shutdown from the Start menu, choose Restart the Computer, and click on OK. Windows 95 starts up again.

# "A Document1 Backup File Exists?"

If WordPerfect crashes (or another program crashes and takes WordPerfect with it) or if you turn off your computer while WordPerfect is running or if lightning strikes your house and causes a temporary blackout, WordPerfect doesn't get a chance to do the housekeeping chores it usually does when you exit. One of these chores is deleting the timed backup files it creates (assuming that you use timed backups; refer to Chapter 20).

The next time you run WordPerfect, you get the bizarre message that a Document1 Backup file exists. This message means that WordPerfect has discovered the timed backup copy of one of your documents — probably one of the documents you were editing when WordPerfect went west.

These timed backup files can be a godsend if you did a bunch of editing and didn't save your document before disaster struck. See the section "Getting back your timed backups" in Chapter 20 to learn how to use timed backup files to recover from these types of disasters.

# Part V
# The Part of Tens

The 5th Wave — By Rich Tennant

"YOU KNOW THAT GUY WHO BOUGHT ALL THAT SOFTWARE? HIS CHECK HAS A WARRANTY THAT SAYS IT'S TENDERED AS IS AND HAS NO FITNESS FOR ANY PARTICULAR PURPOSE INCLUDING, BUT NOT LIMITED TO, CASHING."

# In this part . . .

You would think that humanity would have gotten beyond its fascination with tens by now. Yes, it is an utterly amazing fact that we have ten fingers and ten toes. Big deal. If you count on your fingers in base 2, you can count to 1,023, but do you see "1,023 Ways to Please Your Spouse" in *Reader's Digest*? No.

So, because we seem to be stuck with ten, here's the Part of Tens. This part provides more-or-less useful facts that are so small they might get lost if they didn't have a place of their own. Some of the tens, like "Ten (or So) Awesome Tricks" and "Ten Features We Don't Use but You Might" easily could have been "1,023 Ways . . . " but our environmental sensitivities don't allow us to waste that many trees. So take off your mittens and count along with us as we explore the fascinating world of WordPerfect trivia.

# Chapter 24

# The Ten Not-to-Be-Broken Rules of WordPerfect

. . . . . . . . . . . . . . . . . . . . . . . . . . . . . . . . . . . . . .

## In This Chapter

▶ Tell WordPerfect what you have in mind

▶ Do not use extra spaces or tabs

▶ Do not keep pressing Enter to begin a new page

▶ Do not number your pages manually

▶ Save early and often

▶ Save before using the Edit⇨Find and Replace command

▶ Back up your work

▶ Do not turn off your PC until you exit Windows 95

▶ Turn on the printer before printing documents

▶ Always keep printer supplies on hand

. . . . . . . . . . . . . . . . . . . . . . . . . . . . . . . . . . . . . .

*O*kay, you unbelievers. You don't have to follow the rules explained in this chapter, but don't blame us if lightning strikes you (or, more likely, strikes somewhere near your office and knocks the power out, destroying your valuable documents)!

## Tell WordPerfect What You Have in Mind

Tell WordPerfect what you have in mind for your document. If you want multiple columns, use WordPerfect's Columns feature. If you want wide margins, tell WordPerfect to widen them by dragging the margin guidelines around or by using the Format⇨Margins command. Don't think that it would be easier to skip all that and just use extra Enters, spaces, or tabs to put the text where you want it. This method always means extra work in the long run when you edit your text.

WordPerfect's word-wrap feature, for example, enables it to begin a new line whenever it sees you getting perilously close to the right margin. In WordPerfect's mind (such as it is), a bunch of text that ends with an Enter is a paragraph, so type your paragraphs like that and let WordPerfect do the rest of the work. Don't press Enter until you get to the end of a paragraph (refer to Chapter 1).

## Do Not Use Extra Spaces or Tabs

In high school, your typing teacher taught you to type two spaces after each period. Other than that, you should never type more than one space consecutively (with rare exceptions). If you want to move across the line and leave some white space, use tabs. (See Chapter 9 to learn how to set tab stops and use different types of tabs.)

In the world of typesetting, which includes proportionally spaced fonts, it is considered good form to type only *one* space after each period. Somehow, after the text is typeset, it looks fine. But we can understand if your ingrained two-space habits are too hard to break.

Incidentally, if you are using tabs to create something that looks like a table, adjust the tab stops so that there is one tab for each column. This technique enables you to press Tab just once between entries (refer to Chapter 8). Better yet, use WordPerfect's table feature (refer to Chapter 15); remember the first rule.

## Do Not Keep Pressing Enter to Begin a New Page

When you decide to begin a new page, tell WordPerfect so in no uncertain terms: Press Ctrl+Enter. Don't pussyfoot around the issue by pressing Enter repeatedly until you fill the current page with blank lines. This technique is yet another example of the first commandment in action — if you want a page break, say so. (Chapter 9 explains why the Ctrl+Enter method works best.)

## Do Not Number Your Pages Manually

WordPerfect can number your pages for you and place the page numbers at the left, center, or right of either the top or bottom of the page. What more could you ask? So don't type page numbers yourself; they become a mess if you edit your document and the page breaks move around. Chapter 9 tells you how to number your pages and print other information in headers and footers.

# Save Early and Often

Be prepared for disaster! Every time you squirm around in your chair, scratch your foot, or take a sip of coffee, press Ctrl+S to save your document. 'Nuff said. Yes, a timed document backup helps (refer to Chapter 20), but are you really willing to lose your last 10 minutes or so of work?

# Save Before Using the Edit⇨Find and Replace Command

WordPerfect's find-and-replace feature (described in Chapter 5) has awesome power, either to make lots of wonderful updates throughout your document or to trash it big-time. What if you mean to replace *Smith* with *Smythe,* for example, but you type a space by mistake in the Find box just before you click on Replace All? Poof — all the spaces in your document are replaced by *Smythe.* Your important letter has just been transformed into performance art.

Just in case, save your document before you use the Edit⇨Find and Replace command (also known as Ctrl+F2).

# Back up Your Work

Saving is good, but saving your documents on your hard disk doesn't help if your hard disk dies. We don't mean to sound alarmist here, but it can happen. Talk to someone in your office about setting up a backup system for you by using either disks or backup tapes. At least you can use the Send to option in the Open dialog box (right-click on a selected document, click on Send to, and choose a floppy drive) to copy your important documents to floppy disks occasionally (refer to Chapter 14).

# Do Not Turn off Your PC Until You Exit Windows 95

Oops — you're running late. Time to go! Don't just turn off your computer. If you turn it off while Windows 95 is still running, you can cause problems. Leave the computer on (just turn off its screen). Or, if you prefer, shut down Windows 95 by choosing Shut Down from the Start-button menu and then pressing Enter in the dialog box that lists the myriad ways in which you might want to shut down the computer; you want the first choice, Shut Down the Computer? Windows 95 displays an easy-to-read message, telling you when it's safe to turn the computer off; you just have to wait for it.

# Turn on the Printer Before Printing Documents

If your document refuses to print and you see strange error boxes on-screen, the first things to check are whether your printer is on, whether the on-line light is on, and whether paper is in the tray. If those checks don't fix things, refer to Chapter 12 and Chapter 22.

# Always Keep Printer Supplies on Hand

Oooh — how does the printer *know* when you are about to print the final draft of something big? But it does, and that is the moment when your ribbon goes dry, your ink cartridge runs empty, or your toner cartridge ejects its last hiccup of toner. Rats!

Be sure to have extra printing supplies on hand so that you can foil the printer when these things happen.

# Chapter 25
# Ten (or So) Awesome Tricks

*W*ordPerfect has more awesome tricks than a troupe of acrobatic elephants. But personal taste varies when it comes to "awesome," so we picked out a dozen tricks that one person may find fabulously useful and another may find completely stupid.

# Cutting, Copying, and Pasting with Other Programs

Part of the overall coolitude of Windows programs is that most of them use the same cut-and-paste feature, the Clipboard. You can copy stuff from spreadsheets to word processors, from databases to "personal information managers," and from graphics programs to page-layout applications.

In WordPerfect, you can generally cut (or copy) and paste from Windows spreadsheets, databases, and graphics programs and from other Windows word processors or text editors.

To cut and paste something from *anything* to *anything else,* follow these steps:

1. **Run both programs.**

   This step isn't absolutely necessary, but it makes life easier. They both must be Windows programs.

2. **In the *anything* program, select the text, graphics, or spreadsheet region you want to copy.**

   In most programs, you can use the mouse to select text.

3. **Copy the selected text to the Windows Clipboard.**

   In most programs, you press Ctrl+C; in others, check the Edit selection on the menu for a Copy command.

4. **In the *anything else* program, click in or select the area where you want to paste.**

5. **Paste a copy of the contents of the Clipboard.**

   In most programs, you press Ctrl+V; in others, check the Edit selection on the menu bar for a Paste command.

   You can paste as many copies as you want.

If stuff doesn't copy as nicely as you want, placate yourself by reflecting on the amazing fact that it can be done at all, considering how different the programs can be.

# Dragging and Dropping Text

The fastest way to move text is just to highlight it, click on it, and drag it somewhere else.

# Returning to Where You Were

If you're moving around a great deal between two places in your document, it's nice to be able to switch easily. To go back to where you were, use the Edit⊅Go To command (or press Ctrl+G). Double-click on Last Position in the Go To dialog box. (That grumbling noise you hear is from old WordPerfect users. No, it's not as convenient as before, but it's still useful.)

# Going Back to That Old Same Place

If you want to keep returning to one important place in your document, try using a QuickMark. Click in that important place and press Ctrl+Shift+Q. Now you can go back there at any time by pressing Ctrl+Q.

If you're dancing around several places in your document, you might try using bookmarks. Highlight a word or phrase unique to that place, such as *little grass shack* (this phrase serves as a name). Choose Insert⇨Bookmark and then Create from the Bookmark dialog box. Click on OK in the Create Bookmark dialog box to accept the highlighted text as a name.

To go back to your "little grass shack," press Ctrl+G for the Go To dialog box, click on the name in the Bookmark box, and then click on OK. You can have several bookmarks in a document.

# Reopening an Earlier Document

WordPerfect keeps track of the last four documents you worked on. To reopen them, click on File and then click on any of the four documents listed at the bottom of the drop-down menu.

# Inserting the Date

WordPerfect gives you two — count 'em, two — ways to put today's date in your document. Choose one of these methods:

- ✔ Insert today's date as though you had typed it. Press Ctrl+D, use the Insert⇨Date⇨Date Text command, or double-click on the date in the status bar.

- ✔ Insert a secret "date code" that changes to the current date every time you open the document. Press Ctrl+Shift+D or use the Insert⇨Date⇨[Date Code] command.

The Insert⇨Date⇨Date Format command lets you choose any format, from European to American to Martian. This command also lets you insert the time, with or without the date.

# Inserting Cool Characters

Use the Insert➪Character command (press Ctrl+W, for "weird characters") to insert anything from a trademark symbol to Passover greetings in Hebrew. This command is also home to those convenient little characters (such as the cent symbol and standard fractions) that were on your $150 typewriter but are annoyingly absent on your $150 computer keyboard.

When you click the button under Character Set and hold down the mouse button, you have your choice of characters: multinational (such as accented vowels), phonetic (such as in the dictionary), box-drawing (guaranteed weirdness), typographic symbols (a mish-mash of stuff, such as trademark symbols and fractions), iconic symbols (happy faces and pointing hands), math and scientific (inequalities and the aangstrom symbol), and such languages as Cyrillic, Japanese, Greek, Hebrew, and Arabic. Drag the highlight to the selection you want and release the mouse button.

You can insert only one character at a time. Click on it in the Characters box and then on the Insert button.

The neat thing about the WordPerfect Characters dialog box is that you can leave it lying around on-screen, ready to provide strange-looking characters at a moment's notice, while you type. You don't have to close the dialog box before you can continue typing your document. Just choose a character from the Characters box and click on Insert whenever you want to use a strange character.

When you finish inserting funky characters in your text, click the Close button to make the WordPerfect Characters dialog box go away.

After you insert a strange character in your text, you can copy it to other places just as you would copy normal text — copy it to the Clipboard by pressing Ctrl+C and paste it from the Clipboard by pressing Ctrl+V (refer to Chapter 6 if this is news to you).

# Using Unbreakable Hyphens and Spaces

Normally, when you insert a hyphen, WordPerfect takes that as a license to break the line there, if necessary. This breaking capability is inconvenient for compound terms, such as *Figure 1-17* or phone numbers, such as 555-1212. For these types of things, you should insert unbreakable (*hard*) hyphens by pressing Ctrl+ –. Likewise, you can also insert hard spaces, which prevent a line break between two words, by pressing Ctrl+spacebar.

# Chasing Speeding Bullets

To "bulletize" a bunch of paragraphs, just select them and click on the Insert Bullet button on the Toolbar. (You can also use the Insert⇨Bullets & Numbers command.)

In the Bullets & Numbers dialog box, double-click on any bullet symbol or numbering scheme. You can even start the numbers from a particular value by using the Starting Value box.

# Converting Tabs to Tables

Sometimes you wish that you could create a table the old-fashioned way: by using plain, old text with tabs in it rather than by using the Table⇨Create command and filling in the cells. This capability is also valuable when you're importing unformatted text from some other program, so WordPerfect doesn't know that the text is supposed to be a table.

WordPerfect helps you create a real WordPerfect table from tabular text. Each row of the table-to-be must be a line that ends with a *hard return* (the HRt secret code; refer to Chapter 11). To insert a hard return at the end of a line, place your cursor there and press the Enter key. Within each line, separate your columns by pressing the Tab key. (Hard returns are displayed as paragraph marks; press Ctrl+Shift+F3 to display paragraph and tab marks if they're not already visible.)

Highlight the entire table-to-be so that the highlight forms a nice, neat rectangle. When you press F12 (which is the same as Table⇨Create), a Convert Table dialog box appears. Click on Tabular Column and then on the OK button. Zap! You're tableized. The last column is probably a little too large. To reduce its width, move your mouse pointer over the right edge of the column until it changes form; then click and drag this edge to the left until the column is the width you want.

# Inserting Other Files

WordPerfect is nothing if not accommodating, including the fact that it lets you insert other document files into your document. This feature is similar in its results to the Windows cut-and-paste feature; rather than copy a piece of another file, however, you copy the entire file.

Use the Insert⇨File command to choose any file. WordPerfect displays the Convert File Format dialog box. Choose the filename and click on the Insert button. WordPerfect asks whether you are sure, sure, sure that you want to insert the file in your current document.

If WordPerfect can recognize the kind of file it is, such as Microsoft Word for Windows, it suggests the file type in the Convert File Format From dialog box. If you know that the suggestion is wrong, you can view WordPerfect's conversion repertoire by clicking on the Convert File Format From box; choose the correct one. Click the OK button when you're ready to go, and watch the lovely Conversion in Progress display pulsate.

If all goes well, the file is converted to text that is at least remotely similar to the original. You may have to fool with the Format commands to get it to look right, though.

# *Linking Spreadsheets and Databases*

When you're making a report that includes spreadsheet or database data, the data often changes even after you have finished writing it. To keep your report up-to-date, you can *link* to the spreadsheet or database file rather than insert it. Choose Insert⇨Spreadsheet/Database and then Create Link. In the Create Data Link dialog box that appears, specify the Data Type (spreadsheet, for example), how you want it to appear (Link As), and the Filename you're inserting.

# Chapter 26

# Ten Features We Don't Use — Much

*W*ordPerfect, like any software package today, has a few features most people will never use — maybe a couple hundred of them. They're not bad features; it's just that if you happen to use them, you're in a definite minority. We figured that we would at least tell you what the commands are for these features and a little about how they work. Many of these features are covered in that perennial classic *MORE WordPerfect 6 For Windows For Dummies,* by Margaret Levine Young and David C. Kay (published by IDG Books Worldwide, Inc.). Because these features haven't changed much since WordPerfect 6, that book can still help you figure them out.

## Comments

The folks at WordPerfect must have felt bad for little orphan features such as comments and made up for it by making them as cute as a bug. *Comments* are a type of annotation to your document but not part of the final document. They serve as a communication mechanism between you and someone else who is working on the same document, such as your editor.

To insert a comment, click on the place in the text where you want the annotation to appear. (Don't highlight the text. If you select text and then choose

Comment, you move the text from the body of the document to the comment.)
Right-click in the left margin and then choose Comment from the QuickMenu.
Type your comment, and when you finish, click on Close on the feature bar.
WordPerfect creates a little block with your initials in it. Click on the block to
view the comment; double-click on the block to edit your comment. Delete its
secret code, `Comment`, to delete it (refer to Chapter 10).

# Cross-References

Miss Manners undoubtedly would disapprove of providing references if they're
going to be cross, but that's today's society for you. We're talking about references that say such things as "See page 7 for the herring cobbler recipe" even
though after editing, the recipe could end up on page 8 or darn near anywhere.

The solution is not to type the page number. Instead, use the Tools➪Generate➪
Cross-Reference command to mark the recipe text with a secret name, such as
*herring cobbler,* and likewise link the words *See page* to the same name. Put
your cursor where you want to refer to the page on which your herring cobbler
recipe appears; then choose Tools➪Generate➪Cross-Reference. When you
choose this command, you get a bunch of buttons (yes, it's yet another
Toolbar). Unless you're planning to get really adventurous, choose Reference➪
Page. You're ready to type the secret name of the page number you want in the
Target box and click on the Mark Reference button. Now move the cursor to the
herring cobbler recipe and click on the Mark Target button. By marking this as
the target for Herring Cobbler, you have told WordPerfect that all page refer-
ences to Herring Cobbler refer to whatever page this target is on. Click on
Generate and watch the fun. Regenerate the cross-reference later if you edit.
Got it?

# Line Numbering

For all you lawyers out there who are writing contracts that have numbered
paragraphs, the Format➪Line➪Numbering command numbers every paragraph. Enough said. You're a smart, highly paid professional — you figure it
out (but don't miss the Turn Line Numbering On option at the top of the
dialog box).

# Make Your Memos Fit On One Page

Suppose that you have written the world's best marketing proposal for your
company president. Cutting even one word of this proposal would make it lame
and incomplete, but your company president reads only one-page memos.
WordPerfect to the rescue!

Choose Format➪Make It Fit from the WordPerfect menu, and you'll see the Make It Fit wizard. First, the wizard tells you how many pages long your document is now. You also see a box in which you can fill in the Desired number of filled pages you want your document to take up when the wizard is finished with it. The wizard can make your document only a maximum of 50 percent longer or 50 percent shorter. There is a limit to wizardry.

Finally, you see a list of things WordPerfect is willing to do to your document to make it fit. If there's any formatting you *don't* want WordPerfect to change when it tries to make your document fit, make sure that the corresponding check mark is left blank. Otherwise, WordPerfect will use every trick it knows to get your document into the space you want it to take up.

# Marking Revisions

Revision markings make it easy for a group to work on a document. People who are reviewing a document can turn on revision markings by choosing File➪Document➪Review and then choosing Reviewer in the Review Document dialog box. Changes made thereafter are marked for the author. The button at the far left end of the feature bar allows the reviewer to see the document without distracting annotations, although annotations are still marked for the author.

The author can look at the revisions made by reviewers and decide whether to accept them by choosing File➪Document➪Review and then choosing Author in the Review Document dialog box. The buttons in the dialog box allow the author to move to each annotation and annotate it some more, delete it, or incorporate the change into the document.

# Equations

You scientists, mathematicians, and engineers out there already know that you're in a definite minority. Yet WordPerfect doesn't forget you; it can create nice mathematical equations with Greek symbols and all that. You can create these equations in-line with the text or in a separate area. Check out the Equation option on the Graphics menu.

# Outlines

You wouldn't think that you would need special features for writing an outline. But the organizationally challenged may appreciate the outline features of WordPerfect. To check them out, choose Tools➪Outline. You get automated numbering, tab settings, and a feature bar with buttons to change the levels and hide levels of detail you don't want to see at the moment. You can write the outline of a document and then fill it out with actual text. At any time, you can collapse the document to a specified level of outline headings or see the entire document.

## Macros

Macros are a feature for people who enjoy spending endless hours trying to get the computer to perform a series of keystrokes correctly when they press some Alt/Shift/Ctrl+key combination. The truly masochistic can use all of the WordPerfect macro programming facilities to compute the reentry trajectory of the space shuttle at the press of a single Toolbar button.

Macros work this way. Suppose that you want to insert a herring icon before every paragraph that contains the word *herring*. A macro is a way to record all the steps you would have to take to perform that task and then play those steps back with a single keystroke. To record or play a macro, choose Tools➪Macro. But don't even get started unless you're willing to waste — ahem, invest — a great deal of time.

## TextArt

As our friend Art says, "Expose yourself to Art." Here's your chance to make swoopy, loopy headings and other artsy typography — buckets o' fun for posters and presentations. Choose Graphics➪TextArt.

## Footnotes and Endnotes

Footnotes and endnotes are among the most useful features you won't use, but we just couldn't resist putting footnotes and endnotes at the end of this chapter. You use footnotes when you have annotations at the bottom of each page; you use endnotes when all the annotations (such as references) appear at the end of the document. WordPerfect automatically positions, orders, and numbers footnotes and endnotes, although you can fool with them.

To add a footnote or endnote, click at the end of a word or sentence and then choose Insert➪Footnote (or Endnote)➪Create. WordPerfect displays the Footnote/Endnote Feature Bar (what else?). Type your note in the space that is already numbered at the bottom of the screen. When you finish, click on the Close button on the feature bar. Or, if you're planning to work on a number of notes, you can leave the bar open and cruise around your document, popping back and forth between the main text and the footnotes or endnotes.

# Index

**THE WORLD OF COMPUTER KNOWLEDGE**

**Title of this book:** WordPerfect® 7 For Windows® 95 For Dummies®

**My overall rating of this book:** ☐ Very good [1] ☐ Good [2] ☐ Satisfactory [3] ☐ Fair [4] ☐ Poor [5]

**How I first heard about this book:**

☐ Found in bookstore; name: [6]                    ☐ Book review: [7]

☐ Advertisement: [8]                    ☐ Catalog: [9]

☐ Word of mouth; heard about book from friend, co-worker, etc.: [10]     ☐ Other: [11]

**What I liked most about this book:**

**What I would change, add, delete, etc., in future editions of this book:**

**Other comments:**

**Number of computer books I purchase in a year:** ☐ 1 [12] ☐ 2-5 [13] ☐ 6-10 [14] ☐ More than 10 [15]

**I would characterize my computer skills as:** ☐ Beginner [16] ☐ Intermediate [17] ☐ Advanced [18] ☐ Professional [19]

**I use** ☐ DOS [20] ☐ Windows [21] ☐ OS/2 [22] ☐ Unix [23] ☐ Macintosh [24] ☐ Other: [25]
(please specify)

**I would be interested in new books on the following subjects:**
(please check all that apply, and use the spaces provided to identify specific software)

☐ Word processing: [26]                    ☐ Spreadsheets: [27]

☐ Data bases: [28]                    ☐ Desktop publishing: [29]

☐ File Utilities: [30]                    ☐ Money management: [31]

☐ Networking: [32]                    ☐ Programming languages: [33]

☐ Other: [34]

**I use a PC at** (please check all that apply): ☐ home [35] ☐ work [36] ☐ school [37] ☐ other: [38]

**The disks I prefer to use are** ☐ 5.25 [39] ☐ 3.5 [40] ☐ other: [41]

**I have a CD ROM:** ☐ yes [42] ☐ no [43]

**I plan to buy or upgrade computer hardware this year:** ☐ yes [44] ☐ no [45]

**I plan to buy or upgrade computer software this year:** ☐ yes [46] ☐ no [47]

**Name:** _____ **Business title:** [48] _____ **Type of Business:** [49]

**Address** ( ☐ home [50] ☐ work [51]/Company name: _____ ) ( )

**Street/Suite#**

**City** [52]/**State** [53]/**Zipcode** [54]: _____ **Country** [55]

☐ **I liked this book!** You may quote me by name in future IDG Books Worldwide promotional materials.

**My daytime phone number is** _____

# ❑ YES!

Please keep me informed about IDG's World of Computer Knowledge.
Send me the latest IDG Books catalog.